D0548251

1933

Philip Metcalfe

1933

BANTAM PRESS

LONDON · NEW YORK · TORONTO · SYDNEY · AUCKLAND

TRANSWORLD PUBLISHERS LTD
61-63 Uxbridge Road, London W5 5SA

TRANSWORLD PUBLISHERS (AUSTRALIA) PTY LTD
15-23 Helles Avenue, Moorebank, NSW 2170

TRANSWORLD PUBLISHERS (NZ) LTD
Cnr Moselle and Waipareira Aves,
Henderson, Auckland

Published 1989 by Bantam Press
a division of Transworld Publishers Ltd
Copyright © Philip Metcalfe 1988

British Library Cataloguing in Publication Data
Metcalfe, Philip
    1933: personal recollections of Hitler's
    rise to power
    1. Germany. Political events, 1933-1945 –
    Biographies. Collections
    I. Title
    943.086'092'2

ISBN 0-593-01661-0

All rights reserved. No part of this publication may
be reproduced, stored in a retrieval system, or
transmitted in any form or by any means,
electronic, mechanical, photocopying, recording,
or otherwise, without the prior permission of
the publishers

Printed and bound in Great Britain
by Makcays of Chatham plc, Chatham, Kent

For Jane

My thanks also to Gale Abrams, Elisabeth Borden, Jeanne Gardner, Ursula Hausen, Wilma Stafford—and especially, Agnes F. Peterson and Diantha Palmrose.

Contents

PREFACE

The story that follows describes the fate of five people, three men and two women, who witnessed Hitler's seizure of power in Germany in 1933 and 1934. The narrative is based on their letters, diaries and published memoirs and recounts the history of the first eighteen months of Hitler's rule as seen by the American Ambassador and his daughter, William and Martha Dodd; Hitler's chief of the foreign press, Putzi Hanfstaengl; a Jewish society reporter, Bella Fromm; and the first head of the Gestapo, Rudolf Diels. On one level it tells their stories, on another the stories of their friends, and finally of Berlin society as a whole during a turning point in the history of the 20th century.

In studying the memoir literature and combing through the wealth of private and public papers from this time, I took careful note of what was personal, emotional, even intimate. I sought to answer questions about my "characters" that only writers of fiction normally ask. What I was unable to learn, I did not make up. The quoted dialogue comes verbatim from primary sources.

I did not want to be a detective so much as a painter who endows a lost world with the personality and the dailiness it once possessed. I wanted to write the history of a revolution as the participants lived it, to portray German society in all its complexity; as more than Nazis, non-Nazis and Jews. I wanted to show that in a revolution there is not one reality but numerous, partial realities. For this purpose I imagined a narrative that could go anywhere: into embassies, private homes, concentration camps, even across the sea to America. For the most part, however, I was content to hover over Berlin and peek into windows and overhear half-remembered conversations.

Rarely did I concern myself with whether people were right or wrong, good or bad. That would have hinted at the greater catastrophe to come. I merely wanted to capture a piece of the past and make of it a complete present, for myself and for whoever might care to read along with me. The assigning of responsibility could come later, when the narrative was done. For that the reader and I need only our moral intuitions.

Soon after I began this work I learned that the daughter of the American Ambassador was still alive, that the papers of the Jewish society reporter had found their way into an archive in Boston, that comical references to the life of Hitler's former chief of the foreign press lay scattered in numerous autobiographies, and that the post-war inter-rogations of the Gestapo's first chief had been carefully preserved by the Modern Military Branch of the National Archives. Even greater good fortune came my way when I discovered a group of men and women all but forgotten now: the American correspondents who covered the Nazi revolution from Berlin. Celebrities in their time, their personality pro-files dot the first volumes of *Current Biography.* Archives holding their papers were easily located, but the greatest store of their insight re-mained to be found in the files of their newspapers in Chicago, New York, and Philadelphia. America's infatuation with foreign news dates from the years between the wars; and collectively these dispatches from Nazi Germany offer perhaps the clearest and most detailed picture of Hitler's day-to-day consolidation of power available to historians.

By far the most provocative sources on the feel of Germany in 1933 and 1934 turned out to be the eyewitness accounts of occasional trav-elers to Germany and the memoirs penned by German refugees who fled the country in the late thirties. Not surprisingly, women produced the most detailed commentaries. Unembarrassed by social detail, less devas-tated by the upheaval that displaced their husbands and sons, they turned out to be remarkably accurate informants. Thus, it is no accident that the best introduction to the life of a foreign correspondent is Lilian Mowrer's *Journalist's Wife,* the most enthralling account of social os-tracism and impending exile Eva Lips' *Savage Symphony.* In a small way I hope this narrative will serve as an introduction to this unique literature whose authors the reader will find listed in the bibliography.

Traditional surveys of the Third Reich cover the Nazi seizure of power in 1933 and 1934 in a few swift pages. Various decrees are mentioned, the burning of books described, the loss of civil liberties enumerated as the authors race on to later years and the persecution of Jews, war and death. The image of the Third Reich encouraged by fictional and cine-matic accounts is still of its final, tortured days. But, like other epochs, it had its infancy when it was uncertain, chaotic, even comical. This, then, is the story of the beginnings of a tragedy. Like most good stories it starts innocently, with the arrival of an American family on German shores.

MARTHA AND HER FATHER

A black and white photograph from the 1930s shows an American family on the first class deck of a passenger liner. Behind them the teak railing and the scupper plates can be clearly made out. No wind ruffles their hair, no ocean wave disturbs their balance. The ship is at dock and a portion of a dockside sign, "United States Lines," can be deciphered beyond the close focus of the photograph. The women, mother and daughter, hold bouquets of flowers and smile for the camera. Between them stand father and son. The father has just made a pointed remark, his right arm gesturing, while his 28-year-old son listens. The two women smile. The camera shutter trips.

The port was Hamburg, Germany, in the summer of 1933. Adolf Hitler had been Chancellor for five months, virtual dictator for four, and the American family posing for pictures on the first class deck of the *SS Washington* belonged to the newly appointed ambassador from America, William E. Dodd.

For 24-year-old Martha Dodd, the crossing had been both lighthearted and somber. Lighthearted because a fellow passenger turned out to be the second son of the newly elected president and when the two compared passports they were struck by the simplicity of his which read: "Franklin Roosevelt, Jr." and the exaggerated grandeur of hers: " . . . daughter of William E. Dodd, Ambassador Extraordinary and Plenipotentiary of the United States of America to Germany." Somber because after seeing the Roosevelt party off at Le Havre, Martha searched desperately for a patch of French soil to embrace. She finally found some between two railroad ties and, removing a shoe, touched it with her toe. She had toured Europe with her mother five years before and had fallen madly in love with France.

A month earlier in Chicago when her mother called her at work to tell her that President Roosevelt had asked her father to be the next Ambassador to Germany, Martha never dreamt that in a few short weeks she would be going to Berlin. In Chicago she had a good job reviewing books as an assistant literary editor on the *Chicago Tribune*. Evenings she wrote short stories until early in the morning.

She tried to recall what she knew about Germany. She had toured the Rhineland briefly on her European trip, but she had no interest in politics or contemporary history. According to the newspapers, Adolf

Hitler looked like Charlie Chaplin and behaved like a clown in a country that burned books. She could not imagine her father in such an atmosphere.

Her father was the head of the history department at the University of Chicago and the first professor in the United States to occupy a chair of Southern History. The author of numerous books and papers on Lincoln and Lee and Jefferson, he was a short, precise man with a face weathered from the summers he spent with his family farming in Virginia. His speech displayed the gracious pathos of the born southerner.

"Of course, I was surprised," he told reporters, "but not so surprised that I dropped the receiver or anything like that. I recognized the President's voice, which helped the situation a good deal."

Her father had asked Roosevelt if the leaders of the so-called "New Germany" might not take exception to the appointment of a man who had recently written a biography of Woodrow Wilson. Among conservative diehards in Germany, Wilson was still known as the "War President."

"I am sure they will not. That book, your work as a liberal and as a scholar, and your study at a German university are the main reasons for my wishing to appoint you. It is a difficult post, and you have cultural approaches that could help. I want an American liberal in Germany as a standing example."

The new administration had waited three months before filling the post in Berlin. Roosevelt had wanted an unspectacular man, a shrewd observer whose head would not be turned by fascist flattery or splendor. The President had never met Dodd, but he had read some of his writings and was particularly impressed by the historian's ideas on Jefferson.

"Don't take your household things," Dodd told his family. "Leave most of the furniture and belongings here, because we will be back in a year." Hitler's government was not expected to last, and when it fell the need for a standing liberal in Germany would also disappear. Martha's father fully expected to be back in Chicago, teaching, within twelve months.

But she did not want to go to Germany, Martha argued. She did not want to give up her job on the *Tribune* (as frustrating as it was to review several books in a space hardly large enough to do justice to one). She was earning good money and her stories were beginning to sell.

"Suppose I cannot write over there?"

The prospect terrified her. She knew she was talented and exceptionally lyrical. No less a figure than Carl Sandburg, a friend of the family, had urged her not to be afraid of her lyricism. She wrote effusively but self-critically and both loved and hated her gift and hid its

strain on her under an outward pose of toughness that only poorly disguised her highly-strung nature. If she stopped writing now, after she had begun to produce good work, her father's success would be her ruin. She doubted that her gift could survive the move to a foreign capital and the whirl of foreign impressions. And if it died, who could say it had ever lived outside of her memory of it?

She could of course return if she felt that way, her father promised, to perhaps a better job on the *Tribune*. In the meantime she would make the acquaintance of a great people and a great nation and see history in the making. The experience could only enrich a young woman of her ability and ambition.

Except for a short and unhappy half year at a snobbish finishing school near Washington, D.C. Martha had never lived wholly away from her parents. The family was exceptionally close, no longer quite parents and children but adults living together under one roof. Events had rushed her generation so far ahead intellectually and sensually that she sometimes felt as if her mother and father were her children, her "darlings" as she called them. She was equally devoted to her older brother, Bill, who taught history at the American University in Washington, D.C. Martha and Bill hoped to share an apartment together some day. A recent, ill-fated elopement had only convinced Martha never to let matrimony interfere with her career.

When Bill heard the news he wired back that he was eager to go to Germany where, like his father, he could earn a doctorate at a German university. Martha was left with no choice but to accept the inevitable or stay on alone in Chicago. She tried to see the journey as a lark, but the final weeks in Chicago were an agony of suspense for her.

"Well, you won't need many dresses and certainly not formal ones," her editor at the *Tribune* advised, "because, since the Court life has been destroyed and the Nazis have come to power, there must be no social life." Thinking of the remark later, Martha had to smile. Nobody in America had known very much about Germany or her new rulers.

Roosevelt's first Ambassador to the Third Reich was 64 in the summer of 1933. A plain, toothsome man, Professor Dodd had the unblinking gaze of his idol, Woodrow Wilson, whose public papers he had helped edit. Joy outside of his family came to Dodd only from within. It was an emotion he distrusted and Roosevelt could not have chosen a better man to abjure the blandishments of diplomatic life in Berlin if, indeed, any remained.

A self-made man from the pine brakes and red soil of an impoverished family of North Carolina farmers, William E. Dodd showed an early predilection for the past. Born just four years after the surrender at

Appomatox, he was nicknamed "Monk Dodd" by his schoolmates. Denied admission to the University of North Carolina due to his lowly origins, he passed through a series of military and polytechnic institutes but failed in his quest to secure an appointment to the United States Military Academy at West Point; a tragedy that in his mature years the unmilitary professor considered a distinct blessing.

After receiving a Bachelor's degree from the Virginia Polytechnic Institute he stayed on for two more years as an instructor of history before sailing at age 28 to Germany with money from a rich uncle to study at the University of Leipzig. There he grew his first beard, was seen with a woman of doubtful repute, and wrote a thesis of 90 pages—long for its day—on the origins of the Democratic party. In 1899 he received his doctorate, cum laude, and returned home to see the turn of the century but no job offers.

American history when Dodd came to it in 1900 was largely the history of England in America. Compiled by the patrician sons of wealthy New England families, it traced the influence of English thought and culture in America from the Discovery to the second administration of Jefferson. Geographically, these multi-volumed works saw the pageant of America as unfolding along the rock-bound coast of New England and the gentle inlets of the Middle Atlantic States. The existence of lands west of the Ohio River was recognized but unchronicled. As for the South, it extended no further than Jefferson's pleasant valley plantation in Virginia. Specialized studies such as European or diplomatic history were unknown. America's historians, like her newspaper editors, showed no great interest in the European continent until 1917, when large numbers of their countrymen returned to the Old World to fight and to die.

Dodd's first position was as an instructor of history and economics at Randolph-Macon College in Ashland, Virginia, a town without paved roads, electricity or running water. He lived in a small house by the railway tracks, lectured 15 hours a week and in his first year sent out more than a dozen appeals for employment elsewhere.

Fifty years earlier he might have tried his hand at writing popular history, but by 1905 the historical romance had lost its appeal. To be noticed, an historian had to write for his fellow historians. Dodd's first book, a life of Nathaniel Macon, came out in 1903, to be followed by a second on Jefferson Davis four years later. But his true salvation lay in the historical manuscripts he uncovered in the garrets and cellars of southern courthouses and in the papers and diaries he begged from the heirs of southern gentlemen. With these he founded a local historical society and a journal that he and his students filled with the biographies of notable Virginians. Slowly, the south became aware of its past and American academia of William E. Dodd.

After eight years at Randolph-Macon College and numerous appearances before the American Historical Association he was offered the position of Associate Professor of Southern History at the University of Chicago. He accepted reluctantly, fearing that he might fail in the north. He had married in 1901, above his station, and had two small children.

He need not have worried. For the next twenty years a sea breeze stirred the waters of American history and blew relentlessly in Dodd's direction. Historians, along with the rest of the nation, had no choice but to follow. Its sirens were the popular novelists and the muckraking journalists of the mass subscription newspapers who drew the nation's attention to the sweatshops of America and the fabulous luxury of the country's iron and railroad tycoons.

Why did the New World suffer such inequalities of destiny? The traditional reply was that injustice had always existed and would always exist. Its root causes lay beyond the power of the human mind to comprehend or of the human hand to correct. Elder historians offered little insight. The aloof grandeur of their pose hardly touched the grim reality of America's industrial age.

It was different for historians of Dodd's generation. They had not been born to the powerful families of the Northeast. For the most part they were Southerners and Midwesterners, many of them self-taught men who had made their way in academia against the resistance of Eastern snobbery. To write the history of the deep South or of the California Gold Rush was to set oneself against the interests of an older, established history. The progressive historians, as they called themselves, equated democracy not with Boston's Brahmins or Virginia's one hundred ruling families, but with the inarticulate common man. When they wrote "the people," they meant dirt farmers, indentured servants, missionaries and immigrants, men and women like their own fathers and grandfathers.

To their eyes society had never been permanent or immutable. American history *was* conflict and change and American progress the triumph of the common man over privilege and monopoly and the enemies of change. Democracy had only been given a start at the Constitutional convention; and Dodd often remarked that, even in America, democracy had only been tried for a few brief years.

Enrollment in history courses at Chicago continued slow. Sixty percent of the students left in their first year, siphoned off by the lucrative opportunities in business and finance. The task, as Dodd and the other progressives saw it, was to turn the poorest material into nothing less than the thinking element of the nation. Scholars must concentrate on teaching. Dodd had not preached egalitarianism all his life to disport himself like an intellectual baron in the classroom. He dispensed with the twin goads of the snap quiz and the exhaustive reading list. Instead of formal lectures he delivered narrative, impressionistic soliloquies. Since his platform style was poor—his voice was weak—his new style increased his effectiveness. He talked along as if his students were sitting in his living room, throwing out astonishing insights into the lives of the great figures of the South as if he had been part of their households. His gracious manner and skeptical humor, combined with an easy intimacy, led many of his students to think that they had been remade in his classes. The antebellum South lived in the classrooms of Chicago; and a growing number of history professors and department heads could boast that they had received their graduate training under Dodd's careful tutelage.

Still, after thirty years of teaching, he was disappointed in his career. Unlike many of his colleagues, he had not gone into the government under Wilson's administration. He was old-fashioned enough to believe that scholars should stand aside from political wars. Increasingly, his own work in Southern history was coming under attack by younger historians who saw that its broad sweep was often supported by too few facts. He was inclined to agree. His commitment to teaching had never allowed him the time to dig exhaustively in the historical record. He still had a three-volume history of the Old South to write. He told reporters after Roosevelt's election that if a diplomatic post were offered he hoped it would be in Holland where it was quiet and he could write.

For reasons of his own Franklin D. Roosevelt, America's patrician president, passed over the wealthy financiers of his own party and the hardly less wealthy career diplomats in the State Department to choose William E. Dodd, historian, Southerner, a man of moderate means and even more moderate tastes to be his personal representative and America's "standing example" of the democratic faith in the youngest and most exultantly fascist country in Europe. Outside of Dodd's own family few suspected that the history professor with the erect bearing would evince such a steely contempt for those who refused to believe that God had created all men equal.

The Senate confirmed him without debate, and swarms of reporters descended upon his modest home at 5757 Blackstone Avenue near the university.

"You speak German fluently?" asked a reporter.

" . . . I guess that's what got me into trouble in the first place . . ." Dodd replied.

After some thirty years he did not speak German fluently, but it would have been pointless to explain the complexities of a living language to a newspaperman. He still read it well enough, and he remembered Germany and her history vividly; but then a good memory was part of his equipment. Secretly, he was delighted to be returning. He had once imagined he might return as a minor consular official but never as his country's Ambassador.

After a week of unceasing publicity and hundreds of telegrams and letters from well-wishers he was grateful to escape to Washington to confer with President Roosevelt and the heads of the State Department.

Roosevelt was most gracious. At precisely 1 PM a servant entered the oval office, set a luncheon tray before the President and the Ambassador and quietly withdrew. Roosevelt began with the matter of the $1.2 billion that American brokerage firms had enticed Americans into loaning to German businesses and municipalities after 1926. The brokers had reaped enormous and immediate commissions; but now Germany, like the rest of the Western world, was in the midst of the Great Depression and could ill afford to pay even the interest on the loans. Officially the problem was not Washington's. Unofficially the President urged Dodd to do everything in his power to forestall a moratorium on payments. Otherwise, America's recovery would be slowed even further.

Roosevelt next turned to the problem of the Jews in Germany.

"The German authorities are treating the Jews shamefully, and the Jews in this country are greatly excited. But this is also not a governmental affair. We can do nothing except for American citizens who happen to be made victims. We must protect them, and whatever we can do to moderate the general persecution by unofficial and personal influence ought to be done."

Dodd brought up the subject of the extravagant sums spent by American diplomats abroad. Newspapers in Chicago had recently revealed that American envoys in Paris and London spent $50,000 to $100,000 of their own fortunes each year on palatial residences, servants and social display. Their intention might be to boost American stature abroad, but Dodd wondered if the emphasis on personal wealth and public display did not betray the democratic and egalitarian ideals these men were sent abroad to represent. What were the President's views?

"You are quite right. Aside from two or three general dinners and entertainments, you need not indulge in any expensive social affairs. Try to give fair attention to Americans in Berlin and occasional dinners to Germans who are interested in American relations. I think you can manage to live within your income and not sacrifice any essential parts of the service."

The meeting lasted an hour. When it was over Dodd went over to the

State Department to study the dispatches from Berlin. That evening he dined with the German Ambassador in Washington. Cocktails were served. Dodd did not drink. He went home late, unimpressed with the level of conversation.

At the end of the week he returned to Chicago to close up the house and to pack. At a farewell dinner hosted by the German American Society of Chicago, Martha found herself seated next to Carl Sandburg and his wife in the Gold Room of the Congress Hotel. While others taught her amusing remarks to make to the Fuehrer in German, Sandburg crooned the wisest advice of all:

"Find out what this man Hitler is made of, what makes his brain go round, what his bones and blood are made of. Before your eyes will pass the greatest pageant of crooks and gangsters, idealists, statesmen, criminals, diplomats and geniuses. You will see every nationality in the world. Watch them, study them, dissect them. Don't be frightened or diffident, don't let them or your experiences spoil you or your eagerness for life. Be brave and truthful, keep your poetry and integrity."

At the end of the evening as her father's colleagues came up to shake his hand in farewell, one of them whispered: "Watch your step, *Herr Doktor, Vorsichtig.*"

The German consulate in Chicago wired Berlin that the new Ambassador seemed unduly preoccupied with the tasks ahead; that his wife was a regular *"Muetterchen"* and his daughter an elegant scamp who would soon turn numerous heads in the capital. Only on the Jewish problem did the new Ambassador maintain a discreet silence.

The family traveled by train to Round Hill, the farm in Virginia that Dodd had bought to replace the one his own parents had lost. Dodd took Jefferson's dictum literally: to be a citizen of America meant to cultivate the soil. Instead of playing tennis or golf, Martha and Bill spent their summers in Virginia picking and sorting peaches and apples and bringing in the wheat crop with the farm's tenants and Negro hands. The summers in Virginia always brought the family from Chicago closer and left them strong and tanned and spiritually renewed for the academic year ahead. In Chicago her father suffered from headaches and stomach complaints due to overwork that left him fatigued and with little desire for food. At 64 he looked fragile and at least ten pounds underweight. His doctors could find nothing wrong with him and advised that he get plenty of exercise and fresh air and avoid all mental strain, a regimen he would find all but impossible to follow in Berlin.

As his family strolled along the familiar paths between farm and icehouse, blacksmith shop and dairy pasture and savored the cool evening light over the Southern hills, he motored to Washington each day in the sweltering heat to see Roosevelt again and to revisit the countryside of his birth. He said a final farewell to his 86-year-old father and wandered over the family burial ground in sight of the Valley of Virginia Campaign. At the end of the week they all motored to New York City, where he met with bankers worried about the debt problem and with Jews worried about the Jewish problem.

Shortly before noon on July 5, 1933, after purchasing several dictionaries for his family's use, he boarded the SS *Washington* with his wife, Martha and Bill and turned to wave farewell to America.

As the gangway came up and the tugs swung the great ship into the harbor, the Dodds could not know that their recent brief days at Round Hill and the voyage just beginning would be the last purely pleasurable time they would know together as a family. During the first few days out, as the wake boiled behind the ship, Martha wept bitterly at the thought of her lost life in Chicago, sunken without a trace like the continent behind her. Then she discovered the Roosevelt party and danced and drank and was gay.

The weather was calm, the sea bright.

They had been offered two staterooms, but her father insisted on cozier adjoining quarters where they could all be together. For an hour each day he read to them from a German history to accustom them to the sound of the German language. He had reviewed the deluge of dispatches from Berlin and had an inkling of what lay ahead.

On the crossing he read Edgar Ansel Mowrer's book *Germany Puts The Clock Back*. Mowrer, the Berlin correspondent for the *Chicago Daily News,* had won a Pulitzer Prize that year for his articles on Hitler's rise to power and the fall of the German Republic. The story he told was depressing and obsessed all observers of the day. Its subject was nothing less than the slow unravelling of a fledgling democracy. Germany had been a nation for less than 50 years when the Great War of 1914–1918 ended in her defeat and universal condemnation. The constitution of the newly proclaimed Republic gave equal rights and privileges to every German, but habit and social custom were not so easily rewritten. German society remained a maze of political and social castes. By the winter of 1932, when Mowrer finished his book, the great landowners and the generals, the conservative judges and the aristocratic civil servants were once again in control. The Republic, lacking in tradition, weakened by cynicism and corruption, was denounced as pacifist and materialistic: a soulless machine hamstrung by more than a score of squabbling political parties.

The book read well, and in the warm ease of the summer passage Dodd finished it in a few days. Its author was broadminded, discerning and passionately liberal; a working journalist who had covered Germany since 1924. His text was a ringing denunciation of the conservative figures around Chancellor Franz von Papen who had pruned Germany's democratic constitution to death. The previous July, the villainous von Papen had dissolved Germany's last bastion of democracy, the socialist government of Prussia. To Mowrer's burning indignation, the Prussian government and its magnificent police force capitulated without firing a shot. Germany's largest state, comprising three-fifths of its people and territory, was delivered into the hands of reactionaries. *Germany Puts The Clock Back* was ancient history when Dodd closed its cover in 1933: Hitler was Chancellor of Germany, von Papen his pathetic second in command.

Ireland rose from the sea, green and austere. Most of the ship's passengers disembarked at Southhampton. Across the channel in Le Havre, Martha stepped off briefly to say her goodbyes and to touch French soil. The trip up the Elbe was uneventful. In Hamburg the ship docked at Pier 84. Well-wishers from the embassy and the consulate in Hamburg waved from below. The family waved back. The ship's photographer posed them for a few shots and then the American family disembarked. By then they were wary of newsmen. Photographers in New York had captured them waving, arms outstretched, in a posture they soon discovered resembled the new political salute in Germany. And the *New York Times,* in an editorial, had admonished Dodd for a speech he made in Chicago in which he criticized the administrations' drift towards isolationism. "As he takes up his work in Germany," wrote the *Times*, "the Professor will learn more about diplomacy and politics, which have at least one thing in common. It is to keep opinions to one's self at certain times and under certain conditions." Martha's father would find the advice as hard to take in Germany as in America.

On the dock in Hamburg he preferred to tell German newsmen the story of Bismarck's grant of 250 million dollars to help President Lincoln fight the war between the states. The anecdote emphasized the deep historic ties that united the two countries. The Jewish Rothschilds, Dodd observed smoothly, had handled the transfer.

Elsewhere there was confusion. Bill had not foreseen the complexities involved in bringing a foreign automobile into Germany and found himself enmeshed in permits and licenses phrased in a German that defied translation. To make matters worse, Martha's father had misunderstood a telegram from the Embassy to say that travel arrangements to Berlin had been taken care of and so had done nothing about arranging transportation for his family to the capital. The result was that between dockside and train station there was a considerable delay, during which the American family that had disembarked without butler, maids, or even a personal secretary was exposed to the livid gaze of a gentleman in cutaway and striped pants who by the minute grew steadily more apoplectic. Counselor George A. Gordon was the highest ranking career man at the American Embassy in Berlin, a foreign service officer of the old school and a man steeped in the rituals of diplomatic protocol. A graduate of Harvard with a law degree from Columbia, Gordon belonged to the aristocracy within the State Department whose exaggerated manners and clipped accents set them apart from self-made men such as Martha's father. To make matters worse, Gordon possessed an awesome and uncontrollable temper and he quite disapproved of the choice of an outsider to fill the top post in Berlin although he was much too well-bred to treat Dodd with anything but the most ferocious courtesy. Strictly speaking Dodd was more than just America's representative in Berlin; he was the living, breathing personification of President Roosevelt and deserved all the pomp and obeisance due that sovereign. Gordon sought to instill this concept into the diffident professor with little success on the journey to Berlin via ordinary German railway carriage. Instead, Dodd turned the conversation to the latest developments in Berlin. Gordon, he knew from his reading at the State Department was, by virtue of his training as a lawyer, the ablest and most succinct informant on the Embassy staff.

In a neighboring compartment, Martha and her mother sat amid a profusion of flowers; her mother wishing she could flee back to Chicago every time she thought of the great responsibilities ahead and Martha tenderly and utterly asleep on her mother's shoulder. Following a roughly parallel course, Bill, an automobile enthusiast, piloted the family's modest Chevrolet sedan toward Berlin.

The ordinary German train bearing the ordinary American family arrived at the Lehrte Train Station late that afternoon. Martha was jolted awake by the screech of brakes and the trains' final lurch. She just had time enough to wipe the sleep from her eyes and to straighten her hat before she was whisked out onto the platform to face bursting flash bulbs, dignitaries in silk top hats speaking German, and American newsmen shouting questions in English.

To the horror of Counselor Gordon, who never mingled with the press, Dodd read out a brief statement to the correspondents of the *New York Times,* the *Chicago Tribune* and the Associated Press. He was against mass industrialization, he said; a nation needed its farmers. Nor was he in favor of restricting immigration. "Immigrants are the salt of our country. They bring fresh ideas, strength, brilliant minds, money." Gordon heard all of this without twitching a muscle.

The family was then loaded into several cars and driven to their hotel. Originally, the aggressive management of the Hotel Adlon had offered its hospitality to the new Ambassador, but by tradition American dignitaries stayed at the Esplanade, an airy palace of ballrooms and dining rooms erected by the former Kaiser to house his seasonal guests. The Esplanade on the Bellevuestrasse was close to the American Embassy and offered, with its inner pavillion of cloth-covered tables and peaceful petunia beds, a quiet refuge from the noise of nearby Potsdamerplatz and the chant and strut of Germany's new rulers. So in place of the three bedrooms and a sitting room in a modest hotel that her father had requested, the family was shown into the Esplanade's "Imperial Suite": five magnificent rooms with towering gilt ceilings, brocade-covered walls, marble furnishings, and so many flowers that they thought they were attending their own funerals.

Her father was distinctly embarrassed. One of his objectives was to prove that he could live within his yearly salary of $17,500. That was $7,000 more than he received as a full professor at Chicago but a pittance compared to what the envoys of France and Italy spent each year on entertainment in Berlin. The management, he was told, was charging only a third of its normal rate, in consideration of the great honor of having him under its roof. Mollified, he went to lie down for an hour with a good book. In the future the Dodds simply apologized to visitors for the unnecessary splendor of their surroundings.

They took dinner that night in one of the hotel dining rooms. Dodd was in excellent spirits, bantering in German with the waiters who responded with showers of *"Danke schoens"* and *"Bitte schoens."* Martha tasted her first German beer and ate her first heavy German meal.

Despite the lateness of the hour it was still light over the city when they finished. They strolled up the Bellevuestrasse to the Tiergarten, Berlin's great central park. Once a royal game preserve of some 600 acres, the Tiergarten was bordered on its southern edge by elegant mansions of the last century which now housed the diplomatic set and would soon house the Dodds. They entered the "Siegesallee," or Victory Mall, lined with statues of the former rulers of Brandenburg-Prussia. The Siegesallee was much derided by modern pedestrians who paused to sit on its semicircular stone benches to gaze up at "Margrave Lewis II, the Roman" or "Elector Friedrich II, the Iron . . ."

As the street lights came on and the Tiergarten grew dark and deep, Martha was amazed at how much the city with its innumerable parks and shady alcoves resembled the hushed serenity of a small American town at dusk. It had none of the strutting fanfare she had been led to expect; no pacing soldiers, no officious populace. She sensed the warmth of the people and the hush of the boulevards and decided on the spot that she loved Germany and the Germans.

"We were at the beginning of our task," her father wrote in his diary that night. "The Germans seemed very friendly."

Only once that day had a different note intruded. While riding with a young Embassy secretary from the train station to the hotel, Martha passed the German parliament building or "Reichstag," nearly deserted since the fire that had gutted its main dome some four months earlier. A vagrant Dutchman had been apprehended at the scene of the crime and the new government had been so alarmed by what it took to be a signal for a communist insurrection that it had suspended all civil liberties and arrested thousands of people. In a single night a vagrant's act of arson and the ensuing panic had hoisted Adolf Hitler to near total power.

"Oh, I thought it was burned down!" Martha exclaimed. "It looks all right to me. Tell me what happened."

"S-ssh!" hushed the young secretary. "Young lady, you must learn to be seen and not heard. You mustn't say so much and ask so many questions. This isn't America and you can't say all the things you think."

FIRST IMPRESSIONS

The next day Martha came down with a cold; outside it rained over Berlin. Sigrid Schultz, chief of the *Chicago Tribune* office in Berlin, came to call. Her father had been a famous portrait painter and Miss Schultz, although born in Chicago, had spent most of her life in Europe. She was the only woman remaining in the foreign press corps since the lady correspondent for *Isvestia* had been asked to leave. Miss Schultz told Martha about some of the more unsavory aspects of the new regime which Martha found hard to believe. Miss Schultz, she had heard, was unmarried and lived with her widowed mother. Martha concluded that the plump, blond woman with the breathless delivery must be a bit hysterical.

Another who came to call was the lithe, red-headed H. R. Knicker-bocker, the best known and highest paid correspondent in Berlin. By then Martha was back on her feet, and the two went dancing at the Hotel Eden. Martha was a good dancer although the music at the Eden was not the graceful kind she was used to in Chicago. Knickerbocker was a wonderful dancer and as they glided across the dance floor among oddly hopping German couples he asked her what she knew about Germany and the new regime. She replied that she was still getting a feel for the country. He told her a few stories about some of the leading figures, but when he sensed her indifference he turned to other topics. She found him sensual and alive although she was not normally attracted to redheads. She suspected that he would try to see her again. He was divorced, she had heard, and lived with his girlfriend in the suburb of Wannsee.

A note arrived from Sandburg full of sparks thrown off by the spinning pinwheel of his mind:

So now they have arrived in Berlin says the paper today   and said the New York Times roto last Sunday this is the way they looked in Washington just before they started   watch your notebook you are being told that   it is being hissed in your ear   if you are hard pressed for such spans of time as will get short stories onto paper anyhow: make many notes in any humptydumpty style whatever   put down any and all stray hunches and wisps of ideas   what is useless can easily be sifted out later   and the doing of paragraphs has a practice value   you have been getting into a stride that shouldn't be

lost   and give way to every beckoning to write short things impressions   sudden lyric sentences you have a gift for outpour-
ing   one time we agreed that it will always be hell for you to write
and your main consolation is that it will be a worse hell eventually for you
not to   the roto picture is lovely   alive   caught radiance
   "AND WHY NOT?"

She wanted to keep a diary of her thoughts and travels but it was
impossible: the labor pains of her arrival were too intense. Sometimes
she thought that if she jumped out of her window at the Esplanade she
would wake up on the floor next to her bed in Chicago like that other
young woman from the Midwest who awakened from her dream of Oz.
She ached for someone to hold her hand through the agony of adjust-
ment. Her sensitive, faintly neurotic nature was intensified. She needed a
sweet young man to buoy her up; if not Knickerbocker, then someone
else.

Her father encountered obstacles of his own. The American mission in
Berlin was a large one, 22 people not counting stenographers and code
clerks: eight attachés from the Army and Navy and the departments of
Agriculture and Commerce, three secretaries of embassy and nine consuls and vice consuls. In Washington he had noticed that reports from
consuls and secretaries were seldom curt or objective. Color crept in and
statements of opinion and moral judgment. Many of the reports were so
long and unwieldy that he felt sure they went unread in Washington.
One of the first tasks he set himself was to teach his staff the merits of
clear, factual prose.

He was often depressed when he returned to the Esplanade at noon to
lunch with his family. Given the tumultuous state of affairs in Germany a
number of Americans had gotten themselves into political difficulties.
One of them was Edgar Mowrer, the author of *Germany Puts The Clock
Back*. Mowrer had recently sent an article to his paper in Chicago that
had so infuriated the German Government that the Foreign Ministry
had asked for his immediate transfer. Mowrer wanted Dodd to make an
issue of his case and came to the Esplanade one evening to talk to the
Ambassador in private. Martha caught a glimpse of the newsman as he
entered her father's room: stoop-shouldered and scholarly with a great
wave of graying hair above a lofty brow. His face was full of suffering
like the face of a Christian martyr. She supposed from his passionate
opposition to the regime that he must be Jewish. She knew her father
thought that Mowrer should move on to another assignment; a few
weeks later the Mowrers and their small daughter left for America.
Happily, she thought, since she and her father were rather pro-German.

Her father was in a ticklish position. He had not yet presented his letters of credence to President Hindenburg, who was resting on his country estates and not expected to return to Berlin until late August. The British and Dutch envoys were waiting until then to enter the country, but Dodd wanted to start work right away. The State Department had arranged with the German Foreign Ministry to grant him temporary powers as an "appointed Ambassador." He could draft reports and call on officials, but all written communications between his Embassy and the Government had to be signed by Counselor Gordon. The arrangement was much to Dodd's liking. It gave him time to study the situation before taking up the irksome chore of paying courtesy calls on the other forty envoys in the capital. He decided to take advantage of the anonymity he still enjoyed to make a short trip with his family to Leipzig, the city where he had received his doctorate thirty years before.

So, almost a month to the day after they docked at Hamburg, Martha and Bill and their parents and the Hearst correspondent, Quentin Reynolds, climbed into the family's blue Chevy sedan and headed south along the old Potsdam road. Reynolds had suggested the trip. A former football player and bouncer with a degree from Brown University, Quent had been in Berlin only a few months. In New York City where he had worked as a rewrite man, he had jokingly called for the check at a newsman's tavern in German: *"Herr Ober, die Rechnung bitte!"* Protesting that he only knew saloon German, he was promptly shipped off to Berlin to replace a Hearst man who had run afoul of the authorities. Sigrid Schultz set him up in a sumptuous apartment on the Tiergarten that had once belonged to some Jewish friends of hers, and Quent lost little time in making the necessary connections. A big, bluff Irish type, he was an excellent traveling companion for the Ambassador's impetuous children. Martha planned to take in the music festival at Salzburg, and Bill wanted to rendevous with an old flame in Innsbruck.

By noon they were in Wittenberg where four centuries earlier Martin Luther had nailed his ninety-nine theses to the church door. The theses had been replaced by a bronze plaque and the church was locked. Their progress was further delayed by a procession of Brown Shirts marching through the town. Martha's father noted with satisfaction that a policeman watched the parade with a look of disapproval.

By one o'clock they were in Leipzig, lunching at the Auerbach Keller where Faust made his pact with the devil. While the young people stayed and drank the light German beer, Martha's parents wandered about the old town unrecognized and on the following morning took the train back to Berlin.

Quent and Bill and Martha pressed south on the road to Munich. The most remarkable event of the trip, in retrospect, occurred on the first day out.

Germany that August was doubly festive. In the wave of renewed optimism that followed the inauguration of the new regime, villages dredged bracken ponds, house fronts were painted for the first time in years, chimneys patched, roofs repaired, fields long dormant broken to the plow. As if in sympathy the weather turned hot and dry; one of the most splendid summers on record and one that promised a bountiful harvest in the fall. Villages were decorated with flowers, house fronts with festive garlands. Everywhere they traveled the three Americans saw the red, white, and black banner of the new regime flying from town halls, hostelries, even from the steeples of churches. All afternoon as they motored south, they overtook processions of men in brown uniforms marching and singing and waving their flags in recognition of the Chevy sedan's diplomatic licence plate. Just as enthusiastically, Martha *"Heiled"* back despite the looks Bill and Quent traded and Bill's sarcastic cracks about his sister's maturity. She could not help herself. The enthusiasm she saw was infectious and acted upon her like the strong southern wine she had yet to taste. She was drunk on the ebullience of Germany's national awakening.

They reached Nuremberg around dinner time and checked into a modest hotel in the center of town before going out to see the sights and get a bite to eat. On the Koenigstrasse they ran into a crowd of some 2,000 people surrounding a street tram from which a figure in a white cotton shift was being removed by a number of huge men in brown uniform. The apparition turned out to be a young woman, her face smeared with white powder, her head shaven, her blond braids pinned to a placard around her neck that read: "I have offered myself to a Jew."

From the tram her escort led her through the lobbies of several hotels and in and out of nearby cabarets. When she stumbled they lifted her to her feet; when the crowd cried: "Speech! Speech!" they lifted her to their shoulders for everyone to see.

Martha wanted to follow, but Quent and Bill pulled her back; they returned to the hotel and got drunk on red champagne. Even the hardboiled Quent was unnerved by the sight. He pumped the waiter for facts and learned that the young woman was an Aryan named Betti Suess and that she had been discovered in the arms of her Jewish fiancé. The waiter whispered that "Herr S." was behind the spectacle. Herr Streicher was the mayor of Nuremberg and the publisher of two exceedingly anti-semitic scandal sheets.

Reports of similar incidents had reached the foreign press, but Quent was the first American newsman to actually witness such a spectacle.

With two unimpeachable witnesses by his side, he wanted to cable the story immediately; but Martha begged him not to. It would hurt her father whose relations with the new government were just beginning, she argued. Besides, they did not know the whole story and though the scene had been grim it was outweighed by the many constructive things they had seen earlier that day.

Quent went to his room and telephoned his bureau in Berlin. It was a big story, his editor agreed, but it would be safer if Quent mailed it to New York. He should also avoid any mention of Martha and Bill so as not to embarrass the new Ambassador.

Quent returned to the bar and got drunk.

In the end he was scooped by a group of British tourists who were in one of the cabarets when Betti Suess was hoisted onto the stage. They sent a letter of protest to city officials pointing out that the public humiliation of a 19-year-old girl would only disgust the numerous foreign visitors coming to Nuremberg to attend the upcoming Party Rally. The *New York Times* carried the story of the British protest but made no mention of the presence of the children of the American Ambassador. That was left to the *London Times* as Quent and Bill and Martha returned to Berlin. Entering the city their car was stopped and partially searched and Martha's father had his hands full keeping that part of the story out of the papers. By then Martha had put the affair completely out of her mind. Only later, when her own nerves began to fray, did the pale figure with the powdered face and the shorn head return to haunt her dreams.

Martha was no more prejudiced than others of her generation who proudly proclaimed their Welsh, Scottish or German blood. She had known a number of Jews in Chicago where she had attended the progressive University High School or "Jew High" as it was called by its critics. She even had a Jewish boyfriend for a while and although she did not consider them as physically attractive as her own people and regrettably not as socially acceptable, she admired their intellectual brilliance and their long heritage of literacy.

The Foreign Ministry called to apologize for the unfortunate occurrence; an isolated case they assured the American family. The culprits would be punished; the authorities in Nuremberg had been alerted. Meanwhile the *New York Times* reported that Betti Suess had been taken to a mental asylum, her mind broken by her humiliation.

At a news briefing Propaganda Minister Goebbels tried to excuse the incident to members of the foreign press. They must realize that during the long years of struggle against the Treaty of Versailles many Germans had felt spiritually and politically imprisoned. Now they were free and in power and isolated elements among them were sometimes guilty of excesses. Surely the newsmen must admit that such an occurrence could happen in their countries?

If it did, barked a voice from the front row, the culprits would find themselves back in prison.

Beaten, the Propaganda Minister turned to other topics.

Embarrassed by the extravagance of their apartments at the Esplanade and eager to establish a residence of their own, Martha and her mother toured the elegant homes for rent along Embassy Row. Some were being let for amazingly low sums because their owners, wealthy Jews in many instances, planned to leave the country or welcomed the protection afforded them by a foreign diplomat living under their roof. To the two American women the large mansions with their clutter of bric-a-brac and separate worlds for servant and master seemed strange and stilted. By diplomatic standards the Dodds wanted only a modest residence. They did not want and could not afford a palace or any structure so vast that it resembled Versailles and intimidated the American visitors who came to call.

Eventually they settled on a secluded four-storey villa built by the architect Kristeller for the industrialist Ferdinand Warburg. Located behind a wrought iron fence at the end of a secluded drive off the noisy Tiergartenstrasse, the villa nestled up against the southeastern edge of the vast Tiergarten Park. Martha's father was especially pleased with the location since it was only a short walk from the American Embassy on the Bendlerstrasse.

The ground floor was given over to servants' quarters, porter's rooms and a huge kitchen and scullery. A short entryway between two tall corinthian pillars led to a spiral staircase that rose to an oval ballroom on the second floor and to two adjoining reception rooms, one in pink satin, the other in green, and a dining room that seated 25. In the rear there was a large sunroom with red silk drapes and a stone terrace that descended to a large goldfish pond and one of the finest private gardens in Berlin. Quiet gravel paths disappeared amid azalea bushes and horse chestnut trees that were dropping their mahogany orbs as the family moved in.

The garden, with its winding paths and the birdhouse that Martha's parents built, became a refuge for the family after the manner of "Round Hill." Of an afternoon Martha's father read undisturbed in the fading light on the stone terrace or wandered with his wife in quiet conversation through the deep garden. During Fourth of July celebrations guests felt safe enough in its privacy to share confidences and when Martha and her mother and brother were alone they took their tea along its grassy edge with the butler Fritz Schlappack waiting in attendance. Behind them the house rose, storey upon storey, covered with ivy; a hanging garden in the middle of Berlin's Babylon.

Standing in the middle of a broad, flat expanse of reclaimed marshland under a hot summer sun, her light summer shoes all but ruined, Martha Dodd had to admit that she was hot, tired and frightfully bored.

A young woman, an American sociologist, one of the "social work folk" as her father called them, had invited her to visit an *"Arbeits-dienstslager"* or German labor camp, outside Berlin. Martha had accepted gladly.

By establishing labor camps for young men under twenty-five, the Government hoped not only to solve the immediate problem of unemployment but also to erase the long standing prejudice between "Workers of the Mind" and "Workers of the Fist." A further consequence was also not lost on Germany's new rulers: by moving young people away from their villages and home towns and into different dialect regions, they were creating, for the first time in Germany, a generation loyal to the entire nation and not just to the Rhineland or Bavaria. Service in the labor camps in the summer of 1933 was still voluntary: the young men Martha saw digging drainage ditches were youths working for a decent meal and a chance to enter the ranks of the new ruling class.

While similar public works projects were being carried out in America, it was rumored that Germany's agrarian camps served the dual purpose of public service and military training. Martha was eager for an opportunity to prove Germany's venomous critics wrong.

The Foreign Ministry and the Propaganda Ministry lost no time in arranging the visit when they heard that the daughter of the American Ambassador would be going along. On the drive out Martha sat in the rumble seat next to a young Foreign Ministry attaché while her sociology friend sat up front beside the Propaganda man. As yet Martha could understand only a few words of German and the sociologist had to translate the stream of glowing prospects outlined by the Propaganda man. Again and again Martha nodded her head in agreement.

The four young people trooped out to the huts on the marshes, toured the recreation hall, the dormitories and the common dining room. The sociologist snapped pictures and took statements. The camp boss invited them to sample the noon fare of prunes and cold mush. Afterwards they walked more miles over the marsh to observe the young men digging ditches. There were no military exercises or parades. Everything was as Martha had expected. Bored, her white shoes covered with mud, she was eager to return home and say "I told you so!" to her hypercritical friends among the American correspondents. She pled a previous engagement.

They had not driven far when they saw groups of men running across a field and then falling to the ground to take cover. Others were practicing with rifles. The sociologist insisted on stopping the car and rushed over to take pictures.

"You see, this is what they really do," she whispered to Martha. "The camp we have just been in was forewarned that we were coming, so we saw nothing but the most innocent and constructive activity."

Martha refused to accept her interpretation. She was tired of people looking for the worst in Germany. She agreed with her father: the "social work folk" were intent on seeing just one side to every problem.

The Propaganda man wore a look of deep distress.

As she had sensed from her first evening in Berlin, Americans had a completely false picture of Germany. She had expected to find an officious, impatient people, a nation of martinets. Instead she encountered, from the highest circles on down, a people who were serious and kindly, honest and sincere and obviously sympathetic with her first stammered forays into their language. No one tried to cheat her; everyone was friendly, alert, helpful. She compared them to the French whom she had gotten to know on her first trip to Europe. The French in comparison seemed insincere, superficial, conniving. Their language, she decided, was not beautiful at all but nasal compared to the crisp, rounded tones of German. Without realizing it she had absorbed a good deal of the regime's Francophobia.

Her sympathies did not go unnoticed. A concerted effort was made by several young men in the Foreign Ministry, who had connections with the political police and propaganda, to win her over to the New Germany. They spoke fluent English, knew the latest idioms, one had even visited Washington, but her feminine intuition told her that they were too sly and devious in their attentions and in the end she avoided their company.

Greater success was had by a young fellow in the Brown Shirt organization whose appeal was completely personal. He took her on drives and long walks on Sunday when all of Germany was out walking in the country. He took her swimming and to movies and to nightclubs and sent her notes and flowers. He was passionate and young and middle-class and filled with the ardor of his ideals and his hope for the future. He lent her pamphlets on the menace of Communism and the power of the Jews and although she made little headway with these she found the sweet brown-shirted youth with the peculiar Slavic name terribly endearing. Soon she too was attacking the shamefulness of the Treaty of

Versailles and praising the wisdom of the Fuehrer to Americans who stopped by the Embassy. Her father called her his Nazi daughter, a tactic that only made her more resolute in her conversion. The daily persecutions that robbed him of sleep and appetite she passed off as the excesses of youth, regrettable surely, but negligible notes in the great symphony of the national awakening. She felt as one with the tens of thousands of young people in Germany who saw a new world being prepared for them and rejoiced to be a part of it.

A countervailing angel appeared in the guise of a young secretary from the French Embassy, Armand Bérard. Thirtyish, tall, with brown hair and perfect features, he asked her parents if he might take their daughter out. He spoke excellent English and was an admirer of America. He was understanding and patient; she stubborn and anti-French. They danced and dined and argued and made up and went for long rides in the moody lake region around Berlin. Bérard became a familiar face in the Dodd household; a defender of the anti-fascist faith to a lady who often refused to look his way. After one spat Martha told her mother that Armand was just another moth-eaten Frenchman under a patina of protocol. Protocol was one of the worst slurs in the Dodd vocabulary.

In Chicago her friends read her letters about tea dances, airplane rides, and long autumnal walks in the Tiergarten. In Berlin, she wrote, she was slaying them with her proud, cold gaze, the bankers, the princes and movie stars. But not a word did she say about her writing except that she could do it any time but chose not to. She was swollen with nervous vanity.

She was not writing. She was living.

Martha met her first Nazi bigwig through Tom Delmer of the *London Daily Express*. The corpulent Delmer was famous among the press corps in Berlin for his swank dinner parties. He was also well known to figures high in the new government because he had flown with Hitler on the presidential campaigns of the previous year. Several official denunciations had been filed against Tom for being to all intents and purposes a Nazi himself but that did not keep British Embassy secretaries from dropping by his elegant flat on the Viktoriastrasse for a convening of the "Flying Circus."

To Martha the "Flying Circus" appeared to be a number of rugged young men in their thirties and forties who arrived in dark suits or in the brown uniform of the government's political soldiers. She could only guess at their prominence since their government was so unlike hers. The ones in uniform wore bits of gold insignia on their collars and red bands on their field caps which reminded her of the "kepis" worn by the French military. They were polite to her, briskly shook her hand as they listened intently to Tom's flowing introduction. They held her chair, made sure her wine glass was full but, despite the presence of other chicly dressed women, the gathering was distinctly male. They were courteous but uninterested until they had had quite a bit to drink and then an arm might be draped across the back of her chair as the talk grew loud and flushed.

Martha could take care of herself. She was a married woman after all, in the final stage of getting a divorce. The marriage—to a New York banker, of all people—had been a rash, impetuous act, quickly regretted, and had cost her a number of cherished illusions. But the secret, she felt, gave her a psychological advantage over those who were not married. She was still a sensuous woman in love with clothes and flowers and moonlit walks but wary of being misled again. She was quite willing to sit back and bide her time.

The emergence of the flapper in the Twenties had changed American and European women. The flapper and her excesses, never uncontrolled except in the eyes of *The Ladies Home Journal,* made cheek-to-cheek dancing, drinking, and petting commonplace. Sex became an accepted fact. Men and women languished, even died, from lack of it. Short hair, make-up, flimsy dresses, were the new hallmarks of conformity. Women, even those her mother's age, flashed silken, later bare legs and went out at night in gowns that left their arms and shoulders uncovered. In the moonlight, on long drives, the new woman was lean, sensual, gamine.

By the Thirties the flapper had done her work and retired. Hemlines descended again to mid-calf; Martha had to lower hers even further on arriving in Germany. Women petted with less abandon and smoked with greater intensity. Martha commonly stayed out to all hours of the night, danced in the arms of her partners, drank cocktails and frequently smoked more than was good for her. If a party became too disheveled or sordid with drink she left. Drunkenness was considered unsightly.

Tom's party did not degenerate into that sort of affair although she could not say what happened after she left. The guests did consume great quantities of alcohol as if they had been kept from it for too long and needed it as a narcotic against the great exertions of their work.

Nevertheless, she was relieved by the appearance of a great bear of a man with a huge lantern jaw who crooned English as if he were on the stage which, in a sense, he was. Dr. Ernst Hanfstaengl—everyone called him "Putzi"—apologized, as he took her hand, for not meeting her family at the train station; but that afternoon he had been throwing a party of his own on the Pariser Platz. It was typical of Putzi, who considered himself a self-styled representative of America, to upstage the arrival of the new Ambassador.

In his late forties, well over six feet tall, Putzi was a huge man with large hands and a long nose. The only thing dainty about him was his vanity, which was ever-present and gave to his dark facial expressions a preening, feminine cast. His family had made its money in art reproduction, Martha gathered, and Putzi knew everything there was to know about 19th-century German art and German wines. He had been everywhere and knew everyone: New York, Paris, London, Theodore Roosevelt, Franklin D. Roosevelt, Churchill, Pablo Picasso, people she had not even heard of. He knew scientists and writers and humorists of every description and adeptly appended their pedigrees and credentials to his conversation as he dropped their names.

He was attached to the huge Liaison Office that oversaw the mighty task of meshing the new government with the old. His field was the foreign press, particularly the British and American correspondents who worked in Berlin.

He immediately sat down at Tom's baby grand and began to pound out a medley of Harvard march tunes, Chopin, Beethoven and Wagner, his rich black mane falling over his brow with each surge of inspiration. He was an accomplished, if perhaps too muscular, pianist and rarely completed a composition before moving on to the next. She was told that he was one of Hitler's oldest friends and was frequently summoned to play for the Fuehrer late at night.

Putzi was far more cultivated than any of the others in the room. He dominated the party with his piano playing and his incessant conversation in German and English. His voice could whisper like the wind or outbellow the sergeant major types around him. Putzi was forever making a commotion.

He wanted to see much more of her, he said; Martha could tell that he had an eye for pretty women. He wanted to introduce her to Hitler. Would she let him do that? Martha said she would. No other girl from Chicago was being offered the opportunity.

When he came to dinner at their home on the Tiergartenstrasse he amused even her father who found it hard to be amused by showoffs. Theodore Roosevelt's son had just passed through Berlin and Putzi's face darkened momentarily when Dodd referred somewhat sarcastically to "Teddy, Jr." Putzi said he had known the late President Roosevelt very well. They had been at Harvard together. Once at a stag party at the White House he had broken seven strings on the presidential piano.

He was full of such stories. No one, not even he, could remember if they were true. His personality was so exaggerated that it was possible that life exaggerated itself to fit his mold.

He did not forget his promise to introduce Martha to Hitler. He kept phoning up and saying such things as: "Hitler needs a woman. Hitler should have an American woman. A lovely woman could change the whole destiny of Europe. Martha, you are that woman!"

A marriage between the Fuehrer and the youthful daughter of the American Ambassador was an alliance close to Putzi's heart. Despite endless hours with Hitler, Putzi had never gotten him beyond a certain point in his comprehension of America. Hitler persisted in his belief that America was on the verge of political and moral collapse and that the only truly admirable American was Henry Ford. Lessons from the marriage bed would surely be more effective and—who could tell—perhaps Putzi as the new Foreign Minister, might be able to arrange a state visit to Washington for the Fuehrer.

On the appointed day Martha dressed demurely, without make-up, and wore a veil. For naturalness she added a fresh flower. Her hands were cold with excitement.

In Berlin Hitler met numerous foreigners every day. Some were presented by the Foreign Office, others by his deputy, Rudolf Hess, a few by Alfred Rosenberg, the head of the Party's "Foreign Office." Putzi preferred to work outside the Fuehrer's engagement calendar. So familiar was he with Hitler's habits that he knew just when the Chancellor broke for tea each day and went across the Wilhelmstrasse with a few well-chosen companions to sit quietly in the lobby of the Hotel Kaiserhof. That was the time to catch the Leader's attention, when he was relaxed and responsive and most himself.

On the appointed afternoon Putzi had two introductions to perform: the beautiful Martha and the Polish tenor Jan Kiepura. People who knew Putzi often had the impression that he used his influence to expand his own social connections as much as Hitler's.

Putzi had Martha and Kiepura ensconced in plenty of time at a table among the potted palms. When Hitler entered with a few friends and several bodyguards, he took Kiepura over first to be introduced. Putzi then whispered something into the Leader's ear and hurried back to Martha. The Leader had been told, he said. He brought Martha over. Hitler stood, took her hand and kissed it, said a few words in German that she could not understand and then she said good-bye. He kissed her hand again and that was that. She returned to her table.

Kiepura remained. The Leader's passion was clearly for music, although he kept throwing Martha tentative glances. His charm was in his voice and in his words and these Martha could not feel. Nor was he comfortable with foreign women however lovely. His fame was as a German and he had told Hanfstaengl time and time again that politics was his wife. But Hanfstaengl never listened, and Hitler was baffled by these introductions to pretty creatures whom he could not understand and who could not understand him.

At dinner that night Martha described the meeting to her father. Hitler's face was soft as if it had no bones. She had hardly noticed the little moustache. His eyes were his most striking feature. She described them as pale blue, but others saw them as black or flint gray. Few disputed their remarkable power. There had been nothing distinctive about his dress or bearing. To her he had seemed oddly tender, almost retiring. She found it hard to believe that such a self-conscious man had risen to the pinnacle of power in his country.

It was indeed surprising, her father agreed, but then they had only seen him with foreigners and others of greater education and social distinction. They had not seen him among his followers.

The meeting nevertheless had impressed Martha, if only for the unexpected impression it had left. She had not often had her hand kissed. Her father teased her that she must not wash it or Hitler's delicate autograph would be erased.

PUTZI HANFSTAENGL

The Hanfstaengls were prominent folk in Germany. They supplied three generations of privy counselors to the Dukes of Sax-Coburg-Gotha while distinguishing themselves as patrons and connoisseurs of the arts. The invention of the photographic camera in the 19th century and a new process that put more colored dots to a square centimeter made Putzi's paternal grandfather a wealthy man and the Hanfstaengl name preeminent in the field of art reproduction. Putzi's mother came from Connecticut. Her father had been a general for the North in the American Civil War and later an illustrator with Admiral Perry on the voyage to Japan.

The children were brought up by governesses. When he was two, little Ernst contracted diphtheria, in that day a dreaded killer of young children. To coax the child to eat despite the painful membrane clouding its throat, the family concierge crooned over and over, "Putzi, eat this now, Putzi." In Bavarian dialect "Putzi" meant "little fellow." Little Ernst ate and grew to six feet four inches in height.

After graduating from the Royal Bavarian Wilhelm's Gymnasium in Munich, where his form master was Heinrich Himmler's father, Putzi went to America to attend Harvard College and to prepare to take over the American branch of the family art firm in New York City. Tall, big-boned, with a youthful, lantern-jawed face, the towering German-American stood out in any group of undergraduates as the most boisterous and gleeful, especially if he could get his mitts on a piano. Putzi or "Hanfy," as he preferred to be called in America, was popular with his classmates and regularly accompanied the Harvard football team on its games away from home. At Harvard he added to his list of notable acquaintances T. S. Eliot, Walter Lippmann, Robert Benchley and John Reed. He went out for crew and won the reputation of being a "good oar" as well as some fame when he saved a theology student from drowning in the Charles River.

Whatever Harvard's gift to Hitler may have been, Harvard's gift to Hanfstaengl was not the habit of regular introspection. At the turn of the century, Harvard College gave little thought to instilling in its charges an awareness of lives not their own. At most, the College sought to impart pride of birth and confidence in social position. Putzi arrived with plenty of both, indeed twice as much as other students, since he claimed both the New York Sedgwicks and the Bavarian Hanfstaengls as his forebears.

After nearly not graduating with the class of 1909 for writing a too effusive essay on Goethe's "Italian Journey," Putzi returned to Germany and the bedside of his dying father. He took his military service with the Royal Bavarian Foot Guards and then made the grand tour of the universities of Grenoble, Vienna and Rome.

In 1911, at age twenty-four, he returned to New York City to take over the Hanfstaengl Gallery on the corner of Fifth Avenue and 45th Street. A bachelor, he took his meals at the nearby Harvard Club. Professionally and socially he mixed with the likes of Pierpont Morgan, Arturo Toscanini, Henry Ford, Charlie Chaplin and Senator Franklin D. Roosevelt.

With the outbreak of hostilities between Great Britain and Germany in 1914, Putzi approached the German military attaché in New York, Captain Franz von Papen, with the request to be smuggled home, but tactfully withdrew when he saw how blasé the captain was about such arrangements. For the duration of the war Putzi confined his subversive activities to entertaining musicians off German ships embargoed in New York harbor. He was a fabulous piano player. One of his teachers had studied under Liszt.

An influential firm of solicitors spared him the indignity of internment as an "enemy alien" but could not prevent the Alien Property Custodian from seizing the Hanfstaengl Gallery and auctioning its contents and copyrights for a paltry $8,000. The insult rankled in the American half of Putzi's breast for the rest of his life.

Traveling on an imposingly embossed Swiss passport, he returned to Germany in 1921 with his wife Helene—the daughter of a German-American businessman and like himself a "hyphenate"—and his infant son Egon. He had been promised a partnership in the family art firm in Munich but his older and only surviving brother, Edgar, suggested a brief apprenticeship first. Edgar was a democrat; Putzi, like his mother and sister, a monarchist to the core. It was a classic case of sibling rivalry. Disdainfully, Putzi rejected Edgar's offer and bragged later that he never so much as set foot in the office with his name on the door.

Instead he enrolled in the University of Munich and moved his family into a small flat in the bohemian district of Schwabing. Winter rains drenched the heating coal on his balcony; on better days his wife hung out the family laundry for all the world to see. Life in the flat on the Genzstrasse was a far cry from the Sunday afternoons of his father, Hofrat Hanfstaengl, who in his day had entertained the likes of Richard Strauss, Fridtjof Nansen and Mark Twain in his villa outside Munich.

Chance and a complimentary ticket brought Putzi to Munich's L-

shaped Kindl Keller to hear a speech by an unknown political orator named Adolf Hitler.

A waiter in a railway restaurant, was Putzi's first thought, when he saw the oddly dressed figure in blue suit and leather vest. The Kindl that night was packed with people in Bavarian peasant dress: shopkeepers, artisans, former Army officers, minor civil servants, students.

Putzi, who would hear Hitler speak on innumerable occasions, came to think of him as a *"Sprachmensch,"* a person who lived in the spoken word. Absolutely unimpressive when silent, except for his startling eyes and handsome hands, Hitler was like a Stradivarius violin lying in its case. Put bow to instrument and the man was transformed into a speaker of unparalleled power. Unlike other orators then touring Germany, Hitler never spoke down to his audience. His language was the language of the crowd, the dialect of the trenches, the vocabulary of the street and the public market.

The atmosphere was charged that night. Hitler had just been released from prison for disrupting the meeting of a rival party by leaping onto the stage. The police had their agents in the hall and he had to be careful what he said. Perhaps that accounted for the brilliance of his performance which Putzi would never hear equalled for innuendo.

There was a roar of applause when Hitler was introduced. Purposefully, he strode to the front of the stage and, standing at attention, started to speak. The impression was disappointing at first, tentative and rehearsed. But soon some groups in the audience—housewives, war veterans, unemployed university graduates—began to respond with cries of "Bravo" and *"Ganz richtig."* Hitler shifted his stance slightly and began to employ his face and hands for effect. His words poured forth, infallibly, relentlessly. His rhythm was march time, his insinuations laced with honeyed wit. Interrupted by applause, he held his pose until quiet returned. His voice was strong and supple, not hoarse as it would become later after years of addressing monster rallies.

He reminded Putzi of a fencer who harbored his strength for the next onslaught. His control was complete and mesmerized him as much as his audience. Yet, he was agile and cunning too, suddenly abandoning his own perspective to mimic the arguments of his opponents. He could capture the hesitancies of the bogus intellectual or the liberal politician, hold their characters up to ridicule, and then assume his own demeanor again. A figure eight cut by a rapier was how Putzi saw the technique. When it was done Hitler had the crowd close to ecstasy. A creature of the voice. A *Sprachmensch*.

Cheering, rapping on tables, the audience was on its feet. Hitler cemented the bond by drinking deeply from a stein of beer passed up to him by one of his bodyguards. His face streamed with perspiration; his shirt collar and shirt front were drenched from his efforts. Putzi pushed forward to shake his hand and to tell Herr Hitler that he agreed with 95 percent of what he had heard.

"I am sure we shall not have to quarrel about the odd five per cent," Hitler replied. A gold-plated safety pin held his shirt collar together.

That night it was some time before Putzi could fall asleep.

He took his wife Helene to hear Herr Hitler at the Zirkus Krone, where there were private boxes. Afterwards Helene invited Hitler to visit them at their flat on the Genzstrasse. He was soon a frequent guest at their home for the noonday meal or for afternoon coffee. He broke lumps of chocolate into his coffee and called the mixture "Café Genz."

"He was very respectful, even diffident," Putzi recalled, "and very careful to adhere to the forms of address still *de rigeur* in Germany between—what shall I say?—people of lower rank when speaking to those of better education, title and academic attainment."

The Hanfstaengls were not the only respectable family to take the former dispatch runner under their wing. Herr Hitler knew the Bruckmanns of Munich. The Bruckmann House published Nietzsche, Rainer Maria Rilke and Oswald Spengler. Frau Else Bruckmann was in her early sixties when Hitler met her and still retained much of her former dark beauty. She had been born a princess. It was Frau Bruckmann who persuaded Hitler to purchase a blue suit and to wear white shirts with black ties. She was his admirer, disciple and instructor on how to eat such delicacies as steamed artichokes.

Hitler had already made the acquaintance of Frau Helene Bechstein of the piano manufacturing family. The Bechsteins stayed at the exclusive Bayrischer Hof when they came to Munich. One night, after returning from the Bechstein's, Hitler confided to Putzi: "I felt quite embarrassed in my blue suit. The servants were all in livery and we drank nothing but champagne before the meal. And you should have seen the bathroom, you can even regulate the heat of the water."

These women from Germany's better families applied the finishing touches to Hitler's revolutionary attire. Helene Bechstein bought him his first police dog and presented him with his first dog whip. Hitler wore the whip strapped to his right wrist, its pointed tip just grazing his boot top. Not to be outdone, Frau Bruckmann bought him a heavier specimen with a loaded silver handle. A third, made from rhinoceros hide, came from the proprietress of an inn on the Obersalzberg.

Hitler's dog whips became a hallmark of his civilian attire and, like his moustache, were much copied by his closest companions. Needless to say, the dogs that crossed Hitler's path were usually of the two-legged variety. Wandering the streets of Munich in his old raincoat and floppy artist's hat, his dog whip trailing from one wrist, his German shepherd scouring the pavements ahead, Herr Hitler looked to Putzi like a perfect desperado.

Unaccountably late for appointments, forever behind schedule, eating on the run, sleeping until noon, Hitler spread his network of political contacts from beer halls to police precincts. He lived in a small room at the end of a narrow entryway at No. 41 Therischstrasse. So many people came to see him that his landlady let him use her entryway as a reception room. His bedroom could not have been more than nine feet across, Putzi guessed, and his bed's headboard blocked part of the room's only window. Worn linoleum and a couple of scatter rugs covered the floor. The only piece of furniture in the room, other than a small table and chair, was a homemade bookcase. Visiting one day, Putzi made a mental list of the volumes that nourished Hitler's mind: illustrated encyclopedias, histories of Frederick the Great, works by Treitschke, Clausewitz and Houston Stewart Chamberlain. On the bottom shelf, among cheap editions of Edgar Wallace, lay the bachelor's expedients: illustrated guides to the history of erotic art and western morals. From these Putzi became convinced that as long as Herr Hitler remained unmarried he must work out his passions on the masses.

Helene was not so sure. "Putzi, I tell you that man is a neuter," she said. But her extrovert husband ignored her feminine intuition and wasted many hours in the coming years searching for the right woman for Hitler.

An unused piano in Hitler's entryway provided the bond that held the two together, despite their dissonant natures, for the next decade and a half. One day, due to appear in court for some outrage he had engineered, Hitler grew increasingly depressed as the hour drew near. Putzi, whose Schwabing flat was too small for a piano, sat down at the toothless instrument and began to bang out the overture to Wagner's "Meistersinger." Within minutes, Hitler's spirits had lifted, and he was marching up and down the worn linoleum, swinging his arms in time to the music like an orchestra conductor.

"You must play for me often," Hitler told Putzi. "There is nothing like that to get me into tune before I face the public."

In an age when the mechanical gramophone was still a plaything of the rich, Hanfstaengl's pounding energy, his crooning lips and thrashing hair earned him a special place in Hitler's Machiavellian entourage. With his piano playing Hanfstaengl soothed the nerves of the man who roused the multitudes and gained admittance to the homes of Party members who could barely stand his eccentric antics, his liberal ideas and his obsession for puns no matter where they fell. Putzi became the jester in Hitler's court and, like the jesters of old, frequently came brazenly close to offending his lord.

In the early days, they were still extremely close. Putzi once accompanied Hitler and his driver in their green Selve on a fund-raising mission to Berlin. As secretary they brought along Fritzl, the 18-year-old son of a Party member.

On the old Leipzig road through Red Saxony their car was stopped by a group of Red militia. As a nationalist agitator, Hitler had a price on his head; he gripped his dog whip tensely as the car drew to a stop. With unusual presence of mind, Putzi leaped from the car, his old Swiss passport flapping in the wind. In his worst American accent he explained that he was an American paper manufacturer from Milwaukee on his way to Leipzig with his valet, chauffeur and the young son of a business associate. Without bothering to scrutinize the document, the militiamen waved the car through. Years later, whenever they were in the neighborhood, Hitler would turn to Hanfstaengl and ask if he recalled the incident. "That was a nasty situation you got us out of," he would say, but by then Putzi wondered if Hitler didn't begrudge having been introduced as his valet.

As they entered Berlin, Putzi realized that people in the capital who knew him would be shocked to see him in Hitler's company. Hastily, he commanded the driver to pull over to the curb and informed his companions that he would arrange his own accommodations for the night.

The following day he was relieved when Hitler fetched him in a closed van that one of his Berlin backers had loaned him. As their business was not pressing, the erstwhile art dealer and the artist manqué vied with each other to show a wide-eyed Fritzl Berlin's artistic sights. At the Imperial War Museum the advantage was clearly Hitler's, as he had often visited there on leave during the War.

"I can tell you, Hanfstaengl, when you have seen war from the front lines as long as I did you are lost in admiration for Schlueter," said Hitler, pointing to the death agonies of Schlueter's warriors on the cornices above the museum courtyard. "He was unquestionably the greatest artist of his time. Even Michelangelo did nothing better or more true to life." A tall statement, Putzi thought, which said more about Hitler's fascination for war than his knowledge of art. But Putzi let it pass. He had missed the Great War and did not wish to call attention to the fact that he had not faced the test of fire.

They went next to the National Gallery, where Putzi was sure he had the advantage; but once again Hitler took the lead, marching past the

Dutch and Italian masters to a statue of John the Baptist, erroneously ascribed, Putzi thought, to Michelangelo. " . . . the most monumental, the most eternal figure in the history of human art," Hitler pontificated to a wide-eyed Fritzl before setting off in search of further Michelangelos. When they came across him again, he was lost in reverie before a large Renaissance work depicting nudes frolicking in water around a long-necked swan. "There you are Fritzl. There's no end to his genius."

But the work was by Caravaggio, Michelangelo Amerighi da Caravaggio. The oversight was so fundamental that Putzi was speechless. From that moment on Hitler's claims as an art expert meant nothing to Putzi.

Since they seemed to be without further appointments Putzi suggested they go to the Luna, a large amusement park built in the American style. One of the side shows at the Luna featured female boxing. Putzi, who had an eye for the female figure, suggested they take in a match. Although Hitler raised no objection he looked on with indifference, commenting when Putzi had had enough: "Well, at least it is better than this dueling with sabers that goes on in Germany."

They garnered not a penny from their three-day stay in Berlin, although on their last evening in the city Frau Bechstein presented Hitler with an expensive yellow fedora that had once belonged to her husband.

Hitler was by no means an uninteresting traveling companion. He could hum entire passages of Wagner, and he amused Putzi and the others in the car with his superb comic turns. He could mimic the frenetically gesturing publisher, Max Amann, with his sputtering repetitive sentences and the Party printer Mueller whose voice was so high that it threatened to shatter glass. He could reproduce the voices of market women and children. One of his star turns was the impersonation of a type of high-flown national orator, then very much in vogue, whose speeches invoked Siegfried's flashing sword and lightning striking mountain peaks. He knew by heart a long laudatory poem sent to him by a female admirer who had looked up every word in the dictionary that rhymed with "Hitler." The poetess must have missed a few because, as the green Selve rumbled and rocked through the night, Hitler kept his companions in stitches with couplets of his own invention, each surpassing the last in lugubrious idolization.

Hitler often joked later that prison was his "education at government expense," but his true university had been the trenches of the Great War, a world unimaginable to the patrician Hanfstaengl who had confined his peregrinations to New York's Central Park in those years.

The world had never seen such an arena of instruction: blasted woods, slag heaps, shell craters, fire trenches that extended diagonally across France for five hundred miles, from the English Channel to the Swiss Alps. It was estimated that if all the trenches were stretched end to end they would have reached once around the world. Millions of men made the long march up through the French farmland, where the brooks ran clear and the flowers bloomed, to that wearisome, ominous, greasy zone of battle, that "floor of Hades," as one British poet put it. Poets of other nations called it a "meatgrinder," a "pounding organ," a "storm of steel."

Its contemporaries knew it simply and horribly as the Great War. Only the Battle of Vicksburg in the American Civil War, witnessed by few Europeans, presaged such a callous slaughter of human life. In just four years more than 1,800,000 Germans were killed, 4,000,000 wounded and 1,000,000 carried off to prison camps. The statistics for the French were the same. When it was over one out of every seven Europeans was either dead or wounded.

A German combat unit spent four days at the front followed by two days in the support line and four days resting in the rear. The trip up through the shallow, ill-concealed communicating trenches was often the most hazardous journey of all. The forward lines could be smelled for miles. Everywhere one breathed the scent of putrefaction. Lice, vermin and trench rats fed among the carnage of No Man's Land, an agonized terrain of earth and sky festooned with autumnal hedges of rusting barbed wire.

Cinematic recreations aside, there was little hand-to-hand combat. Rarely did one see the enemy's face unless it was transmogrified by death. Fewer than 1% of the casualties of the Great War were caused by bayonet. Shell splinters accounted for a staggering 70%. The great killer was not poison gas as propagandists made out, but sepsis, the slow onset of infection in the bodies of men who lay helpless among the shell craters of No Man's Land. Lucky was the soldier who received a sniper's wound in his own trenches. From there he could be carried to a dressing station under cover of darkness. There the wounded were separated by aproned field surgeons into three groups: those who could make their way to the rear unattended, those with torn limbs who might survive if the ambulances could get them through and the rest, by far the largest number, with abdominal or head injuries who were set aside and left to expire unattended. Surgeons in the Great War observed for the first time the working of organs that in peacetime they would never have dared expose to the knife.

The comparative peace of the rear presented hazards of its own. By night it was a landscape of ruined farms and deserted villages. By day the Great War soldier could peer down at his leisure into the sun-dappled trenches of previous years and gauge the date and season of bygone campaigns by the shape and color of rotting uniforms. He became an archaeologist of his own fate. Compared to the advanced trenches, the rear zone was simply an older, drier boneyard whose peace was shattered occasionally by an artillery shell fired blindly by the enemy into that peaceful country of dandelion, chamomile blossom and white cup.

Adolf Hitler took part in one of the most costly and senseless battles of the war, the Battle of the Somme; if "battle" is the correct word to describe a conflict that began in July of 1916 and raged for three and a half months, until the November rains turned the contested zone into a sea of mud and stagnant water. The British prefaced the attack with an artillery bombardment that lasted the better part of a week. Over 50,000 British gunners laid down a barrage of more than 20,000 tons of high explosives along a fifteen mile stretch of German front. As the storm of steel churned the earth above, the Germans huddled in dugouts 30 feet beneath the surface, watching nervously as the walls of their caverns swayed like the sides of a ship, alert for the smell of gas, praying, as the force of the concussions blew out candles, that a lucky hit did not seal the entrances and entomb them by the thousands.

When the bombardment was lifted, a young British subaltern signalled the start of the attack with a spirited kick of a soccer ball high above No Man's Land. He was dead before it touched the ground. So poor were the munitions of the day that the Germans emerged exhausted but alive from their subterranean strongholds to answer the British attack with machine gun fire so precise that gunners could write their names in the earth with bullets. The British forces fell in waves, cut down like sheaves of wheat, 21,000 in the first hour. A third of those lay for days in No Man's Land, expiring of their wounds. Three months later when the "Battle of the Somme" petered out in mud and exhaustion, only a few thousand yards of contested territory had changed hands.

Hitler was wounded on the Somme near Le Bargue. By then he was a lance corporal and had won the Iron Cross, 2nd Class. Later he would win the Military Merit Cross and the coveted Iron Cross, 1st Class. He was a dispatch runner assigned to regimental headquarters, a job he found cleaner, if far more dangerous, than living in the trenches. In an age when field telephones were still primitive and wireless nonexistent, human couriers were the only means headquarters had of keeping in touch with their forces in the field. All day long runners trotted down miles of fire trenches, carrying the report books that every field officer had to sign. If rain or a grazing hit shaved off so much as a few inches of trench wall, the runners were usually the first victims of enemy sharpshooters. The life expectancy of a front line runner was measured in weeks. Incredibly, Hitler survived three and a half years. As he recalled later, he often carried nothing more important than a note of greeting from one officer to another.

The "front experience" united countless thousands of Germans for the rest of their lives. Many would never adjust to peacetime or to civilians who had sat out the War at home. In the dirt and squalor of the trenches, those who did not break emerged purified of the false effusions and second-hand notions they had received from parents and teachers. They became connoisseurs of a wilder, more genuine life. They entered a community of the blood.

Putzi would never belong to the community of blood. He missed Europe's most horrible conflict and the communist revolt in Munich that followed. He had a gift for avoiding violence which some of those close to Hitler would never let him forget. He even missed the Beer Hall Putsch, Hitler's unsuccessful attempt to overthrow the Bavarian government which ended when Hitler led a crowd of demonstrators into a cul-de-sac and a fusillade of police bullets. Putzi was in Munich that December day in 1923 but on a different street. He joined the other conspirators to flee over the border to Austria, where he spent his first night in exile hiding in a greenhouse under a bed of chrysanthemums.

Political exile did not agree with Putzi. He had money, of course, but he refused to lend it. A huge figure in an overcoat drawn up to his ears, he skulked from shadow to shadow, a haunted look on his face. The other exiles tormented him by knocking on his door at night and crying "Police!"

When he discovered that no warrant had been made out for his arrest he returned to Munich in time to attend Hitler's trial. The penalty for invading a public assembly, kidnapping a provincial government at gunpoint and leading a demonstration that killed and maimed scores of people was five years comfortable "fortress" arrest and a fine of 200 gold marks. Hitler served only eight months of his sentence; after his release, he came to the Hanfstaengls for Christmas dinner. Putzi, in an attempt to instill order into his life now that he was pursuing a doctorate in history, had moved his family out of the gloomy flat in Schwabing and into a lovely home that he had purchased from a wealthy Duchess. The house was filled with priceless furniture, paintings and thousands of handsome books. The music library, the enormous Steinway, the complete file of *Punch,* the French Empire clock over the fireplace, the bust of Benjamin Franklin by Houdon, all these led less fortunate members of the Party to think Herr Hanfstaengl a little tight-fisted when it came to distributing loans worth only a few dollars in American money.

"Well now," said Hitler somewhat sarcastically, "after that little flat of yours on the Genzstrasse who would have thought we would meet again in a fine house in the best part of town. You are the most feudal acquaintance I have."

That evening Hitler did honors to the turkey and rich Austrian pastries. Encouraged by Helene to pick up the pieces and begin anew, he replied: "It has all been a terrible disappointment dear Frau Hanfstaengl, but the next time I promise you I will not fall off the tightrope."

CHIEF OF THE FOREIGN PRESS

Hitler still could not speak in the south and others had to carry his message into the north. Sales of his autobiography *Mein Kampf* were only modest. During the next seven years the two friends drifted apart, Hitler to his alpine villa on the Obersalzberg, Putzi to Paris to photograph the collections of the Louvre for his family's art firm. In Paris he met Picasso and Marie Laurencin. Eventually, he obtained a doctorate in history. His second child, a daughter, died after a long and wasting illness.

Adrift with no real place in society despite his family name, Putzi was rescued by a telephone call from Rudolf Hess. The Depression elections of 1930 had increased the Nazi delegation to the Reichstag from 12 to 107. After seven years of struggle, the Munich group had become a national party.

"Herr Hanfstaengl, der Fuehrer is very anxious to talk to you."

Putzi invited them right over.

"Herr Hanfstaengl," Hitler began, "I have come to ask you to take over the post of foreign press chief of the party. Great things are before us. In a few months, or at the most in a couple of years, we must irresistibly sweep to power. You have all the connections and could render us a great service."

Although still not a Party member, Putzi accepted.

A grateful Hitler wrung his hand and promised: "Hanfstaengl, you will form part of my immediate entourage."

Then he left. Not a word about where Putzi would work or with whom. Hitler, typically, was too busy to bother with such details.

What fiefdom of foreign consciousness had Hitler so eagerly bestowed and Putzi so humbly accepted? For the most part it consisted of a handful of young men and women who had arrived in Vienna, Munich and Berlin in the twenties to study or to escape personal disappointment at home. Americans flocked to Europe after the Great War to view the battlefields and to enjoy the Riviera at inflation rates. Encouraged by the cultural criticism of H. L. Mencken and Sinclair Lewis, they fled the cold, unadorned towns of the American Midwest to haunt Europe's museums, read her classics and drink the wines she was too wise to prohibit. Bright, literate, many had gone to college. Some even had a year or two of newspaper experience.

With its peace conferences and experiments in new ideologies Europe was the center of the world's big events. A young reporter with a facility for languages, a stout heart and strong feet could make a name for himself. The red-headed H. R. Knickerbocker arrived in Munich to study psychoanalysis, John Gunther came over on a cattle boat, Dorothy Thompson arrived with the American Red Cross, Louis P. Lochner to start life over again after the death of his first wife.

With radio still in its infancy and the written word undergoing a renaissance in clarity and new meaning, foreign correspondence entered a Golden Age. Vendors of the news, correspondents became legends in their own right: Gunther with his *Inside* books, Dorothy Thompson in evening dress traipsing down a moonlit road in pursuit of a story, Edgar Ansel Mowrer delirious in seven languages from the influenza in Rome. It was an arduous calling ducking Sparticist bullets in Berlin, covering separatist riots in the Rhineland, and worker's revolts in Vienna. Each day the local papers had to be scanned, legmen dispatched to cover train wrecks and press conferences, background material collected and memorized. The barber shops of the large hotels and the gardens of government ministries yielded quiet confidences that became the next day's headlines. In the evening there was just enough time to rush home and don the cutaway and tails that the press corps traded among themselves to attend fashionable diplomatic events. With the six hour time difference between Berlin and New York, days often ran as late as 10 o'clock at night. Then they headed for the cracked leather sofas of the Hotel Adlon bar where a visiting editor from Chicago or New York, who had trained on whisky and payoffs in his day, lectured them on seeing Europe from an American perspective; local color and language be damned! The sermon they knew was as out of date as the latest rumors of Joe Stalin's death. They were pioneers of a newer, more advanced, journalism.

By 1930 most had rotated to the top of their profession to become "Chiefs" of their bureaus in Berlin, Paris or Vienna. Representatives of a free press, they watched with alarm as the German Republic wrestled with the complexities of democracy. In Berlin they witnessed first hand the cracks and fissures that eroded a Republic unlucky enough to be born out of military defeat in the unforgiving 20th century. Their rootedness in the country ran deep. They enjoyed Germany's vistas, her culture and people. Of the four Pulitzers awarded to American newsmen in Germany in the thirties all but one went to men who had resided in the country for at least a decade.

The career of H. R. Knickerbocker—the H. R. stood for Hubert Renfro—was typical of the time. Youthful, clean shaven, with carefully trimmed hair the color of cayenne pepper, Knick could be found in any group of reporters waiting outside the portals of the mighty. Born in Yoakum, Texas, the panhandle clung to him like pieces of eggshell to a newborn chick. His goal, as he told an instructor at Columbia University's School of Journalism, was "to qualify as quickly as possible for the most remunerative job possible on a newspaper, preferably in New York, alternatively anywhere. Present qualifications: extremely inquisitive, learned to stay up late on a milk wagon, and had a hard first sergeant in the army."

Knick personified the new breed of foreign journalist: tough, dry, energetic. One week his red head could be spotted bobbing across the Gare du Nord, the next in earnest conversation in the lobby of the League of Nations in Geneva. Restless, competent, impeccably turned out, be it in calfskin gloves or with field glasses for the long view, Knick moved after his stories with relentless impatience. Like the young novelists of his generation he abandoned the altruistic idealism of the war years. He was not cynical or resigned; simply unsentimental and astringent in the gaze he leveled at the world through his brown horn-rimmed glasses.

With more then 30 political parties German politics was exceedingly difficult to forecast, even for an experienced observer like Knick. A few attempted to compare what was occurring in Germany to the vaguely understood ideology of "fascism" in Italy. However, few correspondents had first-hand experience of the Italian variant, and Hitler seemed totally unlike the successful Mussolini. For years National Socialism was thought of as a distinctly provincial affair; one of several strident offshoots of German nationalism. Little attention was paid to the Party's philosophy of Leadership, Struggle and Race. Few read *Mein Kampf* in the original; if quotations were needed, newsmen turned to the Party's "immutable" but moribund "25 Point Program." One week the movement was portrayed as being ruled by iron obedience; the next, about to disintegrate from massive internal contradictions. Everyone was confused by the diversity of its supporters: post-war youth, veterans, and the sleeping colossus of the non-political.

Hitler did little to advertise himself to the foreign press. A southerner, he was uncomfortable in the Prussian north and rarely appeared in Berlin. An Austrian citizen, he could not run for the Reichstag; he never set foot in that building until after January 1933. From the beginning he was buried beneath caricature, especially in the English language press, which vied with itself for ever more fabulous terms of dismissal. He was variously called a "little man—world menace—messiah of absurdity—reactionary—demagogue—adventurer—desperado—would-be dictator—drummer of a jazz orchestra—fanatic—product of the jazz age—

mystical nonesense-monger—drummer-boy—mischief-maker—dapper quack doctor—German Rasputin—clown—terrorist of the streets—brazen charlatan—mad apostle—bolshevik—monarchist. . ."

To interview Hitler in the years before he came to power, a correspondent had to visit the Party's official residence, the former "Barlow Palace," on Munich's elegant Briennerstrasse. Set slightly back from the road, with extensive gardens in the rear and tall gates in front, the new office building faced the official residence of Monsignor Pacelli, the Vatican's representative to Catholic Bavaria.

Nearly three quarters of a million marks had been raised by special levy on Party members to cover the cost of remodeling the palace ballrooms and reception areas into efficient offices for propaganda, membership and culture. Hitler directed the renovation personally. By wedding classicism to modernism he hoped to create an example for future Party buildings to follow. The result was tasteful, even luxurious but hardly revolutionary: cream-colored walls, brass fixtures, imitation teak panelling. The ubiquitous swastika was repeated everywhere, on window panes, draperies, even on the faces of clocks. Hitler's architectural advisor had decorated a fleet of North German Lloyd liners, and wags called the result on the Briennerstrasse a cross between a steamship stateroom and a Pullman sleeper.

The building was easily recognized from the street by the tremendous red banner billowing from its rooftop and the heavy bronze doors beneath a lintel inscribed with the battle cry "Germany Awake!" Two young sentries in black breeches and brown shirts scrutinized each visitor, be he peasant lad, dusty dispatch rider or elegant former officer. Inside, a third sentry gave the Hitler salute and requested the visitor's identification papers. A reception bureau recorded this information and checked the newcomer through to his destination by telephone. Security was tight, as befitted a political citadel.

From the lobby a magnificent staircase rose to the second floor and the structure's showpiece, the Party Senate Chamber. The Chamber, measuring 60 by 150 feet, enclosed a double row of 42 red leather chairs set in a gigantic semi-circle facing the Leader's throne. Twice daily, tours filed up the staircase and past Hitler's corner suite to the Chamber's entrance, flanked on either side by commemorative tablets listing the names of the Party's first martyrs, the dead of the Beer Hall Putsch. Daily their memory was kept alive by fresh garlands of cut evergreens.

Eventually, offices for Agriculture and Economic Planning took over a neighboring building, while in the garden at the rear a rambling wooden structure was erected to house the legion of typists and stenographers. There were departments for bookkeeping and dues collection and a statistical department that could compute in an instant the Party strength anywhere in Germany by means of a Hollerith machine. Steel filing cabinets as heavy as bank safes and proof against shell fire and Bolshevik invasion held the photographs and case histories of every one of the movement's 600,000 registered voters. In the basement a cozy, *voelkisch* canteen dispensed *Weisswurst* and *Leberknoedel* and vegetarian dishes to the 140 employees of the Brown House from Herr Hitler down to the lowliest office boy.

Knick interviewed Hitler in his corner suite on the second floor while Party Secretary Hess and Foreign Press Chief Dr. Hanfstaengl looked on. The atmosphere was almost military. There was none of the easy camaraderie that Knick had been led to expect among "Old Fighters." Neither subordinate addressed Herr Hitler with the familiar "du" form.

Hitler, on the other hand, was most gracious and waited for the newsman to take a chair before sitting himself. A portrait of Frederick the Great looked down from the wall over his desk. Knick made a note that Hitler's legendary blue eyes appeared flat and unmagnetic.

Knick posed his first question. The answer took all of thirty seconds and if the interview had continued as succinctly it would have been over in a quarter of an hour. But by the end of the first minute Hitler had shifted forward in his seat and set his gaze on deep space. His voice rose steadily until Knick found himself in the center of a typhoon of oratory. The curtains billowed, the walls vibrated. Knick became an audience of 30,000. It was not the subject of German indebtedness that filled the room but rather the injustice of Versailles and the encirclement of Germany.

For the next ninety minutes the storm raged. When he was not taking notes, Knick was appraising Hitler from afar. Hitler's spell had obviously fallen over Hess and Hanfstaengl who listened enraptured. It was a little like witnessing a grown man cry, Knick thought, and he felt the urge to reach over and tap Hitler on the knee and say: *"Ja, aber Herr Hitler."*

With his early training in psychoanalysis Knick was familiar with the theory that held that Hitler convinced others by first convincing himself through a kind of auto-hypnosis. How else could he profess such contradictory doctrines with equal sincerity? Knick was not so sure; over the years he had fallen away from his faith in Freud. But whatever the explanation, Hitler's talent to convince was awesome.

An hour and a half later Knick was shown out, exhausted but impressed. Before he left he asked one final question. How had Hitler won his Iron Cross 1st Class? Nowhere in the military records of the War was there mention of it and Hitler had written nothing about the moment in his autobiography.

"You know I was a dispatch bearer in the war," Hitler began. "One day, toward the first of June 1918, I was ordered to take a message to another part of the front, and had to traverse a section of No Man's Land. Presently I passed a dugout which I thought abandoned, but suddenly I heard French voices below.

"Being alone, and armed only with a pistol, I stopped a moment, then drew my pistol and shouted below in my very bad French, 'Come up, surrender!' Then I shouted in German as though to a squad of soldiers, orders to 'Fix bayonets! Draw your hand grenades!' First one French soldier, and then another, and then another came up with their hands in the air until there were seven. I marched them to the rear and turned them over as prisoners of war. So if they had been English soldiers, or, if they had been American soldiers, I am not sure I would have my Iron Cross or be here today."

To Putzi's dismay he was fobbed off with a cubbyhole on the third floor of the Brown House. He had envisioned more elegant quarters next to Hitler's study, where he could better pursue his twin functions of publicist and personal interpreter. Foreigners, he argued, could wander all over the building in search of his office and uncover heaven only knew what gossip. His appeals went unnoticed until national politics called Hitler to Berlin and Putzi to more sumptuous quarters in the Hotel Kaiserhof across the street from the Reich Chancellery.

The Kaiserhof was an ideal place to meet Germany's leading financiers and industrialists, men whose confidence Hitler needed as much as their money. More important, the Kaiserhof lay within the so-called *"Bann-meile,"* a magic perimeter surrounding Berlin's government district, inside of which all political demonstrations were forbidden. From their base at the Kaiserhof, Hitler and his entourage could gaze out at the Reich Chancellery across the street and be as safe from political molestation as the Greeks inside their Trojan horse.

Soon Hitler and his staff were occupying an entire floor of the hotel for weeks at a time. The management performed minor alterations such as installing bright red carpets in some of the suites and reception rooms. Special telephones were brought in; when the "General Staff" was in town the hotel's paging system was monopolized by Party business.

"Tell me, who pays for it all?" a visitor asked one of Hitler's bodyguards.

"Who pays, I dunno," replied the bodyguard. "Hitler does the paying, but he must get the money from somehwere. Anyhow, that's not my business."

The bill often ran as high as 10,000 marks a week. More than once as the "General Staff" was about to break camp and head out on the road no one had the money to pay. It was then that Putzi proved his worth. Certain members of the foreign press were willing to pay as high as two or three thousand dollars for a copyrighted interview with Hitler. Newspapers continued to sell in America despite the Depression, and press barons such as Col. McCormick of the *Chicago Tribune* and William Randolph Hearst reaped huge profits. Hitler wrote several articles for the Hearst syndicate for three or four thousand marks apiece. A third of this went to Putzi as middleman. When Karl von Wiegand, Hearst's European correspondent, complained to his lord at San Simeon about Putzi's penchant for arranging interviews for a fee, Hearst wrote back that he saw nothing wrong with making money from the news; he did it himself from time to time. Besides, he and Putzi's father had been good friends.

Putzi expected to be paid even if the Party was in dire need of publicity. His parsimony at the expense of the political consequences often drove Hitler to distraction. "Get to hell out of this, you and your damned greed!" Hitler once cried. "Can't you understand that if I want a certain article to appear at a certain time throughout the world, money just doesn't matter." Putzi was miffed on that occasion: he was so close to his asking price of 1,000 pounds sterling.

He was frequently the comic victim of his own impulsiveness. Once, when a Hearst reporter rashly approached the Fuehrer in the Kaiserhof lobby, Putzi unwisely restrained the newsman's advance by grabbing his coattails. The newsman turned and toppled Putzi with a gargantuan shove into a potted plant. An embarrassed Hitler pretended not to notice.

Putzi did threaten to demand satisfaction after Alfred Rosenberg, the Party "philosopher" and Russian expert, gave him a ferocious dressing down at the Brown House. "Get out while you can," screamed the Balt, who had never been heard to raise his voice, "or I'll slap you every foot of the way down the steps into the street!" Putzi retreated in such confusion that for a moment he was seen scurrying down the stairs wearing two hats.

It was a thankless task introducing newsmen from Japan, France, Austria, and Portugal to Hitler; only a man with Putzi's craving for the crumbs of attention could have welcomed it. As Hitler's fame grew, so did the stature of those who came to see him. All of these, in the early days, passed through Putzi's hands and wonderfully expanded his personal network of social connections. Before his critics, Putzi couched his hunger for social distinction in the windy rhetoric of "social infiltration"; a good many right-thinking American and British visitors were impressed that a man of Dr. Hanfstaengl's quality could be found at Hitler's side. People who would never have thought to talk to one of Hitler's brown-shirted aides felt quite comfortable discussing politics, art and fine wines in English with the "Chief of the Foreign Press."

"Democracy has no convictions," Putzi assured them. "Genuine convictions, I mean, for which people would be willing to stake their lives. That is Hitler's fundamental discovery, and it forms the starting-point for his great and daring policies, which will always prove to be right."

One of the worst *contretemps* of Putzi's career was the interview he arranged for Dorothy Thompson, the former correspondent for the *Philadelphia Public Ledger*. A large, oaken woman with the promethian features of a piece of classical sculpture, Dorothy possessed immense vitality and an absolute obsession for everything that had to do with the "Situation," by which she meant the precarious political situation in Central Europe. She lived strongly and imposingly outside of herself, apparently oblivious to the discomforts of travel and drinking and endless notetaking. After her first marriage ended in divorce, Dorothy was courted by the red-headed American novelist Sinclair Lewis who came to Berlin to escape an unhappy love affair and to work on the plot of his next book *Dodsworth*. Knick, who was Dorothy's assistant, introduced the two.

Dorothy became Mrs. Lewis, returned to America and had a child. But she found retirement in Vermont dull and the "Situation" in Europe as alluring as ever. *Cosmopolitan* magazine sent her to Berlin and she pressed Putzi for an interview with his chief.

While waiting in the Kaiserhof to see Hitler, Dorothy told her readers that she became a little nervous.

> And Hitler was late. An hour late. Waiting in the upstairs foyer of the Kaiserhof Hotel I saw him shoot by, on the way to his rooms, accompanied by a body-guard who looked rather like Al Capone. Minutes pass. Half an hour. I go around to the room of the press chief: Ernst Hanfstaengel. . . Harvard graduate, famous among his classmates for his piano playing and his eccentricities. Fussy. Amusing. The oddest imaginable press chief for a dicator.
>
> I waited in Dr. Hanfstaengel's room. An Italian journalist precedes me. . . .
>
> When I finally walked into Adolf Hitler's salon in the Kaiserhof Hotel, I was convinced that I was meeting the future dictator of Germany. In something less than fifty seconds I was quite sure that I was not.

It took just about that much time to measure the startling insignificance of this man who had set the world agog.

He was formless, almost faceless, a man whose countenance is a caricature, a man whose framework seems cartilaginous, without bones. He is inconsequent and voluble, ill-poised, insecure. He is the very prototype of the Little Man.

Worse still, Dorothy gratuitously insulted Putzi's mother whom she claimed to have seen in New York during the Great War defending the sinking of the *Lusitania*.

When Dorothy's piece came out the following spring as a slender book entitled *I Saw Hitler* it was not long before Putzi's enemies brought its contents to Hitler's attention.

"Who is this Mrs. Lewis, anyway?" Hitler asked.

The former Dorothy Thompson of the *New York Evening Post,* he was told.

"*Ja, ja,* now I remember, Hanfstaengl again! He brought this woman to me. I'll get that fellow!"

When he next encountered Putzi at the Kaiserhof he flew into a rage.

"What have you done, you imbecile! Scram—get out of my sight! I never want to see you again!"

Arms windmilling, Putzi fled in confusion.

Putzi told everyone who would listen that the woman had shown up for the interview drunk. Her marriage to Lewis was on the rocks and she was bitter. To cover the odor of alcohol on her breath he had sprinkled rosewater on her hands before sending her in. Obviously she had returned to her room at the Adlon and, fortified with further drinks, vented her anger against all men and against Hitler in particular. Putzi said he had heard that she had been paid $1,000 for the article and didn't care what she wrote.

Some of Putzi's harshest critics came from Hitler's closest associates. "Hanfstaengl! You big lug!" they shouted when they saw him. "You have a screw loose," Hitler's photographer once yelled when Putzi merely asked if anyone had seen Hitler. The Party publisher was no kinder. His face swelling with rage, he trotted around his office with his shoulders hunched up in imitation of Hanfstaengl's furtive walk and called the fellow a jackass, a clown, a hypocrite and finally a crazy kangaroo. Dr. Goebbels was less emotional. In reference to Dr. Hanfstaengl he made a motion as if shooing away a fly.

Putzi's annoying mannerisms became even more difficult to ignore in 1932 when Germany entered a period of permanent electioneering and the entourage spent weeks together traveling by car or flying from city to city by airplane. After nearly a month of indecision, Hitler entered the presidential elections against Field Marshall von Hindenburg who was running for a second term. The minor matter of Hitler's Austrian citizenship was adjusted in a day. The Brunswick state government was heavily National Socialist and when its legation in Berlin took Hitler on as a "Privy Counselor," his German citizenship followed automatically. The British colony in Berlin was especially incensed at the charade since Brunswick was a favourite vacation spot for British tourists in Germany.

"Now at least you can stop singing the 'Blue Danube' and learn the *Wacht am Rhein,*'" Putzi quipped when he shook hands with Germany's newest citizen.

For the first presidential campaign the team traveled by huge super-charged Mercedes touring cars. Hitler, with dog whip and road map, rode in the lead car next to the chauffeur Julius Schreck. In back sat his valet Schaub and his personal bodyguard Brueckner. The second car carried a detachment of thugs dressed in heavy coveralls and armed with rhino whips and rubber truncheons. Putzi traveled in the third auto-mobile with Hitler's chief of the domestic press, Hitler's photographer, his personal physician and an assortment of invited guests. Chrome-plated compressors roaring, the caravan raced over Germany's still primi-tive highways. True soldiers, they traveled with the tops down even when it rained.

In Nuremberg they stayed at the Deutscher Hof, in Augsburg at the Drei Mohren, in Stuttgart at a hospice which furnished a Bible with every bed. They traveled at commando speed, striding into their favorite hotel late at night to catch an hour or two of badly needed sleep. More often they dozed through the night as the drivers did the work, awaken-ing at dawn to the magnificent sight of the rugged Karwendel and the Rotwand on the road to Berchtesgaden. No one bore up better than Hitler on these long rides. He seemed to be possessed of unlimited energy and always arrived refreshed and alert.

In Nuremberg a bomb was hurled from a rooftop. In Bamberg bullets raked the caravan's windshields. In the communist strongholds of Chem-nitz, Kiel and Hamburg they were forced to make artful detours around angry crowds of fist-waving Reds. When they did encounter mobs of workers shouting "Down with Hitler! Down! Down! Down!" Schreck hit the brakes, skidded the lead car into the nearest alley while the second car full of bodyguards screeched to a stop and the "Mars boys" went to work with whips, blackjacks, and knife rings.

The results of the first election were inconclusive, and the campaign had to be run again. This time Hitler took to the air. As his pilot he chose Captain Hans Baur, a short, small-boned Lufthansa officer who had chalked up 600,000 air miles and had crossed the Alps 150 times. Hitler's plan was to visit 60 cities in three weeks, many of them after dark.

The group that posed before the three-engine Lufthansa D was a scaled down version of the one that had toured Germany by automobile the previous month. Baur, short and stocky, is sheathed in leather from head to foot. Hitler, in raincoat and hat, scowls histrionically. Next to him stands Schaub on one good leg, beside him the towering Brueckner in a dark overcoat, carrying a valise. Hanfstaengl, his longish hair parted in the middle, is just as tall but with his drooping posture takes an unexpectedly poor picture. Hitler's personal photographer stares with burning eyes as if incensed at the cameraman's f-stop. Goebbels, emaciated and startlingly short, beams enthusiastically in smart white raincoat and snap-brimmed hat. No longer an itinerant agitator, Goebbels had recently married the former wife of a wealthy German industrialist. His bride, dressed in a black Persian lamb's wool coat, sits just outside the picture frame in the couple's new beige and brown Mercedes convertible.

There was one foreigner present that drizzly morning as Hitler's "Flying Circus" convened; Denis Sefton Delmer or Tom Delmer as he was called. Putzi had prevailed upon Hitler to adopt Roosevelt's habit of setting aside a seat for a representative of the foreign press. As the day wore on Delmer saw that his presence was required more to assuage Hanfstaengl's sense of isolation than Britain's hunger for news about Germany.

Delmer, like Putzi, was another one of those queer fish destined to swim between two cultures. Born in Berlin but educated at Oxford, he took over the Berlin bureau of the *London Daily Express* at the whelpish age of 24. From the outset Delmer courted the prominent personalities in Hitler's party and invited them to his elegant apartment at No. 11 Viktoriastrasse for elaborate dinners. He even installed a black Bechstein piano for Putzi to play.

Delmer was a most suitable candidate for a seat next to Putzi on the so-called "Freedom Flights" of 1932. His German was excellent and he sympathized with the Party's complaint that they were getting a poor shake from the government. Their newspapers were banned on the flimsiest of pretexts and the government, with its monopoly of the radio, refused to grant them air time. For his trouble Delmer was denounced to his embassy as a Nazi.

Delmer soon saw that the air campaign was pure misery for Putzi, who was not built for the cramped quarters of an airplane. There was no piano and no opportunity to work linguistic puns over the engines' roar.

The cabin reeked of hot rubber and gasoline. Airsickness was a very real possibility and the white pre-flight pills did not always do their work if one had been foolish enough to drink coffee with breakfast. No true National Socialist could afford the ignominy of being airsick. Putzi's solution was to douse his hands and face with English lavender water while the bodyguards looked on mirthfully. Hitler finally put a stop to that: "That stuff of yours, Hanfstaengl, smells worse than a pimp parlor. Put it away." After that Putzi had to make do with smelling salts.

Berlin, Wuerzburg, Nuremberg, Frankfurt, Darmstadt, Ludwigshafen. . . They never paused long enough to take in the sights or to visit a museum. It was like traveling with a touring boxer. Once on the ground there came the exhibition match followed by verbal rubdowns from local Party bosses at the nearest hotel. When he could stand it no longer, Putzi pulled from his pocket two postcards of Goethe's writing room at Weimer and, gazing at these, caught a few moments of classical repose before the catcalls began. Putzi's problem, Delmer saw, was that he could not help giving the impression that he was better than the others on the tour and, Delmer had to admit, he was.

Airborne, Delmer watched as Hitler sat torpidly next to Baur. Offers of chocolates, sandwiches or gossip were turned aside. Only after the plane had touched down and the door was wrenched open to reveal the crowds of spectators, city fathers, municipal judges and waiting Army and police units did Hitler's lassitude lift. Then into his eyes came that light that Delmer remembered from his German school books, that "gracious shining" of the Hohenzollern emperors as they gazed down upon their loyal subjects.

"Hurry! Run!" shouted Putzi as the entourage charged into a crowded factory. The sea of upraised hands parted at their approach. A woman who meant to kiss Hitler's hand made a grab for Delmer's instead but was interrupted by fullback Hanfstaengl's running block.

On the flag-draped dais Delmer gazed over the sea of upturned faces. Hitler was no longer the belligerent rabble rouser of earlier days but the buoyant philosopher lecturing on the coming millenium. Never had he seemed more confident, more righteous, more respectable. Gone were the attacks on the Jews, the villification of opponents. If the crowds listened without quite comprehending, it made no difference. They provided their own spectacle; Hitler's presence was only a final, messianic vision.

In the end the Presidency went to Hindenburg for a second term, and the "Flying Circus" returned to earth and the corridors of the Kaiserhof. The Party had gleaned 230 of the 608 seats in the Reichstag to become the largest party in Germany. Disdainfully, Hitler turned down an offer to become Vice Chancellor. Sooner of later, he knew, Hindenburg must offer him the chancellorship.

One of those who watched the brown shift at the Kaiserhof was a short, slim 42-year-old divorcée, Frau Bella Steuermann-Fromm. Frau Bella, as she was called, was another Bavarian who had moved north after the War only to watch her family fortune waste away under the Inflation. Eventually she found a job on one of Berlin's most prestigious daily papers where she supported herself and her teenage daughter writing a society column called "Berlin Diplomats."

The Kaiserhof had never had the Adlon's glamor or the Bristol's sparkle. During most of its long history, the Kaiserhof had catered to provincial nobility and country families who came to Berlin to enjoy the winter social season. At tea time Bella watched the brown hordes in the Kaiserhof grill, talking strategy and snubbing each other according to their private pecking orders. They strutted about the tawdry lobby with an air of exaggerated belligerence, their military jodhpurs so outrageously cut that it seemed as if their thighs had sprouted wings.

Later, when she encountered Dr. "Putzi" Hanfstaengl, the introduction was typical,

"I play the piano for Hitler late into the night," he told her.

"Who cares?" she almost said. Bella had little patience with the "Nazi struck." She had heard that Hanfstaengl had neglected the family business for years to chase after Hitler and play the part of clown in his royal court.

Bella was known for her uncompromising realism. She had not read all of *Mein Kampf* but she had read enough to know that if the Brown Ones ever got their way, life for her set would be finished in Germany. Not a particularly remarkable conclusion for Bella. What was remarkable was that so few of her society friends were able to face that fact in 1932, or later.

BELLA FROMM

Looking back on that bygone age of sunny vineyards and purple forest paths when she sat, a small child in a white dress, next to her mother under a favorite walnut tree, it seemed to Bella that there had never been a cloudy day in her youth. Her father was a prosperous vintner whose vineyards on the Main and Mosel rivers sent wines and champagnes to countries as far away as Poland, Russian and Africa. The family came from Spain originally but had lived for eight generations on estates near Kitzingen, a town some fifty miles northwest of Nuremberg.

In that sunny time before the Great War, Ludwig III of Bavaria, still a prince, roamed her father's vineyards and wine cellars, solitary and informal, without the plague of bodyguards and private detectives a later age of political strife would make so necessary. She remembered the Prince as a kindly figure in baggy pants who wore around his neck a permanently knotted cravat joined to his collar with a rubber band. Ludwig's "Iron Necktie" Bella called it.

She was ten when she began keeping a diary. In it she composed long letters to her mother whom she adored. Later it became a repository for social and political gossip too acerbic to include in her newspaper columns. After January 30, 1933, her diary became a lone confidant in an age grown hoary with personal betrayal.

She attended a music conservatory in Hannover and passed examinations in literature and music composition. In 1914, at age 24, she was betrothed to young Herr Steuermann, a textile manufacturer from Berlin. To commemorate the event her father presented Kitzingen with a new town fountain.

With no brothers to volunteer for the front, Bella joined the International Red Cross. In a series of hospitals and aid stations in Wuerzburg and Berlin she nursed the survivors of Langemark, the Somme and the Marne. In their eyes she read the horrors that were kept so carefully out of the public press. In swift succession a daughter, Greta-Ellen, was born, her father died and her marriage, to the fine-featured Herr Steuermann, disintegrated. From the start it had been full of diappointment and misunderstanding. Bella had been raised to obey but not to bow before narrow-minded ways. When she could stand her heartbreak and that of the world's no longer she returned with her infant daughter to the comforting hills around Kitzingen.

In the last year of the War her mother, who had always been weak and frail despite her "cures" in the south, fell fatally ill. Bella moved into a room next to hers. The doctors administered morphine until one day her mother refused her morning injection, sensing that the end was near. When she closed her eyes for the last time she was only 48 years old and Bella was alone, as she would be for most of her life, without parents or husband. Later, even her daughter would be taken from her.

For some time Bella continued to hold long conversations with her mother in the cemetery and under the old walnut tree until one day she knew that she must disturb her mother's memory no more. "Mother!" she wrote later, "Two syllables, one world."

Frightened by Bavaria's growing radicalism and dismayed by the sorry state of her nerves, Bella moved north to Berlin. With her she took her daughter, her medals and her mother's eighteenth-century writing desk with its numerous drawers and secret compartments.

Berlin and Bavaria had long been quarrelsome cousins and "Prussian Pig" was a favorite epithet among Bavarians for foreigners who raised their ire. When Bella arrived in the capital in the spring of 1919, Berlin, like other regions of Germany, had gone socialist and the northern aristocracy had withdrawn in disgust to the provincial courts of Darmstadt, Meiningen and Hannover. With more than 90 daily newspapers, museums of every description and expatriate colonies of British, White Russians, and Jewish refugees from Poland, Berlin was the crossroads of Central Europe. The city boasted more statues and public monuments than Rome, more bridges than Venice, more theaters than Athens and more psychoanalysts than Vienna. In area it was the sixth largest metropolis in the world but more than half of its territory was given over to parks and private gardens. Only three or four buildings were over ten storeys and within its limits could be found some 20,000 cows, 30,000 pigs, and 12 working windmills. On some evenings, as the sun set through the horse chestnut trees it seemed as if one breathed the air of a rural farming community. Nevertheless, Berlin was a thoroughly modern city with renowned hospitals, scientific institutes, colleges of design and one of the most progressive police forces in the world. With only 20,000 automobiles for 4,000,000 inhabitants it lagged far behind the congestion of the New World, but its thoroughfares were crowded with bicycles, double decker buses, electric street trams, and green taxis. Street traffic ran at a frenetic, lurching pace as the green signals at intersections changed every 30 seconds. Each day 250 trains arrived through five train terminals. Tempelhof Airfield, to the south, was the largest airdrome in Europe with its own restaurant hotel and rooftop observation garden.

Straight as an arrow through the city's heart ran Berlin's great White Way, the gaudy Kurfuerstendamm, a blazing broadway of neon lights, restaurants, and cabarets. At night the "Ku-Damm" lit up the city sky for miles until it entered the cool greenery of the vast Tiergarten Park. The Tiergarten had once been a royal hunting preserve and its forested landscape of bridle paths, duck, and goldfish ponds was as dense as any Bavarian wald. When the avenue emerged again at the Park's eastern end it encountered the ramparts of imperial Berlin and Berlin's foremost landmark, the Brandenburg Gate, a Roman victory arch in soot-blackened sandstone rising over a hundred feet in the air and topped by a golden Goddess of Victory.

Under the Kaiser no mortal could pass beneath the Gate's central arch but when Bella arrived in the city the Kaiser was gone and the towering arch was host to double lanes of traffic flowing onto Unter den Linden, imperial Berlin's main thoroughfare and most fashionable promenade, lined with elegant hotels, night clubs and high priced shops. South of the Brandenburg Gate ran the Wilhelmstrasse, Berlin's embassy row, a staid street of 18th century mansions housing the British Embassy, the Hotel Adlon, the President's Palace, the Reich Chancellery and the Kaiserhof Hotel.

As for the Berliners themselves, the shopkeepers, the taxi drivers, the hotel waiters, Bella found them a worldly breed of metropolitan observers who viewed the violent events shaking their city with a droll and fatalistic wit. Their street slang or *"Berliner Deutsch"* was legendary. When astonished they said "I think the monkey takes lice off me." An *"Amerikaner"* was a cookie with icing. A woman in a cheap, showy dress was said to be wearing a "flag." They had scores of words for money: "wire," "moss," "gravel," "thread," "shavings." Reichsmarks they referred to as "eggs."

In Berlin, Bella was a woman of means. She spent her evenings in the company of government ministers, foreign envoys, successful entrepreneurs. She had a house on the Tiergarten and belonged to the prestigious Rot-Weiss Tennis Club. A horsewoman, she cantered daily through the Tiergarten in the company of government officials or members of the general staff. Her spare time she devoted to charity teas and other affairs that relieved the consciences of the rich in troubled times. Dressed in the latest Paris creations she attended opening nights, concerts, and the innumerable professional balls that in the Protestant north took the place of the religious carnivals of the south. Politically, Bella was a liberal monarchist. She believed in parliamentary democracy but feared its excesses unless it was guided by the firm hand of someone like her beloved King Ludwig. She knew and respected the Republic's first

President, Friedrich Ebert, and his successor, General Field Marshall Paul von Hindenburg. Mammi von Carnap, the wife of the Kaiser's former chamberlain, introduced Bella to the towering, bass-voiced von Hindenburg.

Hindenburg's election to the presidency had filled German liberals with alarm. It was rumored that he had not read a book since his days as a cadet in the previous century. He rarely received journalists and never held press conferences. Still, he was impressed enough with Frau Bella to remember her later when she filled his cup at a charity tea.

"Well, well we meet again," the aged President remarked. "And what are you doing these days?"

"I'm afraid I am one of those looking for a regular job," Bella replied. The ravages of inflation had eaten up her inheritance and left her with only the house in Berlin, her two horses and her automobile. Rents on the estates in Kitzingen were not worth the trouble to collect as the government printed more and more money and beggars on the street threw away bills that would have made them millionaires a few months earlier. To support herself and her daughter, Bella wrote an occasional piece for the *12 Uhr Blatt*. Winters, she covered fashion and society; summers, tennis and sports car racing. There was never enough work to make ends meet, but she refused to sell her mother's heirlooms.

"So it is like that?" Hindenburg replied. "But I don't understand. I heard that you are a good writer. See here, if you wish, I can recommend you to the Ullsteins."

The Reich President had a tender spot for the Ullstein publishing concern and especially for its paper the *Vossische Zeitung*. In 1847 "Auntie Voss" had carried a notice announcing the birth of Paul von Reneckendorf und Hindenburg.

Bella forgot the conversation, until, at another party, she chanced to meet Louis Ullstein, the second oldest of the five Ullstein brothers.

"Bella Fromm? Ah, yes, I remember. I've been hoping a long time that you'd visit me. Some months ago, I got a letter from President von Hindenburg. He suggested accepting your services when you offered them—but you never showed up. Would you like to join our staff?"

And so the association was formed. Her years of study had paid off. The taunts of her schoolmates that she was a bluestocking lost their sting. Bella had found a home in the north, a refuge on the Kochstrasse, in the legendary House of Ullstein.

The editorial fortress on the Kochstrasse covered an entire city block. Almost 10,000 people worked for Ullstein. The dusting and polishing of this empire alone demanded the services of some 300 charwomen. It was really a city within a city, a beehive of editors and assistant editors, floor managers, secretaries, and messenger boys. One story told of three lions that got loose and fed on Ullstein's flock of 200 editors for half a day before anyone noticed. Each editor had an office or at least a cubicle of his own. Some editors had oriental rugs on their office floors, others only Axminster reproductions. The most lowly had a modest mat. But each of them had a little green curtain on the frosted glass door for privacy. Each had a telephone, four or five for the most important editors, a single telephone for those, like Bella, who were just starting out. On the street below, the doorman with the symbolic Ullstein owl embroidered on his greatcoat was taller and wiser even then Emil Jannings in the movie "The Last Laugh."

Inside, all was cheerfulness, wit and undaunted optimism. At Ullstein hard work was a tradition; rarely were employees praised for a job well done. The brothers were kind in other ways. They furnished club rooms for their employees, an excellent beer garden and a superb canteen that served inexpensive hot meals. Pressmen and compositors in the rumbling printing plant near Tempelhof had hot showers at the end of their shifts. Greater Berlin was also the recipient of Ullstein generosity: exhibitions of model suburban homes, monthly vaudeville shows instructing housewives in the latest household arts, and the best travel bureau in Berlin.

In 1913 the brothers had purchased one of Germany's oldest cultural monuments: the stately *Vossische Zeitung*. "Auntie," as the *Vossiche Zeitung* was fondly called, had seen a lot of history. Tucked between her fine rag pages in her 70th year was the announcement that General George Washington had defeated the British in North America and in 1821 that Napoleon Bonaparte had died on the island of St. Helena. The grande dame was 210 years old when the Ullsteins bought her shortly before the Great War. Under their management her admirers increased from 25,000 to nearly 80,000, and she became the leading gem in the Ullstein's string of democratic newspapers. They spared no expense on her and she cost them plenty; nearly two million gold marks out of pocket annually. The brothers were businessmen, and Tante's purchase price of eight million gold marks had made them gasp. But they could not give her up. She was a cultural institution, and they were too committed to the Republic to let this most elegant of republican ladies fall into less scrupulous hands. Fortunately for the brothers, their other publishing enterprises were shamefully lucrative.

Besides the tens of thousands who read *Tante Voss*, the *B–Z am Mittag*, the *Morgenpost*, the *Gruene Post* and the *Berliner Illustrirte*, tens of thousands more read the brothers' *Berliner Allgemeine Zeitung*, a workers' daily; the *Blatt der Hausfrau* which taught middle and lower class women how to look chic for a few pennies; *Die Dame,* an ultra-modern fashion magazine; *Tempo,* an evening paper; *Sieben Tage,* a radio paper; *Der Heitere Fridolin* for children; *Die Koralle* for nature and science; *Uhu,* a monthly mix of fiction, fact and humor; and the very literary *Querschnitt,* which offered the works of Pirandello, Proust and Thomas Wolfe in their original languages. Special Ullstein carts sold Ullstein paperbacks in every railway station and for the discriminating collector the Propylaeen Verlag offered deluxe editions of Greek and Roman classics.

"That's charming, Bella, very charming, indeed, but much too flippant," commented her editor after reading her first efforts. "There's a great deal you will have to learn about social reporting. A social reporter does not write realistically. Just remember this: every ambassadress is a beauty. Every Minister is an excellent politician—the best in the world, in fact. Every newcomer in the Diplomatic Corps is always the shining star of the homeland's Foreign Office. If you remember these things you can never go far wrong."

The rebuke was unusually gentle for an editor at Ullstein. Some who came to labor at the Kochstrasse watched as their first efforts sailed, without comment, into the nearest wastebasket.

With over 2,000 dailies, Germany published more newspapers than Britain, France and Italy combined. A squadron of aircraft brought the Ullstein's *B–Z am Mittag* to Leipzig in half an hour, to Munich in two hours. But that only meant that a resident of Leipzig or Munich could read news fresh from the capital on the same day. Germany had no national papers of the likes of the *Times* of London or New York. Ullstein employed some 30 foreign correspondents but rarely did these report on a regular basis. When they did, America meant Washington and American politics the latest utterances of President Herbert Hoover. The brothers sent thousands of words to the *New York Times* each day, but rarely did they feature cables from Reuters or the Associated Press in their own papers. There was little international news of a non-financial nature in German newspapers, and objective political reporting was practically unknown. Germany, in the American sense, had no papers devoted exclusively to the news; a fact that made the German press all the more vulnerable to a centralized censorship later.

Bella's paper was no exception. Compared to American productions, Auntie was a slim creature: no more than fourteen or fifteen pages. On her front page came news from Prussia interlaced with an occasional piece from abroad such as the Hoover moratorium on reparations payments in June of 1931. Inside one found news from France—when it pertained to Germany—and on the facing page, short items from central and northern Europe. Turning further, one came to the heart of the German press, the paté de fois gras of belles lettres, the *"feuilleton"* or cultural section. This might be the latest installment of a stateman's memoirs or the reflections of a German *"Dichter"* walking in the footsteps of Heinrich Heine across the Harz mountains. Whereas American publishers pointed with pride to their foreign coverage, the *"feuilleton"* was the glory of the German press. To see his midnight reveries printed in the cultural section was every German writer's dream.

After the *"feuilleton"* came the financial and business sections and pages on vacation and travel; the Mediterranean in June, the Alps in January. Toward the back the reader entered the realm of brief, objective reports on Berlin color: the latest suicide dredged from the Landwehr Canal, the businessman caught at the border with his company's profits, or the latest escapades of one of Berlin's colorful criminal gangs such as "The Forget-Me-Nots" or "The Harmless Thirteen"—in short, the tidbits of local scandal that assured the Berliner that his city was the most alluring in the world. In this landscape of court proceedings, traffic collisions and mysterious events, Bella's column, *"Berliner Diplomaten,"* appeared several times a week, identified simply by her initials: "b. f."

Life on the Kochstrasse was hectic. Bella soon found herself working sixteen hours a day, attending three or four teas every afternoon, followed by a formal dinner and then a musical evening that might last until midnight. Often her deadline forced her to find a quiet corner away from the glittering company to compose her pieces. Berlin's cabbies knew her by name and the traffic cops by sight as she raced across town in her roadster to yet another charity ball or cocktail party. She employed two secretaries, one to keep her engagements straight, the other to see that she did not offend by misspelling the names of celebrities such as Ghulam Siddiq Khan, Kazys Skirpa or the Marchese Maurigi de Castelmarrigi!

The author of *"Berliner Diplomaten"* was among the figures in black awaiting the arrival of the new Ambassador from France on the platform of the Friedrichstrasse Train Station on September 21, 1931. Professor André François-Poncet alighted from the Blue Express at precisely 8:37 AM. Dressed entirely in modish gray, down to his doeskin spats, he sported a diminutive moustache in the style of the actor Adolf Menjou. His shoes and the black notes of his tie delicately offset the soft gray of his elegant suit. Careful combing hid a small bald spot. France's newest envoy believed that a diplomat should dress with such distinction that he could be recognized in any crowd; that morning André François-Poncet's attire struck just the proper note of Gallic dapperness amid the solemn black of diplomatic pomp. With him on the train he had brought his limousine, also gray, strapped to a flatcar. Barely an hour later Hindenburg had his credentials. It was one of the smoothest diplomatic arrivals Bella could remember.

France could not have sent a man more conversant with German ways. The son of a successful Parisian prosecutor, young André early displayed his remarkable intellectual gifts. He could read at four; by fourteen he was ready to enter the university. Instead, his father sent him to Germany to study at a German gymnasium. The experience was pivotal and awoke in the young Frenchman an awareness of the life of the mind. From that moment on Germany became the center of his professional career, the lodestone of his personal destiny. He easily completed a thesis on Goethe's *Elective Affinities* and became a professor of German literature at l'Ecole Polytechnique and a recognized authority on the poetry of Goethe. He was one of the few envoys in Berlin who had not the slightest need of an interpreter.

After the War he married the imposing Jacqueline Dillais, the daughter of a military family with extensive steel holdings in Lorraine, and started one of those seemingly clairvoyant information services whose daily bulletin was so eagerly studied by French investors. From 1924 until his appointment as Ambassador he represented Paris's 7th Arrondisement in the French Parliament and, as a spokesman and lobbyist for the powerful "Comité des Forges," argued persuasively against social security, the minimum wage and the eight-hour day. The "Comité," an alliance of French industrialists, had their deputies and ministers in French politics and their directors on the boards of *Le Temps* and *Le Matin.* Their wish was that Germany, poor in capital but rich in technology, would join French industrialists in the common goal of keeping organized labor down and prices up. François-Poncet considered himself a pragmatic conservative. He rejected all utopias, believed in no absolute truths and considered socialism an absurd modernist religion.

With her eye for fashion, Bella read François-Poncet's personality in his clothes. He was the perfect headwaiter, she thought: distinguished, well paid, elegant. The only question was whether his German hosts would enjoy the meal he had come to serve. The Comité's dream was of a customs union between France and Germany and within a matter of months François-Poncet was wooing German industrialists through one of their principal contact men in the National Socialist camp, Captain Hermann Goering.

"The Ambassador cannot give you an interview for publication but in a few seconds he will be here in person to give you his reasons," Bella was informed as she entered a drawing-room of the French Embassy near the

Brandenburg Gate. Then the door opened and François-Poncet entered, quickly and smoothly, the youngest envoy in his country's foreign service. Eyebrows arched, head cocked, he recognized her immediately.

"We have already met," he said. "I have to thank you—the only lady who welcomed me. That must be a good omen."

Regrettably, however, it was true that he could not give her an interview.

"Je ne peux malheureusement rien vous dire! Rien, Il est trop tôt pour publier quelque chose. Trop tôt!" He switched to a German as immaculate and smooth as steel. "It is much too early to say anything significant. It is also much too dangerous at the present moment."

"Imprudent," was the word he used in French.

She saw that as a former journalist he understood the power of the press. Well, she asked, what were his feelings as he took up his mission in Germany?

"I find it, I find it very interesting, very in-ter-est-ing . . ."

EMINENCE IN FIELD GRAY

Unobtrusive and charming, Bella was invited everywhere and soon had her share of admirers. Chief among these was General Kurt von Schleicher, head of the Army's Political Bureau. Schleicher was a general with political gifts, but he was first and foremost an officer who saw the Army as the guarantor of Germany's domestic tranquility. In the Indian summer following the Great War, as Germany's armies marched home, it was Captain Kurt von Schleicher who persuaded Germany's first President to acknowledge the Army as the State's guardian against the revolutionary "Worker and Soldiers' Councils." In 1920 when units of the People's Marine Division surrounded the Chancellery and held the President and his cabinet hostage, Schleicher sent in government troups to crush the mutiny. When the young Republic asked veteran organizations to suppress Communist insurrections in Bremen, Berlin and Munich, Schleicher was among the figures who misled the nation into believing that the vigilantes acted on their own. When Poland attacked Upper Silesia, Lithuania and the Ukraine, Schleicher sent defense forces, disguised as agricultural workers, to the great landed estates along Germany's eastern border to guard against a possible invasion. In 1923, when Hitler's putsch in Bavaria and French violence in the Rhineland caused the government to evoke the constitution's emergency powers, Lieutenant Colonel Kurt von Schleicher temporarily took control of the government, restored order, and fed the hungry. Later, when dummy companies were set up between Germany and the Soviet Union, Kurt von Schleicher was among the military figures who traveled to Russia disguised as civilian businessmen to oversee combined Russian and German tank maneuvers. For his services Schleicher was made chief of the Army's Political Bureau. He attended cabinet sessions and drafted speeches for the Defense Minister. "My Cardinal in politics," the Defense Minister called him. All but unknown to the man on the street, and holding no elective office of his own, General Kurt von Schleicher was one of the most powerful figures in German politics.

Schleicher held a visionary idea close to his heart. He dreamt of an alliance between labor and the military that would do for capitalist Germany what the revolution in Russia had failed to do for the Soviet Union: usher in a new era based on progress and tradition. From his vantage point in the Ministry of Defense, Schleicher imagined that he could bend Hitler to his will. He would steal the Party's raw dynamism by offering Hitler a Cabinet post. If Hitler refused, Schleicher would woo Hitler's lieutenants and split the Party. Hitler would lose his movement, the masses would join the Republic and the Party's incessant carping would cease.

"An interesting man with an outstanding ability to speak," Schleicher recorded after his first meeting with Hitler. "In his plans he ascends the loftiest peaks. One must only pull him back to earth with the facts."

"The Eminence in Field Gray" was what the foreign diplomats called Schleicher and, in truth, there was hardly a conversation on the Wilhelmstrasse that Schleicher did not hear of within a few hours. He had personal friends in every ministry, and Bella often brought him bits of information. To her he was Kurt of the mellifluous voice, Kurt of the resonant laugh. His appearance in uniform was striking, at once erect and relaxed. His lopsided smile revealed startlingly white teeth. With his beautiful hands and his pale face, he was irresistibly attractive to women. Bella was slightly heartbroken when he married a much younger woman. That Kurt was very much in love with the lovely Elizabeth, Bella could see. At the French Embassy one evening when the orchestra struck up a dance tune, Kurt asked François-Poncet to excuse him for a few minutes. "I want to have a dance with my wife," he said. "Then I'll come back to dirty politics."

He danced so smartly that night that when he finished François-Poncet led the room in a round of applause. The second dance Kurt saved for Bella.

Socially, Kurt knew everybody. His *Bierabends* on the Alsenstrasse were attended by bankers, journalists and actors. Kurt knew how to manage people. If he was uneasy with strangers, among friends he was eloquent and, most unusual for a man of his position, an attentive listener. He was a particularly close friend of Lieutenant Colonel Oskar von Hindenberg, the President's son and personal secretary, and it was through their influence that the upright Catholic, Heinrich Bruening, was appointed Chancellor in 1930.

Modest and reserved, with the refined good looks of an intellectual, Bruening immediately won Bella's respect when he announced that he would continue to live in his small, two-room pension in a Catholic retreat in Berlin. In the grand triumvirate, Bruening was the ethical, farsighted administrator, Hindenburg the symbol of authority and Schleicher the backstairs manipulator. The problem was that in order to keep the National Socialists out of power, Germany no longer dared elect her Chancellors. Instead, Hindenburg appointed them under the emergency powers granted him by the constitution. The new Chancellor had only to gain the support of the Reichstag and keep the President's trust. This Bruening hoped to do by scoring a foreign policy coup.

In Switzerland he met with representatives of America, Britain and Italy. Absent was the representative of France, Prime Minister André Tardieu, who was busy with elections at home but who promised to return if the others reached a preliminary agreement. Bruening's mission was to request a reduction of the term of enlistment in the German Army from twelve to five years. He needed a greater reserve of trained militia, he said, to protect the Republic from National Socialist and Communist violence. Impressed by the modesty of Bruening's proposal, his listeners cabled Tardieu to return, but the French Prime Minister replied that he was ill. No agreement was reached, and Bruening returned home, empty-handed, to resign.

Kurt von Schleicher had arranged Bruening's fall with the help of François-Poncet. At a dinner party at the French Embassy Schleicher let it be known that Germany would soon have a Chancellor more friendly to French interests. François-Poncet immediately wired Tardieu not to return to Switzerland. All of Berlin buzzed with François-Poncet's joy at Bruening's demise. The French Ambassador came from a rigidly anti-clerical family and considered Bruening a crafty Catholic and a secret chauvinist. In any case, Germany's republican institutions were not France's worry, or so the French Ambassador thought then.

Schleicher and Hindenburg's next choice as Chancellor was Franz von Papen, an old friend and a man with close ties to French industry. The choice was flabbergasting. A dapper former cavalry officer who still dressed in suits of a military cut, von Papen was a political featherweight who had never risen higher by his own efforts than a seat in the Prussian legislature. Fastidiously anti-democratic, his sole distinction was as an equestrian: he had won a medal for his country in that sport in 1911. Brave and discerning in the steeplechase, he showed no judgment when faced with political barriers. Hindenburg and Schleicher had replaced a diamond with a cut glass imitation.

A popular joke told of von Papen's attempt to enter the Reichstag only to find a porter blocking his way.

"But I'm Chancellor," von Papen protested.

"Any chiseler can say that," replied the porter.

Bella considered von Papen a windbag and his wife one of the most inelegant ladies in Berlin. Frau von Papen always wore the same black dress, faded almost to green. The couple had two insipid daughters. "A family ill-favored enough to go far," Bella wrote in her diary.

If the Ambassador from France was pleased with the substitution of the meddlesome von Papen for the resolutely anti-fascist Bruening, Bella could not tell. Diplomats of François-Poncet's persuasion wore masks of icy control. At the end of June he and the regal Jacqueline attended Bella's river party on the steamer *Juvena*. Bella's "Tea Dance on the Wannsee" was a charity affair for needy Berlin children. Each guest paid $5, and the Juvena swim suit company contributed a further $2,500 to hire leggy models to display the latest swim wear. While the "White Ravens" played and the "Wedding Boys" sang, François-Poncet, in dark coat and homburg hat, sat on deck with his wife. The *Juvena* slowly cruised up the River Havel. Bella, who felt a summer cold coming on, braved the wind that afternoon to sit outside with the French Ambassador and his wife.

The French Ambassador was one of the most fascinating creatures in her diplomatic aviary, and she studied him whenever she got the chance. Professor François-Poncet was a puzzle. He was certainly passionate despite the monocle he so loftily pressed to his eye, but he revealed nothing he did not choose to reveal. At his country home on the Wannsee, as the black swans cut curves in the bright lake, he could impulsively drop whatever he was doing to play trains with his four young sons. He had a lively intelligence and an inexhaustible fund of arguments on every subject. One of the most skillful conversationalists in Berlin, his cynical *bon mots* were quoted everywhere. But that day on the steamer *Juvena*, the French Ambassador hid any misgivings he might have had about Bruening's fall behind a mask of perfect inscrutability.

Bella's cold worsened, and her doctor recommended a cure at Bad Reichenhall in the south. As her health improved, her convalescence turned into a vacation and from the Pension Burkner she basked in the warm scent of the pine slopes. But even away from Berlin and the brown figures strutting in the lobby of the Kaiserhof, she could not escape German politics. Prominent figures in the military, heavy industry and banking stopped at the spa on their way to Berchtesgaden to confer with Hitler. One afternoon hundreds of Brown Shirts staged a monster march through the sleepy town, their boots pounding on the cobblestones until Bella could stand it no longer and her fever returned.

Back in Berlin, she took Louis Ullstein aside and told him of the mesmerizing power of those marching men. The portly editor only laughed at her premonition. "You're beginning to hear voices, Bella. You ought to do something about those nerves of yours."

During her absence, von Papen and his conservative backers had overthrown the government of Prussia. Army officers with rifles and hand grenades occupied Berlin police headquarters on the Alexanderplatz and arrested the Police President and Vice-President. All of Prussia's liberal ministers were summarily dismissed and a special decree was drawn up naming Franz von Papen "National Commissioner" of Prussia. Overnight the Reich government had absorbed Germany's most liberal state. The last great pillar of the Republic was no more.

Bella was none too pleased, therefore, when she ran into "Fraenzchen" at one of her racetrack fashion shows in September. She was talking to Kurt von Schleicher in the grandstands and had almost convinced him to pose for a picture when von Papen appeared and deftly leaped over the railing to join them.

"Oh, please! Let me in this picture, too," he lisped.

Bella could have slapped him for his boldness. Rumor had it he and Schleicher were on the outs. Helpless, she could only signal her daughter, Gonny, to snap the picture.

On December 2, 1932, Hindenburg dismissed von Papan and appointed Kurt von Schleicher chancellor.

"Dangerous times are ahead, Bella," Kurt von Schleicher warned. "I must rely upon my faithful friends as never before-so don't forget to come to me whenever you hear anything. The same hour, from twelve to one." The General was wearing himself out negotiating with dissidents in Hitler's party. At the same time, he had to guard against the intrigues of the dethroned von Papen. The General who had pulled the strings now stood on the political tightrope himself. It was one thing to drop the curtain on others, quite another to keep it from being rung down on oneself.

Bella took him a bouquet of lilies but Kurt was busy, so she left the flowers with an aide.

"Who told you that these are his favorite flowers?" the aide asked.

"I guess it must be love," Bella quipped like a true Berliner.

That evening Kurt sent her a short note: "It was sweet of you. Please come again."

But she did not see him again until the start of the Christmas operetta season. Her box was next to his, and he leaned over and invited her to Christmas dinner. He looked tired and pale.

The dinner was an intimate affair, and the talk was exclusively political. She waited her chance to bring up a conversation she had had with Karl von Wiegand, the Hearst correspondent in Europe. An aviation enthusiast, von Wiegand had recently arrived in Europe aboard the Graf Zeppelin. Bella ran into him at a party at the Egyptian Embassy.

"Now tell me," she had said, "when will the Nazis take power?"

Von Wiegand seemed a bit taken aback by her bluntness. He had first interviewed Hitler in 1921 and had predicted then that one day he would triumph.

"It won't be long now," he replied.

That night she repeated von Wiegand's prediction to Kurt over dinner.

"You journalists are all alike," the General reported. "You make a living out of professional pessimism."

"These aren't just Wiegand's ideas, or mine alone," Bella objected.

"I think I can hold them off."

"As long as the Old Gentleman sticks by you," Bella asserted, meaning Hindenburg.

Later, when they were alone, Kurt told her of his plans to lure dissident leaders from Hitler's party into his Cabinet.

What about the Party's war against the Church and the Jews, Bella asked.

"You ought to know me better than that, Bella. All that will be dropped entirely. I'd like to have your friend Bruening back, sooner or later."

Christmas was an especially festive time of year in Berlin. The first Saturday in December marked the opening of the ball season. Aside from the opera and Christmas itself, there was Hindenburg's New Year's reception for the diplomatic corps, the Winterhilfe's gala performance and, on the last Saturday in January, the premier charity event of the season, the annual Press Ball, society's night to put itself on review. Some 5,000 invitations were sent out that year to statesmen from the Prussian and Reich governments, members of the General Staff, university rectors, Reichstag deputies, writers, journalists, stars of stage and screen, cabaret and review, in short, to everyone who was anyone in Germany. Towards 9 o'clock on the night of January 28 a long line of cars stood before the brightly lit banquet halls of the Zoological Garden's "Main Restaurant." The men wore tuxedos, the women Paris gowns in pastels. Monocles glittered, faces beamed rosy felicitations, venerable heads nodded and laughed. The ambassadors of England, France and Russia arrived, as well as the owlish German Foreign Minister, Baron von Neurath; the towering mayor of Berlin, Dr. Sahm; the tennis champion Daniel Prenn; and the short, square air ace Ernst Udet with the "Pour le mérite" around his neck. Representing the foreign press was its president, Edgar Ansel Mowrer, and his lovely wife Lilian. Their names and hundreds of others were inscribed in the ball's "Almanac," whose theme that year was "Love Letters Anew."

By midnight it seemed as if not another guest could be squeezed into the seven gigantic banquet halls and still the cars drew up to dispense yet another starlet in quicksilver evening gown. By midnight the Ball had taken on a distinctly artistic note with the arrival of Max Reinhard, Erich Kaestner, Carl Zuckmayer, Wilhelm Furtwaengler, and Arnold Schoenberg. The coat rooms were full; in the banquet halls champagne flowed like water. In every corner a different dance band struck up a tango or a waltz and people constantly pushed into the official promenade that wound among the rows of tables, inch by inch, to view the tiers of private boxes reserved for the leaders of government and Berlin's biggest business firms. In the Ullstein loge sat Erich Maria Remarque and the best selling novelist Vicki Baum.

Bella was present to cover the affair for her paper. Tomorrow her readers would want to know who said what to whom. She looked very gala in a new Paris gown of pale rose velvet with a sweeping train trimmed in chinchilla. Pastels dominated this year, she noted abstractly, hues of rose and pale blue and lilac. She was filled with apprehension. That morning Kurt had told her: "Don't worry so hard, Bella, dear. I'll see you tonight at the Press Ball. I'll come to the Ullstein box to have a second dance with you." But Kurt was nowhere to be seen. The great center box reserved for the Chancellor and his Ministers was empty. Kurt was gone, swept from office after only 57 days!

The bands played on. The crowds in black and pastel thickened. The stairways filled with gatecrashers. The laughter grew deafening, the chandeliers shimmered like mirages. The Ball would continue until long after sun-up with most of the mid-winter merrymakers spending the following day in bed.

Later, the story made the rounds at Ullstein's about an editor who left the Ball early feeling feverish. His wife put him to bed. He slept around the clock. Awakening on Monday, he rolled over and asked his wife, who had already scanned the morning papers, if there was anything new.

"Nothing much," his wife announced laconically. "Hitler has been appointed Chancellor."

Hitler's Youth Leader, Baldur von Schirach, was on the road Monday, January 30, 1933. He and his friends had a rally to attend. They traveled in Schirach's powerful Mercedes with Schirach at the wheel. They wore *"Raeuberzivil,"* white shirts under brown windbreakers. The Party uniform had been banned again, but everyone who saw the youths in the powerful Mercedes recognized them as Nazis. Schirach stopped at a traffic light. A traffic cop saluted. The man must be mad, Schirach thought.

At the next intersection, another policeman saluted. Something was up. They raced to the nearest branch office and heard the news: Hitler was Chancellor.

In Berlin the crowds filled the streets between the Kaiserhof and the President's Palace where Hitler was conferring with Hindenburg. Shortly before noon he emerged. His guards cleared a path for him through the enthusiastic multitude, and he vanished into the Kaiserhof. Minutes later, the door of the hotel lift on the second floor opened and he stepped out. "Now, we are on our way," he exclaimed to his enthusiastic lieutenants. He was in! Hindenburg had appointed him Chancellor. Von Papen was Vice Chancellor. Most of his Cabinet were officials held over from the previous administrations of von Papen and Schleicher. Everyone gathered around to salute and to shake his hand. Even the hotel porters and maids pressed forward to offer their congratulations. "At least I don't have to go on calling you Your Honorable Privy Counselor," joked Putzi Hanfstaengl when his turn came.

Parked in her roadster on a sidestreet that night, Bella was among the thousands who witnessed the National Socialist victory celebration. The SA* in their brown uniforms, the SS in black and the veterans organizations in gray marched through the Tiergarten to the Brandenburg Gate and then south along the Wilhelmstrasse past the British Embassy and the Ministry of Justice to the Reich Chancellery. Like the conquering army, they crossed the invisible *Bannmeile* and entered the government district, their bands blaring "King Frederick the Great" and the "Horst Wessel Song" and their torches turning the Wilhelmstrasse into a river of light. Behind a closed window in the ponderous old wing of the Chancellery stood the aged figure of Hindenburg in a room that had once belonged to Bismarck, his hand waving in time to the words, "King Frederick the Great, you are our King and hero . . ." As the marchers saluted with an "eyes-right," the white-cropped giant raised his hand in gentle recognition and winced once when the powerful glare of a spotlight swept his otherwise impassive face.

Fifty yards further on, the marchers spotted the figure of Hitler standing in an open window of the Chancellery's new wing, silhouetted against the brightly lit blue of the room behind him. He was in evening dress. Despite the January frost, he leaned out into the night and greeted his followers with the familiar outstretched arm. *"Die Strasse frei, die Reihen fest geschlossen,"* they shouted. *"Hoch, Hoch, Ho-o-o-ch."* The at-

---

*The SA were called "Storm Troopers" or "Brown Shirts" and composed the original Nazi paramilitary organization founded in 1921. The SS was an elite guard within the SA distinguished by their black uniforms and police functions within the Party.

mosphere that night reminded some in Germany of the first weeks of the Great War.

"Long live the Chief of the Luftwaffe!" cried a man in a tree when Goering appeared at Hitler's side. The crowd cheered and raised their arms. Only the few communists among them held back.

"Look," someone shouted, "the Communists are here too."

But no move was made to harm them that night. That would come later.

At Ullstein's the next day, the pessimists predicted that the triumph of Hitler meant the end of Ullstein. The optimists argued that Hitler was no more secure as Chancellor than his predecessors von Papen and Schleicher. His Cabinet, after all, with only two exceptions, was their Cabinet. Besides, Hindenburg disapproved of the "Bohemian corporal" who had tried to unseat him in the presidential elections the previous summer and would not even see Hitler unless von Papen was present. Hitler was boxed in, a figurehead who could be quickly sacrificed if economic conditions in Germany did not improve. That would finish him and his party once and for all.

Putzi Hanfstaengl felt singularly unmoved by the demonstrations of January 30. He was grateful of course for the victory after the long years of struggle and the innumerable nights on the road, but he sensed that in the coming weeks the Fuehrer would have little time for the foreign press or its chief. All scheduled interviews had been canceled, and Putzi was kept busy with importunate newsmen and friends who suddenly wished to renew old acquaintanceships. A moderate, who uttered immoderate words only when he was emotionally aroused, Putzi watched helplessly as Hitler turned to Goering, Goebbels and Rosenberg, the radicals in the Party, for advice. For the moment the entourage remained headquartered in the Kaiserhof awaiting the remodeling of the new Chancellery. It was in one of the red reception rooms at the Kaiserhof that Putzi overheard talk of making Rosenberg a Secretary of State in the Foreign Ministry, as a first step toward making him Foreign Minister. Putzi had long hated Rosenburg for his constant whistling, deplorable taste in clothes, and ungrammatical German. In a panic Putzi rushed across the street to the Foreign Ministry to request an audience with Baron von Neurath. Sound the alarm! Beseech the President to intercede!

"I don't understand you, Herr Hanfstaengl," drawled the phlegmatic Foreign Minister in his heavy Wuerttemberg accent, "surely you are one of the better known members of the party?"

"Certainly I am," Putzi replied, "but where the good of Germany is concerned there are limits and this I will not stand for."

The Rosenberg appointment was blocked.

Nor did the electioneering stop as he had hoped it would. Hitler was eager to test his new strength and called for yet another round of Reichstag elections. Once again, Putzi found himself in airplanes breathing diesel fumes and being buffeted about by rough weather. On the 27th of February he was back in Berlin with a severe cold. He had twenty-four hours to purge himself with relays of aquavit and hot lemonade in rooms Goering had lent him in his villa across the street from the Reichstag. Putzi's fever was at its peak when the phone rang in the next room. It was one of Hitler's aides calling from Goebbels' home: "The Fuehrer insists that you come this evening to Goebbels'. He wants you to play the piano for him." He couldn't do that, Putzi snapped. He was ill and taking a cure. He hung up and went back to bed. Again the telephone rang. He ignored it. It continued to ring. This time it was Magda Goebbels. He was ruining her party, she said. Couldn't he postpone his cure? He could not, he replied firmly, and this time he left the phone off the hook.

Back in bed his sleep was troubled by a flickering light. At first he thought he must have left a light on in the next room but the illumination was fitful, like his sleep. Then the maid burst in: "Herr Doktor, Herr Doktor the Reichstag is on fire."

He was up in a flash, peering out the window at the huge building across the street. The German parliament building, ponderous and dark, was burning as if fireworks had been set off within its interior. Immediately, Putzi got Goebbels on the phone: "I must talk to Herr Hitler."

Goebbels insisted on taking a message.

"Tell him the Reichstag is on fire."

"Hanfstaengl, is this one of your jokes?"

"If you think that, come down here and see for yourselves," Putzi shouted and hung up.

Goebbels called right back.

"I have just talked to the Fuerher," he said, "and he wants to know what is really happening. No more of your jokes now."

"I tell you to come down here and see whether I am talking nonsense or not. The whole place is in flames and the fire brigades are already here. I am going back to bed."

A police constable had called the fire in at 9:14 PM. By 9:42 the blaze had progressed to a General Alarm. Tom Delmer of the "Flying Circus" was one of the first foreign newsmen Putzi summoned that night; as Delmer approached the scene of the fire, the sky above the Tiergarten was rosy with flame. Cordons of mounted police sealed off the northern end of the Friedrich Ebert Strasse. Crowds were being kept back as far as the Brandenburg Gate. The massive edifice on the Koenigsplatz was one of the most florid examples of the architecture of the "Founding Years," but that night only the building's bold outline rose majestically against the flames pouring from its great central dome. Its silhouette had never looked more beautiful. Firemen on the roof inched forward to shoot golden jets of water at copper-colored girders that had once supported the huge glass dome over the Main Meeting Chamber. Every fire truck in the city fought the blaze and, from the north, fire boats on the Spree poured down a steady stream of water that could be seen leaching out of the building's several portals in the subfreezing night. Delmer stepped carefully among the firehoses swollen to the size of serpents and showed his police pass to a nearby constable.

"They've got one of them who did it," the officer confided, "a man with nothing but his trousers on. Seems to have used his coat and shirt to start the fire. But there must be others inside still. They're looking for them."

Just then Hitler and Goebbels arrived and Delmer trotted over.

"Mind if I come in too?" Delmer asked one of the bodyguards.

"Make it snappy," was the reply.

Inside, Hermann Goering, Minister of the Interior and chief of the Prussian police, surveyed the damage, like a general overseeing a field of battle. Dressed in a rich vicuna coat, Goering's face was flushed with excitement. He shot a disapproving glance at Delmer but relented when Hitler said: "Evening Delmer."

"Without a doubt this is the work of the Communists, Herr Chancellor," Goering reported. "A number of Communist deputies were here in the Reichstag twenty minutes before the fire broke out. We have succeeded in arresting one of the incendiaries."

"Who is he?" Goebbels asked.

"We don't know yet," said Goering, his mouth assuming a shark-like thinness at the little doctor's interruption. "But we shall squeeze it out of him, have no fear, Herr Doktor."

"Are the other public buildings safe?" Hitler asked.

"I have taken every possible precaution," said Goering. "I have mobilized all the police. Every public building is guarded. We are ready for anything."

Stepping through water and debris, the group toured the building. Firemen rushed to combat the blaze in the Main Chamber. A heavy door opened briefly; they peered into a furnace of burning benches and desks.

Goering lifted a bit of rag from a charred curtain. "Here you can see for yourself, Herr Chancellor, how they started the fire. They hung clothes soaked in petrol over the furniture and set it alight."

"God grant that this is the work of the Communists," exclaimed

Hitler. "You are witnessing the beginning of a great new epoch in German history. This fire is the beginning.

"You see this building? You see how it is aflame? If the Communists got hold of Europe and had control of it for but two months the whole continent would be aflame like this building."

They climbed to the second floor and encountered Vice Chancellor von Papen, who was making an inspection of his own. Herr von Papen had been dining with President Hindenburg when he learned of the arson.

"This is a Communist crime against the new Government!" Goering called to von Papen.

Resolutely, Hitler wrung von Papen's hand: "This is a God-given signal, Herr Vice-Chancellor! If this fire, as I believe, is the work of Communists, then we must crush out this murderous pest with an iron fist!"

Gently, Herr von Papen withdrew his hand from Hitler's grasp. As usual, he was impeccably dressed in the English manner: a smartly-cut gray tweed coat over a dark suit, and a black and white silk scarf. In one gloved hand he carried a black Homburg hat and his ever-present cane, held at an angle like a military sword. As usual Hitler was dressed in faded raincoat and black velour hat.

"Er . . . Oh yes," von Papen replied shifting to another topic. "I understand that the tapestries have been saved, and that the library most fortunately has not been damaged either."

"We are just about to decide on what measures must be taken next," Hitler said. "Won't you join us?"

"Thank you very much, Herr Chancellor, very good of you indeed. But I think I ought to go and report to the Field Marshall first." The delicate reproof passed Hitler unnoticed.

With von Papen's departure, the group adjourned to Goering's offices in the Reichstag to decide what to do. They were joined by Goering's youthful head of the political police, Rudolf Diels, who had just come from the initial interrogation of the arsonist in a guardhouse near the Brandenburg Gate. The arsonist, Diels had learned, was an itinerant Dutch plasterer named Marinus van der Lubbe who, in quite respectable German, claimed that he had acted entirely alone. Van der Lubbe's hope was that the fire would stimulate others to resist. He denied that he was a part of any plot or conspiracy. In the atmosphere of suspicion and outrage reigning that night Diels knew his report would not be believed, so he did not offer it. Goering was in an heroic mood. Hitler was alternately silent and bellicose, raging one moment against the Communist "sub-humans" who had set fire to a "German monument" and falling into a deep silence the next. With the exception of Diels, everyone believed that a left-wing uprising was imminent. Hitler demanded that every Communist delegate to the Reichstag be arrested and hung from lampposts.

Turning to Diels, Goering gave the order for a full scale police alert, unsparing use of firearms and mass arrests of Communists and Social Democrats. Hastily, Diels scribbled Goering's directives on slips of paper. Later he would worry that he had not been able to catch them all. A lawyer, Diels was not used to collaborating with men who had so little conception of the legal instruments of their offices. His position that evening was a delicate one. Many of his colleagues considered him a turncoat, a Social Democrat who had crossed over to the Nazis. Well-educated and administratively gifted, Diels had risen rapidly under Prussia's liberal governors to become a specialist on Communist affairs. That night he was not only charged with making out warrants for known Communists but also for men under whom he had once served. As he later acknowledged, he could have resigned but he chose to stay on, attracted by the vistas of influence he saw opening before him. He belonged to a new breed of official designated, somewhat synthetically, as "opportunists." To everyone's surprise, the opportunists turned out to be extremely plentiful and alas, unusually talented at their jobs. Without their help, Germany's new rulers would have been as lost among the thickets of bureaucratic tradition as settlers arriving in the New World.

Heavy clouds of black smoke hovered over the motionless trees of the Tiergarten as Martin Sommerfeldt, Goering's press secretary, entered the Reichstag. Sommerfeldt was a Berlin journalist who had come to Goering's attention for a profile he had written entitled: "Goering, What Does He Want?" Sommerfeldt found his chief in one of the lobbies, surrounded by police and fire officials. Rudolf Diels, with his customary sardonic expression, stood nearby.

Calmly, Goering told Sommerfeldt to talk to the necessary officials and to draft an official statement for public release.

The facts, as Sommerfeldt ascertained them, were simple. A theology student on his way home had heard the sound of breaking glass and saw the shape of an intruder entering the Reichstag through a broken window. The student alerted a nearby police constable as the first glow of fire appeared. Within half an hour fire units had arrived and a robust youth, stripped to the waist, was apprehended in the Senate Hall with the remains of nearly a hundred pounds of incendiary material. Diels told Sommerfeldt that he suspected the Communists were behind the fire but stressed that the arsonist was still being interrogated.

The communiqué Sommerfeldt handed to Goering later that night was hardly more than twenty lines long. Quickly scanning Sommerfeldt's words, Goering slammed his fist on the table and shouted: "This is a bunch of bunk!" He didn't want a police report, he wanted a political communiqué to rival the sensational bulletins Goebbels was issuing. Seizing an oversized pencil, Goering raised Sommerfeldt's estimate of the arsonist's incendiary material from 100 to 1,000 pounds.

Impossible, Sommerfeldt gasped. A single man could never . . .

"Nothing is impossible," cried Goering. "One man? That was not one man. That wasn't twenty men! Don't you understand, man? It was a Commune. The fire is a signal for a communist insurrection! The crisis! It has struck!"

In Sommerfeldt's presence, Goering dictated a new version of the arson, describing it as the signal for a Communist insurrection in Germany. He increased all of Sommerfeldt's figures by a factor of ten. A skeptical Sommerfeldt asked Goering to initial the communiqué personally.

"What's the old man shouting about?" Diels asked when Sommerfeldt emerged from Goering's office. Sommerfeldt handed Diels the sheet of paper. Scanning the text above Goering's oversized "G," Diels whistled softly through his teeth.

"You can't have written this . . ."

"Only one word is mine," Sommerfeldt replied: " 'and.' "

RUDOLF DIELS

Born in 1900, the son of a prominent landowner, Rudolf Diels graduated from a humanist gymnasium in Wiesbaden before taking up studies in medicine and law at the universities of Giessen and Marburg. A prodigy in botany, he headed a national association of amateur botanists as a young man. Extraordinarily bright, Diels spent much of his time at Marburg avoiding his studies and participating in marathon drinking bouts with his fraternity brothers in the "Rhenania-Strassburg" dueling corps. That he was a nihilist was evident from the livid scars of numerous saber cuts that covered his cheeks.

At twenty, he passed the State Law Examination "summa cum laude" and after a series of provincial posts entered the Prussian Ministry of the Interior in 1930 as a specialist on Communist affairs. His rivals whispered that the appointment came from his corps' connections, but many of his corps brothers cut him socially for accepting a post in Prussia's liberal government. With his flawed beauty, Diels was fatally attractive to women and a much sought after guest in Berlin salons for his reckless, sardonic wit. His young wife came from the Mannesmann family, a leading manufacturer of rolled steel in Germany. This led to the accusation that he had married for wealth. The marriage was childless and unhappy.

The German Communist Party in 1930 claimed 250,000 adherents, 87 auxilliary organizations, 4,000 political cells and 27 newspapers. In the Twenties the highly sophisticated Soviet underground had chosen Berlin as its headquarters in Europe. The German capital became a clearinghouse for reports from thousands of contact men in Europe's factories, shipyards and businesses. Not surprisingly, Diels' tiny office in the Prussian Ministry of the Interior was no match for such a professional enemy. Under the Republic the Political Police was understaffed, underfinanced and the object of considerable distrust. What did a Republic need with a political police? The very idea conjured up the persecutions of the Czars. Most of Diels' duties consisted of monitoring the careers of prominent German Communists and keeping tabs on Communist Party Headquarters, the Soviet Trade Delegation, and the Communist delegation to the Reichstag. Occasionally, he worked with detectives from Section IA at Police Headquarters on assaults and murders that were clearly politically inspired. Like most of Berlin's citizens, he passed the Fuehrer Publishing House on the Wilhelmstrasse without ever realizing that it too was a center for Communist activity in Berlin.

The accusation that clung most persistently to Diels' career was that he had helped pave the way for von Papen's overthrow of Prussia in July of 1932. Diels never denied that he had taken notes at the confidential meeting between a high-ranking Prussian official and two Communist leaders. The anti-Communist Diels turned the notes over to Schleicher and six weeks later von Papen, who was then Chancellor, announced that he was extending dictatorial rule over Prussia because a Prussian official had conspired with high Communist functionaries to disguise radical terrorism. Martial law was declared, leave for all security police was cancelled, and many liberal officials were furloughed or transferred to the provinces. *Regierungsrat* Diels was promoted and for the first time his police group began to gather material on the parties of the middle class.

When Goering and his friend Pilli Koerner entered the quiet corridors of the Prussian Ministry of the Interior on the afternoon of January 30, 1933, the first person they asked to see was the youngest official there, *Oberregierungsrat* Rudolf Diels.

"I don't want anything to do with the rascals in this building," Goering told Diels. "Are there any decent men here?"

Diels mentioned the name of an official who dealt with personnel matters . . .

"I don't ever want to lay eyes on that fellow," Goering shouted. "He's the first one I intend to send home."

Most of the Ministry's liberals had been removed under the von Papen and Schleicher administrations. The ones who remained belonged for the most part to the Catholic Center Party, the party of Heinrich Bruening. Diels, a Democrat and a member of the "Democratic Club" also stayed on because Goering preferred to work with men he knew even if they did not belong to the Party. Goering fully expected a revolt from the left similar to the one that had gripped Russia in 1917, leading to civil war, entrenched positions and bloody barricades. He therefore, appointed SA and SS leaders to the posts of Police Presidents in the provinces and turned the Prussian State Police over to the head of the Berlin SS. The Berlin Police he placed in the hands of an old friend, a retired Rear Admiral. Fifty thousand SA, SS and Steel Helmet veterans were sworn in as "Auxilliary Police" and one of Goering's first orders was to shoot to kill if resistance was encountered.

With the burning of the Reichstag, civil liberties in Germany came to an abrupt end. Without warning, tenement blocks were cordoned off and searched house to house. Crowds, sensing the danger, turned and fled. Bonfires blazed across Germany, from the Rhine to the eastern

© Ullstein

provinces as the March 5 Reichstag elections took place. Surprisingly, Hitler's party obtained only 44% of the vote; for a while longer Hitler must tolerate the unrevolutionary von Papen and his "Cabinet of Barons" as co-regents.

The 400,000 man army of Brown Shirts were not so patient. Germany belonged to them—or so they interpreted the election results—and they rushed to settle old scores. Punitive expeditions broke into homes and apartment flats. The correspondent for *Isvestia,* a woman, was threatened at gunpoint. German authors who had raised their pens in the cause of pacifism lost their passports. Only a lucky few managed to escape to Switzerland. For speaking of such acts, the *Berliner Tageblatt* was banned. Three Americans were mistreated, and the American Embassy protested to the German Foreign Ministry and to the police.

Diels' life also changed on the night of February 27 when flames engulfed the Reichstag. He and his police arrested all Communist officials who had not already escaped across the borders to France, Czechoslovakia or Switzerland. Soviet oil and shipping companies in Germany were shut down, and the Communist offices in the Reichstag and the Soviet Trade Delegation were raided. Organizations such as Rote Hilfe, the Revolutionary Trade Opposition, and the Communist Youth League were crushed. This was the easiest of Goering's directives to fulfill because the arrest lists had been drawn up long in advance. Against the experienced and well-trained Communist underground Diels did not fare so well. That was a war he would never win; there were successful skirmishes but never an ultimate victory.

Following the von Papen coup of the previous summer, Moscow had sent word to its underground in Germany to prepare for a fascist take over. Courier services were organized, revolutionary cells tightened, lodgings cleansed of incriminating material. Communist informants rarely defected. When they did or when confessions were beaten out of them after January 30, they had only code names to divulge. Infiltration was the only reliable method but took months of preparation and frequently led only to other undercover agents. Meanwhile, opposition groups in Paris and Prague carried on a war of their own. Anti-Nazi literature was smuggled into Germany by balloon, bicycle, even between the pages of travel brochures. Hidden radio stations broadcast anti-Nazi sermons from remote valleys in Czechoslovakia and, in Berlin for a time, there was a flourishing underground literature on how to construct home mimeographing machines.

In an effort to crack down on the fake passport trade all of Berlin's print shops were watched, but Honduran birth certificates and Brazilian passports of excellent quality continued to surface. "Passology," as the Soviets called their craft, could duplicate the signature of any consular official in the world. Among the items turned up in one raid—aside from numerous blank Nazi Party membership books—was the signature of Party Treasurer Xavier Schwartz. Diels no sooner closed down one illegal passport factory than another took its place. He soon came to see that somewhere beyond his reach there lay a master series of stamps and facsimiles from which molds could be pressed and other factories quickly equipped.

Attempts to interrupt the flow of illegal funds fared little better. One raid netted only 14,000 marks, a mere drop in the counter-revolutionary bucket. Throughout 1933 the German Communist Party in Prague continued to smuggle "senior advisors" into Germany and by the end of the year felt confident enough to rededicate itself on German soil.

To the colorful array of second-storey men, prostitutes, cocaine traffickers and common thieves awaiting sentencing at Berlin's Police Headquarters on the Alexanderplatz, the arrival of the National Socialist revolution was a vivid experience. Overnight, familiar warders were replaced with brown-shirted youths wearing the white arm bands of the "Auxilliary Police," youths who ordinarily would have ended up on the other side of "Alex's" prison bars. Alex's dungeons and corridors resembled scenes from bedlam. Transports of arrested suspects of both sexes arrived under SA guard at all hours of the day and night and were unloaded and driven into the building with kicks and blows and made to line up with their noses to the wall until their turn came to kneel painfully on the barrel of a carbine and recite their sins. The atmosphere was thick with the cries of command and the moans of outrage and despair. Exhausted detectives slept on tables covered with confiscated literature and overflowing ashtrays. Lucky was the citizen with bloodied nose who thought to blurt out Diels' name and found himself brought face to face with an exceedingly pale young man in dark suit, rumpled tie and sweat-soaked collar, who distractedly filled out a building pass with an ironic look. Clutching the pass, the suspect could get through the SA guards watching the building's entrances and escape, a free man, into the maze of Berlin's foggy streets.

American correspondents in Berlin were relentless in their criticism of the violence in Germany. In his columns the correspondent for the *Chicago Daily News,* Edgar Ansel Mowrer, persecuted the persecutors and fell silent only when he was away from his desk. When a German paper announced that Germany was again a country worth living in,

Mowrer tacked that statement onto an item from a Catholic paper which claimed that the terror continued. Both were correct, Mowrer wrote: "Germany is worth living in for persons of terrorist inclinations."

Edgar Ansel Mowrer was a Midwesterner who arrived in France before the Great War to study literature and philosophy. He fell into newspaper work when his brother, who was the Paris correspondent for the *Chicago Daily Mail,* left to cover the fighting on the western front. When his brother returned, Edgar moved south to Italy where he described the retreat at Corporetto, married a British actress, and nearly died from the Spanish influenza. His first big assignment was Mussolini in Italy; later he covered the years of prosperity in Germany. The Mowrers shared their home on the Tiergarten with Dorothy Thompson, and Mowrer's best friend in Berlin was H. R. Knickerbocker. Knick's speciality was economics in simple figures; Mowrer's was morality in human terms. He was an emotional, almost overwrought, liberal who would not for a moment think of giving a dictator the benefit of the doubt. His face, lean and ascetic, reminded some of the face of a young Lincoln.

The Mowrers spent their last Christmas before Hitler with Dorothy and Red Lewis in Austria, skiing and drinking. In January the Nazis came to power. In February Mowrer left for a holiday in the Dolomites, and the Nazis received a brief respite. Eight days later Mowrer was back, limping on a broken leg. As his physician he chose the son of the Grand Rabbi of Berlin and within the doctor's dispensary received the latest word on the Jewish persecutions. Jews and other liberals that winter were taking their holidays early. Switzerland, Scandinavia and the Saarland reported a sharp increase in tourism.

When his cast came off, Mowrer began to suffer from periodic sore throats until his doctor warned him that their consultations had been noticed. Thereafter the two men met every Wednesday at noon in the public toilets beneath Potsdamer Platz. The incriminating evidence—a ball of tightly rolled paper—was dropped unobtrusively on the floor. The two never spoke and left by separate exits.

The day after the March 5 elections—whose results Mowrer described as nothing less than the rejection by Germany of 1,000 years of civilization—the correspondents received their first censorship scare. Berlin's Main Telegraph Office on Oranienburgstrasse held up part of Knick's background report on the persecution of Socialists and Communists. In Germany the telegraphic facilities belonged to the government and both Knick and Mowrer sent out ominous warnings that theirs might be the last uncensored dispatches to leave the country for some time.

The scare was premature. Only a dozen of the roughly 150 foreign correspondents in the capital reported any interference. Two of Knick's cables were stopped under an international agreement which held that a foreign government could "stop the transmission of any private telegram which appears dangerous to the security of the State or which is contrary to public order or to decency." A more recent agreement stipulated that a newsman must be promptly informed by the government when a cable was blocked. The Main Telegraph Office did this immediately for Knick's first cable, but waited nearly seventeen hours in the case of the second. In any case, a cable stalled by the Main Telegraph Office could be freely telephoned to bureaus in London or Paris.

The tactic of censors Sebastiani, Kommermann and Hildebrecht at the Main Telegraph Office was to delay and thereby to kill the timeliness of any story they felt pictured Germany as a "wild or bloodthirsty country." The stack of blocked cables that Knick saw at the Telegraph Office was only half an inch high. On such a small scale the tactic was not censorship but interference or, as the German authorities liked to put it, "supervision."

How bloodthirsty was Germany that March? During the March 5 elections even foreigners felt the force of the National Socialist "Day of Reckoning." Nathaniel Wolff, a painter from Rochester, New York, was kidnapped by a band of Storm Troopers after he was heard to say that both the "Nazis" and the "Commies" should be blown to kingdom come. Wolff was taken to an apartment in an obscure part of Berlin and forced to sign a statement that read: "I am a Jew. I will leave tonight for Paris. I promise never again to set foot on German soil. I certify that no physical violence has been done to me and none of my property has been stolen."

In some cases the excitement of the electoral victory proved too great a strain on the emotionally unstable. Edward Dahlberg, an editor for *Scribner's* magazine, had been in Berlin only a few days when he was attacked by a cane-wielding Nazi late one night while walking down the colorful Kurfuerstendamm. Dahlberg, his face bleeding, produced his passport to prove that he was an American but only received further blows from the berserk man's cane. A police officer intervened and took both Mr. Dahlberg and the Nazi—who continued to thrash Mr. Dahlberg—to a police station where Dahlberg was released. The following evening, the wife and daughter of the assailant came to Dahlberg's hotel to beg him not to press charges against their husband and father, a butcher's apprentice who had been drinking.

Storm Troopers broke into the apartment of one American woman and ordered her husband to sign incriminating statements while she was forced to stand naked before them.

Another American woman was forced to watch as her husband was severely beaten for having four suits of clothes in his closet.

"Four suits," cried a Storm Trooper, "while for fourteen years we have been starving. Jews. We hate you. For fourteen years we have been waiting for this and tonight we'll hang many of you." After striking the wife in the face with a rubber truncheon they fled with her passport.

Throughout their fourteen years of struggle, the Nazis had derided the Black-Red-Gold banner of the Republic as the banner of the "Soulless System" of parliamentary democracy. In song, invective and chant they dubbed the colors of the liberal visionaries of 1848 the "Black-Red-Mustard" or, in German, the "Black-Red-Nonsense." Two days after the elections, all Berlin watched as the Nazi banner was hoisted above Berlin Police Headquarters and unfurled from a turret of the damaged Reichstag. By noon calmer heads must have prevailed for the two banners were replaced with the less revolutionary colors of the Kaiser. But by the week's end the Nazi flag flew uncontested over the Stock Exchange, the Reichsbank and in the district around the Brandenburg Gate. Only Hindenburg's residence continued to fly the republican "Black-Red-Gold," probably because no one dared invade the Old Gentleman's palace and pull it down.

The task of ridding Germany's closets and attics of the Mustard banner fell to those most eager for it: the adolescents of the Hitler Youth. House to house searches were conducted and the confiscated banners torn and trampled underfoot and dragged through the dust of the boulevards and burned to chants of *"Heil Hitler."*

On the 10th of March swarms of SA youths invaded the quiet neighborhood around the Hohenzollernkorso in the southern part of the city looking for "Mustard" flags. Late in the afternoon they found one neatly folded in the attic of a nearby hospital and proceeded to drag it outside and along the street until they came to a driveway large enough to accommodate the ceremonial burning. By chance, they chose the driveway belonging to Bella Fromm. That day, she was hosting one of her cocktail parties for the diplomatic set, entertaining the mayor of Palermo, the wife of the Italian Ambassador, as well as the envoys of Belgium, Czechoslovakia and Rumania. François-Poncet and his wife put in an appearance although the French Ambassador typically could not stay long. In all, some 26 guests from the highest ranks of society chatted amicably in her ground-floor music room completely unaware of the fiery celebration taking place on her doorstep.

Discreetly, Bella excused herself and went outside to speak to the crowd: "What's going on? What do you want?"

"Passersby called us here," a youth replied. "They have seen that arms and ammunition have been delivered to the house. They have seen spies driving up in these cars. We know very well that this house belongs to non-Aryans. Now we are going to fumigate the place."

Bella almost laughed, but she wanted to cry. She told the youths to contact the local police precinct; meanwhile they could post a guard at her door if they wished.

To avoid alarming her guests, she drew the drapes and turned on the interior lighting, thankful that the March air was chill, her terrace and formal garden uninviting.

The police officer sent to investigate was an elderly captain in charge of five officers. He wore the Iron Cross, 1st Class and immediately adopted a badgering tone: "I am from station Kreuzberg. We have word that this is a meeting of political agitators. I have orders to search your house."

Bella pleaded with him to wait until her guests had left. The captain relented. He knew that the automobiles with low license plates and pennants flying from their radiator caps belonged to foreign diplomats.

From an upstairs telephone, Bella quietly put a call through to Ru Bassewitz, Chief of Protocol at the Foreign Ministry. When Ru's soft voice came on the line she begged him to send help immediately.

"But I can't believe it," he said. "You're so calm."

"There's nothing else for me to be. For Heaven's sake, Count, get busy."

Almost immediately her protector at the Foreign Ministry, von Buelow, called. He was on his way to see von Papen, he said. The Chancellor would be informed.

Bella told the crowd outside that the Fuehrer had been alerted.

"Everybody can say that," voices muttered darkly. "Give us a proof that Hitler really has been informed."

She returned to her guests. Only the French naval attaché and the Czech Minister knew what was going on. From the ornamental bushes on the terrace they watched as the crowd collected combustibles with which to set the house on fire.

Hitler's Chief of Chancellery, telephoned next, to say that Hindenburg had been informed. Then von Papen telephoned: "Frau Bella, fifteen mounted police are on their way out to you with orders to shoot; tell the crowd."

"Shoot at whom?" Bella asked sarcastically. After all, it was not her revolution. But before the Vice-Chancellor could get over his surprise, she was again summoned outside. One of the Hitler Youths had torn the pennants from the radiator caps of the French and Rumanian limousines. He was challenged by the two chauffeurs. All three men were rolling and kicking in the dust to the delight of the crowd.

Just then four Mercedes limousines from the Reich Chancellery roared up Bella's drive carrying twenty Storm Troopers under the command of Group Leader Schaefer. Bella knew Schaefer. They had attended some of the same parties. He was not the worst of his kind.

"Why, it's you, Frau Bella. What's the matter here?"

Bella replied that the trouble was not of her making; he should ask his own people. Schaefer turned to the nearest youth—the one who had removed the pennants—and holding him by the throat choked out a story about weapons, spies and non-Aryans.

"You blasted idiots!" Schaefer bellowed. "Do you want all of the foreign powers on our neck? Get out—before I line you all up against the wall and fill you full of lead."

The mob dispersed into the night.

They were country lads, Schaefer explained, who had been brought into the city to help celebrate the election victory. He asked if he might come in and apologize to her guests.

To his astonishment Bella refused; the Group Leader was in uniform. A chastened Schaefer ordered the elderly police captain with the Iron Cross to see that the house and its occupants remained undisturbed.

"Zu Befehl," snapped the police captain.

Bella returned to her guests. The Czech Minister, who had observed the entire scene from a spot on the terrace, kissed her hand saying: "I am most obliged. I have just now experienced a page of world history. I have had the chance to study the Nazi soul."

With that the story was out. Madam François-Poncet fainted, while another society matron could be heard shouting into the telephone: "Otto, Otto—I'm still alive."

Later, after the crowd had gone, von Papen's mounted police arrived. But there was nothing left for them to do but turn around and make their weary way back to their stables. The Kaiser's forces were no match for the sleek Mercedes of the revolutionaries.

As Bella dressed to go out that evening, both phones were ringing with queries from foreign newsmen. She begged them not to print the story, but men such as Edgar Ansel Mowrer could not be dissuaded. In her kitchen three of Schaefer's men sat eating cake and drinking coffee. They complimented her on her cooking; she complimented them on their taste for non-Aryan fare.

Von Papen begged Bella to do what she could to smooth over the affair. André Francois-Poncet kindly consented to forget the entire matter, but the Rumanian Ambassador sent a formal note of protest to the German Foreign Minister. Baron von Neurath, in top hat and cutaway, had to tender the Reich's apologies. The Government issued an edict against the mistreatment of foreigners and their automobiles which the foreign correspondents quickly dubbed "Fromm's Act."

Rudolf Diels had a hand in drafting "Fromm's Act," but he was as surprised as anyone at the version that finally appeared. He had compiled a long list of SA excesses—among them the lawlessness outside Bella's home—and submitted these to Hitler along with a draft proclamation calling the SA to order.

Hitler was not impressed.

Diels then produced a list of foreigners who had been assaulted, most of them Poles, but a few Americans also. Most were Jews; again, Hitler would have none of it. He was not interested in protecting Jews, not even foreign Jews. Shrewdly, Diels suggested that if such excesses continued the outside world would say that Hitler could not control his revolution. Hitler turned the report over to Goebbels. Goebbels issued a proclamation warning loyal SA and SS men to be on the lookout for criminal elements dressed in Party uniform who were attempting to damage Germany's relations abroad by molesting foreigners in automobiles flying foreign pennants.

The peppery H. R. Knickerbocker took to repeating the phrase "men dressed in the uniform of the SA" so often that it soon became a damning litany. Mowrer went one step further; he wrote that it was indeed difficult to distinguish between the behavior of SA men and common criminals. The demure Sigrid Schultz of the *Chicago Tribune* worked yet another variation on the theme when she wrote: "Woolworth five and ten cent stores in Berlin today felt the sting of the anti-foreign campaign by storm troopers, or, as the authorities term them, 'agent provocateurs in Nazi uniforms.'" The Government was not amused. The tactic of cloaking an admission of guilt in an outright lie did not work with the foreign press.

From refugee circles abroad came horrible tales of SA brutality. In the middle of March the prestigious *New York Times* printed a selection of these:

> The *Anhalter Zeitung* relates today how Nazi storm troopers broke into the house of Socialist Deputy Sollmann in Saarbruecken, beat him unconscious, revived him by burning his feet with a torch, spat in his face and then threw powdered mustard in his eyes with the remark, "That's your right color, you pig." They again beat him until he became unconscious. They dragged him into a Nazi cafe, where they revived him, only to beat him again. Finally the Nazis threw him into a coal cellar. . .

The *Times* went on to quote from an interview that had appeared in a Viennese paper with a refugee it described as "one of the best known personalities in Germany":

> I spent fourteen days in cells in Spandau Fortress and then a night in a cell in Berlin Police Headquarters with sixty-two other prisoners. These men, mostly working men and Jewish passers-by had been beaten half to death.
>
> I saw men whose eyes had been gouged out. The teeth of most of them had been knocked out with rifle butts. Their hands had been burned. All the Jews had been thrown on the floor and Nazi storm troopers had jumped on them until they fainted.

To German ears such tales smacked unpleasantly of the atrocity stories concocted by allied propagandists during the Great War. In numerous post-war memoirs American and British reporters had confessed to their part in creating such fabrications until the word "atrocity" had come to mean the same as "lie" and men and women on both sides of the Atlantic were determined not to be tricked again. When a newspaper such as the *Cleveland Plain Dealer* compared the anti-Semitic outbursts in Germany with the sinking of unarmed merchant vessels during the Great War, German suspicions increased. Once again, Germany was about to enter an allied propaganda blockade.

Indeed, there was a discrepancy between appearance and reality. Visitors to Germany and most Germans never witnessed a single incident of public brutality. As Lilian Mowrer recalled: the flowers continued to bloom in the window boxes and the traffic to flow without interruption along the great boulevards of Berlin. Edgar Ansel Mowrer told his readers that no foreigner would notice anything out of the ordinary unless he went among the victims of the terror. Knick compared the atmosphere in Berlin to Moscow; a visitor to either capital would see nothing out of the ordinary unless he knew how to read the expressions of veiled fear on the faces around him.

Foreign correspondence necessarily simplified. A single tale of woe might stand for a thousand such tales or only for itself. Rarely did the correspondents press the point that most of the assaults occurred late at night in Storm Troop barracks, deserted parks or isolated apartment flats, by bands of youths in Storm Trooper garb who fled afterward, often with their victim's money and other valuables. The emphasis was always on the suffering of the innocent rather than the desperation of the attackers.

For the most part the stories were true, if not widespread, and were profoundly shocking to American newsmen who had no experience of pogroms and had always known the Germans to be almost overbearingly law-abiding. It was not the number of dead and wounded that appalled them so much as the failure of Germany's new rulers to take steps to curb the lawlessness. Instead, threats were made by powerful figures in the Party that for every SA man slain three Communists would be murdered in retaliation. Worse, the Government issued a blanket amnesty to all Party members who had broken the law in their zeal to attain the Day of Reckoning. Americans who had been injured were left without legal recourse.

On the opposite side of the Atlantic the stories were amplified by the megaphone of distance and lingering anti-German feeling. The weekly and monthly journals of public opinion were the worst transgressors. They quoted stories at third and fourth hand from the hysterical refugee press in Warsaw, Paris and Amsterdam. Germany had entered a second Dark Ages, half the population was either dead or in chains, the streets ran red with the blood of murdered rabbis. "The world will probably never know how many Jews were murdered and disappeared in the fateful months of February and March 1933," wrote the *New Republic*.

On the contrary, some astonishingly educated guesses on the extent of the violence appeared in the foreign press. The *Manchester Guardian* and the *Chicago Tribune* estimated the number of dead at the beginning of March to be close to 100. Knick, with his talent for employing simple figures to describe complex events, calculated that since German Jews outnumbered foreign Jews 100 to 1 and since 9 American Jews and some 100 Polish Jews had filed complaints with their embassies, it was no exaggeration to say that the number of German Jews beaten and tortured since January 30 ran into the hundreds. A Swedish newspaper claimed to have seen a report from the Secret State Police which put the number of dead at 247: 17 Nazis, 14 Jews, 216 Communists. The Government protested that not one tenth that number had lost their lives.

Not surprisingly, it was Hitler who offered the most robust figures; after all, he had read Diels' report on the excesses of the SA. Early in April, in a speech before diplomats and newsmen, Hitler claimed that 300 people had been killed, 40,000 wounded and 100,000 thrown out of their jobs.

In a fifteen-minute telephone hook-up to New York City, Putzi Hanfstaengl branded reports of violence in Germany as barefaced lies. In the course of the recent national revolution—the most peaceful the world had ever known, he hastened to add—unavoidable skirmishes had occurred. But never had any prejudice been shown in the treatment of

Jews, non-Jews, Christians or members of other faiths, stocks or races. The new regime, Putzi said rather confusedly, made no distinction between supporters or opponents.

In Berlin, Hermann Goering, Minister without Portfolio and Chief of the Prussian State Police, sowed contradictions of his own. Summoning more than a hundred representatives of the foreign press to his apartments in the Prussian Ministry of the Interior, he gave them a furious tongue lashing. The gist of Goering's harangue, as Knick put it, was that in the first place beatings of Jews and liberals had not occurred, in the second place they were under investigation and in the final place they would not happen again. "There is not one person in all Germany from whom even one fingernail has been chopped off," Goering declared, and then admitted that it was true that Storm Troopers had beaten terribly "this one or that one" but that the world should be grateful to the National Socialists for saving Germany from Bolshevism. "Where there is planing there are shavings," he asserted in what was to become the most celebrated expression of the year.

He then made good his promise to take a group of foreign newsmen including H. R. Knickerbocker and Edgar Ansel Mowrer on a tour of Berlin-Moabit remand prison. *L'humanité* had reported that Ernst Thaelmann, leader of the German Communist Party, had been blinded in prison and then strangled. Rudolf Diels, head of Goering's anti-Communist branch was instructed to show "Teddy" to the foreign journalists. Led up staircases and along steel gangways, the newsmen were shown into Thaelmann's cell.

"You will observe that Thaelmann looks physically fit," Diels began. "That he is not spiritually comfortable need not surprise you, for Thaelmann does not like it that he, who regards himself as a political prisoner, is in the same jail with criminals.

"However, as he has been the leader of the party accused of inciting the Reichstag fire, that cannot be helped. Thaelmann further complains that he does not like the reading matter given him."

Thaelmann, a tall, scholarly man went to his cot and returned with a book entitled: *Jolly Tales From Swabia*.

"We can talk about that afterward," Diels commented.

Asked if he had any complaint to make about the prison food or his treatment, Thaelmann shook his head. He asked only that his picture not be taken.

A few steps further down the hall was the cell of Werner Hirsch, the former editor of the Communist newspaper *Rote Fahne*.

"Have you anything to complain about?" Diels asked.

"Nothing," Hirsch replied, "except that the evening papers yesterday claimed I had denied having seen anybody badly handled. On the contrary, I saw people with bloody eyes and other injuries delivered here from Storm Troop barracks."

"That was during the first days of the revolution," Diels explained, "when, to save these people from further violence, we took them into protective custody."

Hirsch said the food was adequate and that he was allowed to smoke but that he had yet to be formally charged and had been denied permission to see a lawyer.

The reporter for the *London Times* thought the prisoners looked uninjured, if obviously depressed by their present situation. When the newsmen asked how many liberals and Communists had been imprisoned since January 30, Diels estimated 5,000 to 6,000.

The exhortation of prominent personalities for fairer reporting continued. Vice-Chancellor von Papen wrote the Board of Trade for German-American Commerce in New York City and the American Chamber of Commerce in Berlin asked Americans to withhold judgment on the revolutionary events unfolding in Germany. Putzi's friend, Dr. Karl-Otto Bertling, director of the Amerika Institut and the "Harvard man" in Berlin, cabled Nicholas Murray Butler, president of the Carnegie Endowment for International Peace: "Shocked at gross misinterpretation of recent German events. Save for a few molestations by individual toughs, no harm done to Jews. Latter continue undisturbed in business and office. No leading Jewish papers suppressed. Government has population well in hand. Strict discipline is maintained. Present movement is against bolshevism, not against Judaism."

Even the owlish Baron von Neurath, career diplomat and Germany's Foreign Minister, broke his customary diffidence to grant an interview. In a subdued but passionate voice von Neurath spoke about the exaggerated reports of the last few days.

"As concerns Jews, I can only say that their propagandists abroad are rendering their co-religionists in Germany no service by giving the German public, through their distorted and untruthful news about persecution and torture of Jews, the impression that they actually halt at nothing, not even at lies and calumny, to fight the present German Government.

"Why, even a prominent Jewish banker told one of your American colleagues, 'We reject all foreign interference. German Jews are he-men enough to help ourselves.'

"Actually, every visitor must agree that when he walks through the streets of Berlin even today he encounters Jews, poor as well as elegantly dressed, who are attending their business. Nobody has barred them."

As March drew to a close, the Government could take some satisfaction in having successfully raked the enemy's flanks. The foreign press had had its tour of the Hades of Moabit and saw that the dead yet lived. Symbols of Germany such as von Neurath and von Papen had worked in tandem with moderates such as Putzi Hanfstaengl to dampen the hysteria. With calmer heads prevailing, tempers might yet cool.

BOYCOTT

Revolutions, alas, obey laws of their own. Elements within the Party meant to wreak a rougher justice. Just as the patient showed signs of recovery, he was ordered purged and blistered again. On March 28 Party headquarters in Munich issued a call for a national boycott of all Jewish businesses, goods and professionals.

"Until Governments abroad take measures against the anti-German Jewish propaganda, the Government of the Reich will take no measures against the National Socialist anti-Jewish defence movement in Germany," the Brown House announced, pledging and pardoning itself in the same breath in its dual role as antagonist and protagonist.

The revolutionaries had succumbed to their own propaganda. Germany was not to blame for the public outcry; the Jews and the foreign correspondents were to blame. As the correspondent for the Jewish *Daily Forward* put it from his sanctuary in Prague: if the world rebelled against Germany's little pogroms then the world would be treated to a big pogrom.

In some areas the boycott began at once. In Berlin, Storm Troopers chased pedestrians down the Kurfuerstendamm shouting: "Down with the Jews! Out with the Jews!" Knick's cable describing the scene was blocked by the Telegraph Office, the third one that month. In Goerlitz, Jewish judges and lawyers were placed under protective arrest. In Heidelberg, a Jewish physician on his way to see a patient was attacked and beaten. Jewish shops in Essen, Duisburg and Bochum were closed. Jewish businesses in Schwerin-on-the-Warthe were forced to pay each Aryan employee two months salary in advance.

In Munich, representatives of the SA, the Hitler Youth, the Nazi Party Factory Cells, the Labor Front and the Combat League of the German Middle Class formed the "The Central Committee For Defense Against Jewish Atrocity and Boycott Propaganda." Every newspaper carried the Committee's instructions: that the boycott would begin on Saturday, April 1, at 10 AM and would continue until all Jewish life in Germany was eradicated. Nazi employees of Jewish firms were to demand two months' salary in advance. Jewish employees were to be dismissed. Firms that refused would be dealt with. The airways bristled with vituperation against the "World Enemy" and "Blood Sucker." Thousands of mammoth black signboards appeared with the yellow plague stain.

Foreign observers were astounded at how quickly the prejudice spread. "The boycott is only a beginning," the chameleon-like Putzi Hanfstaengl told an American visitor. "It can be made to strangle all Jewish business. Slowly, implacably, it can be extended with ruthless and unshakeable discipline. Our plans go much further. During the war we had 1,500,000 prisoners. 600,000 Jews would be simple. Each Jew has an SA (man). In a single night it could be finished." Putzi had suffered a loss of influence after January 30 and he was doing his best to make up for it. Revolutions are hard on personalities who crave attention.

Stocks on a jittery Boerse fell as much as eight points.

A Jewish dentist told one American correspondent that after preaching anti-semitism for fourteen years the Government could not call for restraint now that the Day of Reckoning had arrived. Edgar Ansel Mowrer put it more succinctly: look no further for the inspiration behind the Storm Troopers hawking tracts with titles such as "The Jews Want Hitler Murdered" and "Kick the Jew Out" than the editorial offices of *Der Angriff* and the paper's vitriolic director, Dr. Paul Joseph Goebbels.

Knick, Mowrer's crony, saw things differently. Knick had always accorded Goebbels a special place in his dispatches; despite the professional animosity of the moment, the two were still on speaking terms. Knick held Goebbels to be the genius of the Party, a figure who, despite his frail frame, was Hitler's equal as a speaker and his superior as a shaper of public opinion. During the presidential elections of the previous year, Knick had sent Goebbels a complimentary copy of his book *The German Crisis,* and Goebbels had responded with a short note of thanks and the promise that when the elections were over he would come to "grips" with it. Knick continued to treat the Propaganda Minister to an occasional spread at Horchers, one of the great restaurants of Europe, where a meal lasted hours and every pheasant was numbered. Knick enjoyed good food and, as the highest paid correspondent in Europe with royalties pouring in from numerous books, he could afford it. He had the metabolism of the chronically active and always appeared exuberantly underfed.

With the April 1 boycott looming, Knick thought it high time to take Mowrer in tow and pay a visit to Goebbels' offices at the Prinz Leopold Palace. Since, in Nazi eyes, the foreign reporters were as much to blame for the boycott as the Jews, perhaps Knick could patch up relations between the ruler of public opinion in Germany and the poisoners of public opinion abroad before it was too late.

The Leopold Palace was one of the most sumptuous on the Wilhelmstrasse and Goebbels was having it redecorated. Knick and

Mowrer were kept cooling their heels for a while before they were shown in. A small man, Goebbels seemed much smaller in the immense room filled with huge vases of costly orchids.

"You claim to have a reason to speak to me?" he asked, eyeing the two Americans.

Knick and Mowrer explained that they wished to make their position as journalists clear in light of the acrimony of recent weeks. As journalists representing a free press it was their duty to report everything they saw . . .

"We will not have you swindle the public out of our hands," Goebbels snapped. "We know just how that sort of thing is done."

End of interview.

In the hours remaining, President Hindenburg's intervention was sought and there were signs from Munich that the Nazi leadership was having second thoughts. But preparations had gone too far. No government figure had the power call off what had been begun. Instead, it was announced that the boycott would be "interrupted" after the first day, Saturday, and resumed on Wednesday if international Jewry and the foreign press had not ceased their agitation. In Berlin, Goebbels refused to moderate his tone. He told the Jews that they could blame the likes of Albert Einstein for their present misery, and he promised that if the boycott were continued on Wednesday they should expect complete annihilation. His speech, carried over the radio, was interrupted repeatedly with cries of "Hang them!" from the audience. The tension could be felt on every street corner. "The hour of 10 Saturday," Knick wrote, "may prove to be one of the most critical hours in this country's recent history."

No power on earth could have kept Bella Fromm home on "National Socialist Saturday." Early Saturday morning she drove to the Markgrafenstrasse entrance of the Ullstein complex and relinquished her car to the towering Ullstein doorman in his gray greatcoat with the gold-embroidered "U" on the chest. The doorman saluted as he did every morning before folding himself into her small sports car and parking it.

The Ullstein corridors bustled as usual with secretaries and editors, although the gentiles on the staff seemed unusually alert. In Berlin the boycott did not get started until nearly 11 o'clock. It was not until the *Berliner Zeitung* came off the presses at noon that the sound of tramping boots could be heard in the corridors accompanied by the chant: "To hell with the Jews" and the strains of the Horst Wessel Song. Ullstein employees, Jewish and gentile alike, filled the halls and doorways as the procession of office boys, hall porters and a few junior editors marched behind the gigantic doorman who had changed into brown for the occasion. Bella caught the doorman's eye and he blushed and looked away. Only a few days before she had given him one of her coats as a gift to his wife.

The procession marched through the circulation department, the cartoonists' studios, the archives, the employees' canteen, the book department, and the radio station and pneumatic post on the top floor, demanding that all non-Aryan employees be dismissed. They visited each of Ullstein's thirteen buildings that day as well as the printing house out near Tempelhof airfield. After three solid hours of demonstrating, the Ullstein doorman pronounced the boycott officially over.

No employee had been accosted or dismissed. None of Ullstein's Christians received a check for two months wages in advance.

When Bella went to retrieve her car that afternoon its windows were intact, its paint unscratched. The doorman, once again in his gray greatcoat with the Ullstein "U" embroidered on the chest, doffed his hat to her as he always did and handed her the keys.

What was happening in Germany, Bella wondered, as she pushed the gas pedal to the floor. Germany, like Ullstein's doorman, was changing colors by the hour.

To everyone's relief, the day passed with little violence. On the fashionable Ku-damm nearly every shop dripped the pink word *"Jude,"* while on Unter den Linden, under the staid gaze of the Foreign Ministry and the President's Palace, the yellow plague signs seemed almost demure and withdrawn. In upper-class districts husky housemaids bent on fulfilling their daily rounds brushed past SA pickets with a scornful "Nonsense!" to enter the shop of the local tailor or druggist. The shops of orthodox Jews were closed that sabbath Saturday and by noon the other Jewish shopkeepers had locked their doors and rung down their iron grilles.

Most people had taken the precaution of doing their shopping on Friday night after work. On Saturday a holiday mood prevailed, and the crowds assembled more out of curiousity than enthusiasm. Since most of Berlin's classier restaurants were owned by Jews, the city's beer halls did a flourishing business.

Like others in the American colony, the correspondents and their wives went out that day to buy something even if it was only a bar of soap. Mowrer went to his doctor to have his foot cast removed and found the physician hiding behind locked doors. Lilian Mowrer spent the morning shopping at Kaufhaus des Westens and wished she could have bought out the entire store. Wertheim's department store opened as usual but remained largely empty except for its terrified sales clerks. A cordon of some twenty-five Storm Troopers surrounded its block-long building. When Knick's bearish assistant tried to enter he was marched roughly to the curb, punched and called a "Damned dog." Knick took the precaution of showing his passport first.

If pressed, the pickets usually gave way, often to the delight of spectators. Wives of foreign diplomats used their extra-territorial status to demonstrate their disapproval. On the corner of Leipzigerstrasse and the Wilhelmstrasse a large crowd watched as a splendid automobile drew up before a Jewish shop. A smartly dressed society lady emerged and brushed past the pickets with hardly a glance. The crowd broke into shouts and whistles. Pickets rushed to surround the automobile.

"Remain outside!" an SA leader shouted. He went in briefly and then returned.

"Everything is in order," he announced. "The lady is from an embassy."

The boycott lasted only 14 hours. Reportedly, von Neurath and von Papen informed Hindenburg of the public outrage abroad and Hindenburg summoned Hitler and reminded the Chancellor of his oath to uphold the constitution. No doubt Hitler was also mindful of Hindenburg's power to declare martial law if necessary. Defense Minister Blomberg also protested, as did Count Lutz von Schwerin-Krosigk, Minister of Finance and Alfred Hugenberg, Minister of Economics. Hitler was confronted with a divided cabinet. Reichsbank President, Hjalmar Schacht, told the Chancellor that some 200 million marks rested in the hands of Jewish borrowers.

Munich announced the painful news: "The battle (boycott) will not be further taken up on Wednesday. This will prove a disappointment to millions of Germans, but discipline must be observed in any event. It was not easy to yield but Adolf Hitler can only proceed one step at a time."

The correspondents laid bets that the Government would come up with some face-saving excuse. They were correct. On Monday, a banner headline in the *Acht-Uhr Abendblatt* announced: THE UNITED STATES STOPS THE AGITATION COMPLETELY. There followed a garbled version of a Reuters dispatch from New York: "Complying with the wish of the State Department and leading members of Congress, American Jews have decided to take an attitude of silence toward the situation of the Jews in Germany." The State Department had said nothing of the kind. The actual dispatch stated that the American Jewish Congress had decided to refrain, for the time being, from commenting on the "tragic" situation of the Jews in Germany.

While the boycott had proceeded with unexpected restraint in Berlin, Sigrid Schultz, the doughty correspondent for the *Chicago Tribune* and a figure well known in Berlin Jewish circles, pointed out that there had been ugly incidents elsewhere in Germany. In Gladbach the manager of the Tietz department store and his wife had shot themselves. They were in grave condition and might not live. In Hamburg a bomb had exploded at the local Party headquarters but no one was injured. The worst incident occurred in Kiel where a lawyer shot and seriously wounded a Storm Trooper picketing his father's furniture store. An angry mob demolished the furniture store and then, hearing erroneously that the Storm Trooper had died, stormed the jail and murdered the lawyer. In all her years in Germany, Miss Schultz wrote, it was the only case of vigilante justice she could recall.

It had been a strange week for Bella. Three days before the boycott Hitler had twice kissed her hand.

Everyone wondered how Germany's new men would accomplish their coming out. The Chancellor, it was known, preferred automobile unveilings to high society. The suspicion was mutual; the new men came from the lower ranks and had few good things to say about the *"feine Leute"* as they derisively called their social betters. Politically dominant, they were still social outcasts. Berlin society was a closed world to them. With the Foreign Ministry still in the hands of Baron von Neurath, the diplomatic set felt no special need to court Germany's new men and most of the better homes in Berlin were reluctant to be the first to open their doors in welcome. Bella's royalist friend, Mammi von Carnap, spoke for her class when she remarked: "I hope we won't have to accept them socially."

President Hindenburg's state dinner for the Chancellor in February had been a purely official affair. Signora Cerruti, the raven-haired wife of the Italian Ambassador, had been Hitler's dinner companion that evening. Afterwards, while the men were taking their coffee and cigars elsewhere, she was beseiged by ladies who wanted to know if the Chancellor's table conversation had been charming. In reply Signora Cerruti could only roll her eyes heavenward, a gesture her admirers mistook for the highest of tributes. Signora Cerruti had been an actress before the war. She was also Jewish, Bella knew.

Since Hitler's wing of the Chancellery was being remodeled, he could not entertain. The von Papens were no better off. They lived in straitened circumstances in Berlin, in a ministry that resembled a boarding house for comfort. In order to introduce the new men, the von Papens were forced to borrow other quarters for the evening.

It had been toward the end of March, as preparations for the boycott were getting under way, that Bella had the pleasure of feeling Hitler's lips twice touch the back of her hand.

Vice-Chancellor and Frau von Papen request the pleasure of Frau Bella
Fromm's company, Wednesday, March 29, 1933 from 9:30 PM on, at the
Palais Prinz Friedrich Leopold.

The Prince Friedrich Leopold Palace, across the street from the Chancellery, belonged to Goebbels. When Bella opened the pasteboard invitation, her heart sank. One of the most charming buildings in Berlin would
be the scene of Hitler's coming out, an edifice designed in the 18th
century by one of the few great architects Prussia had produced.

That night Bella and her escort, an old friend from the Ministry of the
Interior, dined at the Kaiserhof. Afterwards they crossed the street to the
Palace. Bella was surprised to see that the building looked much the
same despite its new occupants. The stucco had been pulled down and
the floor-length curtains removed. Expensive crystal chandeliers highlighted the bright uniforms of the men and the jewels of the women.
Only the occasional patch of brown or black marred the color scheme
while the jackboots dinned unpleasantly on the parquet floors.

Without thinking she joined the circle of women around Frau von
Papen and Mammi von Carnap. It was rumored that the Chancellor
would pay a surprise visit that evening. Bella had ample warning when
"Fraenzchen" darted into the hall, rushed up to his wife, and whispered
excitedly in her ear.

"The Fuehrer has just entered the palace," a flustered Frau von Papen
whispered to the ladies around her.

The room and the people in it seemed to turn to stone. Black uniformed members of Hitler's bodyguard appeared; the room's great folding doors were flung open. Hitler paused on the threshold, plain-looking
as always but in evening clothes that were fairly well-tailored. Behind
him loomed Brueckner, coarse and uncouth, and escorting them both
was the debonair Hans Thomsen. "Tommy," quiet and reserved, was the
Foreign Ministry's man in the Chancellery.

Nobody in the room moved. Bella's mind seemed to drift. Several
people stood with their arms raised in strained salute. Even von Papen
seemed not to know what to do.

Hitler looked to Tommy for a signal. Thomsen sent out none. Ignoring the people saluting, Hitler broke the tableau and, like a skater
stepping onto thin ice, crossed the slippery floor, coattails flying, in the
direction of his hostess. Only after he had kissed Frau von Papen's hand
in the Austrian manner did Bella come to her senses. She made a motion
as if to withdraw but only caught his attention.

"May I have the pleasure of bidding you good evening, *gnaedige*

Frau?" he asked, turning to Bella and kissing her hand. Over his shoulder Bella saw the faces of her friends, grinning at the Chancellor's mistake.

"Are you having a good time?" he asked.

She was, she replied.

"Where did you gain these decorations?"

The Ludwigkreuz had been given to her personally by the last King of Bavaria, she said.

"You enjoy being here?"

Yes, she replied. It was also her job; she was the diplomatic correspondent for the Ullstein papers.

At the sound of the Jewish name "Ullstein" Hitler winced. He took her hand once more, kissed it a second time, said he hoped they would meet again and departed.

One of Bella's friends turned to her and asked if she would let anyone else kiss her hand that evening. She made a gesture as if to rub the kiss off on his sleeve.

She went over to Tommy who was standing with State Secretary Lammers.

"Your Fuehrer must have a cold," she said.

"Why?" asked Tommy.

"He's supposed to be able to smell a Jew ten miles away, isn't he? Apparently his sense of smell isn't working tonight."

Both men laughed, but not before they looked around the room to see that no one else had heard. That glance over the shoulder was becoming a common sight in the new Germany. Wags dubbed it the "German look"; it was soon indistinguishable from that other quick turn of the head known as the "Jewish survey" which checked faces for improper racial makeup.

For the remainder of the evening Bella observed Hitler's peregrinations about the room. He was at once aloof and nervous. Restlessly, his right hand searched for the security of his soldier's belt. From the buffet he accepted only some lettuce and a drink of orange juice. Toward members of the nobility he was abjectly respectful. He fetched food for the unbeautiful Princess Luise von Sachsen Meiningen, contributing thereby to her already ample girth, and nearly leapt out of his chair when she offered to introduce him to her family. He ogled comely young women.

The wife of the Rumanian Envoy commented: "One can buy patent leather shoes and don a well-fitting tuxedo, but one cannot purchase good manners in a shop."

Seated in a corner, Bella composed her report of the evening. Tommy checked it over before she phoned it in. She gave Hitler a paragraph all to himself.

Very much to the surprise of the guests, Adolf Hitler appeared, at about 10 o'clock. This constituted his first formal social appearance at a large party since his assumption of his duties as Chancellor. He was warmly welcomed by his hosts. They used the occasion to present those diplomats whom he had not yet met, especially the ladies of the international set.

But when the papers appeared on the news stands the next morning, Bella's paragraph on the Chancellor's social debut was missing. An editor at Ullstein's had cut it. The Foreign Ministry was frantic.

"I didn't think the fact of Adolf Hitler's presence important enough to give it special mention," the editor told Bella.

"Are you *that* dumb?" she snapped. "Are you trying to get me into trouble, or are you trying to annoy the Nazis?"

It didn't matter; the effect was the same. The boycott struck the following day.

Not until June would Tante Voss sully her skirts with the word *"Fuehrer"* and then only as a notion attached to something called a "Principle." Until then Hitler was referred to merely as the Reich Chancellor, never Hitler.

Many important people apparently were finding themselves in jail. Tante listed their names daily in short items under the headline: "Arrested." She had no alternative but to print these announcements, as they were very much part of the news of the day. In May, "Arrested" was changed to the less emotional "In Custody." The headline "Forbidden" appeared with increasing frequency too. Many things were "Forbidden," among them many newspapers of the liberal persuasion. In May, an even more ominous category of headline made its debut: "Shot While Trying to Escape." That item came from Munich, from a place called Dachau. Through it all Tante continued to list each week the religious services of the Berlin Jewish community.

THE FOREIGN PRESS

The upheaval that spring made the news vastly more difficult to collect. In the past, the correspondents had been able to rely on the domestic press to stay abreast of events in Germany. The Berlin bureau of the Associated Press, for instance, subscribed to every major paper published in the capital as well as an assortment of papers from the provinces. Along with his other duties, the night man had the job of reading the morning editions as they reached the newsstands. In the afternoon two German assistants spent three hours scanning the rest of the day's papers for items of interest to American readers. Their gleanings were then reviewed by the American staff, who made the final decision on what material to cable to New York.

Under Goebbels' direction, Germany's newspapers were soon printing the same stories under the same headlines. Studying the domestic press became a game of looking for slip-ups. The provincial papers, much less strictly coordinated, were an especially good source for these. A paper from Stuttgart, for example, might mention that two "auxiliary" policemen had been disciplined for having "handled very roughly" Communist and Republican prisoners under their care. A correspondent could transmit that item with little risk of self-incrimination. If challenged, he could easily prove that his source was the Government itself.

In the old days assignments to Leipzig or Nuremburg or Kiel often led to the recruitment of local German newsmen who had a feel for international news and needed a little extra cash. When the Nazis came to power these networks of stringers, nurtured over the years with much care and patience, collapsed overnight. Stringers whose principal employers had been Socialist or Communist newspapers suddenly found themselves without jobs or, worse, disappeared into the still nameless concentration camps. Others, out of fear, simply severed all contact with foreigners.

Much the same fate befell Republican politicians whose offices had always been open to foreign newsmen. Their places were taken by National Socialists who were frequently men of little ability and no experience: leaders and subleaders from the cliques around Hitler and the SA. Requests by foreign newsmen for interviews or information were lost in the shuffle or, in the time-honored bureaucratic fashion, were passed on to other offices across town where they received even less attention.

Louis P. Lochner, the highly respected chief of the AP bureau in Berlin, had to wait 22 days for an exclusive interview with Hitler that had been agreed to immediately by the Leader's closest advisors. Lochner, who was familiarly called Louis P. by his German friends, found that he had to assemble his stories with infinite care. A tip, even from an official source, had to wait until it was cleared by the Government. Sensational reports from Hamburg or Munich were frequently denied by authorities in Berlin who had yet to hear of them. Every organization seemed to have its own press bureau. Ministers, State Secretaries and Party bosses vied with each other in issuing directives and political pronouncements that were often wildly contradictory. The Government was soon releasing as many corrections and disclaimers as news; it was impossible to know who, other than Hitler, had the final say.

Germany's official wire service, the Wolffsches Telegraphen Buero, was afraid to release any news critical of the new regime. A Nazi "controlleur" sat in the Buero's office. Only rarely was Lochner allowed to read the copy as it came off the machines. Even then, he could not print the story without inviting criminal prosecution or worse. Just to keep up with all the ad hoc decrees from all the ad hoc offices regulating the foreign press was a task that would have taken up the entire efforts of his staff.

Lochner had to pass up some of the most damning atrocity stories of the first days because the victims or their friends begged him not to add to their woes by printing their names. He felt that he had no choice but to pass up sensational material if his sources would not come to his defense should the Government demand a showdown. He was forced to walk a fine line between his professional and his private conscience. At all costs, he told himself, he must keep his office open. He dared not imitate the "special correspondents" who breezed into town, culled a wealth of unsubstantiated rumor from their colleagues, drafted an inflammatory article and then, in the time-honored technique perfected in Italy and Russia, filed and ran. If the Government bellowed they were safely out of the country and had proven their point.

If expulsions did come and courageous reporters such as Knick and Mowrer were thrown out, their papers in New York and Chicago could fall back on the AP wire service until replacements could be found. In Lochner's eyes he was the last line of defense for American news in Germany and he dared not run the risk of printing unsubstantiated reports. The flap over the death of Louis Ullstein on March 20 had proven that.

The AP office in New York had put out a report that the second oldest son of the Ullstein empire had succumbed to injuries received when a gang of Storm Troopers entered his home and beat him unconscious. The story had originated with opposition circles in Warsaw. By the time Lochner could correct it—the 70-year-old Ullstein brother had died from complications following gallstone surgery—the harm had been done. In an official broadcast the Government denounced the Associated Press for joining the crusade of atrocity mongers. Lochner had no alternative but to bow his head and take the storm of abuse.

Since a formal order of expulsion only attracted attention and made the expelled newsman newsworthy and his dispatches credible, the preferred tactic was to sever a newsman from his sources by barring him from meetings with Government officials. That was what Goering did in March to Edward Deuss of the Hearst news bureau when Deuss sent out a story about the discovery in a cemetery of the bodies of three Jews who had been beaten to death. Goering personally telephoned Karl von Wiegand, Hearst's ranking correspondent on the continent. Goering said he would let Deuss produce the sources for his spurious report and, if he could not, then Deuss should be transferred to another post. Goering hinted that Goebbels knew that Deuss was half Jewish and was willing to wage a vendetta against him.

Since Deuss had no wish to throw his sources to the wolves, he agreed to be quietly shifted to London. Quentin Reynolds came over from New York to take his place.

Although neither side wanted a showdown, the German Government made no secret of the fact that it suspected even such upright newsmen as Louis P. Lochner of working against them. In March, Rudolf Diels sent a squad of detectives to search the files of the AP photo service for a picture of a Jewish gentleman sans pants with a placard around his neck reading: "I Am A Jew But I Will Not Complain About The Nazis." The photo had been offered to a number of correspondents and had appeared in the press in France, Spain and Switzerland. The cautious Lochner had wisely turned the offer down as being precisely the sort of risk he wished to avoid. Let other newsmen send out that sort of news; he meant to hold on to his post in Berlin.

The raid did not catch him unprepared. Louis P. had married into a prominent German family and had contacts everywhere in Berlin including a relation by marriage in the secret police. This time the tip came from a friendly official in the Foreign Ministry. When the detectives arrived they were cordially met at the door and guided through the volumes of prints on file. They left much impressed with the splendid photographs they had seen and deeply apologetic over the intrusion.

Lochner was shocked, therefore, when he received a cable a few days

later via London that read: NEW YORK CABLES QUOTE INFORM
BERLIN NAZI ATTACKS ON JEWS PLAYED BIG. LICKED
HERE FIRST PICTURES UNQUOTE. New York was complaining
that it had received no pictures of the sort that would have shut down the
AP's photo office. They had been "licked" by the competition. Worse,
they had transmitted their complaint via open cable through Berlin's
Main Telegraph Office where it had certainly been read by the censors!

In a seven-page letter sent out with a friend Lochner pleaded with his
bosses in America to understand that conditions in Berlin were not the
same as in New York. Germany was passing through unusual times. In
the future, such instructions should be *telephoned* from London and
communicated in such a way that the unseen listener on the line would
think that only routine business was being discussed.

To their surprise, Lochner and his colleagues found that they were left
a free hand to write as they pleased about Germany. Dr. Goebbels had
personally assured Knick that there would be no attempts to hinder the
fair reporting of events in Germany and von Neurath had repeated the
promise publicly. True, foreign newsmen were pressured to dismiss their
Jewish employees and occasionally their German assistants were arrested,
but despite such unpleasantness there was no organized effort to impose
censorship on them. Their residences were watched and strangers
stepped up to catch their instructions to taxi drivers. Eavesdroppers took
seats at nearby tables and suspicious characters turned up to apply for
nonexistent jobs. Their office phones were tapped, but then all the
phones in Berlin were tapped, or so it was commonly assumed. These
were merely psychological problems. The big news services, such as the
AP and the *New York Times*, found all the news they could wish to print.

Their refuge from the greater storm lashing the society around them
was an Italian restaurant called "Die Taverne" run by a big bluff German
and his timid Belgian wife on the corner of the Kurfuerstenstrasse. What
the cracked leather seats of the Adlon Bar had been to newsmen during
the Republic, the heavy tables of "Die Taverne" were to the same crowd
during the gathering dusk of the Third Reich. In a corner of one of the
Taverne's low-ceilinged rooms, filled with the smell of beer and coffee
and the strains of the noisy jazz band, the correspondents reserved a
Stammtisch each night between 10 PM and 2 AM. Germany was six
hours ahead of New York; seven hours ahead of Chicago. American
correspondents, accordingly, worked late, since it was much earlier back
home and since the telephone rates to their bureaus in London and Paris
went down after 7:30 PM Berlin time. They would phone in the last
stories of the day and then walk or take a taxi to the Taverne where the
journalist's round table was large enough to accommodate ten, and often

as many as twenty, journalists and their wives and guests drinking beer and whiskey sodas and eating plates of spaghetti and fried sausages and gossiping about the stories they had sent or not sent that day.

Of course, there were spies at the Taverne, faces that showed up night after night, who casually turned their chairs to catch what was said. Putzi Hanfstaengl and Rudolf Diels occasionally dropped by. Diels was invited everywhere and could pick and choose his invitations. To listen to the talk of the Anglo-American correspondents at the Taverne was the job of a man like Diels. He generally remained silent until a break came in the conversation and then he would insert a remark startling for what it revealed about the omniscience of his organization and the cynicism of its Inspector General.

Diels enjoyed his reputation as one of the most outspoken figures in a regime known for its furtiveness. But that spring he labored under an uncharacteristic handicap. He could not reply to the many queries directed his way about the origins of the Reichstag Fire. A distrustful Goering had severed him from the case. Although Diels was shrewd enough to keep himself fully informed, he could only respond with an embarrassed silence and an unforgiving look at enquiries made in his direction.

Hanfstaengl would arrive long past midnight, saluting and shaking hands as he made his way through the noisy rooms and the groups of youthful singers and actors who dropped by for a bite to eat after the night clubs closed. Spying a new face at the round table, Putzi would take a seat for a moment next to the journeying newsman and fall into his familiar routine.

"I want to talk to you!" he would say. "I've been away in Munich with Hitler." The visitor would be impressed by that. And, because Putzi was the kind of person who was too busy to do much business at all, he would conclude with, "We must certainly have a good talk," and then he would be up and off, waving and saluting and circulating out the door.

The importance of the Taverne as a refuge increased after January 30. There was strength in numbers and moral support to be gained in meeting nightly over coffee and alcohol to swap bits of disturbing data gleaned from the regional press. The stories of Knick and Mowrer were often as similar as peas in a pod. Notes were compared; strategies refined. An attack on one was an attack upon them all and would have been reported in every major paper in the world.

In January, Mowrer's book, *Germany Puts The Clock Back,* came out in England and America. As the Nazis celebrated their triumph on the streets of Berlin, Mowrer took his readers on a tour of the Brown House, to a Party rally to hear Hitler speak, and through the pages of *Mein Kampf,* which Mowrer had read down to the last turgid word. Even the raw brew of the Party's hatred of the Jews was served up in one of the book's stronger chapters. *Germany Puts The Clock Back* went through three printings that year. Reviews were favorable, especially in Britain, where the book was applauded for its fairness and clarity.

When an official from the German Foreign Ministry told Mowrer that Hitler had taken a positive dislike to the book, Mowrer retorted: "That's all right, I feel the same way about *Mein Kampf.* He writes for Germans, I write for Americans."

Mowrer's position in Berlin was a strong one. Ten days before Hitler came to power, Mowrer was elected president of the influential Foreign Press Association of Berlin. The Association, founded in the decade before the Great War, represented more than a hundred newsmen from all over the world who worked and lived in Berlin. Only fully accredited correspondents writing general news for daily papers could become members. The Association elected its president and directors in parliamentary fashion, carried out its business in German and maintained clubrooms at No. 1 Potsdamer Platz. Members received Reichstag passes, police credentials, tickets to theater openings and trade fairs, as well as inexpensive health insurance. But more than easing the life of the foreign newsman in the capital, the Association arranged for him to meet with important government officials in a variety of informal *Bierabends* and luncheons. The annual "Founder's Banquet" in June was traditionally the occasion for an important foreign policy address by the German Foreign Minister or the Chancellor himself. During the social season in November the Association held its own small but exclusive fancy dress ball, named each year after a different flower: "Festival of Mimosa" or "Chrysanthemum Dance."

The Association rejected all attempts to bring it under government control. Its president, Edgar Ansel Mowrer, was vigorous in his defense of any member who came under attack by Germany's new rulers. The Government put pressure on Mowrer to resign. Privately, he was told that he need not give the real reason; he could simply claim ill-health. Typically, Mowrer did just the opposite. Early in April he called a special meeting of the Association and told his colleagues: "I was asked to resign for reasons of health and to maintain silence regarding the real reason. I was told that later, perhaps next year, when the displeasure over my book had disappeared, I might be able to resume my presidency.

"My standpoint is this: Responsible foreign newspaper correspondents must by no social or other personal pressure of whatever nature be hindered in the freedom of their criticism in so far as they report to their country on the basis of unchallengable material.

"To clarify this point, I offer my resignation. Please decide for yourselves."

In the discussion that followed, support for Mowrer came from an unexpected quarter when the correspondent for Mussolini's *Popolo d'Italia* rose to say that he had read *Germany Puts The Clock Back* with great interest. Although he did not agree with Mowrer's democratic bias, there was nothing in the book that any journalist in the room should feel ashamed of writing. In a vote of 60 to 7, with 3 members abstaining, the Association overwhelmingly chose to retain Mowrer as president. Goebbels was reported to be furious. The Government announced that it was thinking of dissolving the Association. Putzi Hanfstaengl spread the rumor that Mowrer was a disguised Jew.

"Edgar a Jew?" Knick retorted. "Of course! As Jewish as Ludendorff."

For a time the Association was ostracized by the Foreign Ministry and the Ministry of Propaganda; but there were so many other sources of news in the press bureaus of the greater and lesser departments of the Reich and Prussian governments that the problem remained, as before, one of separating fact from fiction.

June 7th approached, the date of the Association's annual "Founder's Banquet." Because of the existing tension, no Government official and certainly not Hitler or Baron von Neurath would make a major foreign policy address at the occasion. The Hotel Adlon had always pulled out all the stops for the journalists on that night, seating newsmen, statesmen and diplomats at a great horseshoe-shaped table in one of the hotel's largest and most splendid banquet rooms.

That year Mowrer made the affair less formal and arranged for a leisurely luncheon at the Adlon. He sat the newsmen and diplomats at small tables where they could exchange quiet confidences; a tender point with the new Government which frowned on contacts between journalists and foreign diplomats.

Only the papal nuncio declined to attend at the last moment, pleading illness. The nuncio, a favorite of Goering's, was in the middle of delicate negotiations with the German government. Reichsbank President Hjalmar Schacht and Dr. Heinrich Sahm, the towering Lord Mayor of Berlin, the only Germans invited, both accepted. The nuncio's place as speaker for the diplomatic corps was taken by the Turkish ambassador.

Mowrer delivered the opening address. Deploring the absence of official representatives from the Government, he feigned difficulty with his German: "In this country where we are—I mean *have been*—so happy

. . . that some of us have sought relief—I mean recreation—abroad . . ."
The guests roared with laughter; Ambassador François-Poncet especially
seemed in danger of falling out of his chair. When an angry Schacht
demanded permission to reply and rose to say that the foreign press
should stick to facts, not opinions, Mowrer solemnly thanked him for his
words of support. The diplomats roared anew, and Schacht sat down
red-faced. It was a most delightful afternoon that the ambassadors in top
hats and the ambassadors in shirtsleeves spent together in the heart of
Nazi Germany. The Government had been outwitted and rebuffed. Two
weeks later, Alfred Rosenberg, the Party's "Foreign Minister," officially
brought the boycott to an end when he hosted a tea for the foreign press
at the Hotel Adlon.

The boycott had ended, but not the Government's ruses. As the
reporters emerged from Rosenberg's tea they were greeted by banner
headlines in the German press: FOREIGN AIRPLANES THROW
MARXIST LEAFLETS OVER BERLIN. Evidently, a foreign airplane
of a type unknown in Germany had flown over Berlin and dropped
leaflets insulting to the Fuehrer. The Germans, with no aircraft of their
own, were unable to give chase.

"Every bird is allowed to protect its nest," crowed the *Voelkischer
Beobachter*. "Only Germany, with clipped wings and pulled claws, must
sit idly by while its nest is befouled." The entire German press spoke of
the "brazen provocation to the German Government and the German
people." An official investigation was launched. The German delegation
in Geneva demanded that Germany be granted parity in aircraft. Overnight, thousands of posters appeared in Berlin: "This time Hetz-blaetter!
Next time bombs! Germany must have planes! Air defense is a necessity!"

According to the Air Ministry, there had been not one but three planes
of a design unknown in Germany. Two private aircraft had taken off
from Templehof airfield in pursuit but had been unable to keep up.
When the newsmen made enquiries at Tempelhof no one there knew
anything about the incident.

"We were warned in advance of yesterday's raid," the Air Ministry
announced. "Today we received another threat to the effect that the next
visit by the foreign craft would result in dropping not pamphlets but
other things." Airfields along Germany's borders were put on alert.
Refugee circles in Prague were suspected.

The correspondents enquired at the Propaganda Ministry as to precisely where the offending leaflets had landed. In the Wilhelmstrasse and
on the Alexanderplatz, they were told, where they were hastily gathered
up by government clerks and police.

The correspondents asked to see one of the leaflets.

"Its wording is so insulting to the Fuehrer that we do not propose to show it to anybody."

"But how did the leaflet look?" Louis P. Lochner insisted. "You might at least give us an inkling of their appearance."

"Well, they were very poorly printed by hand, with one of those rubber stamp outfits where you put the letters together yourself."

That was the most outrageous assertion of all; that a foreign enemy who could afford to hire three biplanes of the lastest type to fly hundreds of miles into German territory could not afford to have its insurrectionary leaflets printed professionally!

The correspondents checked with government employees and residents along the Wilhelmstrasse for anybody who had seen one of the leaflets. No one had.

Louis P. phoned an aeronautic friend of his and gave him the altitude of the aircraft and the wind velocity over Berlin on Friday and asked if the leaflets could only have fallen on the Wilhelmstrasse and the Alexanderplatz. Louis P. thought he knew the answer. On the contrary, his acquaintance replied, given the conditions of the drop, the leaflets would have blanketed the landscape around Magdeburg, ninety miles to the south!

For a week the foreign press reveled in the hoax.

America had not yet recognized the Soviet Union, but on the evening of May 10 the correspondents gathered at a reception at the Russian Embassy. All day the radio had been filled with news of the great burning of books against the "German spirit" that was to take place that night on the plaza between the Opera House and the University. Similar *autos-da-fé* were to begin at the same hour in Kiel, Frankfurt-Am-Main, Breslau and Munich.

That night, the students of Berlin, in their green and purple fraternity caps, began the slow five-mile march through the city. Accompanying them were vans and private automobiles piled high with confiscated books. The books had been removed in recent days from libraries and institutes throughout Berlin. A four-page list of some 160 proscribed authors had been prepared, many of them known only to professional academicians. Tons of books had been collected and assembled at the students' headquarters on Oranienburgstrasse. Some of the books and pamphlets, deemed too important to destroy, were turned over to the State Library; other volumes with expensive and ornate leather bindings were voluntarily removed by the students themselves. An unknown quantity was sold to a pulping mill at $2.50 a ton to help defray the cost of the banners and brass bands and the hundreds of torches that made up the pageant. The rest were loaded onto vans and into automobiles which, like tumbrels, accompanied the chanting, singing students along the parade route.

The procession did not reach the Brandenburg Gate until close to midnight. The correspondents leisurely made the seven-minute walk from the Russian Embassy to the Opernplatz to join the crowd of spectators, Hitler Youth and Brown Shirts. The crowd was not very large; the hour was late, and Germany was a literate nation that held books and authors in high esteem. By the time the correspondents arrived a light drizzle had begun to fall. The granite plaza had been strewn with sand, and a pyre of logs twelve feet square by five feet high had been erected. As the students entered the square, they tossed their torches onto the pyre; the logs, soaked with gasoline, burst into flames. The flames lit up the building fronts and smoke wafted high above the rooftops of the Opera and the University until the gasoline burned off. Then the flames died down and left only a dull red glow, and the other mood of the evening, a somber uneasiness, took over. Germany was burning its books.

A speakers' platform had been set up in the plaza and decorated with flags. From it hung five huge klieg lights for the camera crews who would commemorate the event. The bright spotlights further dimmed the fire's rosy glow.

"Against the overevaluation of instinctual urges that destroy the soul, for the nobility of the soul! I surrender to the flames the writings of Sigmund Freud," a youthful voice cried over the loudspeaker as an armful of books and pamphlets, presumably from the pen of Dr. Freud, was cast upon the flames.

"Against literary betrayal of the soldiers of the World War, for the education of the people in the spirit of truthfulness! I surrender to the flames the writings of Erich Maria Remarque." The crowd cheered at first but soon settled into a watchful silence.

Writers who had written critically of war were high on the list; Ernest Hemingway's *A Farewell To Arms* was burned that night. The next most hated writers were the internationally minded authors, sophisticates such as André Gide. Of course, the works of anyone who had attacked National Socialism or Adolf Hitler were burned, as well as many contemporary German writers who were Jews and all the great Communist authors such as Marx, Engels and Lenin and even Helen Keller's little book: *How I Became A Socialist*. Lastly, came works of a pornographic nature including the papers of Dr. Magnus Hirschfeld, the founder of the continent's first scientific institute for sexual inquiry. Louis P. noted that many of the students examined the folders of the Institute's photographic collections before consigning them to the flames. Wryly he thought of his own youthful pacifist book, *Henry Ford—America's Don Quixote*. He should have turned it over to the students, he thought, then perhaps it would be reissued in America and make him some money. America had recently gone off the gold standard and, what with the other measures that the Associated Press had taken to economize, Louis P.'s salary had been reduced by nearly one third. His eldest daughter was attending college in America. Selfish thoughts.

The students sweated and slipped on the heaps of books that they carried by the armload or passed hand to hand from the semicircle of waiting vans. The books did not burn well since the students did not take the time to tear the pages from the bindings. While pamphlets and letters burned, the heavy volumes choked the fire and caused it to smolder. The drizzle was no help either. The crowd watched as some pages, liberated and only slightly singed, rose in the column of hot air to dance in the sky above the plaza. One young burner of books grew so weary of his task that he settled back on a pile of waiting literature like a farm boy resting on a broken haystack.

A student made a short introductory speech and then Dr. Goebbels stepped forward. That night, Goebbels gave one of his best speeches although the electrical equipment amplified his voice too loudly and the idiom he used rang strangely to an older generation. Dr. Goebbels was only 35 and knew his audience.

"These flames do not only illuminate the final end of the old era," he cried, "they also light up the new. Never before have the young men had so good a right to clean up the debris of the past. If the old men do not understand what is going on, let them grasp that we young men have gone and done it."

"Oh, my century," Goebbels concluded, "it is a joy to be alive!"

There were cries of *"Heil Hitler"* followed by singing. Then the ceremony was over, and the crowd dispersed in silence while the students went about the dreary duty of working the fire until dawn.

Some 20,000 volumes were burnt that night on the plaza in front of the Opera; not many for a country like Germany where an educated citizen might have as many as five hundred or a thousand volumes in his personal library. The ceremony with its torches and cheering students sweating under the klieg lights had been mostly symbolic. The victors of January 30 meant to show the world that not only a political but an intellectual revolution had taken place in Germany, although some would wonder how intellectual any revolution could be that depended upon fire to erase the past.

Knick viewed the public burning that night with horror. He recalled another night when, as a small boy in Texas, he had stood next to his father and watched as a mob of angry whites burned a southern Negro to death.

May had been a chilling month for Knick although he managed to sail through it with typical outward insouciance. At the end of March he had sent out a series of seven special articles about the new Germany that had minced few words.

He asked his readers to imagine that the Ku Klux Klan had suddenly swelled in numbers, due to the Depression and to the stirring oratory of an obscure political figure from Louisiana, until its leaders were so powerful that the country had no choice but to hand the executive branch of the government over to them.

Then, shortly before upcoming congressional elections, the Capitol building in Washington, D. C. was set ablaze. A Cuban was arrested who confessed that he worked for the Communists and was supported by the Democrats and a wave of political arrests ensued. Boldly, the Klan captured most of the seats in Congress.

Within two weeks the Klan removed the Democratic and Republican governors of all the forty-eight states and replaced every county and city official with one of their own. Thousands of American refugees poured into Mexico and Canada. Within six weeks all public officials, from police chiefs to postmen, were Klansmen. Judges, lawyers, doctors and teachers who refused to join the Klan were forced out of their jobs.

The Constitution was rewritten and the Republic was replaced by a dictatorship. Old Glory waved over the Capital emblazoned with the initials "KKK."

Worse, Knick lampooned the figure of Premier Goering in his story on Dr. Islonsky, a Jewish physician in Berlin, who had been beaten and led through a mock execution. The doctor had been taken to a Storm Troop barracks, blindfolded, stood up against a wall and told to say his prayers as a volley of bullets was fired into the wall just inches from his head.

Dr. Islonsky was still a Soviet citizen. He complained to his embassy, which passed the story on to Knick.

Dr. Islonsky remained in Berlin but his troubles were not over. On March 20 he received a mysterious telephone call. "Are you still there?" asked an unidentified voice. "We'll finish you yet!"

Storm Troopers returned to his home and fired shots through the door. Dr. Islonsky called his embassy, and a squad of riot police was dispatched. And it was on that very night, Knick noted, that Hermann Goering assured the foreign press that the terror which had never occurred had been brought to an end.

Knick was also the first newsman to think of visiting a hospital to interview a victim of the terror. The Government would have given a lot to know who gave him the tip to visit the Saint Antonius Hospital on boycott eve.

There Knick interviewed a 46-year-old welfare worker named Frau Marie Jankowsky. Frau Jankowsky had been beaten in a manner no journalist until then had described, although it would have taken a medical specialist to detail the full extent of her injuries. Storm Troopers had taken Frau Jankowsky to their barracks on the Dorotheeinstrasse, stripped her and held her face down across a table draped with the "Mustard" banner of the Republic. They ordered her to insult the banner and when she refused they caned her. They asked her how much she had been paid as a welfare worker and when she replied that she had worked for nothing they caned her again. They accused her of stealing from the unemployed and continued to strike her on the buttocks and thighs with wooden whips. They accused her of feeding "Bolsheviks" in her soup kitchen and when she weakly identified two of her tormentors as recipients of her charity she was struck in the face with a riding crop so violently that she was thrown across the room and injured her knee.

Knick saw that her knee bore a special bandage and that her face had been cut by the riding crop. The wounds on her back and buttocks, swathed in dressings, were harder to make out.

"They took me for a Jew," Frau Jankowsky said, rising painfully on one arm. "I am not. I am a Social Democrat who has worked many years without pay in the city charity department that gives doles to the unemployed after they have exhausted their Government dole."

The Government responded by barring foreign journalists from hospitals, but not before Knick's story had persuaded Defense Minister Blomberg to denounce the boycott to Hitler; one of Frau Jankowsky's five sons was a soldier in the German army.

It was only a matter of time before Knick landed in hot water but no one expected his adversary to arrive in the guise of Kurt Ludecke, the debonair, gold-penned *roué* who had attempted in 1921 to persuade a wavering Putzi Hanfstaengl to commit one dollar a month of his American fortune to Hitler's movement. After the failure of the Beer Hall Putsch, Putzi and Ludecke, by then bitter enemies, went their separate ways; Ludecke to America as a reporter for the *Voelkischer Beobachter* and Putzi to the galleries of Paris and London. In 1930 Hitler came to Putzi with the offer of a job, but when Ludecke returned to Germany in March of 1933 he had nothing to show for his years of loyalty but a checkered past and a low Party number.

That spring, there were hundreds like Ludecke making the rounds of

Party offices in search of sinecures. Hitler sent Ludecke to Alfred Rosenberg whom he had just made head of the Party's new "Foreign Ministry." Rosenberg's "Foreign Ministry" was a sorry affair: a kingdom of clippings from the world press administered by a handful of regional experts. Hitler's habit was to create offices and then see how his appointees filled them. Rosenberg was given a title but no money. He put Ludecke in charge of the "North and South American Bureau." Ludecke had hoped for a diplomatic post, such as German Ambassador to the United States.

To demonstrate the power of their "Foreign Ministry," Rosenberg and Ludecke decided to make an example of Knickerbocker since it was obvious that Mowrer was too powerful to dislodge. Ludecke took his plan to the Propaganda Ministry, which referred him to the Prussian Ministry of the Interior, which sent him to the Reich Ministry of the Interior, which sent him back to the Propaganda Ministry. No one thought to send him to Putzi Hanfstaengl, and Ludecke would not have gone if anyone had.

This was precisely the chaotic condition which Ludecke and Rosenberg meant to remedy. Nobody had final authority over the foreign press, and the censor had passed every one of Knickerbocker's acrimonious stories out of the country. Ludecke sent a telegram signed by Rosenberg to Knick's editors at the *Philadelphia Public Ledger* and the *New York Evening Post*. The telegram accused Knickerbocker of spreading insidious lies and anti-German propaganda and advised his editors to recall him before harsher steps were taken.

In America, Knick's editors, who had no idea who Rosenberg was, replied: "we have every confidence in mr knickerbocker stop we must respectfully decline to recall him stop." Wisely, they did not mention the threatening telegram in their papers fearing that to do so might truly jeopardize Knick's position in Berlin. Rosenberg meanwhile made news of his own in London when he tactlessly laid a swastika wreath on an English war memorial. The wreath ended up floating in the Thames.

After ten years in Germany, Knick knew how to take care of himself. His editors sent him copies of the entire exchange and he took these to Putzi Hanfstaengl. Visibly upset at the idea that Ludecke was meddling in his domain, Putzi put a call through to Dr. Goebbels. The two agreed to take the matter up with Hitler over lunch the next day. Putzi assured Knick that he had nothing to worry about.

Putzi was as good as his word. By dinner time the following evening, Kurt Ludecke was sitting in a cell in the basement of Police Headquarters on the Alexanderplatz and if Rosenberg had been in Berlin he would have been keeping Ludecke company. By the time Ludecke was freed,

Knick had become the best protected newsman in the capital. He was taken to see Diels, who promised Knick that he would not be troubled further. There was even talk of an exclusive interview with Goering to be printed in the German press. And to complete his rehabilitation, Putzi escorted Knick to a formal dinner attended by Hitler's deputy, Rudolf Hess, and saw that pictures of the evening appeared in the illustrated press. Putzi boasted all over town of his triumph over the "alien Balt" and took care to demolish Ludecke's reputation in America by having the Berlin correspondent of the *New Yorker Staatszeitung* run a story under the headline: LUDECKE ARRESTED FOR SWINDLE AND EXTORTION.

As the books burned on the night of May 10, Knick was free and Ludecke was in prison. One of those who had helped Knick out of his troubles was the slim, almost emaciated, Dr. Goebbels, whose amplified words rang above the flames and reverberated off the building fronts. The vagaries of Germany's new rulers were difficult to fathom.

NO. 8 PRINZ ALBRECHT STRASSE

One morning at the end of June, Consul General George S. Messersmith arrived early at his office at the American Consulate across the street from the Hotel Esplanade. The office was a large one and finely appointed, with a smiling Negro butler and a window that looked out on the Bellevuestrasse.

The bespectacled, sharp-eyed Messersmith was one of the best-informed observers in Germany that spring. He had begun public life as a superintendent of schools for the state of Delaware. It was in Delaware that Messersmith had first tasted the humiliation of political pressure when two state politicos threatened to oust him from his job after he tried to expel a wayward pupil. Messersmith had persevered and eventually triumphed, but the anger and fear he was forced to endure made him set his head down on his desk one afternoon and weep from the sheer bitterness of the experience. In Berlin he was known as a staunch defender of the oppressed, whether American or German. Never for an instant did he flinch or turn away from the sight of injustice. No one who met him in Party or Government offices would have suspected that the determined American Consul General with the drawling voice and the glinting, combative spectacles had ever shed a tear on his own behalf.

That morning Messersmith had enough work on his desk to keep him busy until long after nightfall. There were only so many hours in a day, and Messersmith chose to begin his at daybreak when the Consulate was empty and quiet.

The American Consulate in Berlin was a large establishment. Messersmith's duties included drafting reports on finance and business as well as writing a weekly letter on the German political situation for the President and officials in the State Department. He enjoyed drafting reports or dictating them, rather, for he kept at least one stenographer busy throughout the day. Partly because they were dictated, his dispatches were lengthy and loosely organized, and they irked some readers by their circumlocution. William E. Dodd, when he arrived in Berlin the following month, would remark that Hitler could not leave his hat behind in a flying machine without Messersmith cabling a thousand words on the incident.

That morning, after an hour of work, Messersmith was interrupted by his butler who announced that the Vice-Consul wished to have a word with him. Overburdened with work, Messersmith looked up impatiently as the Vice-Consul entered. The officer appeared calm but pale. There was a matter in the Visa Section, he said, that required Messersmith's immediate attention.

The large room where the American public health officer gave visa applicants their physical examinations was bare except for two rows of curtained booths; one for women, the other for men. The public health surgeon looked grave as he led Messersmith to the men's side of the room and drew back the linen curtain. What Messersmith saw there made him turn aside and spew his morning's breakfast into a white enamel hospital bowl.

Like Knickerbocker who had interviewed Frau Jankowsky, Messersmith had chanced upon a living casualty of the revolution: a 31-year-old white male whose back from the shoulder blades to his buttocks had been flayed so savagely that the skin and subcutaneous tissue had been torn away to reveal the living muscle. The victim was an American physician named Dr. Joseph Schachno who had come to Germany as a child, made his way through the German educational system, and eventually settled down to practice medicine in Koepenick, a suburb of Berlin.

A week earlier, a group of Storm Troopers had arrived at Dr. Schachno's home. He had been denounced, they said, and they meant to search the premises. When they found nothing incriminating, they escorted him to his dispensary nearby but found nothing there. They then took him to their barracks in Koepenick where some twenty or thirty other victims were assembled. The victims were made to strip and were whipped, one by one, in the cruelest manner possible.

Some time after midnight, Dr. Schachno was turned out on the street and, with the help of his aged father who had not been beaten, made his painful way home. For seven days he lay in bed in his wife's parent's home in Berlin, too weak and too afraid to return to his own domicile. That morning he had come to the Consulate to request an American passport.

In a recent letter to Under Secretary of State William Phillips, Messersmith had attempted to explain the type of men in positions of power in Germany: "With few exceptions, the men who are running this Government are of a mentality that you and I cannot understand. Some of them are psychopathic cases and would ordinarily be receiving treatment somewhere. Others are exalted and in a frame of mind that knows no reason. The majority are woefully ignorant and unprepared for the tasks which they have to carry through every day. Those men in the party and in responsible positions who are really worth-while, and there are quite a number of these, are powerless because they have to follow orders of superiors who are suffering from the abnormal psychology prevailing in the country."

Dr. Schachno received his passport and promptly left for Stockholm with his wife to await a steamer to New York City. Messersmith filed a formal complaint with Rudolf Diels, one of the worthwhile men, who seemed embarrassed and apologetic.

Two weeks later, Messersmith's attention returned to Dr. Schachno when a cavalcade of SA vehicles drew up outside the American Consulate. His staff hurriedly informed him that Group Leader Karl Ernst, the youthful leader of the 80,000 man Berlin-Brandenburg SA, had just entered the building accompanied by his adjutants and bully boys.

Leaving four of his men outside Messersmith's door, Ernst came in alone and announced haughtily that Dr. Schachno was not an American citizen and that he had the evidence to prove it. Dr. Schachno's American passport had lapsed in 1925, and he had voted in the March 5 elections as a Bavarian citizen. Dr. Schachno's foremost allegiance as an adult was clearly to Germany and, Ernst concluded in a tone that made the Consul General's blood freeze: "In Germany we can do with a German citizen whatever we please."

Twenty-nine-year-old Karl Ernst was a former elevator operator who had risen swiftly in the ranks of the SA. Young, arrogant and ruthless, his threats against Consul General Messersmith were the least of his misdeeds that spring. Rudolf Diels first met Ernst when the youthful leader led a raid on the office of the Berlin Police President. Goering's choice of Police President for Berlin was a former Rear Admiral whom he knew would act as a foil to the radical SA. The Admiral, a military man of the old school, had quickly earned the ire of the Berlin SA by routinely releasing each morning when he came to work the crowds of Communist suspects hauled in during the night. To cries of "Boycott Police Headquarters," the SA leaders tore pictures from the Admiral's walls and hurled furniture out the windows. They then pushed into Diels' office and demanded that he inform Goering that unless the Admiral were replaced with a man more friendly to the SA there would be hell to pay. That was Diels' first meeting with Karl Ernst and the "illegal SA," but not his last. To protect Diels from the sort of pandemonium that Ernst had wreaked on the Admiral's office, Goering moved Diels' anti-Communist branch into an abandoned arts and crafts school on the Prinz Albrecht Strasse. As Minister President of Prussia, Goering created an entirely new agency out of Diels' office and called it the *"Geheimes Staatspolizeiamt"* or Secret State Police Office. Since the initials GPA

131

resembled too closely the initials of the dreaded Soviet Secret Service, the GPU, the German post office came up with the acronym "Gestapo" when it coined a new franking stamp for the agency.

Organizationally, the Gestapo still reported to Police Headquarters, but practically speaking it was under Goering's control. It brought together all the political departments of the Prussian State Police as well as the political police in the countryside. At its lowest levels, the new agency meshed with the SS and SA auxiliaries who guarded its entrances and drove its vehicles. It had full powers of arrest and interrogation and was formally removed from Germany's legal system. Even National Socialist lawyers had trouble freeing their clients from the clutches of the Gestapo. With nine Divisions ranging from "Protective Custody" to "Cultural Politics," it first employed some three hundred people. By the end of the year, its staff had grown to twice that number. Its budget of nearly four million marks accounted for nearly one-sixth of Prussia's entire budget for police affairs. Renovation of the building on Prinz Albrecht Strasse alone cost 180,000 marks. Goering clearly meant to feed his new creation well.

Goering appointed Diels "Inspector General" of the Gestapo but kept the position of "Chief" for himself. As yet, Goering was too powerful for his rivals in the SA and the Party. If they should ask for Diels' post, he could reply that only a very unimportant man occupied that position and they surely could not be jealous of him. In Diels, Goering had a first-rate legal mind and a young attorney hungry for power. Diels was formidably intelligent, the intellectual superior of almost everyone he met, and a figure who materialized, infallibly, at important meetings and conferences. Intuitively, Diels gauged the limits of other men's minds and counted himself an expert at recognizing Freudian types, a pastime he not only found amusing but turned to good advantage in the Third Reich. Capable of bursts of prolonged labor, he followed these with periods of withdrawal and self-absorption when he moved silently through Berlin society appraising people and personalities. Diels had one of the widest circles of acquaintances in the capital and entry into all the right houses.

To help him run the new agency, Diels called upon the services of a number of young justice officials from the Prussian Ministry of the Interior, young men like himself who had survived and even prospered under von Papen's cleansing of the Prussian police the year before. Many were Catholics, only a few were Party members. One was a fraternity brother.

Their new quarters at No. 8 Prinz Albrecht Strasse were not without their terrors. With armed SA and SS men patrolling the entryways and corridors, Gestapo officials had to take every precaution to guard against their own arrest. Offices with black doors were especially coveted. Officials took the precaution of letting each other know by telephone when they left their offices or stepped across the hall to use the lavatory. One wily detective even carried the warrant for his own arrest in case he was surprised by a gang of Storm Troopers. Every official carried a gun. It was wise when climbing the stairs to ascend along the inside wall so as not to present too easy a target. The shrewdest among them arranged to b: met each evening after work by an automobile belonging to an imposing figure in the new Reich. On foot, one ran the risk of being taken on the street.

Diels cultivated the aura of terror that clung to his office. That summer he told a group of American correspondents gathered at Putzi Hanfstaengl's home that to date he had received eight challenges to duels to the death by pistol and a score by sabre. Diels' corps had written just the other day to enquire when he meant to satisfy his challengers.

"I must reply—alas!" Diels confessed with mock regret, "that although I am ready, my opponents are at the present in no position to meet me. They're all unfortunately in concentration camps."

The newsmen chuckled uncomfortably.

But what if he were killed in a duel, the burly Quentin Reynolds asked.

"What of it?" Diels replied. "That would be fate."

Louis P. had a more serious question. Why retain para-military organizations such as the SA and the SS now that the opposition parties had been dissolved? Couldn't the regular police be counted on to maintain order?

"The value of the SA and the SS," asserted Diels, "seen from my viewpoint of inspector-general responsible for the suppression of subversive tendencies and activities, lies in the fact that they spread terror. That is a wholesome thing."

The *New York Times* and the Hearst Press printed Diels' reply verbatim. After that Diels was careful to speak more guardedly in front of "court journalists." Yet, he rather liked the gentleman of the foreign press. They brought him useful information now that the German press was no longer at liberty to print objective news. The gentlemen of the foreign press were part of a plan Diels had formulated. He was willing to let Hitler and his Party have their revolution. He admired Hitler although he did not always understand him. But Hitler's revolution must obey the laws of Prussia as enforced by officials such as Diels. He would permit the foreign press to broadcast the revolution's worst excesses in the hope that Germany's new rulers would be shamed into curbing the violence of the SA and SS.

That was perhaps the single weakness of Diels' extraordinary mind: he believed a clever plan cleverly executed by a few officials could bridle a revolution led by thousands.

Beneath "the most peaceful revolution in history," Diels discerned a vendetta of the victorious against the vanquished. Berlin's 80,000-man SA was heated to fever pitch by the flames of the Reichstag Fire. In the fratricidal war of the right against the left, countless old grudges were settled by SA bosses with names like "Sow Back" and "Cold Calves" who meant to repay with interest every dent and knobby scar on their brutal faces. Diels had nothing in common with such men. He did everything in his power to see that the SA and SS auxiliaries in his office were employed in such lowly tasks as clerks, translators and drivers. Rank in the SA or SS could have no bearing on appointments with the Gestapo, Diels stressed; only technical ability and industriousness counted.

Of the two, the black-shirted SS were the best disciplined. The SA were rabble except for their officers, who had frequently seen service in the Army. That spring the SA was swollen with criminal elements and many of the toughest remnants of the outlawed Communist Party. The SS had visions of aristocracy and were educated or at least drawn from good families; but that distinction did not always hold. Some in the SA also belonged to the SS, and many in the SS had once belonged to the SA before they tired of the lawlessness of their comrades. Neither necessarily belonged to the National Socialist Party whose functionaries seemed to fit Dr. Goebbels' mold: youthful intellectuals who preached violence but lived the staid lives of civil servants. The only bond that held the three groups together in their fight for power was loyalty to the idea of Adolf Hitler. The SS with their sinister black uniforms provided protection during his huge rallies.

That spring, rumors of SA brutality at a camp for political prisoners in the village of Sonnenburg reached Diels. A number of liberals, among them the attorney Hans Litten, the writer Erich Muehsam, and the editor Karl von Ossietsky, had been roughly handled in full view of the town's citizens. The camp at Sonnenburg, although under police jurisdiction, was manned by local SA men. The camp's police unit had evidently been too small to prevent the violence. Diels sent Dr. Hans Mittelbach, a young attorney with the Prussian Ministry of the Interior, to investigate. After touring the camp, Mittelbach asked to see Litten, Muehsam and Ossietsky. Litten's face was grotesquely swollen and his left eye closed shut. The author Muehsam, a man nearing middle age, had had his dentures broken. Ossietsky was unharmed, probably due to his international reputation as a journalist. Mittelbach ordered Muehsam taken to a dentist. Litten he brought back to Berlin in his own car.

The Government did little to hide the existence of such camps. In April the *Berliner Illustrirte* published an article entitled: "In The Concentration Camp Oranienburg Near Berlin." Pictures portrayed the inmates performing exercises similar to those practiced in the German Army: push-ups and deep knee bends. There were daily discussion groups, even a reading room for studying political developments in the daily press. The camp seemed to deserve the title of "re-education center." The article gave the schedule for a typical day: up at 5:30 AM, coffee at 7:00, work until 12:30, mid-day meal followed by rest until 1:30, followed by exercise, then an hour and a half of something called "sport," supper at 7:00, and lights out at 9:00 PM. With eight and a half hours of sleep every night, plenty of daily exercise plus two big meals and breaks for bed-making and washing and cleaning, what malnourished Communist from the slums of Berlin would object to such a life? The article went on to mention that Oranienburg in Prussia was only a medium-sized "re-education center." Two larger camps were situated in southern Germany. Heuberg near Stuttgart held 1,500 men. Dachau, under construction in Bavaria, would accommodate 5,000 prisoners.

The rumors about Sonnenburg were so persistant and so ugly that the correspondents, who lived only an hour and a half away, could not ignore them. The night Goebbels burned Germany's books, a pitiful lady in gray called on H. R. Knickerbocker to beg him to visit Sonnenburg, where her husband and hundreds of other prisoners were rumored to be confined under the most inhumane conditions. Knick and Louis P. pestered the Government for permission to visit the camp until Martin Sommerfeldt, Goering's press chief, arranged an excursion for a small group of newsmen and state officials.

The village of Sonnenburg lay some eighty miles north of Berlin, near Kuestrin. The prison, a huge gray building with narrow, heavily barred windows, had formerly been a penitentiary for hardened criminals. It now housed several hundred Communists, pacifists and other political "undesirables" who were overcrowding Berlin's jails and remand prisons.

The small caravan of correspondents and state officials came to a stop under the prison's entrance vault. The camp commandant asked the reporters to leave their cameras outside. The massive gate swung open to reveal several hundred men doing military drills and singing Nazi songs. At the sight of the commandant the inmates sprang rigidly to attention.

The place was scrupulously clean, although a certain primitive smell pervaded the grounds due to overcrowding, the newsmen assumed. They were told that the camp held some 443 "leftists." Knick and Lochner inspected the kitchens. The menu seemed reasonably complete.

They asked a prisoner, the former head of the Communist delegation in the Prussian legislature, about the quality of the food.

"Oh," he replied, "*for the past two days* it has been quite good."

The guards, Knick and Lochner saw, were SA youths in their twenties, members of a generation whose life had been one long catastrophe of inflation, joblessness, and economic depression. They were the scum of Germany, toughs recruited from the Party's soup kitchens, uneducated and unwanted, whose only coin of trade was their ruthless ardor as twenty-year-olds. They had been taught that the men they guarded would kill them if they turned their backs, and they behaved accordingly.

"I give every fellow a thrashing when he first comes in," one youth admitted. "That has a very salutary effect. After that he is more likely to obey orders implicitly. We don't try first to find out whether a man is guilty or not, or whether he will submit to discipline or not. It is much better from the viewpoint of keeping everybody in check to give each new arrival a hiding first. It is safe to assume that he is guilty of something or other, else he would not have been arrested and brought here."

Knick and Lochner asked to see the journalist Ossietsky, the former editor of the weekly *Die Weltbuehne,* famous under the republic for its political and cultural criticism. What, they asked Ossietsky, did he do to pass the time.

"Chiefly reading," the editor replied. "Unfortunately, this place has only just been opened so there is as yet no prisoner's library. I must therefore rely upon my wife to send such books as the censor will permit us to have."

Knick said he would send books if Ossietsky would tell him what subjects were permitted.

"I don't suppose there is any objection to history," Ossietsky replied carefully.

Any particular period of German history, Knick asked.

"Well," said Ossietsky with a smile, "I think medieval history would be very apropos!"

They saw no one who was obviously ill or injured but then their visit had been arranged in advance. It was truly shocking to see well-known authors, lawyers and statesmen dressed in prison garb and ordered about like raw recruits, one of the German officials admitted; but then the party that loses must expect such treatment. Had the Communists triumphed, the parties of the right would have been dealt with just as severely. So ran the excuses for such places.

Lochner and Knick and Quentin Reynolds wrote nothing about Sonnenburg or Ossietsky when they returned to Berlin since "protective custody" was nothing less than judicial limbo. The State held all the cards and the prisoner none. Freedom came only at the State's convenience. Lochner and Knick and Reynolds did not wish to add to the stations of Ossietsky's cross. They killed the story, buried their visit to Sonnenburg in silence and left the ugly rumors of what transpired behind its walls to stand as history. There were worse places than Sonnenburg, they suspected. Their appeals to visit Gestapo headquarters on Prinz Albrecht Strasse were routinely turned down by Putzi Hanfstaengl and other officials. The big camps, Oranienburg, Buchenwald and Dachau, remained strictly off limits.

SUMMER VIOLENCE

When Louis P. Lochner heard that Willaim E. Dodd would be the next Ambassador to Germany, his first thought was that Roosevelt must have some sense of humor to send a Jeffersonian democrat to the Third Reich. A man of Dodd's tastes, Lochner predicted, would feel about as welcome in Berlin as a Christian in Mecca. But it was not long before Lochner came to see that the new Ambassador was a man of culture and possessed a keen mind; within a week after Dodd's arrival the two were conferring every few days. Lochner even came to appreciate the wisdom of Dodd's decision to turn down all invitations to social events so spectacular that serious, intimate conversation was all but impossible. Other American correspondents were similarly impressed and found the new Ambassador just the right man for the job.

Bella Fromm could not remember when she had awaited the arrival of a new envoy with greater anticipation. Since January 30 jealousy, distrust, and duplicity had characterized Germany's relations with other countries, especially America and the American press. From what Bella had heard, the decent, upright Dodd would show little patience for such rigamarole. She wished she could say the same for others in the diplomatic corps. She had never turned a blind eye—except in her columns—to the foibles and follies of the diplomatic set. She counted herself worldly and a bit of a cynic, but the length to which some of her diplomatic friends went to accommodate themselves to the chicanery of Germany's new rulers was simply shocking. Some of her oldest acquaintances revealed themselves to be slippery as eels. If rumor were any indication, Ambassador Dodd would be the exception.

Bella, the lady in black, was among the officials who greeted the Dodds' train on the evening of July 13. The new Ambassador paused only long enough to tell the solemn crowd that the Depression in America was quite as deep as in Europe and that he was against restricting immigration to America. Messersmith introduced the new Ambassador to Frau Bella. Bella noted that Dodd's slender, restless daughter looked the perfect example of her generation while the quiet Mrs. Dodd seemed a dear.

The following day Dodd read a brief statement to Bella and other members of the German press gathered in his office at the American Embassy on the Bendlerstrasse. When he finished, the ranking member of the group, a Party man, asked if it were true, as the *Hamburger Israelitisches Familienblatt* had reported, that Dodd had come to Germany to invervene on behalf of the Jews. Dodd smiled his ironic smile and, recalling Roosevelt's instructions, answered with a curt *"Nein."* Throughout the interview, Bella felt that Dodd had to fight back the urge to seize the gentlemen of the German press by their collective collars and throw them out. As he escorted her to the door he remarked: "A most unpleasant job" and invited her to come again.

Although Dodd was not yet acting Ambassador and would not hand his letters of credence to President Hindenburg for several weeks, he immediately felt pressure from Germany's new rulers. An invitation was circulated inviting him to board a special train on the evening of September 1 that would convey him and others of the diplomatic corps to the Party Congress convening that year in Nuremberg. Chancellor Hitler in his capacity as leader of the National Socialist German Workers Party extended the invitation personally. The train, equipped with special dining and sleeping cars as well as a separate compartment for each envoy and his staff, would be furnished at government expense.

The invitation was without precedent. The leader of the German nation was inviting foreign diplomats to be his personal guests at a polititcal caucus.

Transatlantic cables hummed with appeals to London, Washington and Tokyo for instructions.

Unless the State Department gave him a direct order to the contrary, Dodd had every intention of avoiding the show. He found its organizers personally distasteful and saw that the invitation was a clever ruse to use the prestige of the diplomatic corps to prove to the world that the National Socialist German Workers Party *was* the German nation and the German people. As an honored guest, he would be compelled to witness endless hours of military display and to listen to the Chancellor's speech on the "New Culture" which doubtless would have little good to say about democracy. A performance afterwards of "Die Meistersinger" at the Opera House seemed scant recompense for sitting through a day of insults.

Accompanying the invitation was the news that President Hindenburg would return to Berlin on August 30 or 31 to swear in the new chiefs of mission in time to make the journey to Nuremberg. It was hinted that if only a few or none of the new envoys accepted the invitation the official swearing-in might be postponed until October. With eight new chiefs of mission waiting to be sworn in, Dodd was sure the Government was bluffing. His idea was to boycott the Congress. He asked the State

Department to sound out London's attitude, and he sent Counselor Gordon over to talk to the French Embassy.

The British Embassy was inclined to accept. Its new chief, Sir Eric Clare Edmond Phipps, had yet to arrive in Berlin, but the Party Rally in Nuremberg seemed a blazing good opportunity to get his mission off to a running start.

London was of a different mind. The British Foreign Office promptly sent a telegram to Berlin declining the invitation in Sir Eric's name. Sir Eric would remain for several more weeks in London on "urgent family business."

Washington was not so courageous. Under Secretary of State William Phillips wired Dodd that the Department did not want to get involved. Dodd should use his own judgment and take care not to embarrass his government.

Dodd urged Phillips to reconsider. There were at least two precedents he could think of in American history against accepting: one under President Madison, the other under Cleveland. To attend the ceremony would set a vicious precedent and deal a severe blow to the disbanded parties that had once opposed Hitler.

Rather than sound out London or Paris, the Undersecretary replied, Washington wished to avoid influencing other governments in any way.

An angry Dodd was unrepentant. He would not attend.

The only question that remained was what to do if the invitation were extended downward to Counselors of Embassy or Chargés d'Affaires? When the Papal Nuncio finally let it be known that he was declining, everyone breathed a sigh of relief.

The "Festival of Triumph" at Nuremberg that year was not a diplomatic success. The *"Sonderzug"* that departed Berlin at 8:15 PM on September 1, carrying protocol officials, stenographers, a physician and a squad of armed Brown Shirts, had to be reduced from fourteen to nine cars. The Ambassadors of America, France, Britain, Spain, Japan and the Vatican all declined to attend on the pretext of prior engagements or, in Dodd's case, due to the "press of work." Italy sent only a Chargé d'Affaires. When the special train from Berlin pulled into Nuremberg's North Station it was greeted by the flags of lesser principalities such as Haiti, Santo Domingo, Siam and Persia.

Toward noon on August 30, Dodd, dressed in morning coat and top hat, accompanied by members of his staff similarly attired, drove to the President's Palace on the Wilhelmstrasse to hand over his letters of credence to von Hindenburg. Foreign Minister Baron von Neurath escorted him into the reception hall and introduced him to the towering

86-year-old President. Standing, Dodd read from a carefully prepared statement: "President Roosevelt has charged me to avail myself of this opportunity . . ." He took care to stress his country's deep affection for the "German people."

In reply, Hindenburg read nearsightedly from a page of words as black and bold as newspaper headlines.

After the obligatory chat on the "preferred sofa," Dodd rose and introduced the President to members of his staff waiting in the next room. Then he left. His family had not been present. Martha saw only the picture of her father standing on the steps of the Palace with the envoys of Siam, Hungary and Greece who were also received that day. In his black cutaway, high collar and silk top hat her father with his country face looked like a six-year-old in fancy dress.

His "receivemento" or official reception for the diplomatic corps had to wait until the train from Nuremberg had returned and its occupants had had time to recover. Some fifty invitations had been sent out, but as each diplomat brought several members of his staff, the guest book in the American Embassy on the Bendlerstrasse had more than 200 signatures in it before the evening was over. The "show" started at 5 PM on September 6. A great punch bowl was prepared and flowers placed in every room. Dodd and Gordon and the German Chief of Protocol greeted the guests as they arrived. Baron von Neurath came, and Hjalmar Schacht and the French Ambassador, André François-Poncet. The German guests were a mixture of men in morning coats and men in black SS uniforms. Germany's black-clad elite were just then entering the Foreign Ministry as liaison officers and observers. Dodd was not afraid to let a look of disdain show through his smile when he shook hands with these figures in black.

George S. Messersmith, the highest-ranking American consular official in Germany, did not attend. He had not been invited. Counselor Gordon told Dodd that protocol did not permit the presence of consular officials at a receivemento. Messersmith left town so as not to embarrass the Ambassador. Later, when Dodd learned that Gordon had misled him, his embarrassment was compounded when he recalled an earlier incident. Messersmith had invited Dodd, Gordon and several other American officials to a conference in his office at the consulate. At the appointed hour everyone had arrived except Gordon, who telephoned to inform Dodd that he would not be coming and that he thought the Ambassador was degrading himself by conducting business at the consulate instead of the embassy.

Gordon all but ignored the social significance of the amalgamation in 1924 of the American diplomatic and consular branches into a single

"Foreign Service." Diplomats of his generation, the first generation of career diplomats in America, were drawn from prominent Eastern families with several generations of wealth behind them. Trained at exclusive preparatory schools—Gordon prepared in Switzerland—they "finished" at Harvard, Yale or Princeton. Abroad, as at home, they rarely mixed with the middle classes and never with the lower orders. Consul General Messersmith was a self-made man who had married well but who had begun his professional life as a public school official. Although he had done a good deal of political reporting recently, his responsibilities usually involved such pedestrian tasks as looking after American business interests in Germany, locating lost tourists, even reserving hotel accommodations for newly-appointed Ambassadors. Gordon and Messersmith, spoke the same language and served the same government, but insuperable barriers of birth, poise and style kept them apart.

Temperamentally, they were also exact opposites. The relentless Messersmith was on excellent terms with German officials of every rank; while Gordon was instinctively aloof and had on occasion behaved with such irascibility that he was habitually snubbed when he called at the German Foreign Ministry. An efficient administrator and a brilliant analyst of the German scene, Gordon took his staff to task in his annual efficiency reports for such sins as living below their rank or for moving too exclusively in German society! American diplomats abroad made up an invisible club that excluded Consul Generals as well as Ambassadors from the groves of academe.

The jealousy and rivalry among his staff embarrassed Dodd. He was further prejudiced against Gordon when he learned how much his Counselor spent each year on social pretense. With a salary of $9,000, Gordon was spending roughly $30,000 "living up" to his rank at the Embassy. When Dodd looked into the matter further, he found that there was hardly a man on his staff who was not spending from two to three times his salary attempting to outshine his colleagues. One of the first cables Dodd saw when he arrived in Berlin was a bill from his predecessor, a Pennsylvania coal millionaire, informing Washington that it owed him $2,400 for the cost of shipping his household belongings home; this at a time when the average Ambassador spent less than $400 on his transfer.

The lesser embassies in Berlin were greatly strained to provide equivalent levels of display. The numerous teas, diplomatic dinners and musical evenings kept the diplomatic set up far into the night. Envoys complained of being too fatigued to work in the morning. Dodd regularly retired by 10 or 11 at night, and he was usually the first person after the receptionist to arrive at the Embassy at 9 o'clock in the morning. To his chagrin, many on his staff did not appear until 11 o'clock, some of them clearly exhausted and holding their heads, unable to work at full capacity until late in the afternoon when the blandishments of golf and cocktails beckoned again. As a consequence, their work suffered, and on occasion Dodd had to return their reports to be redone. Late night revelry and dilatory work might have suited a slower, more regal age but the mass subscription newspaper with its penchant for diplomatic comment had changed all that. The delicious isolation of embassy life had passed into history even if the diplomats refused to admit it. The best embassies in Berlin, such as the French Embassy, continued a celebrated night life but still had summaries of the German press ready to telephone to Paris by noon each day. André François-Poncet, another academic, bragged that he crushed his staff with work. Embassy secretaries who broke he sent home. Dodd's people would have rebelled and reported him to the club elite at the State Department. He was forced to move more cautiously. At his request, the State Department issued a directive urging all personnel to be at their desks by nine-thirty in the morning. When he paid his first formal call on the Spanish Ambassador, Dodd took Gordon, in top hat and cutaway, with him. To Gordon's great dismay, Dodd insisted that they walk the short distance to the Spanish Embassy.

Despite the loveliness of the summer, Dodd could not have come at a worse time. Since March some twenty Americans had been manhandled in their homes or on the street by Storm Troopers while official Germany turned a blind eye and the press, under Goebbels' direction, worked overtime to brand the messengers of the bad news as the real culprits. A second outbreak of violence, different from the first, came with summer. Whereas the rampages of the spring had involved invasions of residences, kidnapping, robbery and the beating of known liberals and people of Jewish appearance, the summer's rash of violence set a different pattern. The revolution had deepened. The opposition had been routed and its organizations outlawed. Power could now be unrestrained. The curve of violence that had fallen off steeply after March and faded almost to tranquility in May, rose again, in full daylight this time, in front of crowds of eyewitnesses. Unwittingly, the Government supplied the pretext in July in an official decree:

> It has become common practice to give the Hitler salute during the singing of the anthems Deutschland Ueber Alles and the Horst Wessel Song regardless of whether a person is a member of the Party or not. In

order to avoid the suspicion of non-compliance the Hitler salute should be shown.

The notice appeared with commentary in all the papers, and Messersmith gravely reported its substance to his superiors in Washington.

Storm Troopers and Party members had long greeted each other with upraised arms and cries of *"Heil Hitler."* After January 30th the halls of government buildings fairly rang with the *"Heils"* of passing Storm Troopers, SS men, Party officials, and policemen. By summer, Government officials had taken to answering their phones with the salutation, and foreigners such as Messersmith were frequently welcomed by the greeting. In reply, Messersmith either nodded solemnly or made a slight bow. What non-Aryans were supposed to do, no one knew.

State occasions, even theatrical performances, in the capital frequently concluded with the audience standing at attention with arms raised as the two anthems, one traditional, the other revolutionary, were sung. At a luncheon in Kiel, Messersmith noticed that officials and Storm Troopers, seeing him standing with his arms at his sides, shot him rude stares and took pains to discover his identity. Fortunately, the ceremony took place indoors, the guests were men of culture and Messersmith was the recipient of no obvious unpleasantness. The best ploy was to slip away unnoticed just before the conclusion of such events; but as the weeks wore on and the popular enthusiasm for the practice increased, this became more and more difficult. Crowds broke into song without warning, in restaurants and cafés, or simply when the mood struck them at the end of radio speeches or at the unexpected appearance of a well-known revolutionary figure. Increasingly, the dignified foreigner found himself ducking down a nearby alley or into a conveniently placed shop.

Bella Fromm raised her arm in the Hitler salute for the first time at a formal reception for the "National Socialist People's Welfare Organization." She had withdrawn or been dismissed from most of her other charities but Magda Goebbels had sent her a personal invitation to this one.

Again it seemed to Bella that it was her fate to run into Hitler. As usual he arrived late and took one of the few remaining seats in the hall next to her.

"We have met before, *gnaedige Frau,* haven't we?" he whispered.

It was at the end of the ceremony, as the guests rose to sing the German anthem and then the first stanza of the Horst Wessel Song, that Bella had no choice, considering the company, but to raise her arm too. It was not her "privilege" as a Jew, she knew, to give the Party salute but it was also, strictly speaking, not her privilege to be taking part in a National Socialist charity. She swallowed the indignity and told herself that the salute did not count in her case and could not compromise her inner convictions.

By July, every German understood that it was no longer safe to stand in the presence of SA marchers and not raise one's arm regardless of how one felt. Only a third of those who held up their arms had supported the National Socialists in the years of struggle; most of the others were simple opportunists, people quick to take advantage of the National Awakening. The Storm Troopers called these converts the "March harvest" and they were not deceived by the forest of arms raised along their parade routes. They knew that many of those who saluted had only recently been their worst enemies: Red Front members, men and women, who, under the Republic, had steadfastly adhered to the Communist camp. Beefsteak Nazis, the SA called them: "Brown on the outside, red on the inside."

Tourists and other recent arrivals in Germany were conspicuous by the cut of their trousers and the style of their hats, but the parading Storm Troopers were intent only on remembering the faces of those unlucky enough to be ignorant of Germany's new custom or stubborn enough to believe that it did not apply to them. With the unusually large number of Americans traveling and studying in Germany that summer, Messersmith and Dodd feared the worst, and they were soon proven correct.

Around 10 o'clock on a warm Tuesday evening in mid-August, Dr. Daniel Mulvihill, lately of Long Island Medical Hospital, left his hotel and walked up the Friedrichstrasse in search of a drugstore. The 30-year-old American physician had come to Germany three weeks earlier to study thoracic surgery at Berlin's Charité Hospital. As Dr. Mulvihill entered the broad boulevard of Unter den Linden, he paused to take in the spectacle of huge numbers of marching Storm Troopers. Dozens of bright klieg lights played on the marchers and the cheering crowds. He was especially taken by the stirring sounds of the numerous brass bands.

As he told a sympathetic H. R. Knickerbocker later: "I was simply standing there when suddenly just as the flags were passing, a Nazi in uniform rushed up and hit me as hard as he could on the side of the head."

The doctor, stunned and dazed, his left ear throbbing, had no idea why he had been struck until a bystander gave him to understand that he should have been watching with his right arm raised.

Dr. Mulvihill appealed to a nearby policeman, but his German was so poor that by the time he made the officer understand his plight, the squadron of Storm Troopers was far down the boulevard. The officer said that there was nothing he could do. He took the doctor to a nearby café and with the help of a patron who spoke English took down a full report.

Dr. Mulvihill returned to his hotel. The next day he went to the American Consulate and made out a deposition. A medical examination revealed no serious injury but his ear remained deaf to all sound except for a continuous buzzing.

As usual, the correspondents with their phone lines to Paris and London got the story to America first. In Washington, Under Secretary of State William Phillips held a press conference. A reporter at the press conference observed that this was only the latest in a series of attacks on Americans. The newspapers were speculating that Americans might be warned to stay away from Germany unless they had urgent business there. Had the State Department considered issuing such an announcement?

Phillips said it had not. The Consul General in Berlin had ample power to press for redress of any violent act against an American and had done so in the past.

Might it not be wise to advise Americans to give the Hitler salute when in Germany?

It was considered courteous to conform as much as possible to local practice, observed Phillips, although a foreigner could not be expected to know every local custom.

Were visitors to the United States required to salute the American flag?

Even Americans were not required to salute their flag.

Was there a law in Germany that said everyone must salute the Nazi flag?

The Undersecretary of State said he did not know of one.

With the attack on Dr. Mulvihill, American diplomatic authorities in Berlin thought they finally had a case that would test the good intentions of the German Government. If Germany's new leaders failed to get results in the Mulvihill case, either they secretly did not wish to or they truly lacked the power to control their followers in the streets. Dr. Mulvihill was not only a physician and a professional of note, he was the first American gentile to be attacked. While this did not lead American officials to press any harder in his case, it did give them reason to hope that the culprits would receive swift punishment from a government that exalted the inviolability of the Nordic type.

Thirty-six hours after learning of the attack, Rudolf Diels' office telephoned Messersmith to say that Dr. Mulvihill's assailant had been arrested. This was the swiftest action yet following an attack on an

American. The most startling news came the following day when it was learned that the youthful, arrogant commander of Berlin's 80,000 man army of Brown Shirts, Group Leader Karl Ernst, would apologize personally to Ambassador Dodd.

The attack on Dr. Daniel Mulvihill caused reverberations well beyond the confines of the Prussian government and the Berlin SA. Dr. Mulvihill was in Germany to take a special course of study from the world famous chest surgeon, Professor Ferdinand Sauerbruch. Dr. Sauerbruch was a celebrity in Germany. He traveled extensively between his clinics. When he stopped overnight, the local papers always took note of the fact and printed the name of the hotel where he was staying. Dr. Sauerbruch taught that a surgeon must possess character, and Dr. Sauerbruch demonstrated that he had character when the Government ordered him to dismiss his Jewish assistants. He refused and threatened to take his reputation and his practice to Switzerland. The Government relented, and Dr. Sauerbruch's picture appeared the following year in the Party's official *Fuehrer Lexikon*. Putzi's picture and resumé also appeared in the first official handbook of German leaders; but that was not the only connection between the surgeon and the Hanfstaengl clan. Since his divorce, Dr. Sauerbruch had found consolation in the company of Putzi's unmarried sister, Erna Hanfstaengl. For a time Erna had even moved north to be near the renowned physician. Personal connections were vitally important in the new Germany, and an attack on Dr. Mulvihill was an attack on Dr. Sauerbruch and, through him, on Putzi Hanfstaengl, one of the highest figures in the New Chancellery.

Putzi was involved on yet another level. That summer he fulfilled one of his fondest dreams. He took part in the making of a motion picture, a biopic of the life and death of the Nazi hero Horst Wessel, who had been murdered by Communists in 1930 at age 23. Wessel had penned the words to the first stanza of the song by that name and Goebbels had done the rest, until Wessel's reputation as a Berlin pimp was submerged beneath layers of romantic myth.

A film company was hastily formed; shooting started in July. Putzi was not only the Chancellery's observer on the set, he was also a financial backer and the composer of the film's incidental music. The funeral march he had composed on the occason of the untimely death of his daughter, Herta, appeared in the film as Wessel's funeral dirge.

With the exception of the actor who played a German Communist in the likeness of the mature Lenin, the cast were all unknowns from regional theater companies. The director was certainly not of the first rank. Members of Wessel's old Storm Troop were hired as extras, and from the beginning the battle scenes showed signs of being unusually realistic. There was a near riot when the crew invaded the bleak streets of Berlin's Communist district to film a skirmish between the SA and the Red Front. Authentic Communist banners had been borrowed from the Party's historical museum, and as the crew of real-life Nazis and synthetic Communists began shouting their battle cries, real-life Communists poured out of alleys and tenements. The police, who had also been hired to play themselves, suddenly had their hands full. Fists flew, roof tiles sailed, helmets rolled in the gutter.

Less heroic was the pressure brought to bear upon the Jewish community to take provocative parts in the film. The Grenadierstrasse, a small street in Berlin's Jewish quarter, was sealed off, and a number of bearded Jews and others of pronouncedly Jewish appearance, including two rabbis, were ordered to climb a ladder to a low roof. As the extras in SA uniform paraded by, the unwilling participants were ordered to shout Communist epithets such as: "Perish the Nazis," "Death to Fascism," and "Hail Moscow." So confused were some of these amateur actors that as they shouted their taunts they raised their right arms in the Hitler salute.

Putzi did his best to highlight what was respectable in Wessel's career. A release date was set for early October, the 26th aniversary of Wessel's birth. Directors and producers all over Germany kicked themselves for not having foreseen the goldmine in the biography when it first appeared. "Horst Wessel: A German Destiny" was expected to open to packed houses and to make millions of marks. For Putzi it was a dream come true. His imagination ran wild. He would become a millionaire, a powerful director, an artist in light and sound.

The last thing he wanted was for the foreign press to report that the Storm Trooper who had assaulted Dr. Mulvihill had been one of hundreds of Storm Troopers called out to recreate the torchlit parade of the Berlin SA on the night of January 30. That reenactment accounted for the brass bands, the numerous Storm Troop units, the bright klieg lights and perhaps the overly martial air of at least one of the marchers. Fearful that the sale of the foreign rights in America might be jeopardized, Putzi pressed for the swiftest redress.

The box on Dr. Mulvihill's ear set Putzi's own head spinning. It may have been he who gave Rudolf Hess the cunning analogy that next appeared in the German press: "The raising of the right arm in the German salute could no more be expected of an American that that a Protestant would be expected to cross himself when he entered a Catholic Church."

AN EMBATTLED AMBASSADOR

The day Dodd was to receive the apologies of Group Leader Karl Ernst was a busy one for the American Ambassador. On reaching his office he cabled the State Department a second time for instructions on whether to attend the Nuremberg Party rally, and again the State Department's reply was noncommittal. Dodd decided not to go.

At 10:45, Edgar Ansel Mowrer came to talk over his case. Dodd was familiar with the newsman's problems from his study of the embassy's dispatches in Washington. Mowrer, a passionate man, was close to feeling that he had been betrayed.

His troubles had begun in July when his boss, Col. Frank Knox, the publisher of the *Chicago Daily News,* arrived in Berlin. Knox told Mowrer that he planned to transfer him to Tokyo in the fall. Mowrer had done a courageous job of reporting, but the threats against him were mounting and might erupt into violence. Even so moderate a representative of the Prussian government as Dr. Martin Sommerfeldt had called for Mowrer's resignation as president of the Foreign Press Association in the interest of journalistic camaraderie. A new face representing the *Chicago Daily News* in Berlin would invite less acrimony.

A few weeks later, Mowrer received a late night telephone call at his residence on the Tiergarten from the wife of Dr. Paul Goldmann, the Association's oldest member. Her husband had just been arrested by the Gestapo, she said. They had been celebrating their silver wedding anniversary when the police arrived. The elderly Goldmann had covered the German capital for almost 30 years for Austria's *Wiener Neue Freie Presse.* He was a German citizen, however, and the arrest was legal.

"The sons of bitches. Why don't they pick on someone their size," Mowrer exclaimed as he hung up. Three German journalists had recently been arrested in Vienna on charges of espionage. Goldmann was being held in retaliation.

The ailing Goldmann's predicament was dire. It would be impossible for Mowrer to start negotiations for his release on a Friday evening. Just to get the Gestapo to admit that they were holding the newsman would be a minor victory. On Saturday, most officials would be out of town enjoying the warm August weather. Sunday, all Government offices were closed.

Edgar Ansel Mowrer was not a man to bargain with fascists, but to save the 66-year-old correspondent's life he had to come up with a deal tempting to the Government. Since Goebbels had not heard of Knox's decision to shift him to Tokyo in a few weeks, Mowrer decided to offer to step down as president of the Foreign Press Association in return for Goldmann's release. Knick carried the proposal to Goebbels personally on Saturday.

Meanwhile Louis P. managed to wrangle an audience with Rudolf Diels.

Was Dr. Goldmann's arrest purely symbolic, Louis P. asked.

"Absolutely," Diels replied.

In that case, Louis P. said, he and his friends wanted to take Dr. Goldmann's place in jail one day at a time on a rotating basis.

"You might even get considerable publicity for this stunt," Louis P. hinted, "for the press of the world would publish a daily photo of the foreign correspondent who is taking his turn at satisfying your craving for reprisals."

Diels advised Goebbels to accept Mowrer's offer, and Goebbels agreed. Mowrer stepped down and the *Voelkischer Beobachter* crowed that a "sworn and proven enemy" had been removed. But Mowrer, or rather his proxies, had the last word. Knick drafted a special report to the *Chicago Daily News* pointing out that the conditions of Mowrer's resignation signaled the first time that the German Government had compromised with a figure it wished to remove from public life. Heretofore, such persons had usually been ejected, sometimes bodily, from office. The news that Mowrer's end of the bargain had been empty all along was left to the *New York* and the *London Times* to break. Goebbels was furious.

Edgar Ansel Mowrer, the bitterest critic of the regime, was once again an ordinary correspondent. As the Berlin press celebrated his defeat, he delivered his most thunderous salvo yet against the Government. The pretext was Minister Goering's astonishing announcement that the SA and SS were to be stripped of their police powers.

"Friends of Germany may breathe more easily for the first time in many months," Mowrer wrote, "if the promise just made by the Reich government to dissolve the so-called auxiliary police on Aug. 15 is kept. For these so-called auxiliary policemen were simply brown-shirted lads of the storm battalions with red arm bands. They, and they alone, have been responsible for the most horrible aspects of the German terror—for shanghaiing many of the finest Germans, for beating thousands and killing hundreds of so-called political enemies without the shadow of a trial or real examination.

"Obvious, too, is the fact that not the auxiliary police, not the storm

battalions, but the government itself—Chancellor Adolf Hitler, Prussian Premier Captain Hermann Wilhelm Goering, Propaganda Minister Father Paul Joseph Goebbels and other leaders—were responsible for the terror."

No self-respecting government could tolerate such a sweeping attack on its leaders from a correspondent residing within its borders. In Washington, the German Chargé d'Affaires complained to Secretary of State Hull. The German Government simply could not comprehend why the State Department lacked the power to order Mowrer's immediate recall.

In Berlin, Dodd also grew concerned. Mowrer had seriously overstepped the bounds of journalistic propriety. The American Ambassador could appreciate the newsman's point, but how were reasonable men to prevail if the controversy was continually and recklessly provoked? Goering's decree, after all, was a step in the right direction from the liberal point of view.

The Government let it be known that it could not guarantee Mowrer's safety if he insisted on attending the Nuremberg Party rally in September. Diels assigned extra agents to watch Mowrer's home on the Handelstrasse but even the Inspector General of the Gestapo knew he could not protect the newsman from fanatics within the SA.

Knick appealed to Consul General Messersmith to prevail upon Edgar to leave, if not for his own safety, then for his family's. Reluctantly, Messersmith summoned Edgar Ansel Mowrer to the American Consulate. Messersmith thought Mowrer the most courageous journalist he knew. The two saw eye to eye on most things, and Messersmith was loath to take a stand against Mowrer that would look like a personal betrayal. When Mowrer heard the Consul General's words of advice, his eyes filled with tears and Messersmith knew that his fears had been justified.

When Mowrer called upon Dodd that Tuesday morning in late August he came to ask Dodd to stand behind him and to force the German Government to draw up a formal order of expulsion. Dodd refused. According to the original plan, Mowrer's transfer was scheduled for early September. The Germans wanted Mowrer out immediately. What in the name of good-will was to be gained by a diplomatic collision over a matter of a few days?

Thus it was that Roosevelt's most audaciously liberal Ambassador became the instrument of Goebbels' revenge. Mowrer left the American Embassy bitterly disappointed.

Shortly before noon there appeared a lean, clean cut youth whose every gesture exuded an aura of brutality and power: 29-year-old Group Leader Major General Karl Ernst, commander of the Berlin-Brandenburg SA. Resplendent in brown uniform with swinging dagger, his brown kepi ringed with the scarlet band of the General Staff, his collar decorated with three silver oak leaves, Ernst marched up to Dodd's desk, clicked his heels sharply and gave the Hitler salute. Slowly Dodd rose to his feet.

He had come, Ernst announced, to express his deep regret over the attack on Dr. Mulvihill by one of his men and to assure the American Ambassador that his SA leaders would do everything in their power to see that such incidents did not occur in the future.

Dodd asked the young man to be seated and then proceeded to read him a stern lecture on the effect of such recklessness on public opinion in America. The youthful Group Leader could only protest his sincerity. When Dodd finished, Ernst rose, came to attention, saluted, bowed deeply after the Prussian manner and departed. The meeting had lasted five minutes and left Dodd rather amused. Later, according to the fashion of the day, he would parody the Group Leader's apology before friends and family. But he was also relieved. The apology, freely offered, would do much to lessen his government's outrage.

Messersmith was more pessimistic. "The incidents will go on," he told Dodd that afternoon. It took time for the will of the leaders to filter down to the people; thus far not a word about the attack on Dr. Mulvihill or about Ernst's apology had appeared in the German press.

Dodd thought it was Diels who had arranged the apology, but Diels' relations with the revolutionaries were far from cordial. That spring, he had failed in an attempt to remove the SA as guards from Prussia's official concentration camps. The revolutionaries and their spokesmen in the Prussian government were adamant: the camps were for the protection of the State which was now the Party; therefore it was only natural that the guardians of the camps be SA men. Diels withdrew his demand and secretly began to look for other ways to close down the camps.

The sad part about these apologies of Ernst's, Diels thought, was that they so often led to an invitation to dinner. How grand a foreign envoy must feel to actually rub shoulders with revolutionary mercenaries, to have them come to his home, to toast them across the table! What a thrilling story it made for one's next posting!

Dodd did not invite Ernst to dinner or to tea.

Mowrer's friends from the Taverne and the Adlon Bar threw a farewell party and presented him with a handsome silver bowl inscribed with the words "to a gallant fighter for the liberty of the press." His departure from the Zoo Train Station was an emotional one. Nearly the entire foreign press corps came down to see him off. Goebbels sent an observer, and Messersmith left a dinner party to attend.

Mowrer had spent nearly a decade in Germany; it would be years before he would reconcile himself to his personal exodus from Berlin just when things were getting tough. As he boarded the train to Paris, he turned and looked down at George Messersmith and said: "And you too, Brutus." The words cut Messersmith to the quick. All he could think to say in a loud, clear voice was that he would see that Mowrer's wife and daughter followed safely.

As the train lurched forward, Goebbels' man stepped up to the window and asked: "And when are you coming back to Germany, Herr Mowrer?"

"Why, when I can come back with about two million of my countrymen," Mowrer shouted loud enough for everyone to hear. He and Knick had often rehearsed the reply.

"*Aber nein*. Impossible."

"Not for the Fuehrer. The Fuehrer can bring anything about . . . even that."

On the first day of September, as all of uniformed Germany marched toward Nuremberg, William E. Dodd walked home alone, disillusioned and depressed. The efforts of Messersmith, Hess and Hanfstaengl had been of no avail. That morning news of two more assaults on Americans reached the Embassy. Messersmith had been right. The attacks would continue.

Nor was Putzi Hanfstaengl pleased to hear that the son of the internationally known radio commentator, H. V. Kaltenborn, had been slapped across the face on the Leipzigerstrasse in front of a crowd of witnesses. Putzi and H. V. Kaltenborn were old friends. They had been classmates at Harvard and had once appeared together in a play by Schiller at the annual theatrical production of the Harvard Deutscher Verein. Hans V. Kaltenborn—before the Great War the "V" had stood for "von"—was a founding member of the Harvard Cosmopolitan Club. He recalled that Putzi Hanfstaengl had never made the highest clubs at Harvard such as A. D. or Porcellian. Hitler's theorist of social infiltration had had to be satisfied with a "waiting club," the Hasty Pudding, where undergraduates cavorted about the stage in the dress of women.

Kaltenborn, one of the decade's great travellers, was in Germany with his wife and daughter and 16-year-old son, Rolf, to assess Chancellor Hitler and his movement. The family had been doing some last-minute shopping on the stylish Leipzigerstrasse when a parade of Brown Shirts turned into the street bound for the Lehrte Train Station and the Party rally at Nuremberg. As the Kaltenborns did not wish to be seen saluting the marching men they turned their backs on the procession, feigning a sudden interest in the contents of a shop window. Without warning, a husky individual broke away from the crowd following the marchers, stepped up on the sidewalk, whirled Rolf Kaltenborn around, and slapped him sharply across the face. Kaltenborn Sr. immediately announced in fluent German that they were Americans and demanded to see the man's identity papers. The man complied. He was a Party member. Kaltenborn asked him to accompany him to the nearest policeman, but a jeering crowd gathered. Kaltenborn, reluctant to risk a brawl with his wife and daughter present, told his son's assailant to go on his way.

Back at the Adlon, an agitated Kaltenborn telephoned Messersmith and said he wished to file a report. Kaltenborn wanted to keep the incident quiet, but Messersmith took copies of the commentator's affidavit to a number of Government ministries. The Propaganda Ministry, worried that Kaltenborn might mention the attack in one of his radio broadcasts, handed him a letter of apology as he and his family boarded the boat train that night.

So great was Kaltenborn's respect for the country of his birth that when he and his family arrived in New York on the Swedish-American liner *Kungsholm* he passed the incident off as a misunderstanding; his son was unhurt and the family was willing to forget the matter.

"I was able to understand how it happened," Kaltenborn told reporters. "The man who slapped him must have thought he was striking a German."

The second attack was reported by Samuel Bossard, a 21-year-old student from Pennsylvania. He appeared at the American Consulate, his face bruised and swollen. Bossard had been assaulted on the Stresemann-strasse, shortly before midnight by a group of Hitler Youths who struck him repeatedly—once in the eye—and only stopped when he cried out in English. A crowd came to his defense but two policemen who witnessed the assault told him: "What is done, is done."

In an appeal to Rudolf Diels, Messersmith asked that the two policemen on station that night be identified and punished.

Dodd cabled the State Department for help. Secretary of State Hull called in the German Chargé d'Affaires in Washington and advised him to inform his Government that if the attacks did not stop, the United States, not just its Ambassador in Berlin, would issue a sharp, public protest.

But the full weight of Hull's warning must have been muted in transmission for, on the occasion of Dodd's "receivemento" in September, the moonfaced Heinrich Dieckhoff, head of the Anglo-American desk in the Foreign Ministry, took Dodd's Counselor of Embassy, the apoplectic George A. Gordon, aside to express his Government's regrets over the latest incidents. Unfortunately, it would probably be impossible to locate the assailants, Dieckhoff said, but perhaps the policeman who had stood idly by while Mr. Bossard was beaten could be identified.

In Counselor Gordon's eyes Secretary of State Hull's warning warranted more than a casual *tête-a-tête* at a diplomatic function. There had been not one but two policemen who had witnessed the attack, a white-faced Gordon replied. The time and place had been so definitely established that it was unthinkable that the two officers could not be identified and disciplined.

A beaming Diekhoff then made matters worse when he said: "Of course, such incidents do not indicate anti-American or, I might say, anti-foreign sentiment in Germany."

Gordon was incredulous. Why, he wanted to know, had the beatings in some instances continued after the victims had identified themselves in German and English as Americans? In the case of the Kaltenborns the crowd had grown so menacing that Mr. Kaltenborn had had no choice but to release his son's assailant.

Gordon's relations with German officials had never been cordial, but he was dashed if he would be a party to Dieckhoff's evasions.

Diels did his best in the Bossard case, but the two police precincts involved were so evasive that they foiled any attempt to affix responsibility on their constables.

As for Dr. Goebbels, he was not about to relax his grip on the German press just to make public the fact that a few Americans had had their noses bloodied. His ministry preferred instead to deploy its energies calming the waters after the storm. When Messersmith telephoned Bossard a few days before the young man was due to leave Berlin, Bossard was taciturn, almost rude over the phone. Officials from the Ministry of Propaganda, Messersmith learned, had contacted Bossard and squired him about Berlin and Potsdam and introduced him to young Germans his age. Gifts of a more tangible nature may also have been exchanged. Bossard's head had been turned by this kindness. When he returned to America a German wire service quoted him as saying that there was no ill-will against foreigners in Germany. Americans, ignorant of the great changes taking place in Germany, were to blame for the misunderstandings that led to violence. Bossard said he planned to return to Germany the following year.

Elsewhere a red carpet was unrolled to visiting Americans. Prominent

American academics stopping over in Berlin were led to the comfortable reading rooms of the Amerika-Institut, a semi-official organization, whose head, Dr. Karl-Oscar Bertling was only too willing to arrange reassuring introductions. Bertling had received an MA degree from Harvard and was the president of the Harvard Clubs in Germany and a close friend of Putzi Hanfstaengl's. After January 30 the Amerika-Institut rapidly became a willing instrument of the new Government and Dr. Bertling one of its leading apologists. Bertling and an American expatriate named Lane, who had mysterious connections with circles close to Goering, often picked up minor American journalists and college professors stopping at the Hotel Adlon and arranged to so fill up their time with pleasant diversions that the visitors, upon returning home, denied outright as the grossest fabrications, the other, less wholesome, reports coming out of Germany.

Another American who made his Berlin debut that summer was the youthful Douglas Brinkley, who claimed to be a well-known radio commentator for the Columbia Broadcasting System (although the European representative of CBS denied this to Messersmith). Putzi Hanfstaengl passed Brinkley off as a guest speaker at one of the American Chamber of Commerce's Thursday luncheons, and in July Brinkley addressed Americans via German short-wave: "I came to Germany to become acquainted with actual conditions—to establish the naked facts and to enlighten the American people about the new Germany. Nowhere have I been able to find even the slightest sign of unrest or mistreatment. I am a witness that all disquieting reports about Germany are mere fabrication." Messersmith warned Washington to beware of such informants and worried privately that a growing number of American visitors were being turned into budding propagandists for the New Germany.

Dodd's first audience with the German Foreign Minister, Baron Constantine von Neurath, took place in September. Both Dodd and von Neurath were gentlemen farmers although Dodd was more actively engaged in working the land. Von Neurath's estates in Wuerttemburg had been in the family for generations and he functioned more as an estate manager. Each was a southerner displaced northward by ambition. Both were private men although von Neurath, at age 60, had spent a lifetime in diplomatic posts in Rome and London and had accustomed himself to the tiresome social responsibilities of his calling. The corpulent, bald-headed Foreign Minister was not overly intelligent, but he was wise in the ways of his profession. Disciplined and stoical, his favorite poem ran:

> Think and be quiet
> Feel more than you show
> Bow down before God
> And stay your own master.

Under Germany's new rulers his stoicism would be tried to the limit and his mastery over his own destiny cynically eroded.

During their first meeting Dodd admitted that Americans in Germany could be more careful in the presence of Nazi marchers. They were negligent, it was true, but that was their privilege. Americans rarely saluted their own flag. It was not the custom.

Von Neurath, who wished to avoid a formal warning from Washington, replied that he had spent an entire day with Goering and Hitler discussing how best to deter further attacks. Goering, in particular, had been most sympathetic; Hitler less so. Von Neurath thought the attacks were over. Dodd was sceptical.

Dodd then turned the conversation to American outrage over Germany's treatment of the Jews. Von Neurath said he had sat next to three Jews in Baden Baden a few days before and had failed to notice any hostility. Dodd grew more direct. Public conduct would not moderate so long as Hitler and Goebbels announced publicly, as they had at the Party congress in Nuremberg, that the Jews must be wiped off the face of the earth.

Von Neurath looked embarrassed.

"Is there to be war?" Dodd asked as he rose to depart.

"No, absolutely, no!" exclaimed a horrified von Neurath.

Another war would ruin Germany, Dodd warned.

Afterwards, Dodd was not sure that he had come away with any assurances. The Foreign Minister, like so many other officials in Germany, seemed unable to perceive the historical drift of the times.

The remainder of September passed tranquilly. In October the *New York Times* reported another attack.

> Nothing has stirred American diplomats in Germany for some time as did the spectacle of Roland Velz, a native-born American citizen, standing in the main street of Duesseldorf, with blood streaming down his face from a Nazi assault, and compelled to listen in answer to his plea for the arrest of his assailant to a dissertation by a police lieutenant on the proper manner of saluting the Nazi swastika. The case is regarded as even more serious in view of the fact that spectators of the Nazi parade then passing were standing five and six deep along the curb, and it was behind these Mr. Velz was walking deep in conversation with his wife, quite oblivious to the fact that he was omitting a salute to the flag all but invisible out in the roadway.

Elegantly expressed as was typical of the *New York Times,* the dispatch was none the less subtly distorted. No diplomat had witnessed the attack on Roland Velz and Velz made no mention in his deposition to Messersmith of being lectured on the proper way to salute the Nazi flag. In fact, it had been an outraged bystander, a German citizen, who had encouraged the bloodied Velz to seek the aid of the nearest policeman. This officer actually accosted Velz's attackers but did not use his authority to arrest them. Instead, he referred Velz to his commander who voiced the opinion that Velz should have been more careful. Velz called them both cowards. The two policemen took the insult in silence.

Aside from the Czech Embassy, American authorities were the only ones to vigorously protest attacks on their citizens. In part this was because there were so many more Americans than Englishmen or Frenchmen studying medicine and music and physical science in Germany. Germany had long been a scholastic center for Americans, especially Jewish Americans. But differing diplomatic temperaments also played a part. The French Ambassador, André François-Poncet, thought the American Embassy mistaken when it protested individual acts of violence. There were far larger issues at stake than the fate of a few foreign nationals, François-Poncet thought. The German Government made much the same argument.

Dodd disagreed. American newspaper readers, he knew, were far more concerned with problems at home than with the curtailment of parliamentary democracy in Germany. But attacks on Americans and the German Government's apparent readiness to look the other way outraged even the smallest American farmer and jobless factory worker.

Their countrymen were being mistreated, and thus the mentality of the new regime was brought home to them.

The attack on Roland Velz was the thirty-second since January 30. Thus far not a single assailant had gone to jail although it was rumored that several had been expelled from the Party and the SA. In the only case to come to trial, the victim, an American Jew, had been humiliated in open court and the assailant fined 50 marks or roughly $12. Hull in Washington and Dodd in Berlin were ready for a showdown. Dodd made a second appointment with von Neurath. This time he meant to see Hitler.

Since the start of the Nazi seizure of power, emissaries from America, friends of Germany, had offered open and honest criticism. In July, the American journalist and educator, Sherwood Eddy, arrived in Berlin with his "American Seminar." Rosenberg's "Foreign Office" invited

Eddy to speak at the House of the German Press so at least the flap that ensued did not come to rest at Putzi Hanfstaengl's door.

The audience, German and American, sat through two preliminary talks before Eddy's turn came to speak and there was nothing in his manner as he approached the platform to disturb the saccharine countenances of the assembled guests. Eddy's sympathy for Germany was well known. Two of his children had studied at the University of Freiburg.

Eddy opened with a few remarks about the great educational benefit to be derived from a visit to Germany. Then the unbelievable happened. From his briefcase Eddy drew forth a copy of the *Voelkischer Beobachter*. Bella Fromm, who was in the audience, could just make out the headline: 70,000 JEWS IMMIGRATED INTO GERMANY WITHIN THE LAST 15 YEARS.

"Your laws tend to the extermination of the Jews," Eddy asserted. "Here in a daily paper yesterday is an article on "Why The Influence of Judaism Should Be Broken." Here in my hand is a textbook used in your schools where hatred and contempt for the great Jewish race are instilled into the children of Germany.

"I have myself listened to your orators preaching flaming hatred of the Jews, which was mighty likely to have incited their hearers to pogroms.

"I do not speak of atrocities. These occur in all wars and in the beginning of all revolutions and are always exaggerated in the stories about them. But much more serious is economic elimination, which may lead to the starvation of this despairing people.

"I had hoped to find that there was no longer persecution of the Jews. Instead I have learned from many reliable witnesses, both Jew and Gentile, that the fate of the German Jews is becoming increasingly more hopeless.

"If we cannot excuse or deny or defend the lynching of our Negroes in the United States, although fortunately it is decreasing, you cannot defend or deny the sad fate of all these races and groups and classes.

"I see no hope until together we return to and follow the principles of impartial justice, equal liberty for all and those fundamental principles of moral and economic life upon which the past progress of the human race has been founded."

It was as if a bomb had exploded at a tea party. The Americans present applauded loudly. A few Germans dared to show their agreement but most sat silent and enraged. Eddy's performance had been too cleverly rehearsed to be easily forgiven.

Afterwards Bella rushed up to shake Eddy's hand, but the journalist urged her not to be seen with him. Louis P. agreed. He advised Bella to go home.

The following day Bella took her piece on the Eddy speech to her editor at the *Berliner Zeitung*.

"Very interesting Bella but you know we couldn't print such a piece," he said after reading it through.

She knew that, she said, but she wanted to show that not everyone could be bought.

Her report was filed away for posterity in the Ullstein archives.

Dodd was accustomed to speaking his mind to civic groups in Chicago, the graduating class of Annapolis, and in the pages of the *New York Times*. His hero was Woodrow Wilson, who had gone over the heads of the Eastern gentry and the voices of big business in Congress to address his idealism directly to the people. But when the American Chamber of Commerce invited him to be a guest speaker at one of its Thursday afternoon luncheons, Dodd knew he could not be as ferocious as Eddy. Diplomats might propose toasts and deliver solemn appeals for peace, but beyond that they were expected to keep quiet. That was what their governments expected and what the State Department's handbook prescribed. Under no circumstances were they to involve themselves in the personal liberties of the nation of their posting. Diplomats, after all, neither understood nor enjoyed personal liberties of their own.

In a country steeped in history, Dodd decided to cloak his criticism in historical allegory. Roosevelt had given his consent, but the State Department had only agreed unwillingly. Officials there were already shocked by Dodd's criticism of the inefficiency of the Embassy in Berlin, and they resented the very idea that a schoolmaster would presume to lecture his betters.

All the more reason, in Dodd's mind, to pursue his course.

The American Chamber of Commerce in Berlin was no different from the Chamber of Commerce in Seattle or Topeka or Atlanta. Rarely were its members—representatives of Remington and Hollerith and Ford—distracted from the bracing flavor of their after dinner cigars. Since the Crash, most lecturers from America had confined themselves to the well-worn topic of fearing only fear itself. The Chamber continued to do a healthy business in Germany. In the worst months, March and April, there had been talk of an American boycott of German goods, but the Chamber had sent soothing telegrams to friends in America urging patience and restraint. By the time Dodd arrived in Berlin, the boycott was in disarray and the Chamber had turned its attention to whether American firms which employed Germans could properly add the word "German" to their names. The word "German" after January 30 had become a magic talisman against revolutionary invasion.

Dodd was surprised when he entered the banquet room at the Hotel

Adlon to see more than two hundred guests: diplomats, newspaper correspondents, businessmen, Foreign Ministry officials, even representatives from the Propaganda Ministry. Reichsbank President Hjalmar Schacht was present as was Alfred Rosenberg, who spoke not a word of English.

After a luncheon of green pea soup, roast chicken and sponge cake, Dodd was handsomely introduced and opened with the words: "In times of great stress men are too apt to abandon too much of their past social devices and venture too far upon uncharted courses. And the consequence has always been reaction, sometimes disaster."

On the surface, Dodd seemed to criticize economic nationalism: the enrichment of one country at the expense of another. In reality, he attacked the practice of dictatorship. The German audience, after seven months of Hitler's rule, knew how to listen on several levels. Dodd sensed the tension in the hall as he began but he continued on in the easy-going, expository style he had developed in Chicago.

Since the days when ships began to ply the seas, the well-being of the greatest number over the greatest length of time depended upon free and unrestricted trade. he said. Stuart England, Bourbon France and, recently, America had tried to support its elites in glittering splendor while the peasantry and the common man starved. Economic nationalism was the ploy of autocratic rulers. Caesar might shore up the Roman Republic with dictatorship but only at the expense of exploitation abroad and unsurpassed cruelties at home. The half-educated statesmen of today, Dodd concluded, would do well to look to the lessons of the past.

The 2,500 word speech took barely half an hour to deliver, and Dodd was startled by the strength of the applause when he finished. Reichsbank President Schacht professed surprise that history so strongly supported his economic policies. Goebbels' men told the *New York Times* correspondent that they intended to recommend that the speech be carried in the German press without deletion. Messersmith had listened grinning throughout. In his report to the State Department he had only the highest praise for Dodd's shrewdness.

Bella stopped by Dodd's table afterwards and congratulated him on his choice of examples. Dodd smiled his ironic smile and said he hoped Frau Bella had been able to read his meaning between the lines. She assured him that every enlightened listener had.

In the days following, the speech was the talk of the diplomatic set. Most people praised the American Ambassador for his integrity. A few thought the speech undiplomatic. All were impressed at Dodd's display of invincibility.

"Too bad you were not present to hear it," Bella remarked to André François-Poncet.

The French Ambassador smiled charmingly. "The situation is very, very difficult," he observed. "One is at once a diplomat and must hide one's feelings. One must please one's superiors at home and yet not be expelled from here but I too am glad that his Excellency Mr. Dodd cannot be subverted by flattery and high honor."

The *New York Times,* which had once criticized Dodd for not keeping his mouth shut, printed the entire text in its pages. Roosevelt was reported to be pleased beyond measure while numerous Germans from the academic and business worlds approached Dodd privately to say how grateful they were for his words of support. The State Department, with a longer collective memory, was not so forgiving; ammunition came their way the following day when Dodd's second meeting with von Neurath was abruptly cancelled. Correspondents fumed at the rebuff. In Washington the rumor spread that the schoolmaster had offended his hosts and was being made to stand in a corner.

In fact, as Dodd suspected, something more momentous than a minor diplomatic feud was in the air. Hitler had called an emergency cabinet meeting. Hindenburg had returned to the capital. The following day, Hitler announced to the world that Germany was pulling out of the League of Nations. At this news the State Department turned against Dodd again by complaining publicly that their Ambassador in Berlin had not predicted the move in advance.

Dodd's enemies in Washington meant to permanently damage his reputation. Eventually, an article appeared in *Fortune* magazine that struck him to the quick. Entitled "Their Excellencies, Our Ambassadors," the article listed each of Roosevelt's sixteen envoys with a number of dollar signs before their names to indicate their personal fortunes. That was not to suggest, the authors cautioned, that the Ambassador to France, "$$$$ Straus" was only eight times as wealthy as the Ambassador to Spain, "½$ Bowers." In front of Dodd's name was a single "¢" sign. His speech before the American Chamber of Commerce was raked up anew, and he was told that he lacked the necessary glossiness of tact to be a diplomat. He was also offered some free advice: he should shout more in his dealings with the Germans. The authors then went on to mock his principles and his family. They ridiculed the modesty of his first rooms at the Adlon (which had been neither modest nor at the Adlon) and hinted that he took advantage of Jews by renting from them in their distress. The authors laughed at his son who had agreed to be his father's chauffeur but was now too busy sowing his oats. Dodd, they said, had to beg rides from his aides.

The arrows were so deftly placed that they could only have come from sources close to the State Department. The effect was libelous if not unpatriotic, Dodd felt. He was pretty sure a Washington journalist named John Franklin Carter was behind much of the innuendo. He did not know that Carter was a close friend of Putzi Hanfstaengl.

But Dodd had accomplished more than he knew. Two days after his speech to the Chamber of Commerce, Goebbels loosened the gag on the German press. A German news service announced that the glass blower Paul Eckhardt and the chauffeur Friedrich Wilbertz, the assailants in the Velz case, would be tried by a special court in Berlin. The *Voelkischer Beobachter* carried a report of the trial on its front page. In another release, Group Leader Karl Ernst stated that four SA men who had beaten a Swiss citizen and a clerk in the British Embassy were on their way to Oranienburg concentration camp. Dodd's efforts on behalf of the democracies had succeeded. A hole had been torn in the curtain of German censorship. In their meeting a few days later, Hitler assured Dodd personally that he would see to it that future offenders were punished to the limit of the law.

Attacks on Americans petered out that fall, but at the end of October as the weary American Ambassador walked alone toward the Hotel Esplanade he spied an approaching column of marching SA men. Choosing caution over valor Dodd turned and entered the Tiergarten. He too had learned to bend.

PUTZI IN UNIFORM

With more than a million members entering the Party in the first months of 1933, Germany rushed into uniform. Overnight the country turned brown. Train stations at rush hour resembled military depots, and the Party was forced to issue an edict forbidding civilians from wearing khaki-colored suits. That spring Germany's clothiers ran dangerously low on brown cloth.

Putzi sent to London for a special British weave. Hitler had given him permission to draw a uniform from the Party storehouse, but for a man of Putzi's upbringing the only true tailors were British tailors. The uniform was his own creation and was cut from the finest brown garbardine. Its effect was startling. The tunic was olive, the shirt green-hued, the breeches yellowish. On his lumpish, disproportionate frame, the tight-fitting uniform resembled the skin on a cucumber. With the additional inches that the brown kepi added to his stature, Putzi stuck out in photographs of the time like a hulking, round-shouldered bear.

Dressed in his new regalia, he marched into the Hotel Adlon to take his old friend Hamilton Fish Armstrong, the editor of *Foreign Affairs,* to see Hitler.

"Why Putzi," exclaimed Ham Fish ironically, "I've never seen you in uniform before. How magnificent."

"Yes, it is rather good, isn't it? Don't tell anyone, but it's English stuff. That does make a difference."

Hitler's comment when he caught sight of Hanfstaengl was: "You look like a Turkish whore."

That evening Putzi premiered his creation at the home of Louis P. Lochner and his wife. With their close ties to Berlin's cultural scene, Louis and Hilde Lochner hoped to act as a bridge between Germany's new rulers and the republican past. Their guests that night were the Messersmiths, Sigrid Schultz, several officials from the American Embassy and their wives, two former ministers from the late Republic and a Jewish banker and his wife. The dinner was a black tie affair. Putzi's RSVP had been one of the first to return, but on the evening of the promised event he was nowhere to be seen. The dinner hour of 8 PM came and went; Hilde Lochner was just about to signal the servants to open the dining room doors when Putzi arrived, resplendent in SA uniform and lacquered storm boots. Delicate gold epaulets clung precariously to his rower's shoulders. Several guests winced. One gasped "The Gestapo!"

"My butler simply could not find my evening clothes," Putzi confessed. "So at the last moment I had to put on my uniform."

For a few uneasy moments everyone wondered if he would go through the reception line shouting the Party salute but he settled for shaking hands and clicking his heels. "Good evening, Your Excellency," he said to General Groener who, under the Republic, had several times withdrawn the right of the SA and SS to march in uniform. Putzi kissed each lady's hand and bent double to reach the hand of roly-poly Frau Sobernheim, the wife of the "non-Aryan" banker, Curt Sobernheim. When Sobernheim's turn came, the Jewish banker remarked impishly: "I believe, Dr. Hanfstaengl, we are somewhat related."

Putzi stiffened: "How interesting! What do you mean?"

It seemed that a cousin of Sobernheim's had married into Putzi's family. While the other guests smiled behind their hands, the Jewish banker and Hitler's foreign press chief conferred in earnest on the possible blight to the Hanfstaengl family tree.

Putzi's behavior appeared splendid until about half-way through dinner, when attractive Kitty O'Donoghue, the wife of the 2nd Secretary at the American Embassy, suddenly exclaimed: "I have got to leave, I can't take this." At first Messersmith assumed that she was ill but it turned out that Putzi had been pinching Kitty's leg under the table. Calmly Messersmith leaned over to Putzi and whispered: "If you can't behave like a gentleman I suggest that you leave before I make any scandal about it." As Lilian Mowrer once observed, Putzi was always girl-crazy.

After dinner Louis P. succeeded in getting Putzi and General Groener alone together.

"That man Groener is quite different from what I thought he was," Putzi said later. "He's so nice that I've invited him to have dinner with me some time in my home."

"All my guests are nice," Louis P. replied. "The trouble with you Nazis is that you have strong prejudices against anybody who isn't of your ilk." Unfortunately, the brown shadows deepened that year. Louis and Hilde Lochner had few political evenings after the Party issued an edict forbidding its members from mingling with foreigners.

The "Chauffeureska," as Putzi called Hitler's inner circle, became a permanent feature of the Reich Chancellery after January 30. This watchful phalanx absorbed Hitler's unscheduled moments and gradually excluded other old timers like Hanfstaengl. Venturing among the Chauffeureska on serious business became an exercise in futility. "I have just been down to the Berghof to see the Fuehrer," Baron von Neurath confided to Putzi, "but you know, Hanfstaengl, it is impossible to talk to him alone for more than a few minutes on end. One of those louts is always barging in."

Lunchtime was the worst. Hitler was invariably late. When he finally did arrive at two or three in the afternoon to dine on tomato soup and asparagus omelette, he sat among the Chauffeureska at one end of Chef Kannenberg's canteen to jape and jeer and be amused. That spring Hitler's rancor against the foreign press knew no bounds, and Putzi also frequently felt the sting of his displeasure.

"What is America but millionaires, beauty queens, stupid records and Hollywood," Hitler mocked. "I see America from where I sit much more clearly than you ever have."

So ran the logic of the victorious. Consul General Messersmith was not the only one to despair of ever holding a reasonable conversation with Germany's new rulers.

For relief, Putzi traveled. In June he accompanied Baron von Neurath and the German delegation to the World Economic Conference in London. The rumor was that he came as Hitler's unofficial spy; the British Embassy cabled Whitehall to take anything Dr. Hanfstaengl might say with a large grain of salt. His ideas on history were fantastic; his personality utterly eccentric.

In London he hobnobbed with the mighty, met Elinor Glyn, talked to William Randolph Hearst, and received a picture from Lloyd George inscribed: "To Chancellor Hitler, in admiration of his courage, determination and leadership." At a house party given by Mrs. Richard Guiness he met Unity and Diana Mitford, the comely daughters of the eccentric Lord Redesdale. "He is David to Hitler's Saul," Mrs. Guiness told the two Mitford girls by way of introduction. Putzi shook their hands. His own were huge and overheated.

Later that afternoon, the subject of the Jews came up.

"Oh, the Jews, the Jews, that's all one ever hears in London," Putzi lamented. "What about the Jews? People here have no idea of what the Jewish problem has been in Germany since the war. Why not think for once of the ninety-nine per cent of the population, of the six million unemployed. Hitler will build a great and prosperous Germany for the Germans. If the Jews don't like it they can get out. They have relations and money all over the world. Let them leave Germany to us Germans."

Before he left, he invited the Mitford sisters to look him up if they ever came to Munich. They didn't need his address; everyone knew him.

When Unity and Diana arrived in Munich in August they discovered that everyone did not know Dr. Hanfstaengl. The concierge at their hotel had never heard of him. The *Hausmeister* at the Brown House was more helpful; he would tell the Herr Doktor that they were in town. The next day Putzi telephoned: "You have come at exactly the right moment. We are having our *Parteitag* tomorrow. I will get you tickets and a room in Nuremberg."

From the word "Tag" the girls had assumed that the festival lasted only a day and when they arrived in Nuremberg they were unprepared for the thousands upon thousands of men and women who filled the town and spilled out onto the hills beyond. Putzi met them at the train station dressed in his uniform. Unity giggled behind her hand at the sight of his bulk stuffed into tight breeches and high riding boots. He immediately took them to the Deutscher Hof to meet Hitler, but on the way there he became so alarmed at their heavy makeup that he drew them into an alleyway to explain that it was not the German custom to wear paint. He offered them his clean handkerchief. Diana complied, but Unity refused.

"You mustn't wear lipstick," Putzi implored. "The Fuehrer doesn't like it." He so much wanted Hitler to meet some youthful representatives of the British ruling class.

"I couldn't *possibly* do without it," Unity replied with finality.

They sat in the Deutscher Hof while Putzi watched nervously as members of the Chauffeureska filed past their table to appraise his companions. He was not surprised when Hess eventually appeared to say that the Fuehrer was busy. The failure Putzi attributed to Unity's lipstick.

He squired them about Nuremberg and took them to the speeches and parades and otherwise acted as their bodyguard and protector. Eventually, Unity met Hitler through Julius Streicher. Putzi was careful after that to keep his distance lest the jealous Chauffeureska make the attractive Unity another excuse to libel him. The following year when Diana and Unity asked him to take them to the Party congress again, he refused.

"Why?" Hitler asked them afterwards.

"Because of our lipstick," Unity replied.

Hitler laughed. How typical of Hanfstaengl. Always those American spinsters and what did he do when he had the chance to introduce someone comely? He failed.

Rudolf Hess kindly made room for Putzi with the Liaison Office near the Chancellery. Hess had studied in Munich; he and Putzi were on speaking terms, which counted for a lot in the early days of the Third Reich. Just what the Liaison Office did was not so clear. Its stated purpose was to coordinate the aims of the Party with the agencies of the former State. Party bigwigs besieged Hess with demands for jobs and special privileges. Hess stymied these in bureaucratic bottlenecks until the Liaison Office became a cul-de-sac for revolutionary energies. In retaliation, Party bosses called Hess "Black Bertha" behind his back.

Putzi's job at the Liaison Office was to receive representatives of the foreign press and other foreigners curious to learn more about the recent upheaval in Germany. As his assistant he chose Harald Voigt, a former newspaperman from Dresden, and a Party member. His secretary was Agatha von Hausberger, a German woman who had lived in New York for many years and whose latest husband was a ne'er-do-well former cavalry officer. To support her family, Agatha sold the *Book of Knowledge* to members of Hoboken's German community. In two and half years she sold 304 sets of which 81 were returned, some with letters protesting Frau von Hausberger's relentless sales tactics. Eager to start a new life for herself, Agatha left her husband and journeyed to Berlin with her eight-year-old daughter. To her surprise she received the second highest position held by a woman under the regime when Putzi hired her as his personal secretary. Short and energetic, "Adi" von Hausberger was the perfect personality to take charge of Putzi's turbulent office. She kept his appointment book, transmitted his often outlandish whims, and apologized without embarrassment for his frequent absences.

The task of keeping track of the deluge of letters from America that poured into his old office at the Brown House Putzi left to Rolf Hoffmann, a dandy with bushy black hair and an affected British accent. Hoffmann was good at his job. Through him, proper Bostonians, eastern prep school students and boy scouts from the American Midwest secured hotel accommodations, press passes and special tours. Politely, Hoffman answered the letter of an American fascist leader who wanted to know if there was a place for him in the New Germany, passed on requests for audiences with the Fuehrer to Putzi in Berlin, and filed the scads of letters from American cranks attesting their undying hatred of the Jews: "Out upon you, Israel! . . . Faugh! . . . Phewy! . . ." Even the appeal from a former assistant attorney general of Massachusetts for a copy of *Mein Kampf* autographed by Hitler received Hoffmann's personal attention. The heavy volume was duly shipped off with Putzi's signature on the flyleaf.

No one was better at impressing curious foreigners with a theatrical look, a disdainful snort or a brilliant pun than the ebullient Hanfstaengl. Putzi was at his best with newcomers to Germany, visitors seeing the country for the first time, who were perhaps more eager than they knew to connect with a grandiloquent host, a royal spokesman who could cast their apprehensions aside with a wave of his hand. Patriotic Americans of German descent were especially drawn to him. They came to praise

Germany, not to criticize her, and they were hungry for any sign that their homeland had regained the prestige it had lost under the colorless and faintly disreputable Republic. But Putzi probably drove away as many friends of the New Germany as he attracted with his alternatingly imperious and ingratiating moods. Some were lost in the shuffle, others abandoned in restaurants or left waiting for hours at the Party's Liaison Office. Putzi fished haphazardly in the social currents that flowed his way and, as often as not, when his temper flared, rejected prize catches.

When Frederick L. Schuman, a political scientist from the University of Chicago, arrived in Berlin with his wife and one-year-old son to assemble material for his book *Nazi Dictatorship: A Study in Social Pathology and the Politics of Fascism,* he was rudely rebuffed by Hanfstaengl for his Jewish appearance. The 29-year-old assistant professor concluded that Hitler's court jester was pathetically insecure and tormented by overblown social conceits. When Mrs. Kate Pohli-MacLeod, a pillar of the German community in the San Francisco Bay area, arrived in Berlin she was given such short shrift at a reception hosted by Putzi—after being snubbed by Rosenberg and Goebbels—that she feared that her goodwill toward the New Germany would crack completely.

When Robert Bernays, British M. P. and reporter for the *News Chronicle,* came to Berlin to see Hitler on the Jewish question, he never got further than Putzi.

"Your Press, your law, your finance, your politics, are all controlled by the Jews," Putzi thundered and then as suddenly switched to a denunciation of the writer Lytton Strachey: "What a mean and dirty attack that was on Queen Victoria. Now, Dickens really expresses the soul of England."

Mr. Bernays replied that he was not aware that Lytton Strachey had Jewish ancestors, but that was beside the point. The point was that the entire British nation had been shocked by the cruelty of the Jewish persecutions in Germany.

"There ought to have been more discrimination," Putzi agreed, "but you must realize that it was a revolution last March, not a change of Government.

"Let the French march to Berlin if they like. We have no power to prevent them. You in England do not know what Communism means. You have not a single Communist M. P. We have actual proof that on a certain night all the lights in Berlin would have gone out. Then came the firing of the Reichstag. Can you wonder that we have 700,000 auxiliary troops? They are not armed. They are not Reichswehr. They could not keep order if they were. The psychology would be wrong. What is the alternative to Hitler? Communism. If Hitler goes, Communism comes in. Bruening? My dear Mr. Bernays, he is hopeless. No magnetism; charming, but oh, so feeble! He is not a political leader. Hitler has the power of organizing and inspiring. He is what your Lloyd George was in the war. Hitler will co-operate with anyone to meet Communism and war. It is like a ship—when all goes well, all the passengers quarrel among themselves; then the fire breaks out and they are all one. Hitler realizes the ramifications of the ship and that we are all in the same boat."

Mr. Bernays never got his interview with the Fuehrer. "Herr Hammstaengl," he recalled, saw to that.

One had to really know Putzi to dislike him, Quentin Reynolds decided. Putzi had taken an immediate fancy to the Irish-American graduate of Brown University and lost no time in addressing him by his nickname, Quent. Putzi even helped Quent out with a problem his housemaid was having with the SA. Quent's housemaid was from Bavaria and insisted on greeting shopkeepers in Berlin with the traditional salutation *"Gruess Gott"* rather than the bellicose *"Heil Hitler."* Several SA men wanted to take her down to their barracks for "questioning." Quent asked them to wait until he telephoned Hitler's chief of the foreign press. Luckily, Putzi was in his office.

"Let me speak to one of those nitwits," Putzi demanded. "Have you nothing better to do than to annoy a simple peasant girl who works for the representative of the great Hearst organization? If you ever bother her again, I will complain personally to Ernst Roehm and he will take care of you."

The housemaid was never bothered again.

Looking back on it, Quent decided that it was the trip he took with Martha and Bill Dodd in July and the report he wrote on the sight of poor Betti Suess in Nuremberg that soured his good relations with Putzi. When Quent returned to Berlin, there was an urgent message from Putzi to see him immediately.

"There isn't one damned word of truth in your story!" Putzi thundered. "I've talked with our people in Nuremberg and they say nothing of the sort happened there."

"You're dead right," Quent mocked. "I just wanted to impress my New York office so I faked that story from beginning to end."

With that Putzi, launched into a long harangue on journalistic ethics until he saw that Quent was pulling his leg. What was more, Quent said, he had two unimpeachable witnesses, the children of the American Ambassador! With a moan of dismay Putzi slumped across his desk. Why did Quent torment him so . . .?

Otherwise, how explain Putzi's discourtesy to "Mom" and "Pop" Reynolds when they came to visit Quent in Berlin shortly before his return to New York? With the help of Tom Delmer, the press corps' most lavish host, Quent threw a party for his parents in his nine-room apartment on the Bruecken Allee. Delmer selected the wines, drew up the menu, even donated his cook and butler. Sigrid Schultz, Knick, Crown Prince Louis Ferdinand and Bill and Martha Dodd came to dinner. The German guests arrived later, among them Putzi and that old sea dog Count von Luckner. Putzi was soon crooning like Chanticleer at the piano while Quent, whose high school German had improved somewhat, translated for his mother.

"You do not understand German, Mrs. Reynolds?" Putzi asked. "For you then, I shall sing a song I wrote myself."

Since his first meeting with Hitler Putzi had amused himself by writing marches for the Hitler Youth. "Youth on the March," "Dreams of Youth," and "Young Heroes" were several of his compositions. In 1924 he published a sampling of these in his *Hitler Song Book*. The lyrics did not always set the finest example for youthful imitation. The Rhenish peasant tune, *"Deutsche voran,"* for instance, told of maurading Poles on Germany's east, black men along the Rhein and the wheel of Germany's misfortune greased by Jewish financiers. Time had not improved his choice of lyrics. As Putzi launched into his latest effort, he took care to sing softly so that Knickerbocker and Sigrid Schultz did not hear. For one brief moment Quent, an amateur boxer, considered sending a roundhouse right to Hanstaengl's prominent jaw until the soft voice of Louis Ferdinand intervened: "What could you prove, Quent? After all, bad manners are bad weapons."

Count von Luckner broke the tension by inviting everybody into the dining room to witness a demonstration of how he could tear a telephone book in half with his bare hands. Upstaged, Putzi announced that he had to play for the Fuehrer that evening. Seeing him to the door Quent looked Putzi straight in the eye and said, "Never come to my house again, you louse."

One afternoon in September, a rough cut of Putzi's film, "Horst Wessel: A German Destiny," was premiered before a select audience of old fighters at the Ministry of Propaganda. In his introductory remarks Dr. Goebbels reminisced about Sturmfuehrer Wessel, the first SA leader to form a Brown Shirt detachment in Communist Berlin. The film, Goebbels predicted, would stand as a monument to the conquest of Berlin and it was only fitting that they, the friends and comrades of Horst Wessel, be the first to preview the tribute.

Although the rough cut lacked the final scene of Wessel's burial, the screening left a strong impression. Many an old fighter that afternoon was brought back to former days. "As a former comrade of Wessel's," one said, "who knew him well in life and death, I was deeply affected by the film's authenticity and the historical accuracy down to the smallest detail." Jules Sauerwein of *le Temps* said the crowd scenes surpassed even those of Eisenstein's "Battleship Potemkin." Berkeley Gage of the *New York Times* compared the film to "Birth of a Nation."

In October, the film was shown again to a specially invited audience in the Capitol Cinema next to the Gedaechtniskirche. Among those in attendance were Minister President Goering, Pilli Koerner, Rudolf Diels, Wilhelm Furtwaengler, Lord Mayor Sahm, Hjalmar Schacht and Count von Luckner. Afterwards, Schacht pronounced Putzi's score "splendid." Count von Luckner told reporters: "The tears literally sprang from my eyes and they were honest tears! I was that moved by 'Horst Wessel.'"

It came as quite a shock when, barely a week later, on the evening of the film's official premier and the 26th anniversary of Wessel's birth, Goebbels banned the film throughout the length and breadth of the Reich as unworthy of its subject's heroic stature and demeaning to the reputation of the New Germany.

Under Goebbels' direction, the press did a complete about face: the author of the screenplay was a gutter writer, the film's producers closet literati. The direction stank. Goebbels' paper, *Der Angriff,* left the impression that the Propaganda Minister had seen the film at the last moment. Nothing was said about the earlier premier in September.

"We National Socialists see no value in our SA marching on the stage or screen," Goebbels said in an interview. "Such a blatant show of National Socialist ideology is no substitute for real art. Therefore it is so difficult as to be almost impossible to make a film that is truly equal to the spirit of such an exalted organization as the SA."

Putzi, who had invested his own money in the film, appealed to Goebbels personally, but the little Doctor had a thousand and one excuses why the film could not be released: it was too bourgeois, too Christian, too unrevolutionary, too trite, and, in its depiction of street violence, insulting to the fine tradition of the Berlin police! Putzi and the Party's film company, the Volksdeutsche Filmgemeinschaft, had no choice but to withdraw the film and re-edit. The Central Censorship Board let it be known that it might reverse its decision if the film were to be constructed around an SA man other than Wessel.

In all, 27 deletions were made. The finished product, "Hans Westmar: One Among Many," premiered at the Capitol Cinema on December 13 before the entire diplomatic corps, the German Crown Prince, Baldur von Schirach, Group Leader Karl Ernst, Rudolf Diels and other luminaries.

To ward off a second attack, Putzi told the press in advance: "Leonardo da Vinci painted Christ 1500 years after the Savior's death . . . who knows how much time must pass before the gigantic struggle for Germany's destiny will be portrayed in all its completeness."

Again the German press was ecstatic in its praise, calling "Hans Westmar" a monument, a masterpiece, an unforgettable experience and praising Putzi's score for its elementary beauty. Hitler declared the film's funeral march, "Deutschland trauert," the Party's official funeral dirge. Putzi was in seventh heaven. The Central Censorship Board awarded the film its highest Mark of Distinction: "politically and artisitically especially valuable." But again Goebbels interfered, blocking the film's distribution until after the New Year, causing it to lose valuable holiday revenues, and cutting off funds for the purchase of additional prints. The public did not see "Hans Westmar" until February 1934. By then, disillusion with the revolution and the SA had set in, and "Hans Westmar" showed to chilly, half-filled houses. In desperation, Putzi used his own money to make prints and took these to Stockholm and Rome. The film opened in faraway Tokyo, but on the continent it had lost the spontaneity of the moment. Putzi's dream of cinema renown was crushed.

SUICIDE

In the early days when Bella Fromm was trying to make the move from ice hockey to society reporter she was befriended by the brilliant newspaper columinist, Wera von Huhn. Although more than twenty years Bella's senior, Wera's long hair and high forehead gave her such a look of eternal youthfulness that her friends called her "Poulette," a play on the word "Huhn," which means "chicken" in German. Poulette was fluent in several languages and had traveled all over the world. Her late husband, Arthur, had been a leading political columnist in the Kaiser's day. Poulette taught Bella the trick of making diplomatic reporting interesting by concentrating on the wives and families of foreign envoys. The two were inseparable companions and frequently the only women invited to Berlin's traditionally male diplomatic functions.

One evening late in November, Poulette, Bella's mentor, teacher, and second mother went to her room, wrote a farewell note and took fourteen tablets of the powerful sedative Veronal. It was the eve of the twentieth anniversary of her husband's death. A note she left in the kitchen asked the maid not to disturb her in the morning.

Suicide in Germany was an honorable, if sad end, and on the rise. In June, Poulette's personal physician had taken his life.

"From now on I shall collect sleeping drugs," Poulette told Bella who failed to understand.

In October, Goebbels had announced his infamous "Editors Law," banning any German with one or more Jewish grandparents from practicing journalism after the end of the year. Germany's racial theorists had failed in their attempt to identify "non-Aryans" by blood or body type. Therefore, citizens who hoped to continue to work in the restricted professions of medicine, law, and public information had to consult religious records going back to 1800 to furnish proof of racial purity. In Lutheran Germany, these records were unusually complete. In November, Poulette discovered that one of her grandparents, two generations earlier, had regularly attended synagogue.

What should she do? How would she earn a living? Journalism was her only livelihood. At her age she could not find another profession. She had already endured the passing of the monarchy and the death of her beloved Arthur. It was too much for one woman to bear. Bella, whose

Jewish ancestry had never been in doubt, comforted her friend as best she could. They would survive somehow, Bella promised.

Others took the discovery in higher spirits. At the racetrack one day Bella heard the descendant of one of Germany's princely houses announce loudly: "Children, I am rehabilitated. They have hunted up a non-Aryan grandmother in my pedigree. Thank heaven! It is really a disgrace not to belong to the outcastes."

Germany's Jewish minority of 600,000 was growing by leaps and bounds.

At the end of November, the weather in Berlin turned rainy with raw winds and fog. The night Poulette took her overdose of Veronal, Bella attended the "Little Press Ball" given by the foreign press at the Hotel Adlon. When Poulette said she was too tired to attend, Bella made a mental note to see her friend the next day. Despite the cold weather outside, the ball that year was as light and gay as ever. At the largest table sat the Dodds with Sigrid Schultz, Louis P. and Vice Chancellor von Papen. Afterwards, in the wee hours of the morning, the inner circle withdrew to Sigrid's home to dine on small sandwiches prepared by Mother Schultz.

The next morning, when Bella telephoned Poulette for her customary chat she was told that the "Baroness" was still asleep. Seized by a horrible premonition, Bella dressed hurriedly and raced across town to Poulette's residence on the Beethovenstrasse. Brushing aside the maid's objections, she ran into Poulette's bedroom: "Poulette, Poulette—it's Bella. Wake up!"

But Poulette could not wake up. She was in a coma. Her breath came in ragged gasps.

Doctors were summoned. Windows were thrown open but the poison was not in the air. Through her tears Bella read Poulette's farewell note.

> I can't live any more because I know I will be forced to give up my work. You have been my best friend, Bella. Please take all my files and use them. I thank you for all the love you gave me. I know you are brave, braver than I am, but I know you must live because you have a child to think of, and I am sure that you will bear the struggle far better than I could.
>
> Yours,
>
> Poulette.

The doctors did everything they could, but the powerful sedative had done its work. Poulette died without ever regaining consciousness.

"She did not suffer any pain," the doctors told a distraught Frau Fromm.

The Kaiser and Kaiserin sent a wreath. At the Foreign Ministry a flighty Chief of Protocol, Ru Bassewitz, advised Bella to record Poulette's death as pneumonia. Bella noted Poulette's passing in *Tante Voss* between a description of a dinner at the Austrian embassy and a Thanksgiving celebration at the American Church. Before the foreign correspondents she kept up a bold front, but the funeral was almost too much to bear.

"*Bellachen,* we are all so shocked that the new regulations should have this affect," babbled the dowager Mammi von Carnap. Frau von Neurath advised Bella to accept the rites of Christian baptism. Poor creatures, Bella mused, they mistook the issue for one of religion.

Others, she knew, had found protectors. That was the case with the blue-eyed Erhard Milch, Goering's Secretary of State in the Air Ministry. Censorship had raised gossip to the level of official communication. No sooner were secret agents dispatched to the Jewish cemetery in Breslau to bring back a photo of the Milch family headstone than Berlin society was a-twitter with the latest proof of Milch's suspicious parentage. In the officers' canteen at the Air Ministry, Goering brashly echoed a famous anti-Semitic remark from the previous century: "I decide who is or is not a Jew." Milch's pedigree, Bella heard, had to be doctored for inclusion in the *Fuehrer Lexikon*. Descendent of Saxon and Brandenburg peasants, indeed!

Even history writ large was retouched or erased completely. Since the purging of Jewish and Marxist elements from the professions, a debate had raged over the number of German Jews who had served at the front during the Great War. Those who had, it was rumored in official circles, might continue in their professions for a while longer. The Party press, however, insisted that the term "Jewish Front Soldier" was a misnomer. Those Jews who had served in the German Army, it argued, had been unwilling conscripts who had quickly taken noncombatant jobs in the rear. Those few who actually fell for their country had assuredly displayed a courage that came from the Aryan side of their racial mixtures. In reply, the National League of Jewish Front Soldiers rushed out a *Heldenbuch* listing the names of over 10,000 Jews who had died in the 1914–18 conflict. The Army announced that it could only confirm 7,000 of the dead from its records. The Propaganda Ministry hinted that most of these had died of natural causes. In the end it seemed that not a single German of Jewish descent had been among the millions slaughtered in Europe's greatest conflict.

The lesson to be drawn from the Milch case was clear: the Editor's Law allowed for certain exceptions. One need only find a powerful enough protector. In her grief over Poulette's death Bella turned to

General Werner von Blomberg, the blond, tranquil Minister of Defense. Quiet, unassuming and well-read for a general, Blomberg had toured America in 1930 before going to Geneva as Germany's expert on disarmament. His appointment as Minister of Defense in Hitler's cabinet was Hindenburg's doing. Hindenburg expected Blomberg to hold the Army for the Junker class, but to everyone's dismay Blomberg quickly fell under Hitler's spell. Behind the General's back, his colleagues dubbed him the "Rubber Lion."

"We are very anxious, Frau Bella, to have you keep your job," Blomberg said. "The Diplomatic Corps feels exactly the same way about it. The Nuncio spoke to us in the name of all foreign diplomats. Secretary of State Dr. Heinrich Lammers, chief of Hitler's office, is also on your side. He and Vice-Chancellor von Papen, together with us, have submitted a petition to Goebbels. My adjutant is going to forward the correspondence to you."

Indeed, there was not another journalist in Germany who could call in as many favors as Bella. Von Papen spoke to Baron von Neurath, and Ru Bassewitz appealed directly to the lipless Otto Dietrich, Chief of the German press. The entire diplomatic corps rallied behind her as well as the American colony and the American Church in Berlin. Dr. Stadtler, Ullstein's new "political director," wrote her a glowing recommendation. Bella spent part of Christmas penning appeals to German bureaucrats. She closed her letters "With German Greeting," the most restrained of the revolutionary salutations that year.

The correct procedure, as Goebbels graciously pointed out in his reply to Blomberg, was somewhat different. Part II, Section 9 of the Editor's Law stipulated that the State Association of the German Press might petition the National Association of the German Press for a waiver of the Aryan clause in certain cases subject, of course, to his, Goebbel's, approval. Frau Fromm should not expect her case to be settled in a day. Whether or not she qualified for a waiver would be carefully gone into. Goebbels ended his letter with "Kindest regards"; whereas Blomberg, in his appeal, had closed with the formal "Heil Hitler." Bella had to smile at this reversal of roles.

On New Year's day 1934 she covered President von Hindenburg's reception for the Diplomatic Corps and her report, unsigned, appeared on the front page of *Tante Voss*. She was still working two days past the deadline when her editor summoned her to his office.

"The Ullstein press has received a verbal veto against articles *signed* by you," Dr. Welter said.

"I've been expecting it."

"We need your stuff, Bella. And I think we can fix it, especially in view of the fact that the law doesn't take effect until April. You bring in your material and we'll have it written by people with a style different from yours. And you'll get paid as usual."

For the past ten months Bella's understudy had been a youthful Party member named Brecht who boasted of his acquaintance with Goebbels, whom he resembled slightly, and whom he referred to as "Jupp." Brecht was literate only in the art of manipulation, but Bella pretended to dote on him and occasionally gave him rides about town to hear the latest Party gossip. Brecht had wrangled himself a Leica but still no automobile. Bella was sure he would be marvelous at disguising her prose. Only the other day he had asked her to explain the difference between an embassy and a legation!

Her skirmishes with the Government press associations continued. The National Association denied her appeal to be considered a "free lance assistant" at Ullstein, on the grounds that it would neither increase nor decrease the difficulties of her case. The reply from the State Association was even more evocative of the troubles of Herr K. in the novel *The Trial*. She was informed that her request to be exempted from the Aryan clause could not be granted on the grounds that she was not Aryan!

When Ullstein filed an appeal, the Party press took the attack to the public.

"PRESS MOLES IN DISGUISE," cried the *Deutsche Wochenschau.* "BELLA FROMM AND THE BERLINER ZEITUNG."

In one of her columns Bella had made the blunder of identifying Dr. Eduard Stadtler, Ullstein's new political director, as an "Old Guard" National Socialist. Stadtler was nothing of the kind insisted the *Wochenschau,* whose editor, Gottfried Feder, was one of the mythical seven who had founded the National Socialist German Workers Party in Munich. In the Reichstag, Stadtler had been a free-thinking Nationalist who, only a few weeks before Hitler came to power, went on record as being terribly disillusioned with the Leader. Of course, the Jewess Bella Fromm would characterize Stadtler as an old guard Nazi! The Jewish press knew how to distort National Socialism. The House of Ullstein was only making a pretense of coordination. Jewish liberalism knew how to bide its time.

Bella was innocent. Stadtler had duped the entire House. In a brief meeting with the Ullstein brothers, he had passed himself off as an old crony of Hitler's. The brothers had taken him on as their "political director" at a fabulous salary. Although Stadtler had by then joined the Nazi delegation in the Reichstag, Goebbels was unforgiving and blocked his application for Party membership. So Stadtler fabricated a story and chose one of the largest publishing houses in Germany to bilk. With

Ullstein in his pocket Stadtler hoped to make himself indispensable to the Party. Bella, like the Ullsteins, was caught between the wolves and the opportunists. The story was typical of the times.

The new year also nearly saw the end of Bella's smooth relations with General von Blomberg. A junior editor at Ullstein was foolish enough to print a satirical piece lampooning the army. Blomberg was furious and threatened to shut Ullstein down. Bella's editor called her in a panic: "Bella, dear, as usual, you're the only one who might be able to help, or else it means ten thousand employees thrown into the street."

Bella called the General's home and talked to his daughter Sybille. Her father was still furious, Sybille said. Bella should come by in the morning for breakfast when he was in a better mood.

"Well, what the hell do you want?" Blomberg thundered when he saw Bella the next day. Bella began to cry. The author must be a Bolshevik, the General exclaimed. Swiss? No difference. If he was not back on his Alp in forty-eight hours the Ullstein concern would be dynamited off pulisher's row. Bella nodded and wiped her eyes.

The General softened: "How is your own affair working out, Frau Bella?"

"I imagine I'm going to be fired," Bella said. "There seems to be no other way. Minister Goering spoke to Goebbels about it. He said afterward that it was the worst blunder he could have made, because Goebbels would never help anyone for whom he had intervened."

Bella's contact in Goering's office was the youthful Martin Sommerfeldt, like Rudolf Diels a holdover from a more lenient age. At a reception at the Italian Embassy Sommerfeldt took Bella aside. "The Minister President appreciates your importance as a mediator with the diplomats," he said. "Maybe something can be done. Right now Goering is trying to persuade Hitler to take authority over the press from the dwarf's clutches and put it back into Goering's hands. If he manages to talk Hitler into such an arrangement, you are safe and under our full protection."

In reality the plan was Sommerfeldt's, not Goering's. Sommerfeldt told Goering that as Minister President of Prussia he needed the Berlin press to further his political ends. In his name the Prussian state should demand a financial interest as well as a guiding hand in the publishing houses of Ullstein and Mosse and newspapers such as the *Berliner Tageblatt* and the *Deutsche Allgemeine Zeitung*. A "Goering block" was what Sommerfeldt called it. Goering rubbed his hands together in anticipation of the financial empire to be gained. He telephoned Hitler and made an appointment for Sommerfeldt that afternoon. That had not been Sommerfeldt's idea at all but it was too late to turn back.

When Sommerfeldt met with Hitler he was careful not to mention Goebbels or the notion of a "Goering block." Instead, he conjured up the picture of the international disgrace of a muzzled press in Germany and the necessity of cultivating a "loyal opposition."

Hitler listened in silence. After a minute or two he seized Sommerfeldt's report and tore it to pieces.

"There is no such thing as a loyal opposition," Hitler hissed through clenched teeth. "The last thing I need is opposition of any kind—I don't need agreements—I don't need partners—I need character—system—organization! I will not tolerate any opposition!" Then the old charm returned. Sommerfeldt had only meant well, Hitler said, and left the room.

Goering took the news with a shrug and Goebbels had his revenge when Goering's memoirs "Loyalty in the Air" appeared in the Ullstein's *Berliner Illustrirte*. Goering wrote the first installment himself, and the Ullsteins were only too happy to oblige, hoping to keep Goering as their patron in Prussia. But only one installment of the "The War Experiences of Flight Lieutenant Goering" ever reached the newstands. A furious Goebbels went directly to Hitler and asked if the Fuehrer realized that Goering was publishing his memoirs in the anti-Nazi *Illustrirte*. Hitler asked Goering for an explanation; Goering denied having any part in the unauthorized autobiography and threatened to suspend the *Illustrirte* for its brazenness. Once again the conciliatory Ullsteins had been made to look like troublemakers.

At the beginning of 1934, Karl Jundt, the manager of Ullstein's morning papers, decided to intervene on Bella's behalf. Jundt had been Ullstein's Munich correspondent until Hermann Ullstein, the youngest brother, learned that the Nazis planned to overthrow Bavaria and sent his son down to Munich to warn Premier Held of the impending putsch. Held had boasted that if the Nazis had any thoughts of seizing Bavaria as they had Berlin, they would be arrested at the border. Hermann's son made the mistake of calling on Jundt with the news, and Jundt stepped into a neighboring office where, through the thin walls, he could be heard talking to the Brown House: "We have been betrayed. My firm has just sent a man to Munich to warn the Prime Minister about the Putsch." The Nazis moved swiftly. Held was arrested, Bavaria seized and Jundt promoted to assistant director at Ullstein.

He was not a faithful National Socialist, Bella knew. He had admitted as much to her after a night of drinking. Merely another ambitious journalist who saw his chance to move ahead. Jundt suggested that they talk to the leader of the Nazi cell at Ullstein: "Right now people like that may have more influence than the higher-ups."

Two of the Nazi shop leaders at Ullstein had already been suspended for stealing shop funds and Bella did not recognize the political dandy who entered Jundt's office. The shop leader reeked of perfume and wore a lace hanky in his breast coat pocket. He seemed inordinately interested in the French Ambassador.

Bella was not sure herself precisely where François-Poncet stood. From the moment he arrived in Berlin he had caught her eye with his distinguished dress, sharp wit and icy demeanor. For a time she had even been a little jealous of his wife, the regal Jacqueline. Bella was a severe judge of diplomatic wives.

Unlike the blunt-spoken Dodd, François-Poncet represented the old school of diplomacy. In social gatherings his face, with its glinting monocle, remained an inscrutable mask. Only the force of his arguments hinted at the deep emotional life stirring within him. Unfortunately, his cutting remarks could often be taken two ways, as when he introduced his young secretary, Armand Bérard, to Hitler as *his* young SS man. Germany's liberals found no comfort in François-Poncet's presence in Berlin. Their troubles were not his concern, and he had not protested the attacks on French citizens in Germany with anything like Ambassador Dodd's vehemence. In the French Ambassador's eyes diplomats served sovereigns, not subjects. Only in rare moments did he lash out at the small-minded men who had become Germany's leaders. Yet, he admired Goering, who he believed knew something of the world and possessed a certain social panache. Bella hoped François-Poncet's reports to Paris were more critical, but she feared that life at the French Embassy was too luxurious and its Ambassador too civilized to feel overly anxious about the future.

She said none of this to the fop with the lace hanky. Instead, she played the role of the glib society lady who had only social fluff to offer; descriptions of musical evenings at the French Embassy and the cost of Madame François-Poncet's latest gown. Jundt was dazzled by her anecdotes while the perfumed dandy became more and more frustrated until he rudely broke off the interview by walking out of the room.

Mistaking all the signs, Jundt cried "You win" and proposed that they celebrate Bella's triumph at Kempenski's, a famous non-Aryan restaurant on the Kurfuerstendamm. But Bella was a shrewder judge of her adversaries. As she sat among the mirrors and ornamental china and the dishes of Forelle Blau and Salmon in Lemon Sauce, she reminded herself that the meeting had had nothing to do with winning or losing. Obliquely, she had been offered the chance to turn informer.

She knew other women of social prominence who had become salon spies. One was a baroness, another the sister of the illustrious war ace,

Baron von Richthofen. They had accepted political advances and now entertained on a lavish scale in west end apartments with money they could only have gotten from the Propaganda Ministry or from the secret police. Security, however, was not part of the bargain. Once they had betrayed their friends they would be betrayed in turn and cast aside. All revolutionaries despise loyalty, and Bella's choice was that they despise her from the start.

The interview and its failure revealed to her the battle being waged in the shadows and sent the terror deeper into her soul. In a cupboard in her home lay a small pearl handled revolver from the time when, hardly more than a child, she had worked as a Red Cross nurse. In the Great War, Red Cross nurses were permitted personal weapons, but in the Germany of 1934 people were arrested and taken heaven knew where for lesser offenses. The winter sun set early in January, and one evening on her way to the Spanish Embassy Bella pulled off onto the edge of the Landwehr Canal under the windows of the War Ministry where her protector Kurt von Schleicher had once watched over her. Rolling down her window, she tossed the small revolver into the dark, urban waters of the city that was no longer hers.

A few days later her final attempt to find a loophole in the Editor's Law came to a humorous end. Martin Sommerfeldt had arranged an appointment for her to see the lipless Otto Dietrich, Reich Press Chief, at the Propaganda Ministry. For more than an hour she was kept waiting in an unheated hallway and, when she was finally shown in, Dietrich seemed more interested in what she could tell him about the wife of the Rumanian Minister. Finally, he turned to her case. Her husband had served in the War? Yes, Bella replied. And he had won the Iron Cross 1st Class? He had, she observed.

"And where did he fall?" Dietrich asked gravely.

An astonished Bella replied that Herr Steuermann was still very much alive and working somewhere in the American Midwest.

"In that case," replied a nettled Dietrich, "this conversation is pointless."

Thereafter, Ullstein had no choice but to drop her officially from its roster of reporters. From time to time Ullstein printed an unsigned piece by her and she did what she could to sponsor the goodwill of people outside Ullstein as when she passed on an excerpt of Sommerfeldt's new book *Kommune!*, a study of Communism and criminality, to the Ullsteins for publication. She owed Sommerfeldt that much, she felt, for his trouble on her behalf, and she was grateful that he and his wife continued to invite her to their home. It was at Sommerfeldt's urging that she wrote a weekly column for the *Kleiner Journal*, a crude society sheet she found offensive but which Sommerfeldt hoped might yet convince Goebbels of her usefulness. Bella signed her articles in the *Kleiner Journal,* "Hubert v. Eltuille," Poulette's old pseudonym, thereby mocking the regime and bringing her dear friend to life again.

From time to time Louis P. used one of her news tips. She continued to pay dues to the National Association of German Authors but received nothing in return. In just five months she had lost her best friend, her livelihood and the newspaper she had worked on for more than five years. *Tante Voss's* readership had slipped from 80,000 to less than 50,000, her readers driven off by her errant mutterings about Fuehrer and Fatherland. On the last day of March, 1934, the fine old lady appeared in public for the last time. She had outlived her age.

The next to depart was Bella's 17-year-old daughter, Gonny, who worked as a photographer. She had been talking to "Uncle" George Messersmith about America: "He told me wonderful things about the United States. The freedom, the equal chances, President Roosevelt's program. He promised to help me get to America." Gonny's fiancé had already left for New York, and Bella knew that Germany was no longer a fit place for a young woman of Jewish descent. The Editor's Law applied to photographers as well as journalists.

After Messersmith had prevailed upon the American Chamber of Commerce and its new chairman, Louis P., to write a letter of introduction for Gonny, she promptly received an offer from the *New York Times*. Immigrants to America, no matter how desperate, had to supply proof of employment before they received sanctuary in the New World.

The French Embassy raised 300 marks to buy roses for Bella and something pretty for Gonny, but Bella returned the money with her thanks. There were others who needed it more than her daughter, who was young and vigorous and able to work. The Embassy, nevertheless, insisted upon throwing a farewell party for Gonny.

"America is a hard country, Gonny," said Ambassador François-Poncet. "If it doesn't work out, France is always open, to both of you."

In May, Gonny, sad and pale, boarded the train for the coast. A few days later Bella ran into Putzi Hanfstaengl at a cocktail party. She had not seen the foreign press chief to speak to since the previous year when he had swept Gonny across the dance floor at the Rot-Weiss ball exclaiming: "You should go to the Anthropological Institute for a consultation. I think it is absurd that you should be Jewish. Your skull has the perfect Aryan formation."

When Putzi asked after her daughter, Bella found herself fighting back the tears.

"Now at least help Bella," urged Signora Cerruti, the wife of the Italian Ambassador, "so that she needn't go away also."

With a flourish Putzi summoned his assistant Voigt, in full SS regalia, and instructed him in a loud voice to submit a full report on the Bella Fromm "case." But when she ran into him again outside the American Embassy a few weeks later, he had typically forgotten all about her troubles. The Dodds were throwing a farewell party for Consul General Messersmith who was going to Vienna as the new American Minister.

"I wonder why we were asked today," Putzi complained. "All this excitement about Jews. Messersmith is one. So is Roosevelt. The party detests them."

"Dr. Hanfstaengl," Bella began, "we've discussed this before. You don't have to put on that kind of an act with me."

"All right. Even if they are Aryan, you'd never know it from their actions."

"Of course, if you're going to do away with right and wrong, and make it Aryan and non-Aryan, it leaves people who happen to have rather old-fashioned notions about what is right and wrong, what is decent and what is obscene, without much ground to stand on."

"All right, all right," Putzi relented, lowering his voice. "I have lots of friends in the United States, and all of them side with the Jews, too. But since it is insisted in the party program . . ."

He offered her a fruit drop and before she could stop herself Bella was sucking on a bonbon that bore the imprint of the Party's official seal. The mark of the swastika lasted until the rest of the sweet had dissolved on her tongue.

BEAUS

Since her family's move into the fairy tale residence on the Tiergartenstrasse Martha's days and nights had been filled with a flurry of social engagements. It was the Dodd's first social season and unlike their more experienced British colleagues they did not know enough to flee to the Riviera for a "vacation." The winter season hit them head on, exhilarating Martha, demoralizing her parents. Embossed invitations to elaborate dinners and musical evenings came pouring in from the American Women's Club, the American Chamber of Commerce, and from the scores of foreign embassies and their commercial and consular satellites in Berlin. In turn the Dodds were expected to give dinners and receptions of their own and to receive the wives of Vice Chancellor von Papen, Dr. Goebbels, Mayor Sahm and the hundreds of ladies of the diplomatic set. Martha's mother bore these duties with an air of beleaguered desperation. Pressed for time, she would importune the ladies of her staff at the last moment and soon earned a reputation for helplessness and poor planning. The wives of the military and naval attachés already disliked the new Ambassador because he would not allow their husbands to wear their uniforms and medals to official ceremonies.

Evenings they drove up circular drives to Renaissance residences so bright and festive that the Americans thought they were entering Versailles or one of the doge's palaces in Venice. Both Italy and France remodeled their Berlin embassies that year despite their stated inability to pay their debts to America. Elegant, freshly-painted interiors were decorated with heavy chandeliers, antique trelliswork, mock grottoes and costly French and Italian masterpieces. Untold thousands were spent on tapestries and imported almond and lilac trees. At the Italian embassy the Dodds dined off plates of pure gold. On less formal occasions, they mingled with hundreds of other guests around banquet tables laid with every kind of cold meat and alcoholic beverage. Some evenings a fortune was wasted on uneaten food, Dodd reckoned, as he ate a stewed peach in the privacy of his kitchen before going to bed.

The protocol lady at the Foreign Ministry, with her slotted wooden pallets representing dinner tables and her dozens of name tags, frequently placed the American Ambassador between a diplomatic wife who spoke only French and another who knew only Japanese. Under such circumstances enlightened conversation was clearly impossible. Dodd marvelled at his British colleague, Sir Eric Phipps, who could get through an entire evening without so much as emitting a word that revealed his inner thoughts. In the artfully arranged groupings that followed, the men in their evening attire and the women in their lemon and rose colored gowns sat transfixed beneath bright lights, like so many movie extras waiting for a scene to begin. Only, there was no scene and only a superficial script. Dodd had little inclination to watch the amorous flirtations of the younger set or to gape at the daringly exposed bosoms and backs of the ladies present. In protest he and his family made it a point to depart at the youngish hour of 10:30. If feathers were ruffled, he would send his apologies by letter the next day explaining that he customarily performed work in the morning that required his fullest attention.

Martha was not so miserable among the dance bands of the younger set as her father, but she shared his mischievious disdain for unremarkable people. They were the ribald half of the family; her mother and Bill were much more staid. She and her father teased their butler Fritz about his Jewish blood, and once Dodd threw Messersmith a mock Hitler salute on the street. In Dresden over Thanksgiving, after her father delivered an address to a chilly American Church, he appeared at a ball in his honor without the requisite white tie. The guests were mesmerized by the sight; Martha half expected the males in the hall to rush out and discard their ties forever. Later she and her father broke into hysterics at the recollection of the hall full of people staring neckwards at the great Ambassador from Berlin.

A scholar, Dodd was not impressed by rank or title. During his first audience with the Papal Nuncio, the Vatican was just concluding a treaty with the Third Reich dividing the religious and secular worlds between them. Dodd asked the Pope's representative in Berlin if this meant that there were no more Catholics left on earth! A flustered Nuncio found himself defending the idea of separation of church and state while Dodd listened with an amused smile. Once, at an equestrian exhibition, Dodd rose to leave early only to encounter the disapproving figure of the minister from Northern Ireland who enquired archly if there was something wrong. In a tone of mock amazement Dodd replied: "Why, I never knew that horses could jump!" Dodd sensed the dislike for him growing and bore it like a badge of honor. He would not have been a diplomat among such men for all the money in the world.

He refrained from public addresses that his State Department might find provocative, but in social circles he continued to speak his mind. "The Nazis are cruel but not original," he told Bella Fromm. "Most of their decent economic ideas have been stolen from the assassinated Foreign Minister, Walther Rathenau. They stole the 'First of May' from the guilds; last week's 'Harvest Day' from the United States, where it is called Thanksgiving Day; 'Strength through Joy' from the Russians, the 'Labor Front' from the Italians, and their cruelty from the Huns.

"They did not invent anti-Semitism. They simply were the first to organize it so it could be used as an effective weapon of the state."

As everyone predicted, Martha's blue eyes and delicate pink and white complexion turned a number of heads. Politics mesmerized Berlin society and 24-year-old Martha, behind her haughty gaze, shook inwardly in nervous fascination, like a wild bird that had alighted in a clearing ringed with exotic animals. Hans Bleichroeder, the millionaire *roué* who owned the building that housed the American Embassy, was smitten one evening by the sight of Martha in a revealing pink gown. Although he had several mistresses, Bleichroeder began to woo Martha with bouquets of roses and orchids and slivers of delicious candy and bottles of Danish aquavit. The banker Fritz Thyssen took her for a plane ride over Berlin. Even Putzi Hanfstaengl, for a time, threw his weight into the struggle for Martha's heart and soul until he saw that Martha's heart heeded no revolutionary call. Everyone wanted to meet the Americans, and among the first to send them invitations were the imperial Hohenzollerns, lead by "Fritzi" the youngest son of the German Crown Prince. Martha thought Fritzi sweet and the perfect model for the Arrow collar ads, but his mind was too slow and innocent for her tastes.

She was much more interested in Fritzi's older brother, Prince Louis Ferdinand. Tall and slender, with the artistic features of Frederick the Great, Louis Ferdinand was an accomplished pianist as well as the first member of his family to earn a doctorate. His restless, mercurial nature had taken him all over the world: Spain, Argentina, Hollywood, Detroit. He spoke Spanish like an aristocrat and was learning Russian. Aside from his undeniable charm and the fact that he was frequently mentioned as the candidate most likely to succeed to the throne in the event of an Hohenzollern restoration, Martha found herself attracted by the Prince's Hoosier twang. For the past several years Prince Louis had worked in Detroit as a salesman for the Ford Motor Company and consequently spoke an effortless English with a flat Midwestern accent. The "American Hohenzollern," the Germans called him.

They met at a large diplomatic tea and soon became fast friends, exchanging books, arguing philosophy and art, attending plays and concerts together. He was an excellent dancer. The two created quite a sensation in Berlin with their looser interpretation of American dance rhythms. It was not long before the Prince was dropping in unan-

191

nounced for meals at the Dodd home. After the plates were cleared and the servants dismissed, Dodd would caution the Prince: "If you don't try to be more careful with your talk, Prince Louis, they'll hang you one of these days. I'll come to your funeral all right, but that won't do you much good, I'm afraid." Dodd referred to the Prince's habit, when he was drinking, of taking bets from all and sundry that the regime would not last. Officially, the Prince had returned to Germany to recuperate from pneumonia. He told reporters that the American ice water had done him in. Unofficially, he was under a doctor's care for a malady growing increasingly common under America's stringent drinking laws: alcoholism.

When his cure was completed, the Prince returned to Dearborn and Fordland. He quite enjoyed his status as a celebrated commoner and only returned to Germany in the winter months to celebrate his grandfather's, the Kaiser's, birthday in Holland. Eventually he found a princess of his own and married.

Armand Bérard, François-Poncet's protegé, continued to be a frequent visitor to the Dodd home. In the evening Bill or Martha would invite him over for a drink. The Americans displayed a refreshing curiosity and lack of reserve, Armand thought. They were always well-informed and through them he met many of the American journalists in the capital. A bachelor, Armand's lot was a difficult one. François-Poncet was a harsh taskmaster who began each day with a telegram to Paris and ended it with a long dispatch. A man of the pen, the French Ambassador rejoiced when he scooped *Havas* with the news. The deluge of information that he poured into Paris each day by pouch and telephone threatened to overwhelm his superiors at the Quay d' Orsay. When Paris asked him to limit his phone calls during the April 1st boycott of the Jews, the Ambassador's feelings were hurt. "One day I expect them to tell me they do not wish to be informed," he complained to Armand. Like most diplomats, he secretly wondered if his dispatches were read before they were filed.

On weekends Armand joined François-Poncet at his villa on the Wannsee. The French Embassy issued numerous visas that year to people who wished to leave Germany, and one of Armand's duties was to search the emigrants' baggage for weapons. As the black swans cut patterns in the blue water, Armand would row out to the center of the lake and drop illegal handguns surreptitiously into the deep water.

If only his chief had a hobby, Armand thought. A diplomat's life should be more than his work if only for the sake of his staff. Each day he and the Ambassador partook of a vigorous health walk to the university and back, the Ambassador's sharp cane punctuating their steps. But

Armand was never able to get him to try one of the asphalt trails leading into the "wilderness" of the Tiergarten. With such a resolute and demanding superior, Armand was only too glad to escape to the Dodd's home for cocktails, even if Bill was more attentive than Martha.

To Martha's surprise, Bill went to live with the family of a German professor who taught American history at the university. Bill had enrolled in a course of modern European history and hoped to complete his dissertation in two years. Because he was very busy, Martha only saw him at meal times and occasionally at night when they went out together. Martha audited courses in "American studies" at the university, and it was at one of these that she met Mildred Fish, another young American from the Midwest who was pursuing a literary career in Berlin. Mildred was tall and lovely and seemingly well adjusted to life in Berlin. She had a Masters degree from the University of Wisconsin, where she had met her husband, Arvid Harnack, who was studying economics on a Rockefeller scholarship.

Arvid was an official in the Ministry of Economics, and Mildred was a lecturer on modern American writers at the Berlin City Evening Gymnasium. The Harnack family was a notable one in Germany, and Martha found Mildred and Arvid fine and noble in their shared poverty. In their home, as a candle burned brightly behind a bouquet of pussy willows, Arvid read Malreaux and Mildred studied the stories of Gogol. When they did not see Martha for any length of time, Mildred sent her poetic notes urging her to "write, write, write."

In an attempt to attract like-minded lovers of literature among the American colony, Mildred and Martha began doing a fortnightly book column called "Brief Reviews" for a small English language sheet. Mildred's tastes ran toward proletarian writers while Martha, who reviewed under the pseudonym Wesley Repor preferred the latest in experimental fiction. Her favorite contemporary author was Kay Boyle whose latest novel, *Gentlemen I Address You Privately,* dealt with male and female homosexuality.

Martha's newspaper engagement, when it came, was as a weekly feature writer for the Hearst press. She wrote about Berlin's cultural scene. She had her own typewriter and typed her copy on the lengthy stationery the Embassy used for its dispatches. For herself she wrote not at all. She had no time, and her Chicago sensibility was in disarray. She counted herself lucky to get a letter or two off each month in the experimental prose she had learned from Carl Sandburg in Chicago. In her sanctuary on the Tiergarten she read the works of Faulkner, Stephen Crane and Katherine Mansfield.

One day Mildred invited Martha to accompany her on a trip to meet a

German novelist with the euphonious pen name "Hans Fallada." Fallada, or rather Rudolf Ditzen, was a proletarian novelist whose book *Little Man, What Now?* had just come out in America. Its moving theme described simple people faced with economic catastrophe and political turmoil. Since many of Germany's best known authors had gone abroad when their works were banned, Martha was anxious to meet what was left of Germany's once flourishing literary community.

Ditzen lived in a small peasant village with his wife and two small children. He had been arrested briefly by the SA after Hitler came to power, and Mildred was curious to know if his political views had changed. She and Arvid had been studying the Communist writers lately and were forming a small resistance circle of friends and officials in the Ministry of Economics. Martha was unaware of Mildred's Communist leanings, and she did not accompany Mildred and Ditzen when they sauntered down to the lake. With her poor German, Martha would have missed the suggestive inferences behind Mildred's questions.

"You love your country?" Ditzen asked.

"Oh, very much," Mildred replied. "It is lovely to relax along the shores of Lake Michigan or to stroll through the woods outside Milwaukee."

Ditzen smiled at her overly correct German.

"It must be difficult for you," he said, "to live in a foreign country, especially when your interest is literature and language."

"That is true but it can also be difficult to live in one's own country when one's concern is literature."

Ditzen lit a cigarette and then said very slowly: "I could never write in another language, nor live in any other place than Germany."

"Perhaps, Herr Ditzen, it is less important where one lives, than *how* one lives."

The author fell silent.

"Can one write what one wishes here these days?" Mildred pursued.

"That depends on one's point of view," the novelist explained. "Naturally, it is possible to put a number of difficulties and demands in the way of us book writers. They can ban this or that word but that only affects the surface of things. Language cannot be banned; it is something living which belongs to people like their heart or brain. Yes, I believe one can still write here in these times if one observes the necessary regulations and gives in a little. Not in the important things, of course."

"What is important and what unimportant?" Mildred asked, walking past Ditzen to the shore.

After a wholesome lunch the women hiked up a hill behind Ditzen's house and then returned to take commemorative pictures. Leaving, Mildred shook Ditzen's hand and gave him a searching look. He could not know the reason for her visit nor could any of them foresee Mildred's tragic end ten years later under the blade of the Nazi guillotine.

On October 8 Martha celebrated her 25th birthday with a small party. Her parents did not appear, which was most unusual, and because she wanted to restrain the alcoholic excesses of her guests she served only beer and wine. She invited Wolfgang Stresemann, the musically talented son of the late Foreign Minister, Armand Bérard, Prince "Fritzi," and several young Army officers. Putzi Hanfstaengl was the featured guest, and his reputation attracted a rather bored princess whom Martha had recently met. Putzi was characteristically late, and the princess grew more impatient. Hans Thomsen, the Foreign Ministry's man in the Reich Chancellery put in an appearance. Tommy was a frequent visitor to the Dodd home. He was of Norwegian descent and an accomplished linguist. More and more he was leaving his wife, "Baby," at home to appear in the company of Elmina Rangabe, the dark-haired daughter of the Greek Minister. Miss Rangabe had a doctorate from the Sorbonne and a Mediteranean passion for the Fuehrer. She was studying to be an actress and her pungent, off-color wit provided a sharp contrast to Tommy's blond reserve. Miss Rangabe was the sort of young woman who smoked incessantly and never cleaned her fingernails.

Around midnight Putzi arrived like a cyclone but ignored Martha and the princess to confer solemnly with young Stresemann on the beauties of Schubert's "Unfinished Symphony." Peeved at being excluded, Martha went to the Victrola and put on a recording of the Horst Wessel Song. She did not know that playing the Party anthem at social functions and in places of amusement such as cafés and restaurants was forbidden. In southern Germany a "Schnitzel à la Hitler" had been banned that summer. The New Germany was very sensitive to slights against its revolutionary symbols.

Tommy switched the Victrola off. Martha demanded to know why.

"That is not the sort of music to be played for mixed gatherings in a flippant manner," Tommy replied tersely. "I won't have you play our anthem, with its significance, at a social party."

Martha, who was used to being indulged, was annoyed. Tiergartenstrasse 27 might be foreign territory to some but it was home to her and she would play the Horst Wessel Song or Carl Sandburg's ballads if she wished.

"Yes, there are some people like that among us," Putzi told her later. "People who have blind spots and are humorless—one must be careful not to offend their sensitive souls."

For the remainder of the evening Putzi shook the house with his piano playing and Martha's guests mingled self-consciously. Nobody had guessed that Tommy's feeling for the revolution ran so deep. He had entered the Chancellery in 1932 and his attachment to the new regime had been presumed to be purely formal. Apparently it was not, and from that night on Martha began to retreat from the soft flatteries of gifts and flowers. In subtle ways she saw that the ordinary decencies no longer prevailed. She had heard the ugly stories and recognized the sorrow in her father's eyes when he came home from work. On the eve of her 25th birthday she entered the second stage which some visitors to Germany never reached; the stage where German charm and orderliness no longer sufficed. Another, less audible note intruded; the faint, taut whine of terror.

For one thing she was no longer sure how to behave. She enjoyed shocking her parents and friends with her bright rebelliousness. Her lively spirit echoed through the embassy halls: charming, stubborn, honest. But she began to sense from the way people treated her that conversation in the New Germany served dual purposes. Some people drew her out to discover her father's inner thoughts. Her words were valuable to them and were traded later for privileges and safety. Others, she sensed, were afraid to reveal themselves lest she, unconsciously, betray them in her innocence. Her closest friends spoke in whispers and closed the door before sharing confidences. Dictaphones had recently come into general use. News bureaus in London and Paris used them to catch the hurried messages from correspondents in Berlin, Vienna and Rome. The sound was stored on wire spools and it was rumored that there were dictaphones so sensitive that conversations in a neighboring room could be recorded. Few people knew much about such things; the technology of eavesdropping remained fraught with exaggerated imaginings and dread. Everyone in Berlin—Reichstag deputy, Army general, foreign diplomat—assumed that his telephone was tapped.

On the Kochstrasse, where the Ullsteins fought to keep their empire alive, a man formerly with the political police came to call upon the youngest Ullstein brother, Hermann. Nervously, the man asked Hermann if he would mind fetching a blanket to place over the office phone so that they might speak in confidence. Hermann complied good-naturedly. Wires, explained the visitor, could be run from the telephone to the wall and from there to a main switch. Ah, Hermann said, then that explained the visit a few days ago from a man with the phone company who had insisted that his phone was out of order. In that case, replied the visitor, they should do their talking in the park. Berlin that summer was full of men taking the air in the Tiergarten.

After that Hermann noticed that whenever he picked up the receiver he heard a distinct click. The Ullstein concern had some 3,000 telephones and it was some time before all of them could be cleared, but eventually they found the Gestapo's automatic switching device.

After the dreaded visit from the telephone man, people used the telephone only for the blandest of communications and took care to speak in carefully contrived codes. One hesitated to ring up one's friends for fear of incriminating them or of being incriminated by them. Soon the journeyman at the door was not from the phone company but from the electrical company; dispatched to repair an unreported short-circuit. After that the owner suspected that the telephone resting in its cradle had taken on a life of its own, had become a third ear that overheard every voice and inflection. Shops in Berlin did a rapid business in tea cosies that fit snugly over telephones, sealing them off like children swaddled against the disturbing voices of adults.

In his office on the Bellevuestrasse Consul General Messersmith grew so accustomed to the telephone's click that he always waited for its sound before speaking. With a little confidence, Messersmith discovered, the telephone could be turned against its controllers. One evening Counselor Gordon came to him with the astounding news that Dr. Goebbels planned to visit America as part of the German delegation to the Chicago World's Fair! Gordon had the news straight from the horse's mouth at a party at the Italian Embassy.

The prospect dumbfounded both men and it was Messersmith who thought of a solution. He asked Gordon to call him the next day at his office and to pretend to be telling him the news for the first time. When Gordon complied the following morning, Messersmith pretended utter amazement. Why in America Dr. Goebbels was one of the most hated figures in the regime! It was simply astounding to think that he would risk leaving the safety of his country to travel abroad! There were fanatics in America just as there were in Germany, although not so many fortunately, and an army of police would not be able to protect the Propaganda Minister in Chicago. With that both men hung up and the news of Goebbels' plans to visit America, as announced in the morning papers, was denied vehemently by the same papers that evening. Messersmith had to smile as he imagined his words unrolling from a dictaphone on the Propaganda Minister's desk.

In America wiretapping was associated with crime busting. Law-abiding citizens such as the Dodds never gave a thought to dictaphones

197

turning silently behind living room walls until they arrived in Berlin. Dodd got his first inkling that all was not well when Professor John Firman Coar called upon him at the Embassy. Checking *Who's Who* before the professor was shown in, Dodd learned that Coar had been educated in Germany and had received his doctorate in 1900 from Harvard University. Currently he was a distinguished professor of German at the University of Alberta in Canada.

The man who was shown in was tall and lean in the style of George Bernard Shaw, whom he resembled down to the white goatee. Professor Coar walked with a pronounced limp, the result of polio, and used a cane.

Coar told Dodd that he had known Hitler in the early days and had advised him against his ill-fated Beer Hall Putsch. In a recent two-hour talk with Rudolf Hess, the Fuehrer's deputy, Coar had taken up the subject of the damage Germany was doing to her image with her persecution of the Jews and Hess had suggested that Coar go with him to see Hitler in Berchtesgaden. The meeting would be a purely private affair, Coar said, but Hess seemed to think that the Fuehrer might be led to consider other avenues and that diplomatic discussions might develop. Coar wanted to use the Embassy pouch to send a letter to President Roosevelt outlining his plans.

Dodd was agreeable. As a private citizen Coar could say things to the Fuehrer that he could not. The letter went out, and Coar, after flying to Berchtesgaden, called on Dodd the following week.

The meeting had been nip and tuck Coar reported. Hitler was a fanatic but a sentimental fanatic and could be influenced if handled properly. The greatest obstacle that weekend had been Goebbels, who had showed up with a visitor of his own. Hitler had held out the possibility of hope if Roosevelt would take the first steps. Coar planned to remain another week in Berlin to make sure that the radicals around Hitler did not change his mind. Then he would sail for America and try to arrange an audience with Roosevelt.

In the end Professor Coar's good intentions came to naught, but before he left Berlin he bestowed an invaluable gift upon the American Ambassador. Dodd was touring the house on the Tiergartenstrasse prior to moving in when his butler, *der alte* Fritz, informed him that a "Professor Langbeine" was on the telephone. Dodd knew no Professor Langbeine but he recognized Coar's voice at once and recalled that the professor's legs were indeed long. The voice said that a "friend" and "No. 2" had just returned from a visit to "No. 1" and that "No. 1" still wished to go ahead with the plan.

It was one of the oddest conversations of Dodd's life and the receiver he replaced was not the same one he had picked up. Apparently the residence at No. 27 Tiergartenstrasse already had its secret-sharers. "Such is the German situation, and I am learning," Dodd wrote in his diary that night.

The privacy of postal comunications had been suspended with the burning of the Reichstag, and it was not long before Dodd discovered that at least one letter addressed to him from America had found its way into the hands of the Secret Police. It was not a thought that gave him much comfort, until Martha made the acquaintance of Rudolf Diels.

She could not remember where they had met although she suspected it was at one of the endless afternoon teas or perhaps at a diplomatic dinner where the conversation was all surface glitter. He was certainly unlike any of the young men she had dated in Chicago. His face, with its slightly Asiatic caste, jet black hair, sensitive lips and tribal scars was haunting. He was slim and tall, almost gaunt in carriage and very, very charming. Diels was known for his sexual prowess, and he knew how to make a woman feel as if she were the only woman in the room. His smile was disarming, his eyes too frank, his replies tinged with hints of pleasure. He flirted in the continental manner, without pressure and with amusement and wit. It was impossible not to like him. The pursuit for him was as much an intellectual as an emotional game. If an affair went no further then gracious words, then he was satisfied. His raven beauty would seek other quarry in other rooms and when he returned his look would say regretfully: "I told you so." He could not be hurt, not even by the hurt he caused, and every time Martha saw him he was more gracious and more seductively charming than before.

With his sinister beauty Diels was almost a caricature of a secret police chief. He thoroughly enjoyed his aura of menace. At one of Martha's parties he managed to enter the house unannounced and at his sudden appearance all conversation in the room froze and Diels' eyes sparkled with delight. With his lithe slenderness and formidable intelligence, he reminded some observers of a Bengal tiger let loose in a drawing room.

That autumn as the leaves fell and the nights turned clear and sharp his attentions increased and the daughter of the American Ambassador, intrigued by his ambiguous personality, did nothing to discourage him. It was only slowly that she saw that his interest was not entirely romantic. He needed her and her father's sympathy; for no one had more enemies in Berlin than Diels. Not only was he disliked by liberals for his part in the overthrow of Prussia, but he was also sharply criticized by many within the regime for his adherence to the antiquated legal concepts of Roman law. Diels needed the protection of distinguished foreigners if he was not to join the bruised figures confined in the concentration camps.

The affair that autumn between the daughter of Berlin's most liberal ambassador and the man whose job it was to run Germany's liberals to ground caused a sensation. The news that Martha called Diels "dearie" in public eventually got back to the State Department which could not know that Martha frequently referred to people close to her, such as her parents and Bill, as her "darlings." It was a family term of affection. Besides, she quite enjoyed scandalizing the bluenoses. She was young and adored the attention. Her feminine intuition told her that there was nothing she could do to stop the malicious gossip which earlier connected her romantically with Prince "Fritzi," Putzi Hanfstaengl, and even Hitler.

One night, when she and Diels had been out dancing, she invited him up to the library for a late night drink. Without thinking, she went to fetch one of the sofa pillows to put over the telephone when she caught sight of Diels' amused look. Silently he was nodding his approval. She told her father the next day of the Gestapo chief's mute confirmation. Dodd lined a cardboard box with wads of cotton and took a grim satisfaction in placing it over the telephone in his office whenever a Government official or visiting American came to call.

Diels had to smile when he thought of the meaningful looks his friends cast in his direction as they wordlessly draped their telephones with coats and pillows and tea cosies. He knew that it was a technical impossibility to tap every phone in Berlin. On one of his restless forays across Berlin's political landscape he had shown up at the door of the "Air Force Information Service" on the Behrenstrasse. In that building banks of humorless clerks eavesdropped on the conversations of Berlin's leading citizens. Typists transcribed the most important conversations onto special brown sheets and occasionally, when Diels visited Goering in his villa on the Leipzigerplatz, his chief would be in bed with a stack of brown pages on his mountainous tummy. Goering would read aloud Frau von Schleicher's latest anti-Nazi joke or his own cousin's rebellious reference to him as "Hermann the Terrible." Most of the information never went farther than that. Collecting it was the easiest step, utilizing it took real intelligence, and that Goering did not possess and did not need as virtual dictator of Prussia. So Diels did nothing to allay the apprehension of his friends. He thoroughly enjoyed the mystical power the ordinary telephone had come to assume over human beings. For his part, when he had something sensitive to communicate, he went for a walk in the Tiergarten or for a long drive in the countryside.

Goering tapped not only the phones of his rivals but also the phones of his friends. He tapped Diels' phone and the phones of Diels' acquaintances. "I'm warning you," Goering growled. "I know what you're up to." He tapped Roehm's phone and one day warned Diels: "You are seeing too much of Roehm! Are you simply trying to protect yourself or are you taking part in a conspiracy? I warn you Diels, you can't sit on both sides of the fence!" To which the Gestapo inspector replied impertinently: "Herr Minister President, the Head of the Secret State Police must sit on all sides of the fence at once."

In December Martha wrote a friend in Chicago:

> The snow is soft and deep lying here—a copper smoke mist over Berlin by day and the brilliance of the falling moon by night. The gravel squeaks under my window at night—the sinister faced, lovely lipped and gaunt Diels of the Prussian Secret Police must be watching and the gravel spits from under his soft shoes to warn me. He wears his deep scars as proudly as I would fling about in a wreath of edelweiss . . . The smell of peace is abroad, the air is cold, the skies are brittle, and the leaves have finally fallen. I wear a pony coat with skin like watered silk and muff of lamb. My fingers lie in depths of warmth. I have a jacket of silver sequins and heavy bracelets of rich corals. I wear about my neck a triple thread-like chain of lapis lazulis and pearls. On my face is softness and content like a veil of golden moonlight. And I have never in all my lives been so lonely.

BEATING STATIONS

Under the Republic some of Berlin's most delightful costume balls had taken place at No. 8 Prinz Albrecht Strasse. Socialites such as Bella Fromm shuddered to think what transpired behind its walls after the Gestapo took over.

Men were tortured at No. 8 Prinz Albrecht Strasse during Diels' tenure as inspector. Some of the evidence that crossed his desk could not have been obtained any other way. On one occasion when he entered an interrogation room unannounced, he saw a detective hastily hiding a rubber truncheon in a desk drawer. The suspect's face bore the bright welts of recent blows. With his class prejudice, Diels tolerated the application of third degree tactics on people he considered hardened enough to deserve it. He boasted that his job demanded extreme measures and he delighted in the wide-eyed amazement, even envy, that this admission produced on the faces of journalists and embassy secretaries.

Diels did not believe in violence as a way of life. He might look the other way when it was applied to the rough-hewn, but he despised it when it was used on the sensitive and the well-born. In his own way he did what he could to see that men of his calibre did not end up in the dragnet that converged on the dungeons of the Prinz Albrecht Strasse. He was especially concerned for the safety of his former boss, Karl Severing, who was still at large in Berlin. Former Chancellor Bruening lived in seclusion in a Berlin convent, and General von Schleicher and his wife had wisely chosen to take a holiday in Italy. Von Papen had chosen perhaps the safest refuge of all; a position with the Government.

To Diels' astonishment, Dr. Bernhard Weiss, Vice President of Police under Severing, showed up one day at Police Headquarters to turn himself in. While in Prague, Weiss had been accused of "theft of government documents." He had returned to clear his name.

The tiny, bespectacled Weiss was a nationally-minded German Jew who had risen to prominence under the liberal Republic by dint of hard work and talent. Ever ready to accompany his men on raids, he had created the technically efficient criminal and political police. With a scholar's absorptions, prominent nose and pince nez, "Isidor" Weiss became the target of Gauleiter Joseph Goebbels' vicious jibes in the last days of the Republic until the Police Vice President was swept from office by von Papen's putsch of Prussia.

Diels was appalled to see the well-intentioned Weiss in Berlin and amazed that the former police official had been able to enter the building unrecognized. Hastily, he checked for outstanding warrants and, when he found none, advised Weiss to return to Prague immediately if he valued his life. Under no circumstances was he to return to his residence in Berlin where the SA were lying in wait in for him.

Even prominent foreigners were not safe from Party fanatics. Twice, Consul General Messersmith was nearly run down by an unmarked car as he left his office late at night. The police on the streets, Diels suspected, were only safe from SA attack because they carried weapons.

Diels himself had made the announcement that there were some 10,000 political prisoners in Prussia. Foreign estimates put the figure at three times that number. If Police Headquarters on the Alexanderplatz held some 600 prisoners and the holding cells at Prinz Albrecht Strasse another 12 and Prussia's overcrowded remand prisons and penitentiaries some hundreds more, where were the other thousands?

Diels had only to step out of his office to find the answer. A flood of women—wives and mothers of men in protective custody—filled the ante-rooms of the building on the Prinz Albrecht Strasse which operated around the clock and was noisy with men coming on and off duty. Tempers were short, language was foul. The women were not always well-received, and most never got a chance to speak to an official.

"The carrion can't open her mouth enough to say 'Heil Hitler,'" complained one clerk, "so I gave her what for. She'll learn soon enough."

The paper work showed that the husband or son had been arrested and taken either to Spandau or Moabit but according to the wife or mother the prisoner was no longer at either place. Nor had he returned home.

Gestapo officials were slow to comprehend that political prisoners in their care were being removed during the night by bands of Storm Troopers and SS men. That is what happened to Paul Loebe, a former President of the Reichstag and the man who had delivered the oath of office to President Hindenburg in 1925.

Loebe had been in Belgium when Hitler became Chancellor and to everyone's surprise had returned. He was a German citizen, Loebe declared, and had nothing to hide. Thereafter, Loebe frequently visited Diels to protest the summary arrest of former Republican officials and the supression of his newspaper the Social Democratic *Vorwaerts*.

"We'll permit a number of Social Democratic papers to resume publishing soon," Goering promised Loebe, "but you must wait awhile yet. What good would it do you to be able to print the *Vorwaerts* now if your vendors were attacked by the SA and the editions burnt?"

In June, Loebe was arrested for "embezzlement" and joined the law-yers and doctors and journalists confined in Spandau. Life in Spandau was spartan but humane. Unfortunately, Spandau was also a clearing house for squads of Storm Troopers and SS men on the lookout for former opponents. Prisoners were handed over by willing SA warders on the flimsiest of excuses. In August, a Storm Troop arrived from Breslau and took Loebe to Duerrgoy in Silesia, one of the worst concentration camps in Germany.

"Hey, there's Pauly. Hey, come on in, we'll soon make you feel at home," shouted a guard as Loebe was marched through the prison gate. "Where did you leave the three million marks that you brought with you?"

So chaotic were the Gestapo's records that Diels first learned of Loebe's removal from Louis P. Lochner. The omniscient Diels, the best informed man in Germany, had to depend on foreign reporters to tell him what went on in his own jails.

Berlin Police Headquarters so frustrated the SS and SA auxiliaries by releasing their political prisoners that the SA and SS soon adopted the tactic of taking their captives to their fortified barracks or "Bunkers" on the General Pape Strasse, the Kantstrasse, and the Hedemannstrasse. Berlin soon had more than fifty such "beating stations" from which came truly appalling stories of sadism and torture. Other rumors told of abandoned factories near Oranienburg, Koenigswusterhausen and Bor-nim, where local SA bosses had erected private prison camps. No one knew how many of these illegal camps there were. Every county and municipality seemed to have one or two run by a local Party boss and his SA strongmen. The inmates, former democratic town officials and Com-munist tradesmen, were leased out on a per head basis to county and village governments eager to take advantage of the cheap labor and to curry favour with Germany's new rulers. As much as a mark and a half was paid for each man delivered daily under guard to dig ditches, drain marshes and repair roads. The camp officials pocketed the money and kept the prisoners alive on a starvation diet and food parcels sent from home. Of the better known camps, legal and illegal, there was Dachau in Bavaria; Heuberg in Upper Baden; Kieslau and Rastatt in Baden; Koenigstein, Hohenstein, Ortenstein and Zittau in Saxony; Oranien-burg and Sonnenburg in Prussia; Ginsheim and Roedelheim near Frank-furt; Langen and Osthofen in Hessen; Fuehlsbuettel and Wittmoor near Hamburg and other camps in Braunschweig, Thuringia, Schleswig, Pomerania and the Lueneburg Heath. The police were continually dis-covering new ones in their attempts to trace missing persons.

Diels could scarely believe the reports that came in from Silesia, the

Rhineland, and Pomerania. At first he thought the stories could not be true, that the wanton cruelty which had characterized the French Revolution could not be occurring again in the twentieth century in a country as civilized as Germany. Why, to believe some of the stories was to imagine that Germany had returned to the chaotic days of the Thirty Years War.

Loebe's wife eventually persuaded the head of Hitler's Chancellery to telephone Duerrgoy in Silesia where her husband was incarcerated. It was not so easy to kill a man who had friends in high places. Loebe was summoned and told that he was free to go. He refused. Like Police Vice President Dr. Bernhard Weiss, Loebe came from a generation that prided itself on its good name. His newspaper had been a bastion of his party and many of its readers were in Duerrgoy with him. Perhaps he also feared a bullet in the back and a notice in the papers that he had been shot while trying to escape. Incredibly, Loebe turned his back on freedom and reentered Duerrgoy.

The mother of the imprisoned attorney Dr. Hans Litten appealed to Prince Wilhelm of Prussia, but the Prince confessed that his own situation was precarious. He was a Steel Helmet member, and the National Socialists were waging a campaign of intimidation against that monarchical veterans organization. When it came to the Gestapo even the eldest son of the German Crown Prince had no influence he could bring to bear. Litten's mother turned next to General Blomberg, but that worthy only laughed her worries away as absurd.

Her son had spent his short career—he was younger even than Diels—defending the impoverished and the radical. Ten hours after the Reichstag burst into flames he was arrested and taken to Spandau where he was treated decently for a time. His martyrdom began at Sonnenburg.

The National Socialists had never forgiven Dr. Litten for humiliating Adolf Hitler on the witness stand in May of 1931. For two hours Litten had grilled Herr Hitler on his assertion that the Nazi Party was law-abiding.

Litten: Did not Dr. Goebbels once declare that adversaries be crushed to a pulp?

Hitler: That, of course, is not to be taken literally.

And so on.

From Sonnenburg, Frau Litten received a letter from her son, ostensibly about his clients, now bereft of legal counsel, but actually about his own sufferings.

What with my own troubles I have quite forgotten certain very important cases. You absolutely must see that they receive careful attention. Baer (Litten's friends called him Bear) positively must be allowed to cancel his leave. He is on such bad terms with the other tenants that they constantly attack him when he comes home at night. They have repeatedly thrashed him with a violence that might very well be fatal. Since all attempts to obtain redress have been unavailing, one must find another house for him. And then I am greatly concerned about the Hali case (Ha-ns Lit-ten). In his unfortunate situation the man has already made several attempts at suicide.

In the kindly State Attorney, Hans Mittelbach, Litten's mother finally found a Gestapo official willing to investigate her son's plight. In April, a month before American newsman had their tour of Sonnenburg concentration camp, a horrified Mittelbach brought Litten back to Spandau in his own car. Litten's smooth, childlike face was haggard and lopsided. His jaw and one cheek bone had been broken. Several of his teeth were missing. His hearing was damaged and the vision in one eye reduced. A leg had been shattered and improperly set. It was by no means uncommon for men released from protective custody to look like utter strangers to their relatives.

In August Litten was taken from Spandau and tortured by a brutal Gestapo detective who wanted a reversal in Litten's last big trial, the Felseneck case of 1932. Fearing that he would break under torture, Litten told the Secret State Police that he would sign anything they put before him. On August 10 his confession appeared in the German press: HANS LITTEN CONFESSES: ACCESSORY TO MURDER. On August 15 he sent a letter to the Gestapo declaring his confession false. Then he took poison and slashed his wrists.

He awoke in Moabit infirmary where he was told that his "interrogations" would continue.

By then Mittelbach had been replaced by Dr. Otto Conrady, a tall, intimidating man who rarely consented to see the relatives of men confined under his care. The Littens, however, were well-known in academic circles. Litten's father was a university professor and a former tutor to the sons of the German Crown Prince. When Dr. Conrady met with Frau Litten he tried to stare her down. He seemed unable to believe that torture was employed by his office. One day, after repeated appeals from Frau Litten, he lost his temper.

"He's lying all the time," Conrady growled. "We shall soon lose patience with him!"

By October Litten was in Columbia Haus, the dreaded SS prison in

Berlin. His distraught mother appealed to Goering's office, and Diels promised to pay a surprise visit to the SS prison in order to rescue the young lawyer. Either Deils' plan went awry or he misled himself into believing that the official camp at Brandenburg would be a safer refuge for the liberal lawyer.

At Brandenburg Litten's martyrdom began anew. So horrible were the beatings he received there that no prisoner would consent to share a cell with him. Inmates who had been his former clients were forced to strike him in the face and the severely injured lawyer was made to wallow in a pond of prison urine.

Diels refused to see Litten's mother or to take her calls. She finally prevailed upon the imperious Conrady to issue a personal order to the commandant of Brandenburg to desist from further mistreating the frail attorney. For a time, Dr. Conrady's order was obeyed.

Many people interceded in Litten's behalf but nobody protected him. That would have demanded constant vigilance from the young attorneys and state assessors Diels brought into the Gestapo who were too traditional in outlook, too ironic by nature, and too removed from the horrors of the day to realize what was happening behind their backs. Some even reverted to the view that liberals and pacifists such as Litten and Loebe deserved their fate. All of them could point to some liberal they had rescued and taken to a hospital or returned to Spandau to begin again the stations of the cross. Diels twice rescued one young man, the son of a Lutheran pastor, and twice lost him again to the SA. When the newsman H. R. Knickerbocker asked him to arrange the release of a physician, Dr. Hans Haustein, from protective custody, it took Diels months to locate the doctor. Dr. Haustein was released but died in his wife's arms twelve days later. He was thirty-nine.

That summer, word reached Messersmith that Walter Orloff, an American medical student at the University of Greifswald had been arrested for engaging in Communist activities. The Government had names, dates, the confession of an accomplice, even a letter from Orloff to local Communist headquarters pledging his loyalty. It had enough on the young American to cut off his head with an ax in the medieval manner. Messersmith's only hope was that the Government would consent to deportation.

He asked Diels to have the young man transferred to Berlin where efforts on his behalf could be more direct. Diels sent two of his best men to Greifswald to see that the American reached Berlin safely. Unfortunately, once in the hands of SA warders at Gestapo headquarters, Orloff was beaten mercilessly.

Diels summoned Messersmith to his office late at night, told the

Consul General what had happened and complained bitterly about the riffraff he had to work with. What should he do?

Messersmith suggested that the young man be turned over to him. He would see that Orloff received medical treatment and, when he was well enough to travel, sent home quietly. Diels agreed. He repeated that he deplored the beatings, but no matter what he did he was unable to prevent them. Messersmith saw that his contrition was sincere. When Diels offered him his hand, Messersmith took it.

"I wonder how you can shake hands with me after what has happened," Diels said.

Diels was not so sensitive about atrocities elsewhere in Germany. To the contrary, it was part of his plan to see that news of them reached foreign ears. When a naturalized American citizen was attacked in broad daylight in Leipzig solely for looking Jewish, Knick's cable describing the incident was held up by the Telegraph Office. Diels immediately ordered the damning dispatch released. He hoped the foreign press could bring Hitler and his associates to their senses. It was no use, he had discovered, to complain to Hitler about this or that German or foreigner who had been molested. Hitler claimed to be too busy to interfere. It was only when Diels suggested that the mistreatment of Americans and other foreigners in Germany cast doubt on Hitler's ability to rule that Hitler listened. Diels was cunning in his insinuations, and a furious Hitler would order immediate action.

That Hitler was aware of the brutality that reigned in Berlin Diels knew first hand. He had been present one afternoon with Hitler and his retinue at the Kaiserhof when Frau Stennes, the wife of a much decorated, if rebellious, SA officer, entered carrying an oddly wrapped package. In 1931, when relations between the Berlin SA and Munich headquarters were at their worst, Captain Walter Stennes had launched a short-lived rebellion against Hitler's authority. Stennes demanded to know why such lavish sums were being spent on refurbishing the Brown House when his men in Berlin were penniless. Although he was a charismatic leader, many in the Berlin SA refused to join him and crossed over to the SS to crush the revolt. After January 30 the Berlin SS ran Stennes to ground in a hut in the woods north of Berlin. Since then, the doughty SA officer had been confined in Columbia Haus, a prison run by the SS on the northern edge of Tempelhof airfield.

With tears streaming down her face, Frau Stennes unwrapped her package in the Kaiserhof lobby and cast her husband's blood-stained shirt before Hitler and his party. Diels was shocked and embarrassed. Hitler only stared at Frau Stennes in stony silence.

Kurt Hiller, a writer for the nonconformist weekly *Die Weltbuehne* was taken to Columbia Haus in the middle of July. Hiller would always wonder if the SS Sturmfuehrer who called him out of the waiting room at No. 8 Prinz Albrecht Strasse was acting on orders or simply on his own.

His nose broken, blood streaming down his face, Hiller was taken to the basement where some twenty SS men stood or sat around a large wooden table. Along the walls hung rawhide whips and scourges. Hiller was pushed down on the table while four men grasped his wrists and ankles and an SS athlete, naked to the waist, seized a nine foot horsewhip and began to deliver the first "greeting" of 25 lashes. At the sixth stroke Hiller cried out. At the twentieth he was screaming for his life.

At the twenty-fifth, he slipped to the floor but was rudely hauled to his feet again and told to drop his trousers. For a second time they pushed him across the table, pulled his shirt up, and gave him another twenty-five lashes across his naked back and buttocks.

By then the sensation of pain had passed. The blows registered in his skull as dull explosions. Sprawling in his own blood, a gaping wound on his forehead, Hiller was barely alive.

"Loss of blood: negligible," an SS leader jeered.

Doused with freezing water Hiller was thrown into a cell. No stool, no bed, nowhere to sit. Hiller moved from wall to wall like an animal in a trance. To use the toilet in the hall he had to summon his tormentors by raising a red flag. Some mornings he relieved himself in his breakfast pail.

With the others he was chased about the muddy courtyard—the "Bear Dance" it was called—in laceless boots to strains of "Once I Had A Comrade" and "Wandering Is The Miller's Love." The prisoners were drilled until they dropped: "Down! Up! March! Down . . ."

Hiller: I am an Egyptian desert-son.

Guard: What? An Egyptian desert-son, did you say? You are an Egyptian desert-pig!

Hiller: Egyptian desert-pig, Egyptian desert-pig, Egyptian desert-pig . . .

He returned to his cell sweat-soaked, covered with mud, his nose still unset, his buttocks in ribbons. He tried to take his life but failed and was put in shackles—a slow death.

The middle classes suffered the worst. They were ashamed to be in prison. It must be a mistake. Their boss, their wife, Uncle Hans must be busy at that moment working for their release. Then would the State's face be red. There would be a scandal and a public outcry.

Only slowly did it dawn on them that they had been abandoned.

Workers who were Communists had it easier, psychologically. They had been in prison before, always for political offenses, they hastened to add. They were proud to be imprisoned under the fascists. Their lives on the outside had been hard. Here it was at least warm and the food was free. The evil-smelling latrine, the dirty clothes, the loss of all privacy bothered them little. They entered with the proletarian's gift of adapting to any situation.

If the Communist chroniclers captured the vulgarity of their lot, the vulgarity of the persecution was too horrible for any social class to put into words. The generation of the Great War had no language for some experiences and never divulged to their wives or girlfriends what they had seen and endured. In sprees that lasted all night, the SS beaters often obtained an almost physical release from their domination of helpless men. With each blow their passion increased, their breathing grew rougher until the victim lay weak and broken and filled with shame at how personally he had been abused. Weeks, months later he tensed at the mere sound of an SS man's voice. All conception of dignity and honor was eroded. For all classes there occurred episodes so degenerate that they could only be confessed later to priests or pastors who had also been prisoners and who on their release made it their mission to comfort their fellow sufferers. Hiller, who was Jewish, was denied even that comfort.

His legs swelled until he could hardly make out his knees and ankles. He asked to see the camp physician, a robust, bullet-headed Nazi. His urine was bloody, Hiller complained. "That surprises you?" asked the doctor. Hiller showed him his flayed backside. "Does it hurt?" the doctor mocked.

The physician was concerned about Hiller's grossly swollen legs. Hiller's kidneys had been damaged by the beating. The doctor recommended water pills, a salt-free diet and plenty of bed rest.

"The doctor has shit to say about what goes on here," shouted the SS guard in the courtyard. "I am in command here!" As punishment the prisoner with the elephantine legs was made to troop around the courtyard seven times without pause. At night his tormentors watched him through the peep hole; a miserable figure crouching on a mattress of straw. "You ass," they shouted, "go ahead and croak in your corner. Do you really imagine that you will leave here alive. We'll put you in a ditch in the courtyard, shit in it, and fill it in."

It was a charnel house in the heart of Berlin, scarcely a kilometer distant from Germany's largest airfield through which ambassadors, movie stars and tourists passed with hardly a sideward glance. From some of the cells, the silver airplanes could be seen slowly crossing a corner of blue sky.

Using his police powers Diels launched sporadic raids against SA barracks and Party buildings in Berlin. One of his earliest targets was the Party Headquarters on Hedemannstrasse, the scene of several "suicides." Police armed with carbines and hand grenades descended upon the Hedemannstrasse and cordoned off the neighboring streets. The SA defenders responded by mounting machine guns in the windows and doorways of their headquarters.

The police lieutenant called for further orders.

The other side sent for Group Leader Karl Ernst.

Diels arrived by car and, in his customary dark suit and slouch felt hat, was conferring with the SA defense unit when Ernst arrived in a powerful black Mercedes. The Group Leader wasted no time in letting Diels feel the wrath of his tongue.

"What do you think you're doing?" he demanded. "Don't imagine that you can come crying to us if we teach this trash a lesson or two. You were sitting in your soft leather chair when my men were having their heads bashed in by these red bastards you want to help now."

Diels told Ernst that Minister President Goering had sanctioned the use of force if resistance were encountered and gestured to the heavily armed policemen behind him. Ernst only laughed derisively.

In the end Diels prevailed, but Ernst stipulated, slyly, that the prisoners must remain in protective custody.

In the building's lower depths Diels discovered a communal dungeon filled with living skeletons, creatures with broken limbs, missing teeth, faces encrusted with blood, mutely awaiting their end on beds of reeking straw. Every one of them had to be physically carried to waiting police vans.

Diels commissioned a full medical report and put the harrowing evidence before Goering and Hitler. Then, with the aid of policemen from the Tiergarten precinct, he raided a pillory in Charlottenberg and after that the headquarters of Goering's personal bodyguard on the General Pape Strasse where Communists and even SA men were drilled until they dropped. He soon became exceedingly unpopular with the Berlin SA.

One afternoon as he returned from Cologne he was met at the Charlottenberg Train Station by several of his most trusted detectives. Even his estranged wife came down to warn him. Under no circumstances was he to go on to the Tiergarten Station. Ernst and his bullies were waiting at the next stop to kidnap him.

Diels moved swiftly. He dispatched a detachment of police to arrest the kidnappers when they returned to their barracks empty-handed. Ernst he confronted face-to-face at SA staff headquarters. The young hoodlum denied any knowledge of the kidnap plan but said that if it were true then Diels had only himself to blame.

To improve his relations with Ernst, Diels prevailed upon Goering to move the charismatic SA leader Walter Stennes to a cell at Gestapo headquarters. Stennes was a close friend of Ernst's and for weeks Diels watched, fascinated, as the various SS and SA liaison staffs split into those who loathed the rebellious SA captain and those who secretly admired him. Reconstructing the history piecemeal from the files, Diels learned that Goering had promised to support Stennes in his revolt of 1931 but had backed down at the last moment. Goering made amends when he allowed Diels to slip Stennes across the border into Holland. Eventually, Stennes made his way to China where he took command of Generalissimo Chiang-kai-shek's bodyguard.

A grateful Ernst sponsored Diels' membership in the Berlin SA but SA Chief Roehm disapproved. "If you do anything," he told Diels, "you should put on the black shirt. It could save your life. I would be doing you a disservice, if by taking you into the SA, I further provoked Himmler's and Heydrich's hatred of you. One day these men will be truly deadly."

A shadow invisible to foreign eyes pushed Diels and Ernst closer that autumn. It loomed from Munich in the unassuming figure of Heinrich Himmler, Reichsfuehrer SS and Commander of the Bavarian Political Police. Himmler, a favorite of Hitler's, dreamt of a national police force with himself as leader. Quietly he spread his power throughout the south and sent his youthful Chief of Intelligence, Reinhard Heydrich, to Berlin. Diels and his wife invited the Heydrichs out for a picnic lunch. Unwittingly ideological, Heydrich's mind was easy for Diels to pick. Frau Heydrich, for her part, was incensed at the high-handed way in which Diels treated his lovely red-headed wife, Hilde; she could see that the union must end in divorce.

A jealous Goering told Diels to arrest Heydrich, but Diels refused. He had no desire to sign his own death warrant, he said.

"Himmler and Heyrich will never get Berlin," Goering boasted. Hitler finally settled the matter when he decreed that the SS Intelligence Service would undertake no missions in Goering's territory that year. Heydrich hurriedly returned to Munich, leaving his house on the Eichenallee to agents who contented themselves with watching Diels' office and compiling an index of 532 persons to be arrested once Himmler took control of Prussia.

Diels now had enemies within the SS. A motorized unit under the command of SS-Sturmbannfuehrer Herbert Packebusch broke into his home, locked Hilde in the bedroom and, after a tumultuous search, made off with Diels' letters, diaries and personal files. Diels, who was working late that night at Gestapo headquarters, only learned of the invasion when his wife phoned him after the intruders departed. Accompanied by police with machine guns and hand grenades, Diels went to SS headquarters on the Potsdamerstrasse. The SS guard opened to them and directed the officials to Packebusch's office. Thirty-one-year-old Herbert Packebusch sat hunched over Diels' papers jotting notes in the margins such as: "Liberal interior furnishings." Packebusch headed the SS Press Office and considered himself a man of culture.

"You're under arrest!" Diels shouted.

Packebusch jumped as if he had seen a ghost.

Later, at Gestapo headquarters, Diels nearly lost control of the situation when Packebusch called him a traitor. Furious, Diels rose from his chair, and Packebusch pulled a gun from his pocket. Diels' brilliant career might have ended that night with a single pistol shot if his loyal sheep dog had not intervened.

Next day there was hell to pay. The SS demanded the release of Packebusch but Diels told Goering that if Packebusch were set free he would resign as director of the Gestapo. Ernst supported Diels in the controversy.

In October, Goering summoned Diels to his office to meet with Himmler. The Reichsfuehrer apologized for the lawlessness of his subordinate. Packebusch would be tried by a special SS honor court. Himmler then asked Diels to raise his right hand, and Diels heard himself being sworn in as a Lieutenant Colonel in the SS, membership number 187,116. The following day he penned the requisite letter of gratitude: "words could hardly express . . . hope to be found worthy . . . etc." No one had mastered the court style better than the ambitious Diels. But his new masters were not fooled. In his SS file they noted that he was cunning and opportunistic. Some of his papers seized in the raid had not been returned, including a file that Diels had compiled on himself.

In November, Diels asked Martha if she would be interested in attending a session of the Reichstag Fire Trial. The 4th Penal Chamber of the Leipzig Supreme Court had moved its hearings to Berlin to investigate the scene of the crime. Refugee circles in Paris had hurriedly published *The Brown Book of the Hitler Terror* accusing the Nazis of setting the fire.

With artfully assembled evidence, the book described how a handful of Storm Troopers had entered the Reichstag on the night of February 27 through an underground tunnel that began in Goering's villa, where Putzi had slept so fitfully. According to the *Brown Book* the Dutch vagabond, Marinus van der Lubbe, was merely their homosexual pawn who had been too slow to escape the police.

Almost no one in Berlin mistook the *Brown Book* for the truth, but as propaganda it was so effective that Minister President Goering and Propaganda Minister Goebbels demanded a hearing before the Supreme Court to contradict its allegations. Diels was offering Martha the chance to witness an historic confrontation: Goering's appearance before his accusers. Martha's German was still too poor to follow the complexities of a legal proceeding, but she had been avidly following the trial in the foreign press. All of Berlin was abuzz with speculation, and seats at the trial were much sought after. She accepted promptly as her father's unofficial observer.

Security around the Reichstag was tight. Policemen armed with revolvers and short swords ringed the building. To get through the police cordon Martha had to show a pass Diels had given her. Inside, detectives went through her handbag and patted her down for hidden weapons. At the door to the Budget Committee Room, where the court had convened, she had to produce her pass again along with her passport photo.

The judges' bench was set up beneath a huge mural of Kaiser Wilhelm I and Bismarck surveying the Battle of Sedan. Some 75 seats had been reserved in the gallery for the scores of reporters from all over the world, but Diels had secured a seat for her on the main floor near the front of the room. Martha felt somewhat self-conscious as she took her place among Cabinet Ministers, Party officials and members of the Prussian government. Nearby, the daughter of Berlin's Police President made salacious remarks about the new Government loud enough for everyone to hear; but Martha had been in Berlin long enough to be wary of *agents provocateurs*. She pretended not to hear.

At 9 o'clock the five defendants, each accompanied by a police constable, entered the courtroom through a side door. Next came the seven Supreme Court justices dressed in scarlet caps and robes. At their appearance, the entire court rose and, with the exception of the foreigners, gave the Hitler salute which the judges returned. Then, for more than an hour, the justices, witnesses and prominent guests waited for Goering to appear. Martha used the time to study the players in the pageant. She could hardly bear to look at Marinus van der Lubbe. The Dutch youth seemed hardly human. His head lolled forward on his chest as if he were drugged; occasionally long streams of saliva dangled between his knees.

Secretly Martha believed the story that he had been duped into the act by homosexuals within the SA. Ernst Torgler, the leader of the German Communist Party, appeared alert and serene. He had lost weight in prison and looked oddly youthful. The three Bulgarians, with the exception of the "writer" Georgi Dimitroff, looked utterly nondescript.

Georgi Dimitroff was the star of the trial. A member of the Executive Committee of the Communist Party he had been arrested in Munich on the night of the fire and charged as an accomplice. Uncowed by Germany's most august court, Dimitroff had demanded and won the right to conduct his own defense. With ferocious concentration, he set about learning the intricacies of German law from the jail cell where he was kept in chains. Unlike the other Bulgarians, he was fluent in German. His audacious remarks frequently drew delighted laughter from the visitors' gallery. As he grew bolder, the judges grew more thin-skinned. Dimitroff was admonished, threatened and repeatedly banished from his own trial. Only the day before he had been removed forcibly by policemen but a higher authority—Martha suspected Diels—had called him back today in view of the long-awaited appearance of Minister President Goering.

It was close to 11 o'clock when Goering arrived accompanied by a crowd of aides-de-camp, police officers, and of course Diels in a simple dark suit. Dressed in the plain brown uniform of Germany's leaders, Goering was not the least bit contrite about the delay and immediately launched into a two hour harangue on the dangers of Communism and the heresies of the *Brown Book*. Martha understood none of it except for a few names. Once she caught the word "Nero" which provoked an outburst of laughter. Afterwards, she read that Goering had ridiculed the allegations in the *Brown Book* by sarcastically describing himself on the night of the fire as standing in the window of his palace dressed in a blue toga, like Nero, but without a fiddle. There followed a long exposition on *"Nationalsozialismus"* and *"Kommunismus,"* interrupted by cries of "Bravo," and beneath it all the soft drone of the voice of the Bulgarian translator. Finally, after what seemed like hours of histrionics, Goering came to the end of his peroration, and peace briefly returned.

Throughout, Diels had stood at the front of the courtroom just slightly behind Goering, one elbow resting casually on the judges' bench, his cold eyes surveying the audience for the effect of his chief's words. As the defendent Dimitroff rose to begin his interrogation of the witness, Diels followed Goering's replies with the intensity of a scientist observing a crucial experiment. Goering seemed aware of Diels' dark presence. As Diels shifted about the front of the courtroom to get a better view,

Goering turned also and sometimes altered his voice as if taking secret stage directions.

Dimitroff: You have repeatedly stated your conviction that the Communists are guilty of this fire, and you, as Premier of Prussia, are the head of the police and the judiciary. May not this conviction of yours have influenced the whole police and judicial investigation, have guided it into this one channel, and closed all other channels of investigation?

Goering: If I did influence the investigation in this direction it was the right direction. It was a political crime, and it was clear that the criminals were in your party.

Gallery: Bravos!

Dimitroff: Yes, of course, bravo, bravo, bravo! Does the witness know that this criminal party rules the sixth part of the earth . . .

Goering: Unfortunately.

Dimitroff: . . . that the Soviet Union has diplomatic, political and economic relations with Germany, and that its orders give thousands of German workers bread?

Goering: I know that the Russians pay with bills: I should prefer to know that the bills are met. What happens in Russia is of no interest to me. I have only to deal with the German Communist Party, and with the foreign crooks who come here to fire the Reichstag.

Court (to Dimitroff): You cannot wonder that the witness gets angry. I have repeatedly warned you not to make Communist propaganda here.

Dimitroff: But he's making National Socialist propanganda.

Goering: Look here, I will tell you what the German people know. They know that you are behaving in a disgraceful fashion. They know that you are a Communist crook who came to Germany to set the Reichstag on fire, and who now behave yourself with sheer impudence in the face of the German people. I did not come here to be accused by you . . .

Dimitroff: You are a witness . . .

Goering: . . . In my eyes you are nothing but a scoundrel, a crook who belongs on the gallows.

1933

Dimitroff: Very well, I'm most satisfied . . .

Court (to Dimitroff): I have repeatedly warned you not to make Communist propaganda. If you continue in this vein, I shall have you put outside. I have told you not to make Communist propaganda, and you cannot wonder that the witness gets angry when you do so. I order you most emphatically to desist from doing so. If you have any questions then let them be purely factual and nothing more.

Dimitroff: I am highly satisfied with Herr Goering's explanation.

Court: Whether or not you are satisfied is a matter of complete indifference to me.

Dimitroff: Most satisfied. I am merely asking questions.

Court: After your last comment, I must ask you to sit down.

Dimitroff: I am asking questions.

Court: I am asking you to sit down. Do so!

Dimitroff: I am asking a purely factual question.

Court: I have asked you to sit down!

Dimitroff: You are greatly afraid of my questions, are you not, Herr Minister?

Goering: You will be afraid when I catch you. You wait till I get you out of the power of this Court, you crook!

Court: Dimitroff is expelled for three days. Out with him!

FLIGHT

That autumn a forester out with his dog discovered the decomposing body of 35-year-old Albrecht Hoehler, professional criminal and occasional Communist, who fired the shot in January 1930 that made a martyr out of Horst Wessel. Hoehler had been brought to Berlin from Silesia where he was serving a life sentence. The SA wanted to reopen the case but Hoehler continued to deny that the murder of Horst Wessel had been in any way politically motivated. He and his friends had merely tried to help a landlady evict two non-paying tenants, Wessel and his girlfriend, from a boardinghouse. When Wessel reached for his gun, "Ali" Hoehler shot and killed him. Diels, whose curiosity was insatiable, visited the tall, raw-boned convict whose arms and chest were covered with pornographic tattoos, in an interrogation cell at Gestapo headquarters.

"You know what has happened, Ali. The National Socialists have come to power. They demand that the case against you be reopened. How do you feel about that?"

"That I'll get it in the neck this time," Ali replied in the rough dialect of the Berlin underworld. Ali was afraid to stay in Berlin and asked to be returned to Silesia. Diels made the necessary arrangements, but on the way back the police van carrying Ali was overtaken by a car full of SA men. For an hour the police driver was held hostage while Hoehler was taken away. When the body was found by the forester and his dog, it was shot full of holes.

When Diels advised the Ministry of Justice not to pursue the case, the rumor surfaced that he had helped engineer the murder, perhaps again to appease the Berlin SA. Hoehler, certainly, was more useful to Diels dead than alive. Diels took the files of the case to Franz Guertner, Minister of Justice under von Papen, Schleicher and now Hitler. Diels knew Guertner to be a man committed to the independence of the judiciary and the preservation of legal norms. After hearing Diels' version of the murder, Guertner looked disturbed. A revolution, Guertner observed, was an extra-legal occurrence, not unlike the crisis fever that gripped an ailing man. One could only wait and hope that the patient recovered.

Diels agreed but expressed concern that a caste of men had arisen—Group Leaders and Gauleiters for the most part—who behaved as if they were above the law. Guertner admitted that he had noticed them too and estimated their number to be around 2,000, not counting their numerous underlings and hangers-on. He recommended that Diels turn to the "Central Prosecutor's Office." To date, the new office had concerned itself primarily with cases of financial corruption in the Party, but it was empowered to investigate any crime of "sabotage" against the ideal of the new state. The Office was located in Berlin but had judicial authority throughout the Reich. Werner von Haacke handled cases east of the Elbe; Dr. Guenther Joel cases to the west.

Party bosses who robbed and assaulted and extorted money from innocent citizens, who humiliated clergymen and threatened local prosecutors soon heard from the Central Prosecutor's Office in Berlin. Dr. Joel interceded in literally hundreds of cases where powerful SA and Party leaders had stymied or physically assaulted local justice officials who were simply doing their jobs. Joel proved himself amazingly adept at getting around bureaucratic hurdles. The young state assessor saw that it was useless to issue instructions from Berlin; consequently, he adopted the practice of driving or flying to Koenigsberg, Duesseldorf or Bonn to bolster the spirits of beleaguered justice officials. With a unit of special Field Constabulary loaned to him by the Ministry of the Interior, Joel often arrested malefactors on the spot. He steadfastly opposed further amnesties for Party officials who had committed indictable offenses. The period of revolutionary intoxication had past, Joel argued, and he refused to make a distinction between ordinary criminals and criminals in Party uniform. If the Old Fighters were the pillars of the new State, then they deserved to suffer the harshest penalties when they transgressed the responsibility of their offices.

Sometimes the crowds outside the courthouse were hostile, sometimes friendly; it was all the same to Dr. Joel, who did not hesitate to bawl out Gauleiters and SA Police Presidents in heated face-to-face confrontations. He was frequently threatened. Protests against him were sent to Berlin and to the Brown House in Munich. But Dr. Joel would not back down and Diels was only too glad to transmit files from his own office to the Office of the Central Prosecutor for action. Sometimes Diels thought that if there had been ten men as courageous and energetic as Dr. Joel, Germany's history after 1933 would have been different. He misled himself. The Central Prosecutor's Office prevailed in the provinces but rarely in Berlin or Munich where the Party was too powerful. It was an uneven tug of war against forces that were determined to erode the edifice of German justice and make of the State an avenging sword against the weak and the politically isolated.

In November, Diels and Dr. Joel turned their attention to conditions inside the four Prussian concentration camps on the Frisian moors near the Dutch border. The camps had been erected by protective custody prisoners from Duesseldorf to great fanfare about useful work, reeducation and land reclamation. Actually, the real reason behind the new camps on the moors was to reduce the number of illegal camps closer to home. The Prussian government estimated a permanent inmate population of 10,000 and hoped to concentrate these exclusively in "Prussian Morocco" as the prisoners derisively called the treeless landscape south of Osnabrueck. Tragically, the four camps, Papenburg, Esterwegen, Boergemoor and Neusustrum were staffed by unemployed SS men drawn from all over the Reich. Tales of the most horrifying nature were not long in reaching Berlin.

Life was harsh in the moor camps. The wasteland of peat proved intractable, the government's boast of "productive" work nothing more than an excuse for slave labor. Bitter storms blew off the Atlantic, the marshlands froze, and the tools the prisoners used to cut and shape the peat were blunt and primitive. The camp at Esterwegen was especially brutal. Its commandant was a known sadist and the SS guards in Esterwegen carried rifles with fixed bayonets. Numerous prisoners were shot while trying to "escape." The former Police President of Altona was finished off in such a manner. He was sent outside the compound to fetch wood and shot five times in the back. Food at Esterwegen was so scarce that inmates from the other camps threw what scraps they could spare to their starving brothers as they passed by on the "Moor Express," the train that transported them into that awful region.

The SS guards had been told that they would be guarding Republican bosses and they were disappointed when they received inmates who were mostly workers and rank and file Communists. To relieve their frustration, the Prussian government sent them former officials from the Social Democratic Party—most of the prominent Communists had fled the country—as part of a traveling political show. A shipment from Oranienburg duly arrived carrying Fritz Ebert, Jr., the son of the Republic's first President and Reichstag Deputy Ernst Heilmann. On their way to prison Ebert and Heilmann were paraded through the town of Papenburg by shouting SS men and displayed on street corners as arch conspirators. At the Boergermoor camp they were made to stand at attention for three hours in front of the assembled inmate population.

"Who are you?" demanded a guard of Fritz Ebert, Jr. Ebert was an old hand at the game. At Oranienburg they had shorn half of his head, and at Columbia Haus he had been made to shinny up a pole to kiss the bust of his late father. "I am Friedrich Ebert, son of the traitor Ebert."

"I am the super-scoundrel Heilmann," Heilmann shouted when his turn came. "I have deceived the German People and betrayed the workers." Heilmann had been the leader of the Social Democratic Party in Prussia. He was also a Jew and therefore treated with double harshness at Boergermoor. He was beaten and forced to push a wheelbarrow carrying a Jewish lawyer through the camp. The two were led to the latrine and forced to heap spadefuls of excrement on each other, and then Heilmann was driven into one of the dog kennels and made to sniff a dog's behind while reciting the ditty:

> I am as treacherous as a cat
> Meow, meow
> And I bark like a dog,
> Bow-wow, bow-wow.

Ebert, Jr. was handed a lath and told to beat Heilmann and the playwright Armin Th. Wegener. Ebert flung the stave to the ground.

"I am willing to do the work of my three comrades as well as my own," he said, "but I won't beat them." The SS guards were impressed. So were the Communist inmates who had been schooled to think of Social Democrats as cowards.

But the unfortunate Heilmann made the mistake of begging for mercy. "I'll join in any joke," he pleaded. "I'll do anything you ask me, but don't shoot me." As a Social Democrat he had always fought the Communists, he said, even more bitterly than the Nazis. Thereafter, Heilmann found himself shunned in the camps where the inmate population was 95 percent Communist. The SS were not impressed by cowardice, and it was not long before they engineered his death. One afternoon Heilmann was summoned to the commandant's hut and afterwards was seen walking slowly out of the camp as if in a trance. Work crews returning from the moors witnessed the murder. The sentry at the gate let Heilmann walk fifty yards before he shouted: "Eh, Heilmann, where are you going?" Guards rushed from their huts and began firing their rifles and revolvers at Heilmann. They were not good shots, but eventually they brought the politician down. An ambulance took him to a hospital at Papenburg, where with his dying breath he described to Rudolf Diels the tortures he endured.

Amid such misery, the Communists in the camps banded together and chose hut elders to argue their grievances with the camp administration. Slowly they won a few elementary rights, and a society began to take shape. The inmates took care of their own, nursed the sick and injured, advised newcomers how to survive the first brutal weeks of "coordination." They also began to work on the guards, concentrating their efforts on the "friendlies" who were as shocked as they at the behavior of the "beasts." In casual conversation during breaks on the moors, they asked the friendlies if the revolution had brought them the rewards they had expected. Didn't their leaders in Berlin drive around in expensive Mercedes? Why were the grafters in the party never punished? Why was it that their better educated SS brothers always got the cushiest jobs in the camps?

The friendlies had plenty of time to think. Their huts were lonely and spartan, their pay pitiful and frequently late. Working outside on the moors they got just as wet as the prisoners. In their own eyes they were little more than another class of inmate. On weekends they walked to the nearest village to dance with the village girls and frequently came home the following morning limping and tattered after being attacked and badly beaten by the local SA toughs, who greatly resented their presence.

At first the townspeople had greeted the arrival of the camps with great enthusiasm. They imagined huge profits from the new construction and the nearly 6,000 new inhabitants in the region. They were sadly disappointed. The camps were nearly self-sufficient. The inmates raised the first huts; inmate barbers and cobblers trimmed the SS men's hair and made them new boots. Local tradesmen were aware of the 1,000 SS guards only when they tried to collect the money owed them and were threatened with violence instead. People in the region were soon up in arms, demanding that the SS be withdrawn.

Berlin sent a commisson of SA leaders, police and Gestapo officials—Diels among them—to tour the camps. The camps were warned in advance of the visit and underwent a thorough housecleaning. Rations were increased, meat unpacked and the SS cooks given white aprons. Lame and crippled inmates were carefully hidden away. At Papenburg, Diels was permitted to speak to the prisoners in person. In reply to his question whether they were well-treated the prisoners stood ramrod straight and announced that their living conditions—straw mattresses beaten into perfect rectangular berths, floors burnished until they shone—were excellent, the food superb.

At Boergermoor, the commission toured two huts. When one hut senior valiantly stepped foreward to give a full report on the horrible food, the savage beatings, and the harsh labor conditions, the commission broke off its inspection. That night the rebellious hut senior was taken out and beaten with sticks and whips by the SS guards.

Diels had no doubt which of the reports was true. The mayor of Papenburg had described how the SS roamed the countryside like brigands from the Thirty Years War. Public houses were smashed, farmers' daughters seduced and abandoned. Once, a local electrical company cut the power to the camps in protest. The Prussian Ministry of Justice decided to send Dr. Joel and fifty heavily armed members of the Field Constabulary to investigate but when Dr. Joel tried to enter one of the camps he was fired upon by machine gun.

In Berlin, Goering and Diels called on Hitler, and Hitler ordered the moor camps taken by force. Two hundred policemen from Osnabrueck, the largest town in the region, were sent to reinforce Dr. Joel, but the rebellious SS refused to surrender and threatened to shoot any policeman who came within their sights. They were shocked by the news that they were to be replaced by units of the regular police, whom they regarded as the guardians of the hated Republic. Discipline among the demoralized SS grew ragged. Prisoners were no longer marched out to work, storerooms were looted, bonfires lit, fraternization permitted. When, in desperation, the guards offered to arm the prisoners if they would support their cause the Communist camp leaders only laughed.

To find out what was happening, the Boergermoor commandant drove over to Papenburg, the administrative center of the five camps, and returned with the upsetting news that scores of policemen with rifles and hand grenades had surrounded the Papenburg camp and meant to take it the following afternoon. Diels and Goering had again appealed to Hitler. Hitler had lost his temper and given the order to reduce the camps to rubble with artillery if necessary.

The next day dawned gray and wet. A squall blew in from the Atlantic. At 10 o'clock a spotter plane circled Boergermoor. At 11 an armoured car appeared with a police lieutenant and ten men. At 1 o'clock police units occupied the camp without opposition. In Berlin, Diels had arranged for back pay, blankets and new coats to be distributed among the SS guards. In return the SS, laid down their weapons and withdrew in good order, singing but unemployed again. The SS commandant was arrested and a police official appointed in his place. Diels and Dr. Joel were lucky; a few months later and Himmler would have been too powerful to push aside.

Later that month, as Diels was driving to work, he saw two of his aides urgently waving to him in front of the Ministry of Justice. He quickly pulled over. SS and Security police had occupied No. 8 Prinz Albrecht Strasse, he was told. His office had been searched and incriminating documents discovered. Goering had sworn out a warrant for his arrest.

Calmly pulling out into the morning traffic again, Diels retraced his route home on the hunch that he was still an hour or more ahead of his pursuers. Quickly he packed a few things. A man and a woman crossing the border, he reasoned, would be much less likely to arouse suspicion.

He did not take his wife Hilde with him. Instead his companion was Frau von Clemm, the vivacious wife of an American importer who lived on the Tiergarten. Frau von Clemm told friends that she was leaving for a rest cure in Czechoslovakia. Consul General Messersmith kindly supplied the necessary papers. Leaving Berlin, the couple drove east along the Potsdam road and then turned south. They reached the Czeckoslovakian resort town of Carlsbad by nightfall, the car's headlights picking out the streets between the snow drifts. Diels placed the car in a private garage.

Czechoslovakia was a haven for German Communists, Social Democrats, Troskyites and other splinter groups fleeing the Third Reich. Those familiar with the border took the train as far as Schoene on the German side and, properly outfitted in hunting jacket, requested a 48-hour border pass. Others, less well acquainted with the region, made the arduous trip across the Grosser Winterberg or along the Zinnwald plateau. But Diels did not have to count his pennies in a threadbare *pension* in one of the poorer districts of Prague. He and Frau von Clemm took rooms along the promenade and settled down to enjoy the winter season. He was easily mistaken for a successful German civil servant taking a pre-Christmas cure with his wife or mistress. Carlsbad permitted any number of liaisons between the sexes. Lately Diels' health had been poor. He suffered from numerous pyschosomatic maladies. His digestion was bad, his heart irregular. His physician asked if he were experiencing difficulties in his professional life. Diels smiled and said a few. In Carlsbad he enjoyed playing the gallant at the side of Frau von Clemm. He studied the refugee press and kept his ear to the ground. He may also have made a few unofficial visits, for when he left two weeks later the Czechoslovakian police, for the first time, began arresting German emigrés.

One afternoon he read an account of his term as Gestapo director in the German language paper *Bohemia*. Happily, no mention was made of his precipitous flight. The article treated him fairly and predicted that with his removal and the installation of Paul Hinkler, the former Nazi Police President of Altona, in his place, the path was clear for a complete dictatorship in Germany. Hinkler had announced publicly that, side by side with the SA and the SS, the Gestapo would be a standard bearer of the revolution.

Such talk, Diels knew, would only alarm Hitler, who was against further revolutionary turmoil. Nor would Goering be pleased to hear that his Gestapo had moved closer to Roehm and Himmler. Hinkler was an alchoholic, Diels knew, with a history of mental instability. There was a chance he might be invited back.

Feigning boredom with her cure, Frau von Clemm telephoned Goering's office in Berlin. The affable Pilli Koerner answered the phone, and the two chatted for a few minutes.

In passing, Frau von Clemm asked about Diels. Koerner confessed that the man had vanished into thin air. Frau von Clemm passed the receiver to Diels.

"For heaven's sake," exclaimed Koerner, "come back at once. Hitler and Goering did a dumb thing when they got rid of you. Everything has been cleared up. Hitler wants you back too. They tried to prove to Goering and Hitler that you were a Communist and that you were collecting evidence against Goering and Frau Sonnemann and against Roehm and the Fuehrer. All that has been revealed to be nonsense. We expect you to return immediately. This Hinkler is an idiot and shouldn't be allowed to remain at his post one more day."

Diels replied that he was not anxious to see the inside of a concentration camp. Before he would return he needed certain guarantees: that he would not be arrested, that he could deal with the SA as he saw fit, that the concentration camps would be closed, that the ridiculous system of political custody would end.

Koerner was sure that Goering would agree.

Diels asked for a few days to think it over. Only recently his life had been in dire jeopardy, his home invaded, his private papers confiscated. Men had conspired to kidnap and kill him. Only the kindness of foreigners had saved him. No one of importance, least of all Goering, had lifted a finger to protect him.

In a few days he called Koerner back. Koerner put Goering on the line.

"Herr Diels," said Goering, "I implore you to come back. I want to get rid of this dummy Hinkler today. I have prepared a directive that gives you complete independence. What you want, I also want. Order must be restored. When can you get here?"

"Late tonight."

"I'll be expecting you."

"One further question; why didn't you give the post to Himmler?"

"I wouldn't think of it."

At ten o'clock that night Diels strode into Goering's villa on the Leipzigerstrasse. All appeared forgiven. The attack on him had been the opening skirmish in an offensive against Goering, he learned. Fortunately for them both, Hitler's loyalty had never wavered. The Fuehrer, Goering said, was very impressed with Diels.

The news of his return spread quickly through Berlin. His enemies ran for cover, the SA grumbled, the SS gathered its forces in the Columbia

Haus. The building at No 8 Prinz Albrechtstrasse had to be liberated by armed guards and Hinkler forcibly ejected. In Diels' absence some of his closest colleagues had been shifted to other posts and replaced by Party members. Of the some 2,000 Gestapo employees, 20% now belonged to the SA, 30% to the SS.

When Martha met Diels, he was fast becoming the most neurotic personality in Berlin. He liked and trusted no one, except possibly Goering, and lived in constant fear of being shot, kidnapped or poisoned. He took Martha out dancing and to night clubs and tried to be seen as much as possible in her company. Once she met him at his office: a large, unpretentious room with few unusual furnishings except for the telltale dictaphones on his desk. He could have arranged for her to visit a concentration camp, but by then she had heard too much about such places. She was having nightmares; sometimes late at night the sound of an auto backfiring on the Tiergartenstrasse would cause her to start up and run to her mother for comfort.

At first she thought Diels' sinister power protected him until she realized how deeply afraid he was. There was no protection in Germany for any public official. After listening to his horrible tales of intrigue and terror, she began to shrink from his powerful intelligence, fearing that through some casual remark she might betray her German friends. She knew that he was always on the lookout for clues. He was not her friend out of kindness or sympathy, she saw, but because he was frightened and knew that his enemies could not get near him as long as he hugged the diplomatic limelight.

CHRISTMAS AMNESTY

After Germany withdrew from the League of Nations, the country went to the polls to ratify Hitler's decision. "Do you, German man, and you, German woman, approve your Government's policies, are you willing to declare them as the expression of your conviction and opinion and solemnly to acknowledge them?" Ninety-six percent of Germany's registered voters cast a resounding "JA" vote, but in the simultaneous vote for a Nazi Reichstag more than three million people, almost one out of every ten voters, deliberately disfigured their ballots. German feeling was not yet identical to Nazi policy.

The inmates in some 90 concentration camps also cast their votes. Out of 363 inmates in Oranienburg, 330 voted "Yes." In Boergemoor, on the Prussian moors, the Communists in control of the camp decided to vote "No" to prove to the world that they remained unalterably opposed to fascism. Boergemoor's commandant, a police general, gave the inmates a fierce dressing down: "Forty-three million Germans have noted 'Yes.' Do you hear me, forty-three millions! I can't really blame you for voting 'No,' but it is a beastly thing to scrawl all over your voting papers remarks like 'Down with Fascism! Up with the Communist Party! The Red Front still lives!' If you think that in future anyone will be released from this camp you are mistaken!" Of the roughly 6,000 prisoners in the five moorland camps only 53 voted "Yes." In releasing the figures, the government simply reversed the order and proclaimed a victory.

At Lichtenburg, a sixteenth-century castle first used as a prison by Napoleon, the prisoners reasoned that as everyone knew the elections in the camps were fraudulent they might just as well vote "Yes" and spare themselves further misery. At Hubertshof, another Prussian camp, the commandant told the prisoners: "Acknowledge National Socialist Germany, acknowledge Adolf Hitler, the worker. Then he will acknowledge you too, and clear the way for you to a new existence." Sixty-seven percent of the prisoners in Hubertshof voted "Yes," and the commandant was pleased until he saw the results from the other camps. Then he ordered renewed floggings.

No one recorded what happened to the valiant three who voted "No" in Dachau.

Perhaps some of Germany's leaders were fooled by the election re-sulted in the camps. When the Prussian Ministry of Justice announced that there would be a Christmas amnesty in Prussia for prisoners with families, Goering was thrown into a quandary. He wanted to close the camps but did not wish to release a flood of Communist fanatics on the country.

The State, Diels argued, was powerful enough to prevent the Communists from rebuilding their former organizations. The police, the SA and the SS were more than a match for them. What State in history, Diels asked, had ever received such an overwhelming vote of confidence from its people?

But Goering refused to take the action on his own. He and Diels went to the Reich Chancellery to see Hitler.

Hitler had the same misgivings; what if the Communists began their conspiracies anew?

There was no evidence that the Communists released to date had returned to their treasonable activities, Diels said. Their literature had been confiscated, their underground presses smashed. Many of the Communists in the camps were harmless members of the rank and file. Hadn't Molotov said: "I have nothing against the Nazi concentration camps. In them German class fighters will have the last bourgeois restraints beaten out of them"? Besides, there were many non-Communists in the camps, former members of the Social Democratic and Catholic Center parties. Oranienburg was full of such men. Their release would be perceived abroad as concrete evidence of Hitler's repeated calls for reconciliation.

Grudgingly, Hitler gave his consent. He could be compassionate when it profited him to seem so. Then he turned to Goering and revealed his true feelings about his former political enemies: "You see, Herr Goering, up to now I have not bothered myself with this affair, but when I constantly hear the excuses people make on behalf of these rogues, these beasts, I cannot remain silent. Have you forgotten the repulsive faces of these villains, these afterbirths from hell, who attacked us like wild animals during the years of struggle. I can still remember their pranks in the beer hall fights during their perverse speeches. Too much sympathy is wasted on these malicious gangsters. One accommodates them with care in special camps, feeds them, pampers them, even gives them work to do. I will not have this scum dirtying German soil. Shovels are too good for such people. This year, the year of the Revolution, is almost over and every one of them, every one of them, is still alive. They should have disappeared in the first housecleaning. I never left the Bolshevists in any doubt as to what we National Socialists had in store for them. I would have put these rascals up against the wall and executed them but if they must live, then I would have provided differently for their health, for their pleasure, which they value so highly. I would have given them Schnapps, raw whisky in open casks, for their uninterrupted enjoyment. They would have drunk themselves to death; that would have been a pleasant way for them to go from the human point of view. Oh, I should have loaded them on the empty hulks in Hamburg and Bremen and sent them to Helgoland; but on the way they would have drowned."

"The prisoners are to be left in no doubt," Goering announced in December, "that if they repay the generosity of the National Socialist State with new hostile activities I shall eliminate them ruthlessly and forever." Diels' first problem was to find out how many prisoners there were in the camps. He guessed there were roughly 20,000 in Prussia with another 7,000 in the rest of the Reich, but he did not know for sure. He sent out a directive requesting copies of each camp's records and the charges against each prisoner. But the camp records were in utter chaos. Inmates had been transferred or released and not crossed off the rolls. New inmates were not properly registered and in some cases could not be located. Camp officials, after all, were not interested in record-keeping but in making a profit on slave labor. As for the crimes the prisoners had committed or failed to commit, not even the prisoners knew for sure. Security Police, SS warders, and SA guards demanded of each prisoner the reason for his arrest, and the prisoner had to come up with some reason or run the risk of not being released at all. He couldn't very well say he was guilty of representing one of the recently disbanded liberal parties or that he had once raised the rent on a tenant who turned out to be a Party member. Communist inmates had good reason to hide the full measure of their opposition to the regime. Still, prisoners had to come up with some safe reason for their incarceration. Failure to salute the Party flag was a popular excuse.

In the third week of December, the inmates in Oranienburg concentration camp lined up to listen to Diels' speech of reconciliation.

"The Minister President has granted this amnesty on the basis of the recent election results. Only a few failed in their duty and the amnesty nearly did not come about due to the numerous atrocity articles coming from well-known emigrés in Paris and Prague predicting that it was only a ruse and that for every man released hundreds of new prisoners would enter the concentration camps. No one expects that upon your release you will immediately become loyal National Socialists. But it is expected that you will reenter the present State order and that you will not return to your earlier Communist, Social Democratic or Jewish leaders."

The flashes from the cameras of the international press yielded little warmth.

Between December 15 and December 23 Diels or his representatives visited the camps of Sonnenburg, Esterwegen and Papenburg. More than a thousand prisoners from the moor camps were brought to Papenburg to open trucks on the night of December 21. It was cold, nearly ten degrees below freezing, and Diels was late. When he arrived shortly before 1 o'clock in the morning with a crowd of photographers and the Regional Commissioner of Osnabrueck he must have been tired from his long train trip or eager to return to his host's warm hospitality for he omitted his customary speech and said simply: "You are free to go!" That was not strictly true. Only 300 men from the moor camps were released, or one-fourth of the inmate population. At Hubertshof 58 men out of 700 were released while 90 new prisoners arrived. Not even Diels could say for sure if the full 5,000 had been released by Christmas as promised. His estimates were only rough visual tallies.

From their inception, the camps had been shrouded in deceit. The prisoners were marched to work singing lustily. Beatings were called "examinations"; injuries were attributed to "a fall down the stairs." Thus, on the day of their release the lucky few were weighed and found not wanting. Miraculously, according to the records, everyone gained weight in the camps! Then they were given two statements to sign. They agreed to ask no compensation for any injury or hardship they had endured, and they acknowledged that any action the State had taken against them had been wholly justified. They swore further that they would commit no further offense, such as speaking of their life in the camps, in either word or deed. Any violation of this agreement, they were told, would lead automatically to their rearrest. They signed the statements eagerly.

The gates were unlocked and, carrying their meager possessions and their red release cards that bore the dates of their captivity and instructions to report regularly to the police, they were restored to a freedom they barely remembered.

Diels was returning from Papenburg on December 23 when he heard the news that the German Supreme Court had acquitted all the defendants in the Reichstag Fire Trial except the Dutch youth, Marinus van der Lubbe, who would be beheaded for the crime. The three Bulgarians were safe in the court jail in Leipzig; but Diels knew that Goering had promised Karl Ernst that he could have Georgi Dimitroff, the hero of the Fire Trial. Diels put through an emergency call to Berlin and learned that Goering had arranged for the transfer of Dimitroff and the other Bulgarians to Oranienburg. Diels issued an order to delay the transfer as long as possible.

At the Chancellery Putzi Hanfstaengl heard the rumor that the Bulgarians would be flown to Russia since no other country wanted them and that Goering intended to have Dimitroff murdered moments before the plane took off. The international repercussions would be enormous, Putzi knew; in the foreign press the Fire Trial had played second only to the beating of Americans. Greatly excited, Putzi confided his secret to Martin Sommerfeldt, Goering's press chief. In the past, the decent Sommerfeldt had helped him avoid several public relations disasters and, putting their heads together, the two came up with a plan. Sommerfeldt telephoned Louis P. and invited the AP bureau chief to lunch with him at the Hotel Adlon the next day. Goering, fortunately, was ill and out of town.

A nervous Sommerfeldt outlined his plan to Louis P.

"I've figured out there is one way of dissuading the general. When the foreign press claims one thing about him, he stubbornly does the opposite. What I'd like to have you do is to write a story and cable it to your paper, to the effect that you have learned on unimpeachable authority that the murder of Dimitroff is being planned by a high member of the government, and that such a murder, if carried out, could have far-reaching international consequences."

Worried that his bureau might be closed down if he went too far, Louis P. turned to Ambassador Dodd for advice but carefully kept Sommerfeldt's name out of the discussion, as even the Ambassador's diary was not secure against prying eyes. Did he have Dodd's permission to act? Dodd consulted with the British Ambassador before replying "Yes." Both ambassadors felt that Louis P. should do everything in his power to prevent Dimitroff's murder. The public outrage in America and Britian would be devastating to continued relations with Germany.

Sommerfeldt's plan had two problems. First, Louis P. risked damaging his unusually good relations with the Government. Second, his cable on the rumored assassination must travel all the way to America, be read by the German Embassy in Washington and then re-cabled to Berlin as part of a weekly press report. That might take as long as a week and by then Dimitroff would be dead.

The alternative was to use the British press and, as luck would have it, Reuters had just sent a new man to Berlin who would readily be forgiven for not knowing the rules. So the next day Louis P., Putzi Hanfstaengl and the Reuters man were sitting in the Adlon Bar when Martin Sommerfeldt wandered in as if by chance. Sommerfeldt was invited to join them, and Louis P. mentioned casually that he had heard a rumor that Georgi Dimitroff, the hero of the Reichstag Fire Trial, was to be murdered before he left Germany.

Sommerfeldt was indignant. Germany was a nation of justice and culture and Minister President Goering was a soldier, with a soldier's code of honor!

The Reuters man was fascinated and asked Sommerfeldt if he could use his denial for his wire service. Louis P. seconded the request. Sommerfeldt pretended to have doubts but finally agreed as long as the item was attributed to a "reliable source." The Reuters man was delighted.

That night the German Embassy in London telephoned the full text of the story to Berlin, and Sommerfeldt sent a copy to Goering. At first Goering was angry; but when he saw himself described as a soldier and a gentleman, his anger turned to delight. He released an official denial of the "horrid rumor" to the foreign press which Putzi read over the phone to Sommerfeldt with great relief. Putzi had not had many successes that year.

In the end Dimitroff and his two countrymen were brought to Berlin and put on a Duroluft flight at Tempelhof airport. No other passengers were allowed on board, and the three arrived safely in Moscow six hours later. Dimitroff had been saved by his democratic and fascist enemies.

Life in Germany was grim that winter. In towns under 50,000 the suicide rate increased by 14%. Refugee circles in Paris calculated that 3,000 people had lost their lives for political reasons in 1933, 119,000 were wounded, 174,000 imprisoned.

Diels' most controversial action that winter was the war on the monarchial organizations gathering to celebrate the Kaiser's 75th birthday. Louis P., whose stories on the Hohenzollern family were always timely, cancelled his trip to Holland that year when he saw that the big story was unfolding in Berlin. The German press was beside itself with outrage after it learned that the royal family refused to bring large areas of vacant moorland under cultivation because it would mean the loss of some 50,000 marks a year in privileged hunting fees! As telegrams and letters of congratulation poured into the exiled Kaiser's residence in Holland, royalist celebrations in Berlin assembled behind closed doors and drawn curtains.

The next to feel the heavy hand of the new Gestapo were homosexuals. All bachelors without mistresses were suspect, and an investigation of their papers usually turned up some remark critical of the regime. Even married men were occasionally run in. Herbert von Mumm, the aristocratic representative of the Protocol Office, was removed from the Foreign Ministry on trumped up charges of sexual inversion. Berlin, once the libertine capital of Europe, was shocked by the repression.

Diels also meant to bridle the excesses of the Hitler Youth. He composed a long list of religious processions disrupted, church windows broken, cruxifixes stolen and, in Goering's company, showed this to Hitler.

Hitler was not impressed. What did Diels expect to accomplish?

Merely to suggest that the Hitler Youth might better be placed under the command of the SA instead of its own youthful leaders.

"That is sheer nonsense," Hitler countered. "That would be like putting the goat in charge of the garden. Herr Goering, I have never raised this subject with you before but the entire country is talking about it. The crowd around Chief of Staff Roehm is completely and utterly perverted. It would be insane to entrust these people with the guidance of the Hitler Youth." He would be much more interested in a report on homosexuality within the SA.

Leaving, Diels told Goering that such a report would spell his doom.

"Come back immediately with me to Hitler," Goering demanded, "and repeat to him exactly what you just told me."

"I only said," Diels told Hitler, "that this assignment will cost me my head. We have ample evidence that the clique around Roehm is sensitive on this point. The bodies of two SA Leaders who objected to the tendencies among Roehm's clique years ago were recently found in Lake Walch. A few weeks ago, Herr von Flatow was found murdered on his estate in Pomerania for the same reason. Police President and SA Ober-fuehrer Graf von Wedel recently requested my protection because he felt threatened due to his criticism of the homosexual clique. Oberpresident and SA Group Leader Lutze also no longer feels safe since he complained allegedly to you about these tendencies. Several days ago two citizens from Breslau appeared before Herr Hess—who passed them on to me— to report on the unbelievable excesses committed by Group Leader and Police President Heines in Breslau. They told of debaucheries of this sort committed in the Hotel Savoy in Breslau that are known to everyone but which no one dares criticize. I had to supply these men with false identities so that they might remain in Berlin because they feared for their lives and dared not return to Breslau."

Hitler promised Diels full protection.

Consequently, the volume Diels prepared for Hitler on all aspects of the SA was as weighty and complete as he could make it. He documented the beginnings of the SA bunkers and beating stations, the illegal concentration camps, the martyrdom of German Catholics, liberals and Jews. In its pages Diels emptied the full pot of the SA's outrages.

He took the report to the Obersalzberg personally, but when he returned home that night all he would say to his wife was: "Don't ask me any questions. They are all murderers."

To an old friend who was also a lawyer he confided that on the Obersalzberg Goering and Hitler had ordered him to arrange the murder of SA Chief Roehm, General Kurt von Schleicher and other prominent figures.

"You come from a decent, landed family," his friend counseled. "None of your forebears were hangmen. You must get away from these creatures."

Diels asked Goering for leave of absence. He was ill.

"You are sick?" Goering rasped. "You had better make up your mind to be *very* sick."

"Yes, I am truly ill. I have done what I could to return the carriage of state to its proper path. I can do no more. I have often asked you to accept my resignation. Now, I cannot go on."

"All right, you are ill. Therefore, you cannot remain in service, not for a single day longer. You are confined to your home since you are ill. You will not make any long distance calls or write any letters. Above all else, watch your step."

Diels had joined the outcasts and like them fled a terror he could not escape. It was a fear worse than the fear he had felt as a youth in the Rhenania dueling corps when he entered the long cold hall where shreds of hair and dried blood dotted the ceiling. Noisily, the servants overturned baskets of swords and the floor was spread with sawdust as the surgeon unpacked his bottles of antiseptic and stitching implements. The youthful duelists donned heavy protective trousers and wound thick pads about their necks and chests. Iron goggles covered their eyes until only their cheeks and chins and foreheads remained exposed. Assistants with swabs of antiseptic gauze stood at the ready.

"*Silentium!*" cried the umpire.

The duelists, dressed like Mongolian warriors, stepped into the sawdust ring, swords in the air, their free hands clasped in their belts behind them. Seconds crouched at their sides.

At the cry "*Los!*" the fray began. Neither youth could alter his stance or move his head. When a second cried "Halt" the duelists stepped back. Their wounds were checked, their brows wiped dry. "*Los!*" and again the sabers swirled through the air, first at the head and then down toward the chin. "Halt!" One more round and the battle was done. After fifteen minutes of terror, the duelists stood decorated in riverlets of blood that ran down their cheeks and hung in shivering stalactites beneath their chins. The conflict over, their mettle tested they were led to the surgeon's table, where their wounds were cleaned and stitched over tureens of steaming water that soon turned the color of oxblood soup. The stitches, like the cuts, were taken without anesthetic.

Revolutionary terror had no end but lingered like a held note through the days and nights of the New Year and left Diels with nightmares, heart palpitations and a wasting digestion. He went to a sanitorium in Switzerland to rest. When he returned, he invited Martha and Bill to his home. They arrived to find him reclining melodramatically on a couch, two loaded pistols nearby. After ordering his wife out of the room, Diels gestured toward a large map of Germany covered with circles and codes in different colored inks: "You know, most of this is my work. I have really organized the most effective system of espionage Germany has ever known."

Then why did he live in fear, Martha asked.

"Because I know too much," Diels replied softly.

She saw him often in the following weeks. He feared for his life and avoided crowds and was often obsessed at how easily he could be poisoned. Yet, a sense of challenge also stirred his weakened body. Could he outwit his enemies, hide himself in a thicket so dense that none could follow? Martha's friends warned her that he was only using her, but she felt unafraid. As a diplomat's daughter she was safer than any German, safer than any official. Diels sought her out. He needed her protection. If half of what he told her were true he knew everything about her and her friends; it was useless for her to worry.

One afternoon he hinted darkly that he had gone to Switzerland for more than a rest cure. Was it to deposit certain papers abroad, she asked? What other protection was there, he replied?

He emerged occasionally from semi-retirement, in one memorable instance to close down a particularly heinous camp run by the local Gestapo office in Stettin. There in an abandoned tire factory on the dockyards, opponents of the regime were "retreaded" in a manner so cruel that a stenographer sent to the municipal hospital to take evidence fainted dead away. The Gestapo officials involved received stiff prison sentences, and Diels' office was further sullied in the public mind.

In March, he made a final appearance before the Berlin Foreign Press Association. Thirty thousand Germans had passed through the camps, he admitted, some 7,000 remained yet confined.

"We are no man-hating organization," he explained. "We believe in humanitarian treatment, not only force. If we have been charged with beating prisoners and other atrocities, I can only say that these charges disturb me less than the friendships that have quickly developed between our guards and our prisoners. Our protective custody, lasting only a few months, has permitted us to deal with many political offenders more lightly than a regular court would have dealt with them under the law. Our very arbitrariness, has turned out to their benefit."

The journalists' pencils must have paused at that statement.

Diels sounded more terrifying than he felt. SS officials within the Gestapo were forging evidence to show that a group smuggling illegal literature into Germany planned to assassinate Goering. Diels suspected a conspiracy against him but was too far from the center of power to act. When more than a hundred people were arrested, Diels was made to appear a fool. His agency had turned against him.

"I have decided to let you go and to entrust Himmler with the Prussian Political Police," Goering informed Diels. "I will remain in command. The press has already been informed."

"Then Heydrich has triumphed," Diels observed.

"Just what is that supposed to mean?"

"You will see in due time. Poor Germany!"

With that, Goering lost his temper: "You don't have to be sorry for Germany. Leave Germany to me. You have disappointed, compromised and abandoned me. Look to your own future."

"I always knew it would end this way."

"Just what do you mean by that?"

"Only that you would be well advised to surround yourself with a trusted bodyguard," Diels said, leaving the room.

The next morning Hitler sent for him.

"Roehm and his creatures have given me enough trouble," Hitler began. "If Goering thinks that he can saddle me with Himmler and Heydrich then he is mistaken. Himmler can have his SS. You are an expert and must remain at your post. If you wish to have greater authority, then I will give it to you. Goering once mentioned that you wished to become Minister of Police. I think such an office is unnecessary but we can consider it."

"I cannot stay. I am ill."

"You are not so sick that you cannot do your work which, in any case, will become easier with time. I know that you have worn yourself out combating the Communists."

At that Diels had to smile: "No, my Fuehrer, 90% of my frayed nerves comes from the SA and the SS."

With burning eyes Hitler replied: "You can rest assured that that won't continue for long."

"I am truly ill and cannot remain. I thank you for the confidence you have shown me."

Hitler fell silent, and Diels departed.

Diels now had to worry about his own skin. Since Ambassador Dodd was in America, he appealed to Martha to intercede for him with Consul

General Messersmith. He told her that he was about to be arrested by Himmler and shot.

With tears in her eyes, Martha pleaded with Messersmith at his office on the Bellevuestrasse to have a word with Goering, but the Consul General was not disposed to do Martha Dodd any favors. He quite disapproved of the Ambassador's two children. Neither was of much help to their parents; Martha in particular was notorious for her night life. He told her that Germany's domestic turmoil was none of his affair. He was an observer only. Any communication with Minister President Goering would have to take place at a higher level. With some difficulty he persuaded her to leave.

Then he began to have second thoughts of his own. Diels was one of the better officials in the Government and had unfailingly interceded in cases involving Americans. As it happened, Messersmith was due to dine at the Herrenklub that day, but first he called up the Air Ministry to see if he could locate Goering. An aide said that his chief had just left for the Herrenklub, where he was to be the special guest of Generals von Seeckt and von Fritsch. Messersmith was in luck.

When Messersmith entered the Herrenklub a little after noon, Goering was seated talking to his hosts. On seeing the Consul General, he rose and put an arm around Messersmith's shoulders. "Gentlemen, this is the man who doesn't like me at all," Goering said, "a man who doesn't think very much of me, but he is a good friend of our country."

Messersmith begged to have a few words alone with the Minister President. In a German as blunt as the German Goering used, Messersmith said that he had learned from a reliable source that Himmler meant to do away with Ministerialrat Diels. Goering's face grew dark. He thanked Messersmith and returned to his hosts. Expressing his regrets, Goering said that something important had come up which he must attend to immediately. The generals' reserve prevented them from showing the slightest sign of surprise.

When the afternoon edition of the *Berliner Zeitung* hit the streets, Messersmith read that Diels, only 34, had been appointed Regional Commissioner of Cologne. His post as Gestapo Inspector would be filled by Himmler. Later, in a conversational aside. Goering let Messersmith know that he appreciated his intercession. Diels' long courtship of the diplomatic community had paid off. He had found his lair.

At No. 8 Prinz Albrecht Strasse there was a thorough housecleaning. The last of Diels' associates were transferred to meaningless posts elsewhere. A few were arrested by Heydrich for not returning the Hitler salute. For the moment Heydrich resisted the temptation to merge his intelligence service with Diels' system. Instead, he insisted that the SS Intelligence Service remain separate, a darker shadow upon the deep gray of the Prussian Secret Police.

On April 20 Diels, in the black uniform of the SS, shook hands with Minister President Goering under a huge emblem of the Party banner as Heinrich Himmler looked on. The transfer of the Prussian Secret State Police to Reichsfuehrer SS Heinrich Himmler was complete.

In a final conversation with a British Embassy official, Diels spoke candidly about torture, officially applied:

"The infliction of physical punishment is not every man's job, and naturally we were only too glad to recruit men who were prepared to show no squeamishness at their task. Unfortunately, we knew nothing about the Freudian side of the business, and it was only after a number of instances of unnecessary flogging and meaningless cruelty that I tumbled to the fact that my organization had been attracting all the sadists in Germany and Austria without my knowledge for some time past. It had also been attracting unconscious sadists, i.e. men who did not know themselves that they had sadist leanings until they took part in a flogging. And finally it had been actually creating sadists. For it seems that corporal chastisement ultimately arouses sadistic leanings in apparently normal men and women. Freud might explain it."

PUTZI IN THE USA

In the spring of 1934 after his disappointing trip to Italy with his film "Hans Westmar," Putzi Hanfstaengl received a phone call from the Reich Chancellery.

"Hanfstaengl, you must come over to the Kaiserhof at once. There is no one to have tea with 'him.'"

So it had come to that. When the rest of the court was out of town he was summoned to amuse the chief. He could remember a time when he would have been the first one called.

A few minutes later, when he strolled into the Kaiserhof lobby, past the fake Hungarian orchestra, he spied Hitler sitting in a corner among the potted plants and a growing number of onlookers.

Over tea, the two old friends trotted out topics from earlier days: Richard Wagner, King Ludwig II, Hitler's inability to dance. They could each have taken the other's part.

Putzi said he was thinking of making a trip to America.

"What do you want to do there?" Hitler asked suspiciously. "Sell that film of yours?"

No, Putzi replied. He wanted to attend his twenty-fifth class reunion at Harvard. Attendance was more or less a point of honor. "It would be a good opportunity to talk to old friends," he angled. "Some of them are very influential by now. I may even see President Roosevelt."

With a yawn Hitler gave his permission.

What Putzi did not reveal—perhaps because he knew it would only awaken old prejudices—was that '09 Class Secretary Dr. Elliott Carr Cutler, the eminent Boston brain specialist, had asked him to be one of the fifty top-hatted, baton-bearing commencement aides in the June ceremony.

"I may even, as a surprise," Putzi told a group of American correspondents, "take with me my film, 'Hans Westmar,' which I showed to Premier Mussolini and to notables in Stockholm. That film can show better than any words of mine what we Nazis stand for."

From across the Atlantic Harvard could only reply, wanly, that reunion ceremonies were in the hands of the alumni and that if some of the class of 1909 wished to view films on the Nazi movement, Harvard could make no objection. But some of Harvard's Jewish alumni did object. Letters of protest poured in. The Harvard *Crimson* printed one that vaguely connected Putzi to Germany's new concentration camps: "If there are those whom his (Putzi's) heart would not delight so to honour, these would, in all policy, be grouped at the tail of the commencement parade and be allowed to witness the ceremonies from the outside, through keyholes and windows." The smart-alecky *Crimson* printed the letter under the caption *"Heil Hitler."* The student newspaper supported Putzi in the controversy and thought it childish to deprive a Harvard man of the company of other Harvard men for purely political reasons.

In Boston, Dr. Cutler was having second thoughts of his own. He had never dreamed that his invitation would stir up so much controversy. He rang up Putzi in Munich, where the foreign press chief was practicing a particularly elusive Chopin étude, and withdrew, however reluctantly, the invitation to be an aide. For his part, Putzi told American correspondents in Berlin that he was flabbergasted by all the furor. "As for propaganda, I have never made propaganda and never will," he declared. Scores of Americans as well as many classmates had written to him in support, but the press of "official business" made a trip to America out of the question for the present.

The month of May passed without further controversy.

In June, when correspondents asked if he had definitely abandoned his plans to visit Harvard that summer, he replied cryptically, *"Que vivra verra*—He who lives will see." Neither Harvard nor Dr. Cutler had raised any objection to his attending the ceremonies as an ordinary alumnus.

On June 10, American correspondents found cause to saunter past Putzi's Berlin residence at No. 3 Pariser Platz. The North German Lloyd liner *Europa,* the last vessel likely to get Putzi to Cambridge in time, was due to embark from Bremerhaven within the hour, and Putzi was throwing a gargantuan garden party. Foreign diplomats, government officials and old friends such as Magda Goebbels and Frau Emmy Goering showed up. It was a splendid affair although the country's three top men failed to appear. Putzi, in dark suit, looked imposing beside the statuesque Helene in flowing white gown. When it was over, the house and its owner remained in quiet seclusion. The reporters cabled their papers that Putzi would not be coming after all.

The ink was hardly dry on the morning editions when the typesetters were handed a second cable. Putzi, in a startling about face, had left his house in raincoat and dark glasses and caught a late train to Cologne where he packed his large frame into a German mail plane scheduled for a last-minute rendezvous with the outbound *Europa* at Cherbourg. Breathless and no longer in disguise, Putzi boarded the ship with five large suitcases and three wooden crates. The crates contained busts from the Hanfstaengl collection which he hoped to present as gifts to the military academy at West Point and to Harvard's philosophy and music departments.

The garden party had been a ruse. Putzi's assistant Voigt had already left for America to make the necessary preparations and the Foreign Ministry had been apprised of Putzi's plans well in advance. The head of the Anglo-American desk at the Foreign Ministry wished he could have blocked Dr. Hanfstaengl's trip abroad but lacked a suitable pretext. His only hope was that Dr. Hanfstaengl, the highest ranking figure in the Government to visit America, would handle any complication that arose with his customary charm and wit. In other words, the gentlemen of the German Foreign Ministry could only cover their heads and await the catastrophe they knew must come.

Miraculously, there was none. Outrageously incautious in his utterances in Berlin, Putzi moved with the grace of a waltzing elephant abroad. A guest at last, he abandoned his role of defensive Berlin host and relaxed and hobnobbed with the other Americans on board ship.

On the opposite side of the Atlantic, all was thrown into a frenzy of preparation. Harvard, fearing a bomb explosion killing and maiming alumni and spectators, consulted with the Governor of Massachusetts who called out the State Police. In New York, the Criminal Alien Squad was alerted to keep watch on subversives who might conceivably try to bring Dr. Hanfstaengl down. The American Jewish Committee and the B'nai B'rith sought to cast oil on troubled waters by issuing a joint statement recognizing Putzi's visit to America as purely personal in nature and expressing the hope that he would meet with no discourtesy.

As the great liner steamed into New York harbor late in the afternoon of Saturday June 16, a mob of almost 2,000 demonstrators waited for Putzi behind police barricades under the 12th Avenue expressway. The crowd brandished signs demanding: OUST NAZI HANFSTAENGL, SHIP THE HITLER AGENT BACK, and FREE ERNST THAELMANN. Nearly 100 of New York's finest and 50 plainclothesmen kept the crowd in line.

As tugs nudged the ship up against Pier 86 the object of all this ferment was giving a jovial interview in the first class salon to a group of newsmen who had come aboard with the quarantine and immigration officials. For the occasion Putzi wore a dark suit and tie with a softly symbolic tan shirt. He displayed not the slightest discomfort. After all, where he came from he was used to dealing with members of the American press.

"Is it true that you have come to American for political reasons?"

"I am very pleased to be in New York again. Actually, Hitler was against my making the trip. 'What sort of reunion is it?' he asked me. 'Can't you postpone it? We have a lot to do.' But then I missed the tenth and the fifteenth reunions of my class at Harvard. This time I wanted to attend. In the end I received permission."

"It is true that you intend to organize a National Socialist Party in America against the Jews?"

"Look, I am getting older and very much want to see old friends from my student years. Who knows if I will ever get the chance again!"

"It is reported that you wanted to arrange a banquet when the news of the sinking of the *Lusitania* reached America."

"At the time I received, quite by chance, word that my brother Egon had fallen in France. It does not seem very probable that I would have been in the mood to hold a banquet."

"You are the first prominent Nazi to come to America. Won't you say something about the Jewish question?"

"Certainly I could write six volumes for you on the political boycott against Germany, but I am on vacation. Perhaps later I will give you something political. When? In a few years maybe."

"Heywood Broun has suggested that you be interned on Ellis Island."

"Heywood Broun?" Putzi knit his brows in a look of profound concentration. "Oh, yes, I remember him. A nice fellow, a very nice young man. He was at Harvard a class behind me. You know, I think he said that out of class jealousy!"

Heywood Broun, in his column "It Seems to Me" in the *New York World Telegram,* had dealt harshly with Harvard's favorite son. Putzi deserved to be removed from the *Europa* and confined on Ellis Island as an undesirable alien, Broun said. Otherwise Washington must bear the blame for the bloody riots that would ensue. In Broun's opinion Hitler's minstrel deserved to be greeted with "thunders of silence and mountain ranges of inattention."

Broun then went on to furnish additional details of Putzi's forced resignation from the New York Harvard Club in May of 1916 following some incautious remarks about the *Lusitania* tragedy. The incident had started in the bar, worked into a fistfight and ended with Putzi lying recumbent and unconscious on the floor. Or at least that was what classmates told Broun. As for Dr. Ernst Franz Sedgwick Hanfstaengl's ability as a piano player, Broun summed that up in a single sentence: "He plays very loudly."

But the mood that afternoon in the first class salon of the *Europa* was jovial. Putzi was in his element. The reporters adored his aplomb. In America he was master of the wit that made him appear a fool in Berlin.

American business in Germany was safe, he said. The Chancellor enjoyed hearing him play but he did not summon him to play every time he was tired. "No, no. I am glad he does not, for he is tired often and I should be playing a great deal." He had not brought along his film, "Hans Westmar," after all and, for the record, his American friends called him "Hanfy" not "Putzi." The newsmen and their darling then trooped out to the sun deck for photographs. At their request Putzi, leaning against the ship's rail, raised his arm in an affable Hitler salute.

Stepping around to the other side of the ship, he addressed the sound cameras. "The situation of the Jews in Germany is fairly normal," he said. When an interviewer mistakenly referred to "Premier" Hitler, Putzi resolutely signaled for a retake.

The only disagreeable note of the afternoon occurred when several Jewish reporters pressed him for five minutes of his time. "I should like to give you 5,000,000 years," he snapped and turned his back.

The crowd of demonstrators on the pier eyed each departing cab expectantly and once mistakenly booed an innocent party. Finally, Putzi alone remained. After examining the situation one last time through binoculars from the ship's bridge, he decided on an alternate route ashore. Accompanied by six men from the Criminal Alien Bureau, he descended with his numerous pieces of baggage to a waiting police tug which took him rapidly up river to a landing near Columbia University.

Later, Goebbels would attempt to embarrass him on his flight:

"Well, Hanfstaengl, you must tell us how you so bravely swept aside the Communist demonstrators at the dock."

"Herr Doktor, what can you be thinking of? Should I have wandered unprotected into that mob? I was a guest in a foreign country after all, and certain security arrangements had been made by the authorities."

"Well, one can hardly claim that your arrival in the Jerusalem of the New World made a very heroic impression."

"You seem to have forgotten," Putzi parried, "how you, during the election campaigns, always paid close attention to detours that circumvented Communist strongholds."

But on the evening of his arrival the little Doctor's jibes were far in the future as he dined at the posh Claremont Inn on Riverside Drive. Afterwards, in the company of Quentin Reynolds, he showed up at the Stork Club on 51st Street. He was scheduled to take the 6 PM train to Boston but was delayed by Miss Olive Jones, a hostess-entertainer, whose piano waltzes bedazzled him for the next four hours. "A decided talent," Putzi opined, leaning heavily on Miss Jones' piano. "But you must practice five hours a day; three hours at the piano and two hours in retrospect."

"He's just a great big Don Juan," she told reporters later. " . . . And he

245

was so kind; he said I ought to go to Berlin to study music—and, what d'you think? He said if I went to Berlin he'd personally supervise my career."

He and Quent caught the midnight sleeper for Boston.

Collier's magazine, which Quent represented, had commissioned a piece on Hitler from Putzi. It was the first of many forays Putzi would make into the field of political reminiscence. In return for his essay, "My Leader," Quent handed him a check for $2,000.

The train pulled into Boston's South Station at 7:30 the next morning to be met by swarms of reporters, an army of police detectives and State Troopers, but not a single protestor.

Ralph Bradley, a classmate and cotton merchant, who had swung aboard in South Boston with a boisterous "Hello, Putzi," drove him out to Brookline and the home of "Naughty Nine's" class secretary, Dr. Cutler. Present at the meal was the elderly A. Lawrence Lowell, Harvard's president in Putzi's time. Lowell asked Putzi to explain his friend Hitler's popularity.

"If a car gets stuck in the mud," Putzi began, "and begins to sink deeper and deeper and the engine stops, and then a man comes along and pours something into the works which starts it up again, you don't ask what it was he put in. You set to and get the damned thing out. It may only have been *Begeisterungsschnapps,* a kind of psychological schnapps, but it is enough for the time being."

"This whatever-you-may-call-it may be all right to start with," replied the canny Lowell, "but what happens when the driver gets drunk on it?"

Putzi had no answer.

When lunch was over there was some consternation that the class of '09 was still some $10,000 short of its $100,000 reunion goal. Grandly, Putzi threw a thousand dollars of his *Collier's* check on the table. In America he was a different man.

All day, as he moved about Boston and attended the second game of a double-header between the Boston Red Sox and the St. Louis Browns, he was surrounded by reporters and a phalanx of watchful police. Four State Troopers had been assigned to him as bodyguards, two of them Jews. Ordered to don typical alumni dress—white flannel pants, sport jackets, striped ties—the four State troopers took a lot of ribbing down at the station. That night when Putzi stepped out into the back yard of Ralph Bradley's home in Back Bay to speak to the press, he saluted his reluctant protectors.

"To the health of my invisible but always alert army," he cried, brandishing a highball. "Gentlemen of the press, I give you gin! I believe with the illustrious Lord Nelson who thus expressed himself: 'Claret for children'—have you got that?—It's very important. 'Claret for children. Port wine for men. And gin for heroes!'"

He beamed at this midsummer pearl.

"Lord Nelson said 'Brandy for heroes,'" a voice chimed in.

"You're right, you're right. But make it gin for heroes anyway, gin is a better drink than brandy. Gin for heroes! I'll stick to that."

"What is the real reason behind your visit?"

"Baseball! Earlier today I watched a baseball game. It was magnificent! What speed! What sliding! What throwing! Intently I followed each move of the contest. I saw the facial agonies of the pitcher and the sardonic satisfaction of the catcher. I just wish I could have had several hundred young Germans to see what I have seen today. It would be a wonderful lesson about a friendly country."

"What is your favorite music?"

"Classical music—Bach, Schumann, Wagner."

"What about American Jazz?"

"Oh no. That I leave to the Negroes. I do not compete with a man in his specialty. The Municker drinks his beer, the Scotsman dances the highland fling, and the Negro plays his jazz. I do not compete with any of them."

"What did you and President Lowell talk about?"

"Bismarck, Demosthenes, the art of public speaking and Hitler as an orator."

"Is Hitler anything more than an orator?"

"A man must be something more than an orator to guide a large nation. Is that not so?" Putzi countered testily. "A man to run merely a clipper must know what he is doing. Is that not so? And to run a large country, to keep his power when not everyone is for him, that takes something, too, doesn't it?"

"Aren't you on a mission for Hitler?"

"Heavens on earth, no. I am here to loaf."

"Have you ever heard Roosevelt speak?"

"Which one? I have heard both, the former President Roosevelt and the present one. But you mean the present one, of course. Yes, I have heard him on the radio. He is splendid! Magnificent!"

"Who is the better orator, Roosevelt or Hitler?"

"That is like asking which is better in a storm, umbrellas or overshoes."

Would he object if he were asked about his views on the Jewish question?

"Oh, no, but I do not think it is good to discuss that question. It

247

doesn't help Germany and it doesn't help the Jews. But I will say this. I will say that the Jew's situation in Germany is going to be normal before long."

"Have you found many Americans to be hostile to you due to your country's policy on the Jews?"

"Americans are like children. You cannot please all of them all of the time." That didn't sound quite right: "Americans are like children in that they are good, too, and they are like children in that you can't fool them. But I didn't come here to fool anybody. I came to fool around—there's a great difference, you know."

What were his plans?

"I don't know when I may be called back," Putzi replied, his voice heavy with fatigue. "I expect to be here for several weeks, until you are sick of me. Tomorrow I am going for a swim. It may be on the North Shore. I won't know until tomorrow. Anyhow I've brought my bathing suit with me.

"Sometime before I leave I want to sleep just once more in the Harvard yard. Harvard has changed a lot. There are many new buildings, but the yard is almost the same. I'm going to sleep there one night this week, but I don't think I shall announce what night it will be."

The thought of a dip in the chilly north Atlantic must have revived Putzi, or else the call he was expecting came through. As policemen stood guard that night on Ralph Bradley's well-lit porch, Putzi, in a surprise move, motored north to Beverly Farms and the home of classmate Louis Agassiz Shaw. There he spent several hours pounding out Bach concertos before turning in. The following day he rose early, played some more Bach and then drove down to Boston with friends to attend a luncheon at the home of a Massachusetts Saltonstall. In the coming days, he continued the tactic of staying in Beverly Farms and motoring down to Cambridge for the festivities, his titanic energies exhausting a fleet of reporters. Society matrons joined his retinue that afternoon, and he sat as advisor to one at a horse race. He bet no money, he told reporters, but he did root for a horse carrying brown colors. The race was hardly over when he rushed off to attend memorial services for the dead of the class of 1909 in Harvard Chapel. As the great bell tolled overhead, the roll of the dead was recited. Sixteen sons of Harvard had fallen in the Great War. When reporters sought an interview with Putzi as he was leaving he said: "I don't feel like talking very much. I knew practically all of those boys whose memory we were honoring in there."

He did agree to a short question and answer session in a shady corner of Harvard Yard. As the reporters from Boston and New York crowded around, Rabbi Joseph Shabow, also of Harvard, cried out: "What did you mean in your interview yesterday that the Jewish problem would soon be restored to normal? Did you mean by extermination?".

"Now, now," Putzi replied, pained by the implication. The Yard police swiftly declared the interview over and, taking Putzi sternly by the arm, led him in the direction of President Conant's house where the traditional tea for the class of 1909 was about to commence. In the background, Rabbi Shabow could be heard protesting that he was just as good a Harvard man as Hanfstaengl. It was the only unpleasantness of the visit.

The affair at President Conant's home was formal. Each alumnus, with name badge and spouse, filed into the ballroom past the president and his wife. When Putzi's turn came, he shook Dr. Conant's hand and said: "I bring you greetings from Professor Hoenigschmid of Munich." Dr. Conant smiled but made no reply. He remembered Hoenigschmid from his sojourn in Germany in 1925. The professor had been an ardent nationalist then and, Dr. Conant suspected, was probably a loyal Hitlerite now. To Dr. Conant's relief, Putzi said nothing about the proffered "Dr. Hanfstaengl Scholarship."

Putzi had made the offer in May when his trip to Boston was still undecided. The code of discipline and fair play "inculcated on the playing fields of Harvard" were vivid memories, he wrote Dr. Conant. By all that was holy in Franklin, Emerson and Longfellow, he wished to double his class subscription of $500 to establish a "Dr. Hanfstaengl scholarship" to enable some young Harvard student—preferably the son of one of his classmates—to come to Germany to study for a year. Accompanied by a number of correspondents, Putzi marched into the Berlin banking firm of Delbruck, Schickler and Co. to draw up a check for 2,500 marks. "I want this check deposited subject to the order of the Harvard president regarding its disposition," he told the teller loud enough for the newsmen to hear.

It was a characteristically impulsive gesture but it put Harvard in something of a quandary. Customarily, class donations were given without restrictions. Gifts, on the other hand, were associated with a donor's name but only if they were in excess of $10,000 and approved by the Harvard Corporation. As for a scholarship, Dr. Hanfstaengl had made no provision for future funding. Did he think he could buy back his post as commencement aide? Was the offer a means of highlighting the niggardliness of his Harvard critics? Would the student chosen return to Harvard a mouthpiece of the German government? That afternoon President Conant was grateful not to have to go into these matters before an audience.

What he could not see from his vantage point in New England was that Putzi's offer was genuine and certainly courageous since foreigners and their sponsors were objects of suspicion in the New Germany. Putzi sought an ally, even a youthful, raw-boned ally, to bring Harvard's liberal light to Munich. But his ideal of intellectual exchange came too late. By 1934 American academics wanted to punish Germany, not enlighten her. At the very least, they hoped to keep their youthful charges safe and uncontaminated on American shores.

On Tuesday a nor'easter blew in. Several events had to be cancelled due to rain; but fortunately not an outing on a 5,000-acre estate belonging to a wealthy Harvard son and railroad tycoon. Putzi was charmed by all the children who showed up. "They look at me in a mixture of admiration and stupefaction," he told reporters.

"What do you think of American women?"

"Let me tell you. I married an American woman, a Long Island woman, the most beautiful woman in the world. I entrusted the very important task of bringing myself into the world to an American woman, my mother. Can I say more than that?"

He was asked about his son, Egon.

"He's going to join the Navy. He's a great friend of Count Felix von Luckner. I come home, and he pays no attention to me. He loves Luckner. He's going into the Navy surely."

How was he spending his time lately?

"You want to know what I've been doing, eh? Well, I've slept, slept, slept. Your President Roosevelt once remarked to me that the time we spend sleeping is the only time we do not waste."

That night the class of 1909 enjoyed a boisterous stag dinner at the Harvard Club. "The rain is a fine thing," Putzi said waving his glass as he disappeared into the Club. "It confines us to indoor sports, which are not without their merits."

Wednesday, the day for which Putzi had traveled so far, dawned warm and clear. Along with more than a thousand other alumni, he broke festive bread at one of the numerous college houses set aside for that purpose and then, toward noon, took his place in the lengthy columns forming up behind alumni marshal Dr. Cutler to make the boisterous trek across Lars Andersen Bridge for the annual "confetti battle" in Harvard's ivy-covered football stadium.

The sky was blue, the playing field bright green, the brass bands plentiful and loud. The classes of 1914 and 1919 commemorated their twentieth and fifteenth anniversaries that year; but the first to be greeted by the more than five thousand wives, friends and proud offspring lining the stadium were the seven surviving members of the classes of 1869, 1873 and 1878 who made their entrance with faltering steps and faded banners. Then came the class of 1914 in white trousers, orange polo shirts and black caps. Close behind followed the class of 1919 in white trousers and blue tunics singing "We haven't seen Hitler in a Hell of a while." Ribboned letters on their backs lampooned the New Deal and America's recent repeal of prohibition: "1919 Supports the NRA—Never Refuse Alcohol" and, "We Have a Code in Our Head." Five of the "Nineteeners" held a placard aloft that presaged the humor to come.

1919
FOR CLASS PRESIDENT
MAX HANFSTANGEL
FOR CLASS VICE PRESIDENT
ADOLF KEEZAR

Poor Mr. Keezar was a Jewish haberdasher on Harvard Square.

No one was prepared for what came next: the sight of the class of 1924 goosestepping into the stadium, arms held high in the Hitler salute. Dressed in authentic Bavarian costumes—shorts, knee socks and green felt hats—they drew a huge beer truck behind them bearing the sign "Harvard Beer and Ale." The class of 1931 followed in white bartenders' aprons.

Putzi's class, numbering 300, was the largest. Preceded by the HANF-STANGEL FOR PRESIDENT banner, its members—wearing straw boaters, white trousers and dark coats—filed across the stadium in pairs. Except for Putzi. He wore a frock coat with a red carnation in his button hole. As he waved and saluted and stood for photographs the banner carriers razzed him with the Hitler salute. Once the banner was seen to go down but reappeared later, apparently none the worse for wear. The graduating seniors in black caps and gowns trailed in, almost as an afterthought. While brass bands churned out a cacophony of Harvard tunes, German drinking songs and traditional American airs, a senior delivered a satirical farewell address and the class of Naughty Nine bestowed frivolous degrees on some of its more illustrious members such as a D.C.N., or "Debunker of Current News," on H. V. Kaltenborn. President Conant, who was unavoidably absent, was enthusiastically cheered and everyone rose to sing a final rendition of "Fair Harvard." As the strains of the last verse died on the air all hell broke loose in a frenzy of confetti and streamer-throwing that lasted a full fifteen minutes and turned the heavens into a rainbow of glittering paper.

Thus refreshed, the crowd withdrew to Soldier's Field to watch the Harvard-Yale baseball game. It was on the walk over that Putzi had his hand shaken by a beaming, roly-poly person whose name he could not for the life of him remember. Later he learned that his admirer was a classmate, Max Pinansky, Maine's first Jewish judge. The afternoon papers printed their own version of the symbolic handshake while Harvard defeated Yale 3 to 2.

Putzi skipped commencement the following afternoon and spent the weekend on the North Shore with an old flame who lived in Beverly Farms. In the middle of the week he appeared in Boston to dine with members of the German consulate and to announce, proudly, that he had received an invitation to attend the social event of the season, the wedding of America's wealthiest bachelor, John Jacob Astor 3rd to Miss Ellen Tuck French. The romance had taken place under the gaze of the entire East Coast and the marriage, on Saturday in Newport, Rhode Island, was expected to bring out America's "Four Hundred" foremost families. Some papers reported that the bride's mother was none too pleased to learn that her former husband had invited Hitler's favorite pianist. Undaunted, Putzi arrived in America's summer capital in a rattling Ford roadster driven by the son of a classmate.

The date was June 30, 1934, and upon hearing the news from Germany telling of the arrest and dismissal of many of the men who had helped Hitler to power, Putzi could only tell reporters that "such things might happen in any country." Surreptitiously, he gathered up all the newspapers he could find and retired to a nearby hotel to study them before rushing off to an informal pre-wedding luncheon in his honor.

"I have no comment to make," he told reporters. "I am here to attend the wedding of my friend's daughter. The wedding is more important than anything else today. I never mix business with pleasure and today I stick to my program."

He stole the limelight again as he entered Trinity Church dressed in black cutaway, striped trousers and smartly polished cylinder hat. Such was the heat that weekend that the other guests were reduced to informal summer wear. One paper commented that Putzi looked as out of place as a nudist at a costume ball. Sitting on the Astor side of the church, he was listening to the organ music and savoring the sensation of having for once penetrated to the center of American social power, when he felt a tug at his sleeve. An intruder had crawled down the isle to ask him to comment on the news that SA Chief of Staff Ernst Roehm had been arrested for attempting to overthrow Hitler. "Not here—later—outside," Putzi whispered. As in so many other moments in his life, he had been upstaged precisely at the apogee of his glory. The heavy aroma of orchids suddenly reminded him of a funeral parlor and he felt fearfully lightheaded as 18-year-old Ellen Tuck French promised to honor and keep her husband. The word "obey" was carefully omitted from the ceremony.

As the young couple hurried off to honeymoon in British Columbia, Putzi told reporters in all earnestness that he had no idea what was happening in Germany. He needed time to think.

His confusion can be imagined. In the coming days he would read not only about Roehm's execution but the execution of others who had belonged to the Flying Circus. A former Chancellor had been executed, another was in exile, a third under house arrest. There were no reliable reports on the number of people arrested.

Before reporters at Beverly Farms he wrapped himself in the cloak of imperial grandeur.

"News that came on Saturday was news to me but it was not entirely unexpected news. My leader, Adolf Hitler, had to act and he acted; thus as always."

Putzi admitted knowing many of those executed but said he felt no sorrow. "There will be others who will fill their places," he said somewhat cryptically. Through the consulate in Boston, he secretly sent a cable to von Neurath in Berlin asking if it was safe to return. Baron von Neurath replied that it was and the sooner the better. The deciding factor for Putzi was that his family was still in Germany; Helene in Berlin and Egon in Munich. He booked return passage on the *Europa* for July 7th and hastened to finish old business.

On a hot summer's day he arrived in Cambridge with two of his crated busts only to discover the folly of postponing generosity until the last moment. Harvard was deserted. Daubing his leonine face with a scented handkerchief, he paced the empty halls of Harvard's music building until he encountered, quite by chance, the head of the music department who had dropped in to gather a few notes before going on vacation. Thus did the bust of Christolph Wilibald Ritter von Gluck, Putzi's favourite composer, find a niche at Harvard. Schopenhauer was not so lucky. After searching in vain for someone in the philosophy department, Putzi and Schopenhauer's bust returned to Beverly Farms by taxi.

On July 4th he chartered a private plane and flew with the crated bust of Field Marshall Paul von Hindenburg to the American Military Academy at West Point. The Point had not been informed of Putzi's visit and said that it must consult with Washington first. A despondent Putzi stood on a promontory next to the statue of his illustrious Civil War grandfather, Major General John Sedgwick, and gazed at the waters of the Hudson below. The bust of that "Grand Old Man of Germany," as Putzi called Hindenburg, also accompanied him back to Beverly Farms.

In New York Putzi's assistant, Harald Voigt, put the best face possible on the misunderstanding. The busts of von Hindenburg and Schopenhauer were only "casts" and would be part of a fall showing of the works of the sculptor Joseph Torak at one of New York's finer galleries.

The West Point contretemps offered one advantage. In a letter to the superintendent of the Academy, Putzi stated that he would be returning in the fall to attend the Harvard-Yale football game. In the meantime he gave as his address the Reich Chancellery in Berlin. Thus was America's oldest military institution put on notice that "E. F. S. Hanfstaengl" fully expected to return in the fall, alive and unharmed. The letter—Putzi's insurance policy—made its way to the press and into the files of the German Foreign Ministry.

Nevertheless, he was in a somber mood when he boarded the *Europa* on the evening of July 7th.

"The art of diplomacy and the art of statemanship differ. But somewhere they meet," he intoned. The jovial son of Harvard, who had arrived flourishing a meaty paw of goodwill, departed in morbid spirits. As he mounted the gangway he came to attention, scented handkerchief to his side, one arm raised stiffly toward the swastika flag flying from the ship's masthead.

"What happens is inevitable," he told reporters. "Is that not true of history?"

MUTINY

On the morning of "bloody Saturday," June 30, while Putzi slept soundly before his drive to fashionable Newport, an American scholar walked across Berlin to return a book to the Reichstag Library and noticed nothing out of the ordinary. Not until 11 AM did the first trucks filled with Goering's green police race down the Stresemann Strasse to the center of the city. As the traffic pulled to the side, it was clear that the men in heavy steel helmets were not participating in a drill. The diplomatic quarter south of the Tiergarten was occupied, Roehm's luxurious residence surrounded and sealed off.

A traffic jam near the Reichswehr Ministry on the Bendlerstrasse trapped a reporter for the *London Times*. Next to him, heading in the opposite direction, was a taxi carrying a young woman who sat weeping. She was an attractive woman and stared straight ahead as the tears rolled down her face. The *Times* man sensed that she was crying over something more tragic than a romantic quarrel.

Louis P. knew something was up when his office boy returned with the news that trucks full of uniformed SS men were converging on Gestapo headquarters and that the Prinz Albrecht Strasse was closed to all motorized traffic. He put a call through to Munich to ask if the Army had occupied the Brown House, but the German stringer there was too frightened to talk. Suspecting that something serious was in the wind, Louis P. alerted the AP bureaus in Paris and London and asked them to telephone his office every fifteen minutes for the next few hours. He had a hunch that the Government might try to disrupt outgoing telephone communications.

At 3 o'clock he was summoned with the rest of the foreign press to the Propaganda Ministry. Goebbels was with Hitler in Munich. It was Goering, surrounded by somber aides, who entered the press hall with the sarcastic remark: "Once again I have to worry about this nightwatchman ministry." Goering was dressed in the light blue uniform of the Air Force. His account of a mutiny within the ranks of the SA was brief and brutal.

"I just want you to keep to the truth," he told the reporters. "No pictures of fantasy for the sake of a story are necessary are there?

"For weeks and months we have observed that a certain clique of Storm Troop leaders tried to misuse loyal Storm Troopers to precipitate a so-called second revolution in order to overthrow the State and establish their own ridiculous regime. For weeks and months there have been complaints from the country that these Storm Troop leaders acted brutally against the population and that things happened that could no longer be brought in line with the sense of justice of the people.

"For weeks this clique has been under the supervision of the secret police. Today the Fuehrer himself determined to set an example. Whoever rebels against him loses his head.

"Roehm and certain others of his more intimate staff tried to exert pressure on the Fuehrer. Because of this, Roehm has been expelled from the party, deprived of all his offices and thrown into prison. The supreme leader in Munich and I, as his deputy in Berlin, struck with lightning speed to suppress any resistance without respect for persons.

"The Storm Troopers themselves are good, brave and self-sacrificing. They will follow their new Storm Troop leader."

With that Goering strode from the room but returned almost immediately: "Ah yes, you journalists always like a special 'Headline' story; well, here it is. General von Schleicher had plotted against the regime. I ordered his arrest. He was foolish enough to resist. He is dead."

Goering's face beamed as if to say: "You see, I've had my revenge."

The reporters rushed to their cars. When Louis P. reached his office, London was on the line. With only his German notes as a guide, he immediately began dictating his story into the phone. He was on the last sentence when the operator broke in to say that outgoing calls in a foreign language would no longer be permitted. Later, when the Paris office tried to reach him it was told: "Berlin does not reply!" Once again Louis P.'s quick thinking had scooped the competition. The other news services in Berlin got no news out that afternoon.

Meanwhile, the Nazi press office in Munich released an intriguing bulletin. At 2 o'clock that morning Hitler had flown to Munich with a few companions and driven to the resort town of Bad Wiessee where Roehm was vacationing. "The execution of the arrest revealed such immorality," the bulletin continued, "that any trace of pity was impossible. Some of the Storm Troop leaders had taken male prostitutes along with them. One of them was even disturbed in a most ugly situation and was arrested."

The task of burying Roehm's name in mud had begun.

In the next 94 hours, with only a few pauses for sleep, Louis P. and his staff cabled more than 30,000 words to America. Realizing that the other news services would rely on the official version of events, Louis P. and his colleagues worked to emphasize the human side of the "blood purge." While one of his staff monitored the flurry of official bulletins, two of his German assistants toured the city's restaurants, markets and night spots to find out what the people in the street had to say. Berlin was bright and peacefully cool that evening as crowds gathered to study the single-page news sheets the Government was releasing. Some citizens were delighted to hear of Roehm's fall; others were apprehensive. Coffee houses and restaurants played catchy tunes and march music. The radio was filled with only the lightest of dance airs. For the most part, the crisis was received with surprising nonchalance.

Never had so many regular police been called out to protect the government district. A police detachment with a machine gun stood guard on the Potsdamer Platz while another rode up and down the broad thoroughfare of the Unter den Linden. Constables constantly urged the crowds to keep moving and only replied with a shake of their heads when they were asked what was happening and why. Taxis were scarce, and for a short time that afternoon the subways had been suspended because so many people were trying to reach the center of the city. Goering's heavily-armed green police were especially numerous near the Brandenburg Gate and around the Ministry of the Interior. No one could get close to Gestapo headquarters. Access to Vice Chancellor von Papen's offices was also strictly forbidden.

Around 6 o'clock, Martha Dodd and Armand Bérard returned to Berlin after a long day of sun and sand at one of the beautiful lakeside beaches outside Berlin. The weather was unseasonably hot and the two young people had spent the day close to the shimmering water, too relaxed to speak or even think about politics. The sun was still high when they started back, hungry and slightly giddy from so much light. They sped through piney woods and down acacia-lined avenues. It was a Saturday evening like any Saturday evening with people strolling in pairs or sitting on balconies among their flower boxes. Enjoying the cool breeze, Martha rode with her skirt up and thought to herself that it would take a good night's sleep to accustom herself again to the claustrophobic world of shaded interiors. She was to reenter that world sooner than she expected.

As they approached the city, they noticed that there were fewer people on the streets than usual and that these stood about in isolated groups as if awaiting some word or news in motionless expectation. Helmeted police in blue uniforms stood at all the major intersections. Black-uniformed SS men were posted in front of the government ministries. Hurriedly, Martha pushed down her skirt. One note, she noticed, was missing: the color brown. Among all the uniforms in black and blue and light green, the brown shirts and caps of the Storm Troops were nowhere to be seen.

As they approached the Tiergarten, they encountered long rows of military vehicles filled with heavily-armed police. The Tiergartenstrasse was closed to civilian traffic but they were let through. Martha got out at the foot of the drive and ran toward the house while Armand hurried off to check in at his own embassy. On the Matthaeikirchstrasse he saw machine guns mounted for action. He was asked to show his diplomatic card. The headquarters of the Berlin-Brandenburg SA, only two doors down, was completely sealed off, and Goering's police were removing armloads of documents from Roehm's villa on Standartenstrasse and loading them into waiting lorries.

Martha ran into the house and down the long hall to the spiral staircase that rose to the second floor.

"Martha, is that you?" her brother's cautious voice called from the floor above. "Where have you been? We were worried about you. Von Schleicher has been shot. We don't know what is happening. There is martial law in Berlin."

For a moment, in her panic, Martha could not remember who von Schleicher was.

Two weeks earlier, a sharp note of criticism had been voiced by Vice Chancellor von Papen in an astonishing speech at the University of Marburg. Without retreating one step from his stance as Hitler's foremost supporter, von Papen attacked the shape of the new Germany. It was the last courageous speech by a public official in the Third Reich.

"If the outside world claims that liberty is dead in Germany, let it be taught by the openness of my exposition that the German Government can afford to make the burning problems of the nation the subject of debate. . . .

"We in Germany have one single party in place of the multi-party system which lately and justly has disappeared from Germany.

"This I regard as only a transition state and justified only so long as it is demanded for safeguarding the revolution and until a new personal selection begins functioning. . . .

"It goes without saying that the supporters of the revolutionary principle will first of all also occupy the positions of power. But when the revolution is completed then the government can represent only the totality of the nation. Never is it representative of special groups, for, if it were, it could not effect a popular union.

"In this connection it is necessary also to abandon false and romantic ideas unsuited to the twentieth century. Thus we cannot think to repeat the division of the people, on the ancient Greek model, into Spartans and Helots. At the end of that ancient development the Spartans had nothing to do except to hold down the Helots, and thus Sparta's external power was weakened. . . .

"The worst sort of intellectualism is the dominance of catchwords. Thus there are persons fundamentally liberal who do not utter a sentence without misusing the word liberalism. They characterize freedom as a liberal concept, whereas in truth it is arch-Germanic. They attack equality before the law, which is pilloried as a liberal degeneration, whereas in truth it is the prerequisite of any just decision. . . .

"It is a wholly reprehensible notion that a people could be united through terrorism. The government will counter any endeavor in such a direction, realizing that terrorism is a sign of bad conscience and that it is the worst counsel to any leadership.

"No organization, no propaganda, however excellent, would be able by themselves to maintain confidence in the long run. I, therefore, all along held a different opinion of the propaganda movement against so-called critics. Not by incitement, especially of youth, not by threats against the helpless part of the nation—only by a confidential talking it over with people can confidence and devotion be raised.

"History is waiting for us—but only if we show ourselves to be worthy of it."

The Vice Chancellor was startled by the roar of applause when he finished. He had first read the speech on the train to Marburg and thought some of its points too sharply drawn. But he was relieved to have cleared the air and felt ready to face the consequences he knew must come.

"Yes, yes, my dear Papen, your Marburg speech was very fine," a colleague chided afterward. "Too bad, though, that you delivered it and not Goebbels."

Goebbels was swift to react. A recording of the speech for rebroadcast was confiscated, and the German press was instructed to keep silent. Only the *Frankfurter Zeitung* and the *Berliner Morgenpost* published excerpts. When von Papen complained to Hitler that a junior minister had forbidden the circulation of an official speech by the Vice Chancellor, Hitler protested that Minister Goebbels had acted only to reduce political tension. Hitler promised to go with von Papen to see Hindenburg to discuss the speech and other matters of State.

Inexplicably, von Papen hesitated and Hitler saw Hindenburg alone. In the end there was no confrontation: von Papen stayed on as Vice Chancellor, and Goebbels' ban on the speech remained in effect. Underground copies of the speech were circulated in pamphlet form. The correspondent for the *Chicago Daily News* lent Ambassador Dodd a copy for twenty-four hours and Dodd, understaffed as usual, labored over a translation to cable to Washington.

After von Papen threw down the gauntlet at Marburg, foreign observers waited for the second round in the duel. Surprisingly, it came in the guise of a comic interlude following a speech by Reichsbank President Schacht attended by both the Vice Chancellor and the Propaganda Minister. In the question and answer period that followed, an American correspondent rose to ask Goebbels if his relations with Vice Chancellor von Papen had been damaged by the Marburg speech.

Goebbels leapt from his chair and cried: "Herr von Papen! Herr von Papen!!"

In the nervous hush that followed, the entire room turned to watch as von Papen hastened toward Dr. Goebbels who lurched the last few steps to embrace the Vice Chancellor, crying: "My dear Herr von Papen, did you hear: the two of us are supposed to be on unfriendly terms, precisely the two of us who are the best of friends!"

Turning then to his audience and holding von Papen's hands in his, Goebbels exclaimed: "Gentlemen, I assure you, there has seldom been such a close understanding between two ministers of the same cabinet, as between Herr von Papen and me."

But the correspondent from America would not be put off: "It has been reported to me that it was you, Herr Propaganda Minister, who ordered the seizure of the printed copies of Herr von Papen's speech at Marburg!"

"A wanton lie and aspersion!" Goebbels shouted. "The Marburg address of my friend Papen was in the best spirit of the regime. Isn't that so, Herr von Papen?"

Von Papen, who did not know what to say, could only nod his head in agreement, moved and bewildered at once. Afterwards, the two took tea together at the same table; signifying, the correspondent from the *New York Times* wondered, that the dispute was merely a tempest in a teapot?

Meanwhile Goebbel's paper, *Der Angriff*, published a cartoon of a Storm Trooper kicking a top-hatted gentleman. The Gestapo moved in and arrested Edgar Jung, the young aide in von Papen's office who had drafted the Marburg address. In his diary, Dodd noted that the atmosphere in Berlin resembled the worst days in Paris during the French Revolution.

He had arrived in Germany hoping to avoid the figure in homburg hat and military cane who occupied the office of Vice Chancellor. To Americans of Dodd's generation, von Papen's career was distinctly unsavory. Not only had von Papen midwifed Hitler's ascension to power, but eighteen years earlier he had been involved in a scandal of epic proportions in America. As a young military attaché in New York during the Great War, Captain von Papen had conspired to blow up key points of the Canadian railway system. Deported in the winter of 1915, the British discovered in his possession the check stubs for his nefarious activities in the New World.

In Berlin, social conditions soon threw the dapper intriguer and the American Ambassador together. At the "little" foreign press ball in November, the von Papens sat with Sigrid Schultz and Louis P. at Ambassador Dodd's table. The atmosphere was tense until Miss Schultz turned to von Papen and asked in her most innocent voice: "Mr. Chancellor, there is something in the memoirs of President von Hindenburg which I am sure you can elucidate for me. He complains that in the last war, in 1917, the German High Command never heard anything about the peace suggestions of President Wilson and that if he had known about them the dangerous submarine campaign would not have been launched. How was that possible?"

The table fell silent.

"There never was such a thing as a peace suggestion by President Wilson," von Papen snapped.

"Oh yes there was," Dodd replied in an accent as dry as cotton. "It was made on December 18, 1916."

"Anyhow, I never understood why America and Germany got to grips in that war," von Papen declared.

"I can tell you that too," Dodd continued patiently. "It was through the sheer consummate stupidity of the German diplomats."

After that, von Papen went out of his way to court the attentions of Ambassador Dodd, who he saw was a man impervious to German disdain. He even hosted a dinner in Dodd's honor at the aristocratic Herrenklub.

On June 29, the day before the mutiny, Dodd hosted a luncheon of his own for some twenty guests including von Papen and Italian Ambassador Cerruti and his wife. The day was stifling hot with storm clouds on the horizon and a burning sun overhead. When Dodd asked Signora Cerruti what she thought of the forbidding atmosphere, the wife of the Italian Ambassador replied that in such heat anything might happen. It was an unfortunate choice of words considering later events. The following week, the rumor made the rounds that the Italian Embassy had been informed in advance of the violence about to break.

After lunch, Dodd and von Papen talked politics in the sun parlor where the walls were mostly glass and the silently turning dictaphones could not pick up their conversation.

"Anyway, I shall not be torpedoed," von Papen told Dodd as he left.

MURDER

True to his prediction, von Papen escaped the first round of executions on Saturday but was placed under house arrest. A secretary and a high-ranking police official turned away all visitors to his home on the Lennestrasse with assurances that the Vice Chancellor was in excellent health but unavailable for consultation. Former Chancellor Kurt von Schleicher was dead; Bruening had been warned in time to flee to Britain. Of Germany's recent chancellors only Hitler and von Papen remained alive.

As an outsider with diplomatic immunity, Dodd could spread a sort of protective rain over a few mortals in the German capital. The secret police were watching his home, he knew, and he had to take care not to distribute his sympathies too widely or his protective powers would be diluted: he might perhaps be mistaken for one of the players in this still mysterious conspiracy. On Sunday, as scores of anonymous assassins were dispatched to bring down prominent officials, Dodd decided to see what he could do to protect the beleaguered Vice Chancellor.

As he and Martha drove toward the Wilhelmstrasse the streets appeared calm. The armed police had been withdrawn and the SS forces confined to barracks. The machine guns were gone from the roof tops and only an occasional police constable or an SS man on a bicycle could be seen pedaling with a rifle slung over his shoulder. In front of the Chancellery spectators milled about under the watchful eyes of the police. Earlier in the day, an Army detachment had paraded beneath Hitler's window to fife and drum. The Fuehrer had appeared briefly to salute them and to wave at the crowd chanting: *"Heil, Heil!"*

The car with its low license number slowed as it passed von Papen's residence; Martha thought she saw von Papen's son standing at an upstairs window. The guard at the door watched them suspiciously as they moved down the street and turned the corner. That afternoon Dodd returned and sent in his card.

"I hope we may call on you soon," it said.

It was all Dodd could do.

At No. 27 Tiergartenstrasse newsmen came and went all day. People were beginning to ask questions, they reported, in cafés and beerhalls. They wanted to know why officials had been executed who only a few days before had been revered as heroes. The story of General von

Schleicher's part in the plot was also unclear. Now it was admitted that he had not conspired with a foreign power after all but had only meddled in things that were none of his business. A severe penalty for meddling: death! And what, people wanted to know, had Goering meant on Saturday when he said that he had "expanded" on Hitler's orders for Berlin?

Dinner that night at the Dodd home was a somber affair. Quite a few people showed up; newspaper friends of Martha's and junior secretaries from the embassy. From time to time one of the younger guests would break the silence to exclaim about the fantastic events of the weekend. The older guests for the most part kept silent.

By then a number of things were clear. In Munich, seven high-ranking SA leaders had been executed, among them the Police Presidents of Munich and Breslau. It was also revealed that Frau von Schleicher had been fatally shot on Saturday while trying to shield her husband. According to an investigation conducted later by the Army, an unmarked car carrying six men in civilian attire had pulled up in front of the General's residence in Neubabelsberg. A figure hopped out, dashed across the street and opened the gate to the General's driveway. The car then backed swiftly up the drive. When the cook answered the door she unthinkingly disengaged the electric alarm. The callers raced through the house and discovered the General seated at his desk in the study. Shots rang out. When Frau von Schleicher rushed in from the next room she was shot down too. The cook ran into the garden screaming.

News of Frau von Schleicher's murder was especially troubling to Martha's mother. Martha's father appeared tense but quiet. Washington had requested brief reports on the crisis as it developed, but as yet there was little to report and nothing on the reasons behind the mutiny.

Only that morning Dodd had received a reply from Roehm's office to a dinner invitation he had sent out for the following week. Both Dodd and Roehm were making an effort that summer to get out more socially. Now the meeting between the two would never take place. The note said simply that the SA Chief of Staff regretted that he could not attend for reasons of ill health. He would be out of town on a rest cure. The bloated SA commander did suffer from severe arthritis although his political troubles, Dodd suspected, were more serious.

When the somber repast was over, the company moved to the ballroom. Elmina Rangabe, the unpredictable daughter of the Greek Ambassador, showed up with Hans Thomsen, who looked calm and self-assured as usual. Armand Bérard also dropped by, restless and ill at ease. His chief had been in Paris when the purge struck and was expected back that night. The upright radio in the corner was turned on. Goebbels was scheduled to address the nation and for the next hour radios all over Berlin were tuned to the Propaganda Minister's well-oiled voice as it floated, melodious and insinuating, over cobblestone streets and gardens slumbering in hushed twilight.

According to Goebbels, the momentous events of the past 48 hours had begun in the town of Bad Godesberg on Friday night as Hitler stood on a hotel terrace overlooking the softly flowing Rhine.

"In this hour he is more than ever admired by us. Not a quiver in his face reveals the slightest sign of what is going on within him. Yet few people who stand by him in all difficult hours know how deeply he is grieved and also how determined he is to deal mercilessly in stamping out the reactionary rebels who are trying to plunge the country into chaos . . ."

The hour struck. Hitler flew to Munich where he received a full report. Assembling the leaders of the Munich SA, he tore the insignias from their tunics. He then raced by car to Bad Wiessee with his SS bodyguard and Goebbels. Entering Roehm's *pension,* he personally arrested the SA commander.

"I may be spared a description of the disgusting scenes that lay before us," Goebbels intoned. "A simple SS man with an air of indignation, expresses our thoughts, saying: 'I only wish the walls would fall down now so that the whole German people could be a witness to his act . . .'"

On the road back to Munich, other SA leaders were arrested. In Munich, Hitler addressed the assembled SA: "His words are a bitter exposure of the small group of arrested criminals who had wanted to grasp the power of the State for themselves in league with reactionary elements and who had not even refrained from establishing relations with a foreign power . . ."

At this Armand blanched. In Nazi eyes the foreign power could only be France.

"His whole life," Goebbels continued, "is devoted to the German people, who love him and honor him because he is great and kind, and because he can also be merciless when it becomes necessary . . . The whole nation breathes easily again as if freed from a horrible nightmare . . . May a favorable destiny bless us so that we can carry out our great task to its conclusion with Adolf Hitler . . . The Reich is there, and, above all, our leader."

Asking themselves what it meant, the listeners adjourned to the library. If Roehm and his closest aides had planned a coup against the Government in Berlin, why had they retired to a remote resort at the foot of the Bavarian Alps? How was it possible for Hitler to enter the conspirators' headquarters without encountering resistance? Where were

Roehm's bodyguards? Why were the conspirators caught napping during the first hours of their rebellion? And how did the deaths of General
von Schleicher and his wife fit into the plot?

The newsmen informed Dodd that at Lichterfelde barracks outside
Berlin, SS firing squads were "liquidating" scores of SA mutineers. The
offices of Berlin's leading psychiatric practitioners were crowded with
people suffering from persecution manias. Weary and saddened, Dodd
went to bed. Martha spent a sleepless night haunted by the sounds of
imagined rifle volleys.

Bella's contact in the Ministry of the Interior called her Saturday. He
used the code they had agreed upon for emergencies. She must come
quickly, he said, and meet her American friend. Bella rushed to her car
and raced to the prearranged meeting place. The official, deathly pale,
slid in beside her.

"Your friend Schleicher was shot this morning," he whispered. "It is
known that he came to see you only a short while ago. You'll have to be
careful, Bella! There is a wholesale butchery in full swing."

Kurt and Elizabeth von Schleicher had dined with her only eight days
before. Since his retirement Kurt had traveled about Germany and
visited Italy. On his return he looked rested and refreshed. Bella had also
invited his old friend and former aide, General von Bredow. They dined
on the terrace, out of earshot of the servants.

Where was his bodyguard, Bella had asked.

"The same old Bella," Schleicher observed. "Alarmist as usual. Good
lord, I've been out of politics and am happy to be out of the dirty mess.
So why should I fear? Of course, I've been very interested in what's
going on."

The subject of von Papen's Marburg address came up. Where had
"Fraenzchen" found the nerve? It was obvious he had not written it
himself. Von Schleicher was not even sure what it meant: "Well, it
looked like a genuine body blow. But frankly, I don't know—whether
Papen was declaring himself against the Nazis; or whether he was just
peeved at something and wanted the Nazis to offer him sugar; or
whether it was all false. Maybe Hitler himself wanted the speech made,
so that foreign countries would hope that the Nazis will be less ferocious
from now on."

General von Bredow heard of his friend's death while taking tea at the
Hotel Adlon. "I am surprised that the swine have not killed me also
before now," he said. A foreign attaché offered to hide him, but von
Bredow declined. "I am going home," he announced loud enough for

everyone to hear. "They have killed my Chief. What is there left for me." His friends never saw him again.

Bella had to decide what to do. She wanted to flee but she was expected at a gala soirée at the Japanese Embassy that evening. She telephoned the Protocol Office and was told that it would look suspicious if she changed her plans. Appearances were everything now.

That evening she dressed in one of her most expensive gowns and pinned on all of her medals. She felt like a condemned criminal as she entered the brightly lit Japanese Embassy. In the checkroom she ran into the Lord Mayor of Berlin, Dr. Heinrich Sahm. "Thank goodness, you are here, Bellachen," he said.

"I was worried about you too," Bella whispered. "You have always spoken your mind very frankly."

Then she put on her brightest smile and somehow the years of practice carried her through the evening. In a way it was a relief to greet old friends and to know they were still among the living. The foreign diplomats looked on, fascinated by the play of emotions.

Afterwards she and Dr. Sahm went to the Wintergreen, a small bar where members of the foreign press sometimes met. The conversation turned to Goering's former Gestapo chief, Rudolf Diels. Bella thought that Diels was as dangerous as any of the others but took greater pains to hide it. Even Martha Dodd, after succumbing to his charms, Bella told Dr. Sahm, now tolerated Diels' flattery only to gain information.

Goering had visited Cologne a few days before the killing started. As hundreds of officials and thousands of spectators watched, Goering's red plane circled the Siebengebirge and landed on the airstrip ringed by Gauleiters, Group Leaders, and numerous high-ranking police and state officials. Among the notables was Rudolf Diels in black SS uniform. When Goering descended in resplendent white uniform, an honor guard more than a half-mile long presented arms with a resounding crack. Goering had come to the ancient city on the Rhine to officiate at Diels' swearing-in as Regional Commissioner, but the former inspector of the secret police saw at a glance that Goering was displeased. Ignoring Diels, Goering went down the line saluting and shaking hands with old friends. Finally, he turned to Diels and without so much as a handshake drew him aside.

There would be no swearing-in, Goering said.

As the band repeated the strains of the parade march and the hundreds of police stood at attention in the hot summer sun, Goering accused Diels of plotting with the Archbishop of Cologne, of conferring with former Chancellor Bruening in Switzerland and of depositing documents abroad critical of the regime. Himmler and Heydrich, Goering's new aides, had assured him of these things.

Diels denied everything and asked the Minister President if these latest accusations were not just as foolish as all the earlier ones against him. The mercurial Goering finally agreed, and the two returned to the long line of honor guards who at last could go to parade rest.

That evening the Lord Mayor of Cologne presented Goering with a three-thousand-year-old Celtic Sword as regiments of the SA and SS paraded in review. When the ceremony was over Goering turned to Diels and said: "Watch yourself in the next few days."

In Berlin, Heydrich was not satisfied with Goering's change of heart. Diels' name was removed from the execution lists, but the Gestapo office in Cologne was not informed. A trusted chauffeur warned Diels in time and Cologne's newest Regional Commissioner spent the first days of July on a secluded estate in the Eifel Mountains until the manhunt ended. Among the list of dead, Diels was pleased to see the names of three SS men who had done most of the flogging at the Gestapo camp in Stettin.

On Monday morning, people returned to work but were careful to discuss nothing more important than the weather. Fear of the secret police was widespread. Observers noted that in the better restaurants a hush fell when the orchestra paused between songs. Heavily-armed police and pairs of SS men kept the crowds moving along the street in front of the Reich Chancellery. Inside, the Cabinet, minus Vice Chancellor von Papen, met throughout the day. Louis P. had stationed a man at the Kaiserhof to watch Hitler's comings and goings. Since his return to Berlin, Hitler had lived in the Chancellery like a man under siege. Armed police barricaded the heavy folding doors that led to the Chancellery's inner courtyard and through the Chancellery's windows the AP man could see SS guards posted in nearly every room. In all that time Hitler emerged only once to drive under heavy guard to the Hotel Adlon to pay his respects to the King and Queen of Siam.

According to the controlled press the "liquidations" had ceased the previous evening. Six more names were added to the list of the official dead, bringing the total to 18. Among them was an SA Division Commander, a District Commander, a Chief of Staff and two SA Commanders. A complete list was promised in 24 hours.

A nameless witness to the executions at Lichterfelde, the barracks housing Hitler's personal bodyguard, described a drum head court composed of a police general, an army general and several lay justices that handed down a guilty sentence every seven minutes. Many of the "traitors" refused to be blindfolded. SA Group Leader Karl Ernst died shouting: "I am innocent. Long live Germany! Heil Hitler!" Ernst had been about to leave on his honeymoon when he was apprehended. In Munich Roehm had refused to take his own life and was executed. Among the other dead was Germany's most prominent Catholic layman, Dr. Erich Klausener. Klausener, a director in the Ministry of Transportation, had been executed by a nameless SS officer in his office on Saturday. The funeral announcement captured the anguish of his grieving family:

> In accordance with the sacred will of God, we stand broken-hearted by the bier of my husband, beloved above all else in the world, truest of comrades; of my protecting father; of our unforgettable son, brother and uncle, Dr. Erich Klausener, Ministerial Director in the Ministry of Transport, president of Catholic Action in Berlin, member of the Order of St. Gregory, Knight of the Iron Cross, First Class.
>
> He was suddenly torn from us on June 30, 1934, after a lifetime of sacrifice for family, church and Fatherland.

Goebbels forced the elimination of "church and Fatherland" in most of the press, while in defiance of Catholic rite, the Government cremated Klausener's body and returned the ashes to the family in a simple cardboard box.

The same fate awaited the remains of General von Schleicher and his wife. As friends and relations of the murdered couple gathered to pay their last respects, Gestapo agents descended on the ceremony and announced that the funeral had been cancelled on orders from above. The floral tributes were seized and the mourners dispersed. The bodies were taken away; by the end of the week they, too, had been reduced to ashes and laid to rest in a corner of a country cemetery among other recent, unmarked graves. Only a few ancient decommissioned officers dared attend the ceremony.

With the new week, Dodd was preoccupied with other troubles. Armand Bérard had passed him a telegram from Wilhelm Regendanz, the civilian accused of having offered his home as a meeting place for the conspirators Schleicher, Roehm and, presumably, Francois-Poncet. Regendanz was a wealthy Berlin banker who frequently entertained members of the diplomatic set. He had been in London when the hurricane of violence broke. His oldest son, an officer in the SA, was arrested and imprisoned. His wife and two small children remained in Berlin.

The telegram was addressed to the French Embassy but Francois-Poncet could do little. He half expected to be executed himself and had left his wife and children in Paris. The French Embassy was relying upon

Dodd to dip into his precious store of immunity to protect Regendanz's family.

Martha and her mother agreed to go to Dahlem to pay their respects to Frau Regendanz. At first she did not recognize them but when they showed her the telegram from her husband she broke down sobbing. She was terribly frightened, she said, and under a great strain. She was sure her husband would be arrested if he returned to Germany. Her house had been searched, her passport confiscated, her oldest son taken away. She worried that he was in a concentration camp or dead. She broke down again, hysterical with grief. Beyond being observed entering and leaving Frau Regendanz's house, there was little Martha and her mother could do.

Herr Regendanz remained in London, but he sent a full report of his harmless social activities to the Gestapo. Never, he assured the secret police, had the General, the SA Chief and the French Ambassador met under his roof at the same time.

After some weeks his son was released and took a night train across the border. The Government had frozen the family's bank account, but Frau Regendanz was able to discreetly sell bits of her furniture and other family objects. The day before she escaped with her younger children by plane she called at the Dodd home to offer her thanks. As she spoke excellent English, the servants were not suspicious. A few days later a postcard arrived from London with the message: "Arrived safe and sound. Deepest gratitude and love. Carrie." It was a story typical of the times.

Vice Chancellor von Papen remained under house arrest. Hindenburg ordered the Army to guarantee his friend's safety and the Propaganda Ministry hastily announced that it had been officially established that von Papen had absolutely no connection with the mutineers, although he still might resign. Most of von Papen's closest associates were either dead, in prison or in hiding. One was last seen scaling a garden wall in his tennis clothes with a band of SS men in hot pursuit.

The Associated Press sent reinforcements to Berlin, and Louis P. took time out to sit on a park bench across the street from von Papen's residence. Other observers sat on other benches nearby. One, in the dress of a homeless vagrant, was obviously from the secret police. Louis P. took out a copy of *Der Angriff* and pretended to read. After half an hour he was about to abandon his vigil when he saw von Papen's twenty-year-old son returning from his law exams in the company of a secretary. They shook hands and began conversing in English. The eavesdroppers on the benches strained to hear.

"Be careful," warned the secretary, "we are being watched."

"How's your father?" Louis P. asked.

"Oh, all right."

"By this time I suppose he is out of office?"

"I don't know anything about what is happening."

"Have your parents and you made any plans for the future?"

"We haven't the slightest idea what is to happen next."

"What is the sentinel there for?" Louis P. asked, nodding in the direction of the grim-looking guard in steel helmet standing in front of the villa.

"For our protection."

" . . . we had better not be seen talking together too long," the secretary admonished.

The Government did its best to make von Papen's life miserable. A unit of Goering's special police was stationed in his home. The von Papens were forced to live without privacy, surrounded by suspicion and hostility. A few days later they were invaded by police detectives who wanted to question their housekeeper.

"Yes, it wasn't exactly nice," Frau von Papen confided to Louis P. during another chance encounter on the street. "We had visitors again last night. Not even the kitchen was spared. Naturally we would like a different 'watch' from the one now posted before our house. Of what good is a watch if it lets persons through?"

By the middle of the week a distinct morning-after mood had settled in. "It's an odd world we live in," an elderly electrician confided to a British diplomat. "If I'd said a word against Roehm yesterday I'd be in a concentration camp. It would be more than my life is worth today to say a word in his favor." Nor could people understand why the deaths of certain debauched elements in the SA were followed by the disappearance of numerous others whose lives and conduct were blameless, at least to nonpolitical eyes.

The official death toll climbed to 50 or 51 and had been doubling every day since Sunday. The foreign press reported that the men executed at Lichterfelde had died shirtless as their comrades refused to shoot at men in the Party uniform. "Well, boys," cried one of the condemned, "I do not know what this is all about, but anyhow shoot straight." Inquiries at Government offices as to the disposition of the bodies were met with a shrug and the reply: "Who cares?"

The shadow of death touched the American colony in Berlin when an official of the German Academic Exchange Service, Dr. Morsbach, who was to have met a group of some fifty American university students and their teachers, was taken off to a concentration camp. Representatives of the group called on Dodd to complain.

"Strange, we can hear nothing about the horrible deeds or about public attitudes from anybody," they said. "Nobody ventures a remark and no newspaper gives any of the facts."

The Embassy traced Dr. Morsbach to Landsberg concentration camp, a camp for sterilized workers near Wittenberg. His head shaven, a large letter "L" painted on his shirt, Dr. Morsbach asked the Embassy official, "Please give my regards to and thank the American Ambassador." The remark, made within the hearing of the camp commandant, saved his life.

On Wednesday, July 4th, the Dodds hosted a large tea for the American colony in Berlin. Sprays of red, white and blue flowers and small American flags decorated the rooms. An orchestra played American tunes as the Dodds greeted their guests in the ballroom. Throngs of people were soon standing about, chatting quietly with glasses of punch and plates of food. The day was warm and many of the guests preferred to walk in the garden or to sit at the tables on the lawn. Martha's mother wore a lovely blue dress that highlighted her silver hair. Her voice was gracious and delicately Southern, but the tenseness of the last few days could be read in her dark eyes. The past week, she wrote a friend in Chicago, had seemed like a century. Martha's father chose to be gently humorous as he greeted friends such as Louis P. and the violinist Fritz Kreisler. Martha and Bill were less diplomatic. They greeted new arrivals with the phrase: "Oh, so you're still among the living?" until several German guests became quite irate. From time to time an American newspaperman drew Dodd aside to whisper the latest news. In this way Dodd learned that the killings had stopped and that the Nazis were again in control. The city crematorium was working around the clock incinerating the dead.

Louis P. was not only tired and wan after four days of nearly continuous reporting, he was bitter too. A number of his personal friends were among the victims. He was especially concerned about the fate of Prince "Auwi," the Kaiser's 4th son, an SA leader and a close friend of Group Leader Ernst. The Prince had been called before Goering and asked to repeat what he had said to Ernst in a telephone conversation a few days earlier. The Prince replied that he had merely wished his friend godspeed on his honeymoon trip.

"Lucky for you that for once you have told the truth," Goering rumbled. His listening service had recorded the entire conversation. Goering sent the Prince on his way with the remark: "He is too dumb to have known anything."

When the butler whispered to Martha that the *"junge Herr von Papen"* was downstairs, she was not surprised. They were occasional dance partners, and she had left word that she would like to see him when his period of confinement ended. The two young people disappeared into the garden behind the house and emerged to slip unnoticed into an open-air café on the Tiergarten. The blond young man with the somewhat cynical smile described his great relief at being free again. His father of course was shocked at the attempt to link his name with that of Roehm and General von Schleicher; the one a political gangster, the other an arch enemy. When Martha told him that her father had left his card at their home on Sunday, young von Papen looked nonplussed: they had received it only that morning. In the intervening days it had been in the hands of the secret police.

Louis P. was busy that afternoon picking up bits and pieces of information from Fritz Kreisler and from Bella Fromm, who had just returned from the country where she had found temporary refuge on an estate belonging to friends. Bella was especially alive to the tension among Dodd's guests. The diplomats were jittery, the Germans shaken. Several people within her hearing expressed regret that it was Schleicher and not von Papen who had paid with his life.

Another group discussed the troubles of Ambassador François-Poncet. An American news agency had identified France as the "foreign power" accused of plotting with the mutineers. When François-Poncet called on von Neurath to demand proof of the "vile affirmations," the Foreign Minister refused to produce any. The Government obviously meant to frighten and humiliate the French Ambassador.

Dodd was certain that Roehm had been involved in some sort of plot from a memo he read of a conversation with Group Leader Rolf Reiner. Reiner had been Chief of Staff in Roehm's Ministry and before that head of the Liaison Office where Putzi Hanfstaengl worked. Several weeks before the mutiny an SA official had handed Reiner a document to be delivered to Roehm. The official advised Reiner to read it before passing it on. The document described a meeting between Roehm and Ambassador François-Poncet where plans for an SA putsch had been discussed. The French Ambassador had placed liberal amounts of cash at the disposal of the mutineers, much of which had found its way into Karl Ernst's pockets. Reiner, a member of the SS, turned the incriminating evidence over to Himmler and an immediate investigation was launched. For his loyalty, Reiner was appointed Himmler's special assistant.

Reiner estimated that 150 people had been executed in Munich on Sunday, 70 in Berlin, another 300 in the rest of the Reich. Arrests he believed approached 15,000.

Martha knew Reiner. He was a rough-looking youth from Bavaria with bushy black hair. He had approached her table one night when

Diels was absent and warned her that she should not be seen in the company of the Gestapo inspector. Diels' fate was sealed, Reiner hinted.

As it turned out, Reiner was not as clever as Diels at evading his pursuers. After talking so openly to foreigners about the purge, Reiner disappeared, a victim of the brutal and far-flung internal investigation that continued for months after the purge. When he reappeared in Berlin society, his head was shaven and his former friends avoided him, fearful that he had compromised them to his interrogators.

For most of the week a tall, blond man in Bella's office had been missing. The "Long One," as he was called, was a photographer and an SS recruit. When he finally reappeared he was a changed man. No longer self-assured and authoritative, he sat at his desk and stared at the door. When friends asked him what was wrong, he broke down and began to weep: "I had to shoot in the Gestapo cellar. Thirty-seven times I shot . . . Thirty-seven are dead . . . Thirty-seven are haunting me . . . I can't escape from those thirty-seven ghosts . . ." After that he was never seen again. Brecht, Bella's understudy, supplied the final piece in the puzzle. "Have you heard about the 'Long One'?" Brecht asked. "He passed . . . He talked too much . . ."

The governments of both Britain and America complained that their ambassadors had cabled no information beyond what was readily available in the foreign press. Dodd informed Washington that the motives behind the purge were still unclear but it appeared that critics on both the right and the left had been silenced and the power of the SA severely curtailed. Dodd refused to speculate further about the motives behind the execution of so many prominent people. He was an historian, not a fortune teller. There were too few facts. He did not wish to apply reason to murder, as so many were doing.

He ventured two theories only: that the mutiny had either been aborted before it had gotten started or that its seriousness had been deliberately exaggerated to cover the Government's crimes. François-Poncet's continued troubles clearly were being used as an excuse for von Schleicher's death while the German people had only the scantiest notion as yet of how many of their countrymen had been killed. For the rest, Dodd advised Washington to study the foreign press. His own sources of information were no better.

He did submit a curious version of the mutiny that he received from Diels. During the past winter, Diels reported, "World Jewry" had funneled 12,000,000 marks into Germany for a monarchical restoration. The German Crown Prince was the recipient of the funds; but when Diels' agency closed down the remaining monarchical societies, the Crown Prince turned the money over to Roehm and fled into the SA.

Diels appealed to von Papen. Von Papen's private secretary, von Bose, compiled a dossier on the affair which von Papen showed to Hindenberg. Angered, Hindenburg ordered Hitler to restrain Roehm or the Army would take over the Government. Von Bose was executed and von Papen held incommunicado because of their knowledge of the plot. That was what Goering had meant when he said he had expanded on Hitler's orders for Berlin.

In his summary of the tale, Dodd added a cautionary note. "World Jewry," he pointed out, could hardly be so foolish as to entrust such a large sum of money to the flighty Crown Prince while Hindenburg's vigor recalled 1914 more than 1934.

Washington's response was to request Dodd to remind the German government of the money it still owed American citizens. A startled Dodd doubted that he could have much effect, but he did as he was ordered. No official ever made a more futile march up ministry stairs than the American Ambassador charged with reminding condemned men that their earthly finances were in arears.

An embarrassed von Neurath promised that Germany would pay if she ever got enough dollars. The Foreign Minister believed the official version of the purge: that Hitler, Goering and Goebbels were to have been killed in a coup originally planned for August but moved up to June 30th; that the Cabinet was to have been arrested and Roehm installed as Minister of Defense. Documents to that effect would be published soon, von Neurath said; however, none ever were.

"My task here is to work for peace and better relations," Dodd wrote in his diary that night. "I do not see how anything can be done so long as Hitler, Goering and Goebbels are the directing heads of the country. Never have I heard or read of three more unfit men in high place.

"Ought I to resign?"

Had France, Britain and America withdrawn their envoys, a painful blow would have been delivered to the regime's prestige. An open note to Hindenburg decrying the events of June 30 would have encouraged some in the Cabinet to resign and perhaps forced the President to intervene. But a diplomatic démarche was never considered. Dodd had to content himself with the remark, widely quoted at the time, that after June 30, 1934 Germany was no longer a civilized modern state.

Dodd boycotted Hitler's address to the Reichstag on July 13, preferring to listen to it on the radio. When Hitler proclaimed that von Schleicher and Roehm deserved to die for meeting in secret if they had discussed nothing more seditious than the "weather, gold coins and like topics," Dodd decided he would never again speak with the Fuehrer except on official business. He loathed the German Chancellor.

Hitler spoke for an hour and forty-one minutes with great passion. The familiar figure of H. R. Knickerbocker sat in the visitor's gallery of the Kroll Opera House. Knick had been in New York negotiating a gold-plated contract with the Hearst press when news of the purge broke and he immediately took ship for Germany. He had heard Hitler speak on innumerable previous occasions but never to an audience so tense. Most of the delegates who filled the immense hall were members of the Storm Troop organization. They sat bewildered and numb as Hitler began his account. More than a score of seats were empty; their rightful occupants either dead or imprisoned. Soldiers with rifles stood at the entrances to the hall, armed SS men in the aisles. It was the toughest audience of Hitler's career.

The plot Hitler described started among men close to Roehm, men who shared his sexual inclinations. Their plan was to launch a true National-Bolshevist revolution with the help of a second and larger group of SA leaders who were sexually normal but who felt themselves bound to Roehm in soldierly loyalty. The rebels planned to seize Government buildings, take Hitler hostage, and issue orders in his name. General von Schleicher would act as their director of foreign affairs.

Given the ghastly code name "The Night of the Long Knives," the resultant civil war would have cost the lives of tens of thousands of people, Hitler said. He had no choice but to strike first in the hope of saving the innocent by sacrificing the guilty.

As the minutes ticked by the audience listened in stunned silence. Knick checked his watch; 20 minutes and still Hitler had not garnered a single handclap. Then, suddenly, Hitler came out with the words that brought the audience to its feet:

"Mutinies are suppressed in accordance with laws of iron which are eternally the same. If anyone reproaches me and asks why I did not resort to the regular courts of justice for conviction of the offenders, then all that I can say to him is this: in this hour I was responsible for the fate of the German people, and thereby I became the Supreme Justice of Germany . . ."

"Heil! Heil! Heil!" chanted the 500 delegates in brown, forgetting under the spell of Hitler's words that he had just promised to kill any one of them who so much as threatened to topple his regime. It was the debasement of the masses, Knick saw, who enthusiastically cheered their own enslavement.

Hitler spoke like a man possessed. He claimed that the dead numbered no more than 77. Of these 50 were SA leaders, six SS-men and five Party members. Thirteen others were shot for resisting arrest; 3 more had died by their own hand. He alluded again to the collusion of a "foreign power" but cleared the Hohenzollern family of any suspicion. In the visitors' gallery Prince Louis Ferdinand leaned over to Armand Bérard and whispered: "Something for you, something for me."

When Hitler finished to a roar of applause, Goering, as President of the Reichstag, called upon the assembled delegates to rise and signal their approval. On the Tiergartenstrasse, Dodd turned off the radio in disgust.

François-Poncet's rehabilitation had to wait several weeks. His superiors in Paris were assured that that he was no longer under suspicion, but von Neurath never forced a denial of the charges in the German press. The Foreign Ministry wanted Francois-Poncet to stay on, but suitably humbled. Twice François-Poncet begged to know if he still enjoyed the Chancellor's confidence but received no reply until one evening at a performance of "Die Walkuere" Hitler invited him into his loge. During the intermission the two were seen chatting pleasantly. The French Ambassador had won his reprieve.

EXPULSION

When Putzi Hanfstaengl returned to Berlin in the middle of July, his first thought was to see Hitler. Representatives of the foreign press were pestering him for a complete list of the dead and he had none to give. Continued silence was useless; the correspondents were compiling lists of their own. Surely, someone, somewhere, had signed the death warrants.

He found Hitler and the "chauffeureska" vacationing on the Baltic with Goebbels and his family. The setting was pure Buddenbrooks by the sea; salt air and spotless bathing cabanas, not at all the atmosphere for an excursion into the bloody past. The chaffeureska vouchsafed him a few moments alone with the chief but kept a foot in the door so that he would not feel too brave. Putzi did not feel brave at all and completely lost his composure when Hitler greeted him with: "Well, here you are again, Mister Hanfstaengl! Haven't they done you in yet?"

He turned his attention instead to the arrival of the publisher William Randolph Hearst on the continent. Hearst regularly spent his summers in Bad Nauheim taking the cure. That summer he arrived with a crowd of the fun set and his mistress Miss Marion Davies. After visiting Rome they drove up to Germany to attend the Oberammergau Passion play. Putzi flew down and attached himself to their party in Munich. He had a number of questions he wanted to ask Mr. Hearst. What did Mr. Hearst think of the Passion Play? What was his opinion of the German press?

"I think the German press has been among the best in the world," Hearst told Putzi, "and for that matter, still is, considering the conditions under which it is published. But if I wrote what I think of those conditions I would be arrested, and if you printed what I wrote you would be arrested. So why discuss the subject at this time?"

Putzi knew that was true. He went home and wrote his own version of the interview and gave it to the *New York Times*. In it he made Hearst sound like a convinced National Socialist: "Germany is battling for her liberation from the mischievous provisions of the Treaty of Versailles and for her redemption from the malicious suppression and encirclement to which she has been subjected by nations which in their avarice and shortsightedness have only shown enmity and jealousy over her advancement."

Hearst was the inventor of that sort of journalism, and he didn't blame

Putzi one bit for writing what he had to. Putzi wanted Hearst to meet Hitler. Hearst was hostile to the idea. Putzi appealed to Miss Davies: "The Fuehrer wants to see Mr. Hearst. He will be glad to come here."

"What a minute—wait a minute," said Miss Davies. "Mr. Hearst has no desire to meet Mr. Hitler. But I have."

"You want to see him?"

"Do I!"

Hitler, however, did not want to see Miss Davies. He wanted to see Hearst. Miss Davies pleaded with "WR" for three days: "Have a heart. I've gone every place to see this man . . ."

In the end it was Louis B. Mayer in Hollywood who changed Hearst's mind. Mayer thought a meeting might ease the plight of the Jews in Germany. In the middle of September Hearst gave in. Four SS men arrived by plane in Bad Nauheim and Hearst, Miss Davies and Putzi flew to Berlin. In the end Hearst saw Hitler for five minutes, without Miss Davies.

"I didn't understand a word Hitler was saying," WR told Miss Davies afterwards, "and I didn't understand his interpreter either."

"Why am I so misrepresented, so misunderstood, in America?" Hitler had lamented. "Why are the people of America so antagonistic to my regime?"

"One reason, of course," Hearst replied, "is that the people of the United States believe in democracy and are adverse to dictatorship. That idea has been inculcated in them from the foundation of the nation."

"But I am entirely a product of democracy," Hitler protested. "I, as a private citizen, appealed to the people of Germany. I was elected to my office by a majority vote of the people of Germany. I presented my proposals, my policies, to the people of Germany. They endorsed these policies by more than a two-thirds majority. We have a Constitution, the Constitution of Weimar, and according to that instrument, the endorsement of a policy by the voters is a positive injunction to the government to put that policy into operation. Not to have done it would have been to deny the will of the people. That is democracy, is it not?"

It might be, Hearst agreed, but Hitler's policies were not.

Putzi bragged all over Berlin about how he had captured the great Hearst: "I only had to convince him that we were interested in justice and he softened right up and went with me to see Hitler. Hitler put on one of his acts—it is amazing how easy it is to impress these Americans. Now he has agreed to write for us about the Third Reich in his press."

Putzi got another taste of power that summer when he arranged for the first formal expulsion of an American correspondent from Germany. The expulsion made headlines around the world since the newsman or, rather, newswoman was Dorothy Thompson, the wife of the Nobel Prize winning novelist, Sinclair Lewis.

Putzi's third book had appeared that spring; a collection of over a hundred cartoons gleaned from the foreign press in the last ten years. Putzi called his book: *Hitler In the Caricature of the World: Deeds Versus Drawings*. On one page he printed the offending cartoon, on the facing page his refutation. Only someone with Putzi's imagination would have dared bring out a collection of cartoons portraying Hitler in *Schurrbart* and jackboots in 1934. And only Putzi's good relations with Rudolf Hess, whom he acknowledged in the introduction, ensured Hitler's enthusiastic support for the project. In America the volume was ignored completely with the lone exception of Dorothy Thompson, whose prediction in 1931 that Hitler would never come to power had made her famous among her newspaper colleagues. Dorothy's review of Putzi's book appeared in the pages of the *Saturday Review of Literature* and was entitled, appropriately: "Putzy-Footing Propaganda." Only Dorothy could have slapped Putzi's face so adroitly for each of his brazen distortions of history:

> Dr. Hanfstaengl has selected these hundred cartoons from amongst thousands. He has selected them with a view to answering them, and he has selected the ones which can most easily be answered. . . . The greater number of these cartoons are reproduced to show, with appropriate crowings, how the prophecies of Hitler's political opponents have been refuted. One group holds up to ridicule the possibility of Hitler coming to power. Well, Hitler is in power, now, and this ought perhaps to be sufficient answer. It is, however, not sufficient answer, for the official propagandists. For there are still a great many perverse people who think that their mistake was not to underrate Hitler but to overrate his opponents. For them Dr. Hanfstaengl uses this book over and over again to repeat the myth that Hitler came into power as the voluntary selected leader and dictator of a majority of the German people. The truth is that the prophets who predicted that Hitler would not achieve a conquest of the power by democratic methods—that is to say by winning a majority of the votes of the people—were right. Hitler did not win the power, it was handed to him by President von Hindenburg and the German nationalists . . .
>
> Another group of cartoons prophesies that Hitler will not fulfill his election promises and indicates that he is misleading the voters. Dr. Hanfstaengl's comment on one of these is that "to the irritation of his opponents, Mr. Hitler made no election promises." . . .
>
> Held up to laughter also are the prophecies of the cartoonists that the Nazi party would split apart because of the contradictory elements contained in it. Obviously Dr. Henfstaengl was premature in ridiculing these predictions.
>
> It is quite futile for Dr. Hanfstaengl to try again to fasten upon the Jews

the responsibility for the reports which came out of Germany of the atrocious happenings to socialists, pacifists, liberals, and Jews in the early days of the regime, or for the consistent criticism which has gone on since then. The rest of the world knows better. The most outspoken critics of the Hitler regime have by no means been only Jews.

The book concludes with a photograph of a laughing chancellor, and an admonition to German readers to follow his example and smile, too. Tell that to sixty thousand emigres, whose sense of humor seems singularly undeveloped. Dr. Hanfstaengl apparently is, but the world is not, amused.

Putzi was furious but he could do nothing until, as if by divine providence, Dorothy entered Germany driving a rented car. Hindenburg had died on August 2 and Hitler had quickly proclaimed himself Reich President as well as Reich Chancellor. Another plebiscite was announced asking the German people to express their approval. To her readers Dorothy tartly explained the difference between elections in America and plebiscites in Germany. "In other countries when there is an election you vote whether you want one candidate or another, but in Germany Hitler made himself President and it was the law, and then people voted whether they liked the law or not. If they liked it, that meant he was President; and if they didn't, that meant he was President anyhow."

She stopped briefly in Garmisch where she met a man from Chicago who had just seen the Passion Play at Oberammergau and still had not recovered from the experience. "The people are crazy," he told her. "This is not a revolution, it's a revival. They think Hitler is God. Believe it or not, a German woman sat next to me at the Passion Play, and when they hoisted Jesus on the cross, she said, 'There he is. That is our Fuehrer, our Hitler.' And when they paid out the thirty pieces of silver to Judas, she said, 'That is Roehm, who betrayed the Leader.' Can you beat it?"

In Berlin Dorothy checked into the Adlon and, like an expatriate abroad, rejoiced again in the simple pleasures of European life: "It was good to be there, like home. There was Fix in the bar, with his shining black hair and his shining smile and his good Dry Martinis. There was the big porter who can always get anything you want—reservations when the airplane is sold out and money when the banks are closed. There was the manager who always remembers how many people there are in your family and what room you had last time. . . . The French doors were open into the garden and the fountain was sparkling and the little lawn was as smooth as the finest broadloom, and a man in an apron was actually sweeping it with a broom. It was all the courtesy, all the cleanliness, all the exquisite order which is Germany."

She took her car around to be serviced and tried to get in touch with

Knick to apologize for some unkind remarks she had made about his latest book, *The Boiling Point*. Several friends had called her a bitch to her face for writing that the book would have been better if Knick had never read a copy of *Time* magazine or worked as a correspondent for the Hearst concern. Knick never returned her calls.

She looked up a number of German acquaintances to find out their feelings about the murder of Roehm and the others.

"In my country we think there should be a trial," she told a young German woman who worked in a bank.

"But if the whole people are in danger?" the woman asked.

She looked up a towering SA man she knew. "The Little One" she called him. This time when they met The Little One wasn't wearing his uniform. After he described the events of June 30 she asked: "What will happen now?"

"There are two and a half million Storm Troopers. How do you think they feel?" he parried.

"I'm asking you."

"It used to be that we were the fighters for the revolution. Hitler still says so. He says it was only a handful that were traitors. But it used to be that we were the men who saved Germany. When we passed people saluted. When we went in a restaurant, we got the best seats. Now people look the other way. It's no honor any more to wear an SA uniform. The people who know the truth are mostly dead, and if you talk you get sent to a concentration camp. The top leaders are almost all dead. Lots and lots of the subleaders are in prison."

"How many did they shoot?"

"About three hundred. But the papers never printed it. Hitler said seventy-seven."

"What will happen?" Dorothy repeated.

The Little One shrugged. "It will be a hard winter. We'll see how the people stand it. It will never be the same again with Hitler. That's true. The heart's gone out of the revolution."

"Hitler sits on a throne more powerful than all the Caesars," Dorothy observed.

"Hitler stands on a tightrope," the Little One corrected.

A German journalist told her over tea: "This revolution follows the classic pattern. Revolutions need Terrorists. Nice respectable people don't make revolutions, they only plan them. Afterward, when the revolutions succeed, the people who made them are in the way. In Russia one could send them to Turkestan or Siberia, and in Italy to Tripoli or the Lipari Islands. It is unfortunate that Germany has no colonies. So there was nothing to do but shoot them. The Storm Troopers were a great nuisance. They cost a lot of money and annoyed people by showing off. I think they probably were definitely plotting something too. Many of their leaders were scoundrels. Now one can recognize the Storm Troopers and get them in hand. It is too bad about some of the conservative people. Shooting the wife of General Schleicher made a bad impression abroad, I believe. The clean-up was not pretty, but it has consolidated Germany."

At the end of the week she dropped in to see Ambassador Dodd. She was in Germany to study the German socio-philosophical system, she said. Properly speaking, Dodd replied, the Germans didn't have one. He had not met Dorothy before but liked her immediately.

No sooner had she returned to her hotel than she was visited by a young man from the Gestapo who carried an order for her expulsion. Mrs. Lewis was being asked to leave because of her *Cosmopolitan* piece on Hitler in 1931 and her recent criticism of Germany's Jewish policy. The order came from the highest authority. There was no appeal although Mrs. Lewis might have an additional 24 hours to plan her departure. An order for Knickerbocker's expulsion was also drawn up, but it was set aside temporarily because his chief, William Randolph Hearst, was in the country.

What puzzled Dorothy most was why the order had been delayed so long. She had visited Germany twice in 1933 on assignment for the Jewish Telegraph Agency and had experienced no trouble. Why had the feud suddenly turned personal? Her false prophecy that Hitler would never be Chancellor was four years old.

"It is difficult to see how an adverse impression at that time could be interpreted as an attack on Germany," she told a group of American correspondents in Berlin. No one suspected that her offense was of a more recent vintage and lodged like a poisoned arrow in the sensitive soul of Hitler's chief of the foreign press.

Her train left at 8 PM the next evening and she had ample time to pack and say good-bye to the Adlon, the hotel where she had met her husband and where, one year, her friends had thrown a birthday party for her on the lawn so carefully manicured that it could be swept with a broom.

"What, are you leaving us already?" the manager asked. "Has everything been alright?"

"Perfect," she replied, "thanks ever so much. Thanks for everything." She went into the bar.

"Auf Wiedersehen," crooned the little hotel page. "Come again soon, *gnaedige Frau. Auf baldiges Wiedersehen."*

Practically the entire press corps came down to the Friedrichstasse Train Station to see her off. They gave her a large bunch of American

Beauty roses, and she held these in her arms as she leaned out the train window, waving good-bye. She refused to cry.

Two hours later the train from Paris arrived carrying William L. Shirer and his wife. By then the newsmen had all gone home, and the only people waiting to greet Shirer were two Gestapo officials who asked to see his passport. Shirer had a good idea what to expect in Germany. His grandfather had been one of the liberal refugees of 1848. Growing up, Shirer had heard only disparaging tales about Berlin and Berliners. Shirer had trained as a reporter in Paris and shared the French view of German ways.

After some consultation, the Gestapo officials returned his passport. and told him to go on his way. They were looking for accomplices of Dorothy's.

They needn't have bothered. In the quiet years of 1935 and 1936 the revolution became familiar and optimism returned. Dissenting opinion from Germany rarely reached foreign ears, drowned out by the jubilant crowds and the march of Germany's rulers down the path of history.

EPILOGUE

Hopeful that his candid reporting might yet change the course of American isolationism, AMBASSADOR DODD remained in Berlin until December 1937, when State Department hostility and German protests convinced Roosevelt to try a career diplomat. Dodd, 68-eight years old and in failing health, embarked on a series of lecture tours across America exhorting a united front among the democracies until his voice was stilled on February 9, 1941.

Hardly a week after the bloodletting in Germany MARTHA DODD departed on a lengthy tour of Soviet Russia which left a lasting impression on her. Returning to America with her parents in 1937, she married a wealthy Chicago philanthropist and published an account of her years in Berlin, *Through Embassy Eyes,* and two novels. In 1957, during the McCarthy period, she and her husband were indicted on charges of Communist espionage and fled to Mexico and eventually to Czechoslovakia, where she lives today.

In 1937, only a few days before his fiftieth birthday, PUTZI HANF-STAENGL was lured onto a military airplane headed for the Spanish front. When he discovered that he was to be parachuted into the war zone as part of a practical joke, Putzi hastily talked the pilot back to earth and fled to Britain. Emmissaries were sent urging his return, but Putzi remained adamant: he demanded a personal apology from Hitler. None was offered. Arrested by the British along with hundreds of other German refugees following Germany's invasion of Poland, he was held in various internment camps in England and Canada until he persuaded the White House to take him on as a clandestine advisor. Ensconced in a mansion outside Washington D.C., Putzi's imperious manner so annoyed his protectors that he was eventually returned to Canada and at war's end shipped back to Germany where a Bavarian de-nazification court cleared him of all complicity in Hitler's rise to power. Putzi Hanfstaengl lived to attend his 65th Harvard reunion and died in Munich on November 6, 1975.

Earning a living as a wine wholesaler to the diplomatic set BELLA FROMM remained in Germany until the "Crystal Night" attack on the

German synagogues in 1938. Escaping with her second husband to New York City, she worked for a while in a glove factory and later as a typist in a relief agency. In 1942 her Berlin diaries were published as *Blood and Banquets* to great acclaim. A frequent lecturer on Germany after the war, Bella Fromm died in New York City on February 9, 1972.

RUDOLF DIELS remained in Cologne for two years and then moved to Hannover as Regional Commissioner. He held that post until 1940, when he was dismissed for refusing to carry out orders against Jews and other persons. Thereafter he withdrew into private industry and became Director of Inland Shipping in the Hermann Goering Werke. Arrested by the Gestapo following the July 20th attempt on Hitler's life, Diels was expelled from the SS and his second marriage to the widow of one of Goering's brothers dissolved. Diels survived the war and was active behind the scenes for the prosecution at Nuremberg. For a time he served as an Under Secretary in the Bonn Ministry of Interior. Diels' vivid memoirs *Lucifer Ante Portas* appeared in Switzerland in 1949 and in Germany in 1950. He died on November 18, 1957 when a hunting rifle he was removing from his car accidently discharged.

NOTES AND SOURCES

Martha and Her Father

10 "Of course, I was surprised": *Chicago Herald-Examiner,* June 12, 1933.

10 "I am sure they will not": Dodd, *Diary,* 3.

10 "Don't take your household things": Dodd, *Embassy Eyes,* 15.

10 "Suppose I cannot write over there?": *ibid.,* 13.

12 "Well, you won't need": *ibid.,* 14–15.

13 Dodd's first teaching position: Dallek, *Dodd,* 27.

15 Dodd's lecture style: Henry Steele Commager to author, Dec. 5, 1981.

15 "You speak German": "Ambassador Extraordinary," *Survey Graphic,* July 1938.

16 "The German authorities": Dodd, *Diary,* 5.

16 luxury loving envoys: *Chic. Daily News,* Apr. 25, 1932.

16 "You are quite right": Dodd, *Diary,* 5.

17 "Find out what this man Hitler is made of": Dodd, *Embassy Eyes,* 16–17.

17 "Watch your step": "William E. Dodd As Statesman: Address of Charles E. Merriam," *University of Chicago Magazine,* May 1940.

17 German consulate's report: T-120, reel 5139, fr. K317497-98.

19 "As he takes up his work": *NY Times,* July 6, 1933.

19 the Jewish Rothschilds: "Ich bin William Eduard Dodd": newspaper clipping, 1934–D, Box 43, Dodd papers.

20 George A. Gordon: Memoir Notes, vol. 1, #1956, Messersmith papers; also Burke, "American Diplomats", 85–87.

20 "Immigrants are the salt": Fromm, *Banquets,* 120.

22 "We were at the beginning": Dodd, *Diary,* 12.

22 "Oh, I thought": Dodd, *Embassy Eyes,* 22.

First Impressions

23 "So now they have arrived": Writings File: Carl Sandburg, Restricted Material, Dodd papers.

24 the American mission in Berlin: Dallek, *Dodd,* 197.

25 an "appointed Ambassador": *Foreign Relations of the United States, 1933,* vol. 2, 383.

25 "Herr Ober": Reynolds, *Quentin,* 107.

26 Germany that August: Hauser, *Time Was,* 253–54.

26 "I Have Offered Myself": Dodd, *Embassy Eyes,* 28.

26 Betti Suess: Dodd, *Embassy Eyes,* 28–29; Reynolds, *Quentin,* 122–23; *Ldn Times,* Aug. 25, 1933; *NY Times,* Aug. 19, 1933.

27 Foreign Ministry apologizes: *ibid.,* 32; also T-120, reel 5674, fr. L521959.

27 Betti Suess in mental asylum: *NY Times,* Sept. 4, 1933.

28 the Warburg villa: "Mrs. Martha Dodd die Gattin des amerikanischen Botschafters," item 202, Box 50, Welles papers; Dodd, *Embassy Eyes*, 33–34; Mrs. Dodd to Bessie Pierce, Aug. 14, 1933, Folder 5, Box 2, Pierce papers.

30 "You see": Dodd, *Embassy Eyes*, 38.

31 description of the "Flying Circus": "A Night With The Circus," Apr. 7, 1933, British Embassy, Berlin, FO 371/16722 4530, Public Record Office.

32 the flapper: Fass, *The Damned*, chapters 6–7.

34 "Hitler needs a woman": Dodd, *Embassy Eyes*, 63.

Putzi Hanfstaengl

37 "Putzi, eat this now": Hanfstaengl, *Unheard*, 25.

38 Edgar Hanfstaengl: Egon Hanfstaengl letter to author, Apr. 23, 1981.

41 "I am sure": Hanfstaengl, *Unheard*, 38.

41 "He was respectful": *ibid.*, 40.

41 "I felt quite embarrassed": *ibid.*, 44.

41 Frau Else Bruckmann: Schirach, *Ich glaubte*, 31.

42 Putzi, I tell you": Hanfstaengl, *Unheard*, 54.

42 "You must play": "I Was Hitler's Closest Friend," *Cosmopolitan*, n. d., File: German Government Officials, Box 37, Welles papers.

43 "That was a nasty situation": Hanfstaengl, *Unheard*, 59.

43 "I can tell you": Hanfstaengl, *ibid.*, 61.

44 ". . . the most monumental": *ibid.*, 63.

44 "There you are Fritzl": *ibid.*, 63.

44 "Well, at least": *ibid.*, 64.

45 casualty figures from sepsis: Kegan, *Battle*, 64.

46 Hitler wounded: Masur, *Hitler*, 323.

47 Putzi in Austria: Ludecke, *I Knew Hitler*, 181–84.

47 Putzi's fashionable new home: Hanfstaengl, *Out of the Strong*, 3–10, Toland papers, Box 45, FDR Library.

48 "Well now": Hanfstaengl, *Unheard*, 125.

48 "It has all been a terrible disappointment": *ibid.*, 131.

Chief of the Foreign Press

49 "Herr Hanfstaengl": Hanfstaengl, *ibid.*, 158.

50 H. R. Knickerbocker: "Red-headed Reporter from Texas," *American Press*, May 1935; *Current Biography*, 1940; Davis, *Shadow*, 149.

51 an implausible political movement: Granzow, *Mirror*, 42.

51 "little man—world menace": Ludecke, *I Knew Hitler*, 531.

52 Brown House: Schirach, *Ich glaubte*, 88; Delmer, *Trail*, 112; Rave, *Kunst Diktatur*, 35; Schuman, *Nazi Dictatorship*, 67; *NY Times*, Oct. 18, 1931.

53 "Ja, aber Herr Hitler": "Adolf Hitler" in Fernsworth's *Dictators and Democrats*, 22.

54 "You knew I was a dispatch bearer": Knickerbocker, *Tomorrow*, 31–32.

54 "Tell me, who pays": Starhemberg, *Between Hitler*, 78–80.

55   "Get to hell out": Trevor-Roper, *Secret Conversations,* 528; also Picker, *Tischgespraeche,* 173.

55   "Get out while you can": Ludecke, *I Knew Hitler,* 399.

56   "Democracy has no convictions": Rauschning, *Voice,* 75.

56   Dorothy Thompson: *Current Biography 1940;* Sheean, *Dorothy and Red,* 34, 46, 207; Shorer, *Sinclair Lewis;* Sanders, *Dorothy Thompson.*

56   "And Hitler was late": Thompson, *I Saw Hitler,* 12–14.

57   "Who is this Mrs. Lewis?": Ludecke, *I Knew Hitler,* 533–34.

57   "Hanfstaengl!": Ludecke, *I Knew Hitler,* 536–37.

58   "Now at least you can stop singing": Hanfstaengl, *Unheard,* 185.

59   Captain Hans Baur: Baur, *Hitler's Pilot,* 17, 27.

60   "That stuff of yours": Delmer, *Trail,* 148.

60   "Hurry! Run!": Delmer, *ibid.,* 150.

61   "I play the piano for Hitler": Fromm, *Banquets,* 90.

Bella Fromm

63   Herr Steuermann: *True Detective,* Feb. 1942; also vitae, Folder 3, Box 48, Welles papers.

64   "Mother!": Welles, *Engel,* 35.

64   more monuments than Rome: Eckhardt, *Brecht's Berlin,* 12.

64   20,000 cows, 30,000 pigs: "Changing Berlin," *National Geographic,* Feb. 1937.

66   "I think the monkey": *ibid.*

67   "Well, well we meet again": *True Detective,* Mr. 1942.

68   little green curtains: Baum, *Quite Different,* 272.

68   Ullstein: Ullstein, *Rise and Fall,* 46–53.

69   "That's charming, Bella": Fromm, *Banquets,* 16.

70–71   André François-Poncet: Solo, *François-Poncet,* 12–82; Kessler, *Twenties,* 407–408, 422; Fromm, *Banquets,* 30–32; Karl von Wiegand to Flick-Steger, Nov. 7, 1931, Box 11, von Wiegand papers.

71   "The Ambassador cannot": *Berliner Zeitung* clipping, Scrapbook, Welles papers.

Eminence in Field Gray

74   "An interesting man": "Ein Bild des Generals Kurt von Schleicher," *Politische Studien,* vol. 10, 1959.

74   "I want to have a dance": *True Detective,* Apr. 1942.

75   Bruening's failure: Wheeler-Bennett, *Knaves,* 50–51; Bruening, *Memorien,* 557–60; Heiden, *Fuehrer,* 460–461; Papen, *Memoirs,* 140, 156.

75   "But I'm Chancellor": *True Detective,* Apr. 1942.

76   "You're beginning to hear voices": Fromm, *Banquets,* 53.

77   "Oh, please": *True Detective,* Apr. 1942.

77   "Dangerous times are ahead": *ibid.*

77   "Who told you": Fromm *Banquets,* 65.

77   "Now tell me": *True Detective,* Apr. 1942.

78   "It won't be long now": Fromm, *Banquets,* 60.

78 "You journalists are all alike": *ibid.,* 66.

79 "Don't worry so hard": Fromm, *Banquets,* 72.

79 "Nothing much": Ullstein, *Rise and Fall,* 7.

80 "Now, we're on our way": Hanfstaengl, *Unheard,* 206.

80 "At least I don't have to go on calling you": *ibid.,* 206.

81 "Long live the Chief": Regler, *Owl,* 151.

81 "I don't understand you, Herr Hanfstaengl": Hanfstaengl, *Unheard,* 207–208.

82 "The Fuehrer insists": Hanfstaengl, *Unheard,* 211.

83 "They've got one of them who did it": Delmer, *Weimar,* 118–20.

84 "This is a Communist crime": Papen, *Memoirs,* 269.

85 Hastily, Diels scribbled: "The Political Effects of the Reichstag Fire" in *Nazism and the Third Reich,* 115–17.

86 "This is a bunch of bunk": Sommerfeldt, *Ich war dabei,* 26–28.

Rudolf Diels

87 Rudolf Diels: Diels' interrogation Oct. 24, 1946; Aronson, *Fruehgeschichte,* 82–83; Orb, *Machtrausch,* 98–99.

88 "I don't want anything": Diels, *Lucifer,* 127.

91 "Passology": Diels, *Lucifer,* 176–78; also Hoehne, *Codeword,* 28; Dallin, *Espionage,* 87.

91 Alex's dungeons: Valtin, *Out of the Night,* 559–60.

91 escape a free man: "Rudolf Diels—Portraet eines verkannten Mannes," *Politische Studien,* 9:475–81, 1958.

92 "Germany is worth living in": *Chic. Daily News,* Mr. 2, 1933.

92 public toilets beneath Potsdamer Platz: Mowrer, *Triumph,* 218.

93 no evidence of doctored cables: "Editors Differ on Censorship," *Editor & Publisher,* Apr. 1, 1933.

93 "supervision" of foreign press: "200 Dailies Are Supressed by Hitler," *Editor & Publisher,* Apr. 1, 1933.

94 "Four suits": Nuremberg Documents, PS-1759.

94–96 "Passersby called us here": Fromm, *Banquets,* 79–85.

95 "But I can't believe it": *True Detective,* May 1942.

96 "Why, it's you Frau Bella": *ibid.*

96 "Otto, Otto": *ibid.*

97 "Fromm's Act": *True Detective,* June 1942.

97 "Woolworth five and ten cent stores": *Chic. Tribune,* Mr. 10, 1933.

97 "The Anhalter Zeitung": *NY Times,* Mr. 15, 1933.

98 German suspicions increased: Dittmann, "Meinungsbildung," 44–45.

98 the flowers continued to bloom: Mowrer, *Journalist's Wife,* 289.

99 "The world will probably never know": *New Republic,* Apr. 12, 1933.

99 Knick's estimate of casualities: *Phil. Public Ledger,* Apr. 5, 1933.

99 number of dead 247: *Chic. Daily News,* Apr. 12, 1933.

99 Hitler's figures on casualities: *NY Times,* Apr. 8, 1933.

99 Putzi's telephone hook-up to New York: *12 Uhr Blatt,* Mr. 26, 1933.

100–101 "There is not one person in all Germany": *NY Times,* Mr. 26, 1933.

101 "As concerns Jews": *NY Times,* Mr. 27, 1933.

Boycott

103 "Until Government's abroad": *NY Evening Post,* Mr. 27, 1933.

104 "The boycott is only a beginning": McDonald Diary, Mr. 28, 1933, quoted in Steward, "U. S. Government Policy," 39–40.

104 Knick and Goebbels dine at Horchers: Agnes Walker letter to author, Oct. 1, 1981.

105 "You claim to have reason to speak to me": Mowrer, *Journalist's Wife,* 296–97.

105 "The hour of 10 Saturday": *NY Evening Post,* Apr. 1, 1933.

105–106 Bella Fromm on National Socialist Saturday: Fromm, *Banquets,* 99–100; *True Detective,* June 1942; Ullstein, *Rise and Fall,* 27–29.

107 "Remain outside!": Anonymous, *Why I Left Germany,* 123.

107 "United States Stops Jewish Agitation": Birchall, *Storm,* 136.

107 "Complying with the wish": *NY Times,* Apr. 5, 1933.

108 "I hope we won't have to accept them": Fromm, *Banquets,* 88.

109 "Vice-Chancellor and Frau von Papen": *ibid.,* 94.

109 "The Fuehrer has just entered": *ibid.,* 95.

109–110 "May I have the pleasure": *ibid.,* 95–96.

110 "One can buy patent leather shoes": Mr. 29 entry, Folder 2 (1933), Box 1, Welles papers.

The Foreign Press

113 chaos under new rulers: "Round Robin," Apr. 30, 1933, fr. 224, reel 15, Lochner papers.

114 erroneous Ullstein obituary: *ibid.;* also *NY Times,* Mr. 24, 1933.

115 Eduard Deuss incident: Messersmith to Secretary of State, May 12, 1933, G/ DEW 811.91262/112, National Archives; von Wiegand cable to Hearst, Folder: Hearst, William Randolph, Box 14, von Wiegand papers; "Men of Cabelese," *New Outlook,* Dec. 1933.

115 Gestapo raid on AP photo service: Lochner letter to Ken Cooper, Mr. 26, 1933, fr. 865–66, reel 1, Lochner papers.

116 "NEW YORK CABLES": *ibid.*

116 "Die Taverne": Shirer, *Berlin Diary,* 40–41; Dodd, *Embassy Eyes,* 100–101; Bernays, *Special Correspondent,* 219; Gibbs, *Journey,* 237–39; Mowrer, *Journalist's Wife,* 286.

117 "I want to talk to you!": Gibbs, *Journey,* 237–39.

118 "That's all right": Mowrer, *Triumph,* 217.

118 Berlin Foreign Press Association: "Shirtsleeve Ambassador," fr. 141–48, reel 40, Lochner papers; also "Verein der Auslaendischen Presse zu Berlin, 1934," Folder 5, Box 48, Welles papers.

118 "I was asked to resign": *NY Times,* Apr. 6, 1933.

119 "Edgar a Jew?": Mowrer, *Triumph,* 219.

119 "In this country": *ibid.,* 220–21.

120 "Every bird": *NY Times,* June 24, 1933.

1933

120 "This time Hetz-Blaetter!": Schuman, *Nazi Dictatorship,* 340–41.

121 "Its wording is so insulting": *NY Times,* June 25, 1933.

121 Louis P. consults an expert: "Shirtsleeve Ambassador," fr. 214–17, reel 40, Lochner papers.

121–123 book burning: *Phil. Public Ledger,* May 11, 1933; "Germany: The Twilight of Reason," *New Republic,* June 14, 1933; "Round Robin," May 28, 1933, fr. 232, reel 15, Lochner papers; Anonymous, *Why I Left Germany,* 207–11; *NY Times,* May 11, 1933; "Germany: Book Bonfire," *Literary Digest,* May 27, 1933.

123 "These flames": *NY Times,* May 11, 1933.

124 Ku Klux Klan analogy: *NY Evening Post,* Apr. 3, 1933.

124 "Are you still there" *Phil. Public Ledger,* Apr. 5, 1933.

125 Frau Marie Jankowsky: "Knickerbocker, *Tomorrow,* 81–83; *The Brown Book,* 211–12; *Ldn. Times,* Apr. 1, 1933.

125 "They took me": Knickerbocker, *Tomorrow,* 81–83.

126–127 Ludecke's attempt to oust Knick: Ludecke, *I Knew Hitler,* 612–47; *Public Ledger* telegram to Knickerbocker, May 8, 1933, Correspondence 1932–33, Knickerbocker papers; Messersmith to Secretary of State, May 12, 1933, G/ DEW 811.91262/112, *Foreign Relations of the United States, 1933,* vol. II, 400– 402; Ludecke letter to Max Amann, Feb. 28, 1933, Ludecke papers; Moffat to Julian Mason, June 8, 1933, 811.91262/112, National Archives.

126 "we have every": *Public Ledger* telegram to Knickerbocker, May 8, 1933, Correspondence 1932–33, Knickerbocker papers.

127 "LUDECKE ARRESTED FOR SWINDLE AND EXTORTION": Ludecke, *I Knew Hitler,* 670.

No. 8 Prinz Albrecht Strasse

129 George S. Messersmith: Kennan, *Memoirs,* 66; Memoir Notes, #206, #1954, #1961, Messersmith papers; *Berliner Boersen Courier,* July 2, 1933; "Der neue Gesandte Amerikas in Wien," *Neue Freie Presse,* Mr. 25, 1934, Scrapbook 1, Box 6, Welles papers.

129 Hitler could not leave his hat: Dodd letter to William Phillips, Nov. 17, 1933, 1933-P, Box 42, Dodd papers.

130 Dr. Schachno beating: Memoir Notes, #1958 & Messersmith to Secretary of State, July 11, 1933, #213, Messersmith papers.

130 "With few exceptions": *Peace and War,* 191–92.

131 "In Germany we can do": Messersmith to Secretary of State, July 18, 1933, #214, Messersmith papers.

132 renovations costing 180,000 marks: Graf, *Politische Polizei,* 175.

132 only a very unimportant man: Diels' interrogation, Oct. 18, 1946, National Archives.

132–133 terror at No. 8 Prinz Albrecht Strasse: Gisevius, *Bitter,* 49–51.

133 "I must reply": *NY Times,* July 16, 1933.

133 "The value of the SA and the SS": Lochner, *What About Germany,* 50.

134 SA and SS employed at lowly tasks: Graf, *Politische Polizei,* 204.

135 Oranienburg: "Im Konzentrationslager Oranienburg bei Berlin," *Berliner Illustrirte Zeitung,* Apr. 30, 1933.

136 "Oh, for the past two days": Lochner, *What About Germany,* 54–56.

Summer Violence

139   Roosevelt's sense of humor: "Round Robin," June 30, 1933, fr. 240, reel 15, Lochner papers.

140   "A most unpleasant job": Folder 2 (1933), Box 1, Welles papers.

140   invitation to Nuremberg: *Foreign Relations of the United States, 1933,* vol. II, 255–56.

141   "Sonderzug": *Vossische Zeitung,* Sept. 1, 1933.

142   "President Roosevelt has charged me": 1934-D, Box 43, Dodd papers.

142   Messermith snubbed: Dodd, *Embassy Eyes,* 96–97; also Dodd *Diary,* 15–16.

143   American diplomats: *Chic. Daily Mail,* May 16, 1932; also Weil, *Club,* chapters 1 and 3.

143   Gordon's critical efficiency reports: see reports, 1933–G, Box 41, Dodd papers.

143   sums spent "outshining" colleagues: annual cost of living accounts, 1934-D, Box 44, Dodd papers.

143   a bill from his predecessor: Dodd to Secretary of State, May 19, 1934, Moore papers.

144   French Ambassador "crushed" his staff with work: Solo, "François-Poncet," 92.

144   "It has become common practice": *Vossische Zeitung,* July 15, 1933.

145   "We have met before": Fromm, *Banquets,* 109–10.

146   Dr. Daniel Mulvihill: Messersmith to Secretary of State, Aug. 21, 1933, 362.1113 Mulvihill, Daniel/11 GC, National Archives.

146   "I was simply standing there": *Phil. Public Ledger,* Aug. 18, 1933.

147   Under Secretary of State Phillips' press conference: Aug. 18, 1933, 362.1113 Mulvihill, Daniel/7 GC, National Archives.

148   Dr. Sauerbruch and Erna Hanfstaengl: Sauerbruch, *Mein Leben,* 404.

149   pressure on Jewish community: *NY Times,* Sept. 11, 1933.

149   torchlit parade reenactment: *NY Times,* Aug. 18, 1933.

149   "The raising of the right arm": *NY Times,* Sept. 12, 1933.

An Embattled Ambassador

151   Sommerfeldt's call for Mowrer's resignation: *Der Angriff,* July 6, 1933.

151   "The sons of bitches": Mowrer, *Journalist's Wife,* 303.

152   "Absolutely": "Shirtsleeve Ambassador," fr. 184, reel 40, Lochner papers.

152   Mowrer's thunderous salvo: *Chic. Daily News,* Aug. 8, 1933.

155   Dodd receives Ernst's apology: Dodd, *Embassy Eyes,* 152; Dodd, *Diary,* 26–27; *Phil. Public Ledger,* Aug. 23, 1933; *NY Times,* Aug. 23, 1933.

155   "to a gallant fighter": Mowrer, *Journalist's Wife,* 308.

156   "And you too Brutus": Memoir Notes, vol. III, #2034, Messersmith papers.

156   "And when are you coming back": Mowrer, *Triumph,* 226.

157   Rolf Kaltenborn slapped: Kaltenborn, *Fifty,* 189; also Messersmith to Secretary of State, Sept. 1, 1933, 362.1113 Kaltenborn, H. V./4, National Archives.

157   "I was able to understand": *NY Times,* Sept. 12, 1933.

157   Samuel Bossard: Messersmith to Secretary of State, Sept. 2, 1933, GRC 362.1113 Bossard, Samuel B./12, National Archives.

158   "Of course, such incidents": Memo from Gordon, Sept. 13, 1933, GRC

363.1113/10, National Archives.

159 Dr. Karl-Oscar Bertling: Colwell, "American Experience," 207; also Messersmith to Secretary of State, Sept. 26, 1933, FP 362.1113/17, National Archives.

159 "I came to Germany": van Paassen, *Nazism,* 240–41; Messersmith to Secretary of State, Sept. 26, 1933, FP 363.1113/17, National Archives.

160 "Think and be quiet": Heinemann, *Foreign Minister,* 2–4, 9.

160 "Is there to be war?": Dodd, *Diary,* 37.

160 Foreign Minister unable to perceive drift: Dodd letter to Bessie Louise Pierce, Oct. 1, 1933, Folder 10, Box 9, Pierce papers.

160 "Nothing has stirred American diplomats": *NY Times,* Oct. 13, 1933.

161 François-Poncet thought the American Embassy mistaken: Memoir Notes, vol. 1, #1958, Messersmith papers.

161 victim fined 50 marks; Messersmith to Secretary of State, Oct. 12, 1933, 362.1113 Velz, Roland/8 GC, National Archives.

162 Sherwood Eddy speech: T-120, reel 2714, fr. H034784 & H034858 & H034870f.

162 "70,000 JEWS IMMIGRATED": Fromm, *Banquets,* 123.

162 "Your laws tend to the extermination": *NY Times,* July 21, 1933.

163 "Very interesting Bella": Folder 2 (1933), Box 1, Welles papers.

164 "In times of great stress": *NY Times,* Oct. 29, 1933.

164–65 "Too bad": Folder 2 (1933), Box 1, Welles papers.

165 Fortune article: "Their Excellencies, Our Ambassadors," *Fortune Magazine,* Apr. 1934.

166 John Franklin Carter behind innuendo: Dodd letter to Judge Moore, June 8, 1934, 1934-M, Box 45, Dodd papers; also Hanfstaengl, *Zwischen,* 280; *Current Biography,* 1941.

Putzi in Uniform

167 a million new members: Orlov, *Nazi Party,* 48–49.

167 "Why Putzi": Armstrong, *Peace,* 534.

167 "You look like a Turkish whore": Hanfstaengl, *Zwischen,* 292.

168 "The Gestapo!": Lochner, *Always the Unexpected,* 187.

168 "My butler simply could not find": Lochner, *What About Germany,* 352.

168 "I believe, Dr. Hanfstaengl": *Always the Unexpected,* 187.

168 "I have got to leave": Memoir Notes, vol. 1, #1962, Messersmith papers.

168 Putzi was always girl crazy: Mowrer, *Journalist's Wife,* 299.

168 "That man Groener": Lochner, *What About Germany,* 353.

168 edict forbidding mingling: T-120, reel 5075, fr. L155606f.

168–169 "I have just been down to the Berghof": Hanfstaengl, *Unheard,* 228.

169 "What is America but millionaires": *ibid.,* 234.

169 "To Chancellor Hitler": *ibid.,* 224.

169 "He is David": Mosley, *Life,* 106.

169 "Oh, the Jews, the Jews": *ibid.,* 107.

170 "You have come at exactly the right moment": *ibid.,* 108.

170 "Why?": Mosley, *ibid.,* 133.

171 Liaison Staff as bureaucratic bottleneck: Orlov, *Nazi Party,* 72–74.

171 Agatha von Hausberger: Freedom of Information Act, Federal Bureau of Investigation.

171 Rolf Hoffmann: Pope, *Playground,* 129–30.

171 appeal for autographed *Mein Kampf:* Roger Sherman Hoar to Hanfstaengl, Apr. 14, 1933, T-81, reel 27, fr. 24351.

172 Frederick Shuman rebuff: Schuman, *Nazi Dictatorship,* introduction.

172 Kate Pohli-MacLeod: T-81, reel 277, fr. 24433.

172–173 "Your Press, your law": Bernays, *Special Correspondent,* 209–14.

173 "Let me speak to one of those nitwits": Reynolds, *Quentin,* 119.

173 "There isn't one damn word": *ibid.,* 123.

174 "You don't understand German": *ibid.,* 127–28.

175 "As a former comrade of Wessels": Horst Wessel Film publicity, Ewers Nachlass.

175 "We National Socialists see no value": *Licht-Bild-Buehne,* Oct. 13, 1933.

175 Central Censorship Board's demands: Hull, *Film,* 31; Schuman, *Nazi Dictatorship,* 367; Welch, *Propaganda,* 75–77.

176 "Leonardo da Vinci painted Christ": *Berliner Lokal-Anzeiger,* Dec. 14, 1933.

176 Putzi pays for prints: Ernst Hanfstaengl, Freedom of Information Act, Federal Bureau of Investigation.

Suicide

177 "From now on": Fromm, *Banquets,* 114.

178 "Children, I am rehabilitated": *ibid.,* 113.

178 "Poulette, Poulette": *True Detective,* July 1942.

178 "I can't live any more": Fromm, *Banquets,* 138.

178 "She did not suffer any pain": *ibid.,* 138.

179 "Bellachen, we are all so shocked": *ibid.,* 139.

179 Erhard Milch: Irving, *Rise and Fall,* 327f.

179 Party press attacks "Jewish Front Soldier": *Voelkischer Beobachter,* Apr. 25, 1933.

179 Army confirms only 7,000 dead: *Vossische Zeitung,* Oct. 31, 1933.

180 Werner von Blomberg: "Blomberg Builds A New German Army," *NY Times Magazine,* June 2, 1935; also Folder 1 (1934), Box 2, Welles papers.

180 "We are very anxious": Fromm, *Banquets,* 139.

180 the correct procedure: Goebbels to Blomberg, Dec. 12, 1933, Folder 3, Box 58, Welles papers; also Pollock, *Decrees,* 29–37.

180 "The Ullstein press has received a verbal veto": Fromm, *Banquets,* 149.

180 "I've been expecting it": *True Detective,* July 1942.

181 exemption from Aryan clause denied: Landesverband Berlin letter, Jan. 20, 1934, Folder 1, Box 2, Welles papers.

181 "PRESS MOLES": "Getarnte Wuehlmaeuse in der Presse," *Deutsche Wochenschau,* Jan. 20, 1934.

181 Eduard Stadler: "We Blundered Hitler Into Power," *Saturday Evening Post,* July 13, 1940; also Ekstein, *Limits,* 288–89.

182 "Bella, dear": Fromm, *Banquets,* 146–47.

182 "The Minister President appreciates your importance": *ibid.,* 149.

1933

183 "There is no such thing": Sommerfeldt, *Ich war dabei*, 44.

183 "We have been betrayed": "We Blundered Hitler Into Power," *Saturday Evening Post*, July 13, 1940.

183 "Right now people like that": Fromm, *Banquets*, 150.

184 "You win": *ibid.*, 151.

185 Bella throws away her gun: *True Detective*, July 1942.

185 "And where did he fall": Feb. 1934 entry, Folder 1 (1934), Box 2, Welles papers.

186 "He told me wonderful things": Fromm, *Banquets*, 161.

186 American Chamber of Commerce letter of recommendation: Mrs. Quay McCune letter to author, Oct. 17, 1982.

186 "America is a hard country": Apr. 13, 1934 entry, Folder 1 (1934), Box 2, Welles papers.

186 "You should go to the Anthropological Institute": Fromm, *Banquets*, 112; also May 1934 entry, Folder 1 (1934), Box 2, Welles papers.

187 "Now at least help Bella": Bella letter to General von Massow, May 30, 1934, Folder 1 (1934), Box 2, Welles papers.

187 "I wonder why we were asked today": Fromm, *Banquets*, 162.

Beaus

190 Dodd throws Messersmith mock salute: Martha Dodd letter to Thornton Wilder, Dec. 14, 1933, Wilder papers.

190 Dresden Thanksgiving address: Martha Dodd letter to Thornton Wilder, Dec. 14, 1933, Wilder papers.

190 "Why, I never knew that horses could jump": "Familie Dodd im Ausland," *Deutsche Allgemeine Zeitung*, Beiblatt, Aug. 27, 1941.

190 "The Nazis are cruel but not original": Fromm, *Banquets*, 131.

191 The "American Hohenzollern": *Chic. Tribune*, Feb. 26, 1933.

192 "If you don't try to be more careful": Louis Ferdinand, *Rebel Prince*, 253.

192 Prince's drinking problem: *ibid.*, 239.

192 "One day I expect": Bérard, *Souvient*, 187.

193 Mildred Harnack-Fish: see Eberhard Bruening. *Mildred Harnack-Fish als Literaturwissenschaftlerin*. Akademie-Verlag, 1983; also undated letter from Mildred Harnack to Ambassador Dodd with Vitae, Folder G-H-I-K, Restricted Material, Dodd papers.

193 edit column Berlin topics: Martha Dodd to Thornton Wilder, Sept. 25, 1933, Wilder papers.

194 "You love your country": Cripon, *Fallada*, 200–201.

195 Elmine Rangabe: Smith, MY LIFE, 51.

195 ban on Horst Wessel Song: *Die Gesetzgebung*, 51.

195 "That is not the sort of music": Dodd, *Embassy Eyes*, 67.

196 the Ullstein visitor: Ullstein, *Rise and Fall*, 39–41.

197 tea cosies to overcoats: Wheeler-Bennett, *Knaves*, 72; also Smith, MY LIFE, 19.

197 Messersmith fools Goebbels: Memoir Notes, vol. I, #1953, Messersmith papers; also *Berliner Tageblatt*, May 4, 1933.

198 Hitler wants FDR to take first step: Coar to L. H. Howe, Sept. 2, 1933, PPF, 3717, FDR Lib; also T-120, reel 2714, fr. H035027f; Dodd memorandum, Aug. 16, 1933, 1933-C, Dodd papers; Coar to W. A. R. Kerr, Aug. 25, 1933, Coar papers.

199 "Such is the German situation": Dodd, *Diary,* 24.

199 Diels' charm to women: Kalnoky, *Guest House,* 67–76.

200 sensational affair: Carr memo, June 5, 1935, Box 12, Carr papers.

201 "I'm warning you": Diels, *Lucifer.,* 171.

201 "You are seeing too much of Roehm": Sommerfeldt, *Ich war dabei,* 57.

201 "The snow is soft": Martha Dodd to Thornton Wilder, Dec. 14, 1933, Wilder papers.

Beating Stations

203 Bernhard Weiss: Diels, *Lucifer,* 164–65; also Liang, *Berlin Police,* 158–60.

204 Messersmith nearly run over: Memoir Notes, vol. 1, #1971, Messersmith papers.

204 10,000 political prisoners: *NY Times,* Apr. 20, 1933.

204 "The carrion can't open her mouth": Litten, *Tears,* 70.

204 "We'll permit": Loebe, *Erinnerungen,* 151–52.

205 "Hey, there's Pauly": *ibid.,* 153.

205 list of better known camps: *Brown Book,* 287.

206 "Did not Dr. Goebbels": Litten, *Tears,* xiii.

207 "What with my own troubles": *ibid.,* 19.

207 HANS LITTEN CONFESSES: *ibid.,* 42.

207 "He's lying all the time": *ibid.,* 55.

208 Diels twice rescued one young man: Diels, *Lucifer,* 202.

208 Dr. Haustein: Diels' letter to Knickerbocker, Oct. 31, 1933, and funeral invitation dated Nov. 12, 1933, Folder 2, General Correspondence 1932–33, Knick papers.

208 German evidence against Orloff: T-120, reel 2714, fr. H034914-19.

209 "I wonder": Memoir Notes, vol. 1, #1958, Messersmith papers.

209 Frau Stennes at Kaiserhof: Diels, *Lucifer,* 184–85; also Drage, *Amiable Prussian,* 97–98.

210 "Loss of blood": Hiller, *Leben,* 252.

210 "I am an Egyptian": *ibid.,* 266.

211 "That surprises you": *ibid.,* 256.

212 "What do you think": Diels, *Lucifer,* 188.

213 Diels frees Stennes: Drage, *Amiable Prussian,* 99; Diels, *Lucifer,* 185; Hoehne, *Death's Head,* 82.

213 "If you do anything": Diels, *Lucifer,* 236.

214 "You're under arrest": *ibid.,* 237.

214 "words could hardly express": Graf, *Politische Polizei,* Doc. 17a, page 426.

215 security at the trial: unpublished MS dated Berlin, October 13, S. Miles Bouton papers.

217–218 "You have repeatedly stated": Reed, *Reichstag,* 227–28.

Flight

219 "You know what has happened": Diels, *Lucifer*, 222.

219 Diels recommends case be dropped: Graf, *Politische Polizei*, 202–203; see also fr. 34, reel 1, Guertner Diaries, Record Group, 978.

220 Guenther Joel: Diels, *Lucifer*, 225–28; Hoehne, *Death's Head*, 80; Altstoerter et al, fr. 113–14, reel 41 & fr. 31, 42, reel 34.

221 murder of former Altona Police President: Langhoff, *Truncheon*, 173–75.

221 "Who are you": *ibid.*

222 "I am as treacherous": *ibid.*, 200–1.

223 civilian discontent: *ibid.*, 227; also Diels, *Lucifer*, 192.

224 camps surrender: Langhoff, *Truncheon*, 232–33; also Diels, *Lucifer*, 193–94.

225 Frau von Clemm: Diels interrogation, Oct. 18, 1946, National Archives.

226 "For heaven's sake": Diels, *Lucifer*, 244.

226 "Herr Diels": *ibid.*, 246.

227 2000 Gestapo employees: Graf, *Politische Polizei*, 184.

Christmas Amnesty

229 "Forty-three millions": Langhoff, *Truncheon*, 218.

229 voting figures for moor camps: *Als sozialdemokratischer Arbeiter*, 60.

229 "Acknowledge National Socialist": Billinger, *Fatherland*, 184–85.

230 "I have nothing": Diels, *Lucifer*, 252.

230–231 "See here, Herr Goering": *ibid.*, 253.

231 "The prisoners are to be left in no doubt": *NY Times*, Dec. 8, 1933.

231 chaotic camp records: Billinger, *Fatherland*, 195.

231 "The Minister President": *Vosssiche Zeitung*, Dec. 21, 1933.

232 "You are free": *Als sozialdemokratischer Arbeiter*, 72.

233 Sommerfeldt plots with Lochner: Sommerfeldt, *Ich war dabei*, 62–65.

233 "I've figured out": "Shirtsleeve Ambassador," fr. 374–76, reel 40, Lochner papers.

234 statistics of grim winter: Schuman, *Nazi Dictatorship*, 293–99.

234 50,000 made on privileged hunting fees: *NY Times*, Jan. 18, 1934.

234 arrest of homosexuals: White to Moffat, Feb. 28, 1934, White papers.

235 "That is sheer nonsense": Diels, *Lucifer*, 274–76.

236 "You come from a decent": *ibid.*, 282.

236 "You are sick": *ibid.*, 283.

236 sabre dueling: Bolitho, *Other Germany*, 144–64.

237 "Because I know too much": Dodd, *Embassy Eyes*, 136–37.

237 concentration camp at Stettin: Diels, *Lucifer*, 288–89; also Therov, *Pommern*, vol. 1, 29–37 & vol. 2, 224–73.

237 "We are no": *NY Times*, Mr. 9, 1934; also *Ldn. Times*, Mr. 10, 1934.

238 Diels betrayed by Gestapo: Koehler, *Inside*, 99–110.

238 "I have decided": Diels, *Lucifer*, 294–95.

238 "Roehm and his creatures": *ibid.*, 296.

239 "Gentlemen": Memoir Notes, vol. 1, #1957, Messersmith papers.

240 "The infliction": British Embassy, Berlin, Apr. 25, 1934, FO 371/17706 XP 3367, Public Record Office.

Putzi in the USA

241 "Hanfstaengl, you must come": Hanfstaengl, *Unheard,* 253–54.

241 "I may even": *NY Times,* Mr. 29, 1934.

241 "If there are those": *NY Times,* Mr. 31, 1934.

242 "As for propaganda": *NY Times,* Apr. 25, 1934.

242 "Que vivra verra": *NY Times,* June 8, 1934.

243 Foreign Ministry's prayer: Dieckhoff memo to Reichsminister von Neurath, June 7, 1934, T-120, reel 4614, fr. K269657.

243–245 "Is it true": *NY Times,* June 17, 1934.

244 Broun's column: *NY World-Telegram,* June 15, 1934.

245 "I should like to give you": *Newsweek,* June 23, 1934.

245 "Well, Hanfstaengl": Hanfstaengl, *Zwischen,* 344.

245 "A decided talent": *Boston Globe,* June 18, 1934.

245 "He's just a big Don Juan": *Ldn. Daily Express,* June 20, 1934.

246 $2,000 check: *Deutsche Allgemeine Zeitung,* Sept. 15, 1934.

246 "If a car gets stuck": Hanfstaengl, *Unheard,* 258.

246–248 "To the health": *Boston Globe,* June 18, 1934; also *NY Times,* June 18, 1934.

248 "I don't feel": *Boston Globe,* June 19, 1934.

249 "Now, now": *NY Times,* June 19, 1934.

249 "I bring you greetings": Conant, *Several Lives,* 142.

249 "I want this check deposited": Associated Press, June 7, 1934, fr. 41, reel 35, Lochner papers.

250 "What do you think": *Boston Globe,* June 20, 1934.

252 "I have no comment": *NY Times,* July 1, 1934.

252 "Not here": Hanfstaengl, *Unheard,* 259.

253 "News that came": *NY Times,* July 2, 1934.

253–254 West Point: *NY Times,* July 8, 1934; Deutsches Generalkonsulat New York to Deutsche Botschaft, Washington, D. C., July 10, 1934 & Hanfstaengl to General Conner, July 6, 1934, Pressestelle, Gesamel-Akten, 1934, Akten aus dem politischen Archiv des Auswaertigen Amts, Auswaertiges Amt.

254 "The art of diplomacy": *NY Times,* July 8, 1934.

Mutiny

255 young woman weeping: Reed, *Insanity,* 163.

255–256 "I just want you": *NY Times,* July 1, 1934.

256 "Ah yes": Wheeler-Bennett, *Nemesis,* 323.

256 "Berlin does not reply": *NY Times,* July 1, 1934.

256 "The execution": *NY Times,* July 1, 1934.

258 Armand hurried off: Berard, *Souvient,* 239.

258 "Martha, is that you": Dodd, *Embassy Eyes,* 144.

258–259 "If the outside world": *NY Times,* June 24, 1934.

259   "Yes, yes, my dear Papen": Wheaton, *Prelude*, 489.

260   "Herr von Papen!": Orb, *Machtrausch*, 270.

261   "Mr. Chancellor": "Winter of 1933," Folder 17, Box 29, Schultz papers.

261   Signora Cerruti at Dodds: Cerruti, *Ambassador's Wife*, 153.

261   "Anyway": Dodd, *Diary*, 117.

Murder
263   "I hope we may call on you soon": Dodd, *Embassy Eyes*, 155.

264   Schleicher's murder: O'Neill, *German Army*, 49; also *NY Times*, July 3, 4, 1934.

265   "In this hour": *NY Times*, July 2, 1934.

266   "Your friend Schleicher": Fromm, *Banquets*, 170; also entry Folder 1, (1934), Box 2, Welles papers.

266   "The same old Bella": *True Detective*, July 1942.

266   "I am surprised": Wheeler-Bennett, *Nemesis*, 324.

267   "Thank goodness": Fromm, *Banquets*, 170–71.

267   Goering in Cologne: Gollo, *Long Knives*, 210.

268   "Watch yourself": Diels, *Lucifer*, 305.

269   "I am innocent": *NY Times*, July 3, 1934.

270   Martha's visit to Regendanz's: Dodd, *Embassy Eyes*, 163–65.

270   Regendanz's report: see report, 1934–R, Box 45, Dodd papers.

270   "Arrived safe": Dodd, *Embassy Eyes*, 165.

270–271   "Be careful": *NY Times*, July 4, 1934.

271   "Yes, it wasn't exactly nice": *NY Evening Post*, July 5, 1934.

271   "It's an odd world": Kirkpatrick, *Circle*, 57.

271   "Well, boys": *NY Times*, July 4, 1934.

271   "Strange": Dodd, *Diary*, 125.

272   "Oh, so you're still among": Dodd, *Embassy Eyes*, 158.

272   "Lucky for you": Koehler, *Gestapo*, 37; also *NY Times*, July 4, 5, 1934.

273   François-Poncet's troubles: *Solo*, "François-Poncet," 276; also *NY Times* July 6, 1934.

273   Reiner's estimate of casualties: Memo prepared by Hugh Corby Fox, July 2, 1934, 1934-R, Box 45, Dodd papers.

274   Reiner's head shaven: Riess, *Espionage*, 256.

274   "I had to shoot": Fromm, *Banquets*, 173–74.

274   Dodd ventured two theories: *Foreign Relations of the United States, 1934,* vol. II, 230–37.

274–275   Diels' version: Dodd to Secretary of State, July 25, 1934, 862.00/33 44 FP, National Archives.

275   "My task": Dodd, *Diary*, 123.

276   "Mutinies are suppressed": Knickerbocker, *Tomorrow*, 39–40.

277   "Something for you": Bérard, *Souvient*, 242–43.

277   François-Poncet's rehabilitation: Solo, "François-Poncet," 280–84; also François-Poncet, *Fateful Years*, 141.

Expulsion

279 "Well, here you are again": Hanfstaengl, *Unheard,* 263.

279 "I think the German press": Coblenz, *Portrait,* 112–14.

279 "Germany is battling": *NY Times,* Aug. 23, 1934.

280 "Wait a minute": Davies, *What Times,* 148–49.

280 "Why am I so misrepresented": Coblenz, *Portrait,* 104–105.

280 "I only had to convince him": Nov. 15, 1934 entry, Folder 1 (1934), Box 2, Welles papers.

281–282 "Dr. Hanfstaengl has selected": "Putzy-Footing Propaganda," *Saturday Review of Literature,* July 7, 1934.

282 "In other countries": "Good-Bye to Germany," *Harper's,* Dec. 1, 1934.

283 "In my country": "Good-Bye to Germany," *Harper's,* Dec. 1, 1934.

284 Knick's expulsion order: Faris to Knickerbocker, Dec. 27, 1934 and enclosures, Folder 1934, Box: Correspondence 1934–48, Knickerbocker papers.

284 "It is difficult to see": *NY Times,* Aug. 27, 1934.

284 "What, are you leaving": "Good-Bye to Germany." *Harper's,* Dec. 1, 1934.

BIBLIOGRAPHY

OFFICIAL RECORDS—UNPUBLISHED

Akten aus dem Politischen Archiv des Auswaertigen Amts, Bonn. Auswaertiges Amt, Pressestelle Gesamel-Akten, 1934.

Archives, YIVO Institute for Jewish Research, New York City. Nahum Greenburg Collection, items 1200–1300.

British Library, Newspaper Library, London. *Daily Express* Cuttings, Hanfstaengl File.

Federal Bureau of Investigation, Washington, D. C. Freedom of Information Acts: Ernst Hanfstaengl, Agatha von Hausberger.

National Archives, Washington, D. C. German Foreign Ministry Archives, Microcopy T-120, reels 2713, 4614, 4615, 4616, 5075, 5389.

Records of the National Socialist German Labor Party (NSDAP), Microcopy T-81, reels 25–31, 35–37.
Records of the United States Nuremberg War Crimes Trials, Guertner Diaries, October 5, 1934—December 24, 1938, RG 978, reel 1 and United States of America versus Josef Altstoertter et al (Case III) reels, 1, 34, 41, 46, 42, 48, 52, 53.

U. S. Department of State, Central Decimal Files, 1933–1939, Record Group 59.

Public Record Office, Kew, Richmond, England. FO371/16718 4490, FO371/16750 4530, FO371/17706 XP 3367

OFFICIAL RECORDS—PUBLISHED

Baynes, Norman, H. ed. *The Speeches of Adolf Hitler, April 1922 to August 1939*. Oxford University Press, 1942.

Degener, Herrmann A. L. *Degener's Wer ist's*. Verlag Herrmann Degener, 1934.

Das Deutsche Fuehrerlexikon 1934/35, Verlagsanstalt Otto Strollberg, 1934.

Die Gesetzgebung des Kabinetts Hitler: Die Gesetze im Reich und Preussen seit dem 20. Januar 1933. Berlin, 1933.

International Military Tribunal. *Trial of the Major War Criminals*. 42 vols. Nuremberg: Secretary of the Tribunal, 1947–1949.

Picker, Dr. Henry. *Hitler's Tischgespraeche in Fuehrer hauptquartier, 1941–42*. Seewald Verlag, 1965.

Pollock, James (ed.). *The Hitler Decrees*. George Wahr, Publisher, 1934.

Trevor-Roper, H. R. *Hitler's Table Talks*. Weidenfeld & Nicolson, 1953.

U. S. Department of State. *Documents on German Foreign Policy, 1918–1945*. Series C, U. S. Government Printing Office, 1949—.

U. S. Department of State. *Foreign Relations of the United States, 1933*, vol. 2, U. S. Government Printing Office, 1945.

U. S. Department of State. *Peace and War; U. S. Foreign Policy, 1931–1941*. U. S. Government Printing Office, 1943.

1933

PERSONAL PAPERS

S. Miles Bouton Papers, Hoover Institution, Stanford, California.

Wilbur J. Carr Papers, Library of Congress, Washington, D. C.

John Firman Coar Papers, University Archives, University of Alberta, Canada.

William E. Dodd Papers, Library of Congress, Washington, D. C.

Bella Fromm Collection, Boston University Library, Boston, Massachusetts.

Hanns-Heinz-Ewers Nachlass, Heinrich Heine Institut, Duesseldorf.

Hubert Renfro Knickerbocker Papers, Columbia University, New York City, New York.

Louis P. Lochner Papers, Wisconsin State Historical Society, Madison, Wisconsin.

Kurt G. W. Ludecke Papers, Hoover Institution, Stanford, California.

George Strausser Messersmith Papers, University of Delaware, Newark, Delaware.

Bessie Louise Pierce Papers, University Archives, The Joseph Regenstein Library, University of Chicago, Chicago, Illinois.

President's Secretary's File, Franklin D. Roosevelt Library, Hyde Park, New York.

Sigrid Schultz Papers, State Historical Society of Wisconsin, Madison, Wisconsin.

Katherine A. H. Smith Papers, Hoover Institution, Stanford, California.

Karl von Wiegand Papers, Hoover Institution, Stanford, California.

Thornton Wilder Papers, Yale University Library, New Haven, Connecticut.

John Campbell White Papers, Library of Congress, Washington, D. C.

PRIMARY SOURCES

Anonymous. *Als sozialdemokratischer Arbeiter im Konzentrationslager Papenburg.* Verlag Genossenschaft Auslaendischer Arbeiter in der USSR, 1935.

Anonymous. *Why I Left Germany by a German Scientist.* trans. Margaret Goldsmith, John Dent and Sons, 1934.

Armstrong, Hamilton Fish. *Peace and Counterpeace: From Wilson to Hitler.* Harper and Row, 1971.

Baedecker, Karl. *Germany: Handbook for Rail Traveler and Motorist.* Karl Baedecker Firm, 1936.

Baur, Hans. *Hitler's Pilot.* Friedrich Muller, 1958.

Bérard, Armand. *Un Ambassadeur Se Souvient: Au temps du danger allemand.* Plon, 1976.

Bernays, Robert. *Special Correspondent.* G. P. Putnam, 1934.

Billinger, Karl. *Fatherland.* Farrar and Rinehart, 1935.

Birchall, Frederick T. *The Storm Breaks.* Viking, 1940.

Bolitho, Gordon. *The Other Germany.* D. Appelton-Century Company, 1934.

Brown, John. *I Saw For Myself.* Selwyn and Blount, Ltd., 1935.

Cerruti, Elisabetta. *Ambassador's Wife.* Allen and Unwin, 1952.

Coblentz, Edmond D. *William Randoph Hearst: A Portrait in His Own Words.* Simon and Schuster, 1952.

Conant, James B. *My Several Lives.* Harper and Row, 1970.

Davies, Marion. *The Times We Had: Life With William Randoph Hearst.* Bobbs-Merrill Company, 1975.

Delmer, Sefton. *Trail Sinister.* Secker & Warburg, 1961.

Diels, Rudolf. *Lucifer ante Portas: Zwischen Severing und Heydrich*. Interverlag, 1949.

Dietrich, Otto. *The Hitler I Knew*. Methuen and Company, 1957.

Dietrich, Otto. *Mit Hitler an die Macht*. Verlag Franz Eher, 1934.

Dodd, Martha. *Through Embassy Eyes*. Harcourt, Brace and Company, 1939.

Dodd, William E. Jr. and Martha Dodd (eds). *Ambassador Dodd's Diary*. Harcourt, Brace and Company, 1941.

Ebermayer, Erich. *Denn heute gehoert uns Deutschland*. . . . Hestia Verlag, 1966.

François-Poncet, André. *The Fateful Years*. Harcourt, Brace and Company, 1949.

François-Poncet, André. *Politische Reden und Aufsaetze*. Florian Kupferberg Verlag, 1949.

François-Poncet, André. *Von Versailles bis Potsdam*. Florian Kupferberg Verlag, 1949.

Fromm, Bella. *Blood and Banquets: A Berlin Social Diary*. Garden City Publishing Company, 1944.

Gibbs, Philip. *European Journey*. Doubleday, 1935.

Gisevius, Hans-Bernd. *To The Bitter End*. Houghton Mifflin Company, 1947.

Hanfstaengl, Ernst. *Hitler in der Karikatur der Welt—Tat gegen Tinte. Ein Bildsammelwerk*. Verlag Braune Buecher, 1934.

Hanfstaengl, Ernst. *Hitler Liederbuch 1924*. Hanfstaengl, 1924.

Hanfstaengl, Ernst. *Unheard Witness*. J. B. Lippincott, 1957.

Hanfstaengl, Ernst. *Zwischen Weissem und Braunem Haus*. R. Piper & Company Verlag, 1970.

Hauser, Heinrich. *Time Was: Death of a Junker*. Raynal & Hitchcock, 1942.

Heydrich, Lina. *Leben mit einem Kriegsverbrecher*. Verlag W. Ludwig, 1976.

Hiller, Kurt. *Leben gegen die Zeit*. Rowohlt, 1967.

Hiller, Kurt. *Profile: Prosa aus eimem Jahrzehnt*. Editions Nouvelles International, 1938.

Kalnocky, Countess. *The Guest House*. The Bobbs-Merrill Company, 1974.

Kaltenborn, H. V. *Fifty Fabulous Years, 1900–1950*, G. P. Putnam's Sons, 1950.

Kennan, George F. *Memoirs, 1925–1950*. Little, Brown and Company, 1967.

Kessler, Count Harry. *In the Twenties: The Diaries of Harry Kessler*. Holt, Rinehart and Winston, 1971.

Kirkpatrick, Ivone. *The Inner Circle. Memoirs*. Macmillan and Company, 1959.

Knickerbocker, H. R. *The German Crisis*. Farrar and Rinehart, 1932.

Knickerbocker, H. R. *Is Tomorrow Hitler's?* Reynal and Hitchcock, 1941.

Koehler, Hansjuergen. *Inside the Gestapo*. Palas Publishing Company, 1940.

Krivitsky, W. G. *In Stalin's Secret Service*. Harper and Brothers, 1939.

Langhoff, Wolfgang. *Rubber Truncheon*. Dutton, 1935.

Lips, Eva. *Savage Symphony*. Random House, 1938.

Litten, Irmgard. *Beyond Tears*. Alliance Book Corporation, 1940.

Litten, Irmgard. *Die Hoelle sieht Dich an. Der Fall Litten*. Editions Nouvelles Internationales, 1940.

Lochner, Louis P. *Always the Unexpected*. The Macmillan Company, 1956.

Lochner, Louis P. *What About Germany?* Dodd, Mead and Company, 1942.

Loebe, Paul. *Erinnerungen eines Reichstagspraesidenten*. Arani, 1950.

Louis Ferdinand, Prince. *The Rebel Prince*. Henry Regnery Company, 1952.

1933

Louis Ferdinand von Preussen, Prinz. *Als Kaiserenkel durch die Welt*. Argon Verlag, 1952.

Ludecke, Kurt G. W. *I Knew Hitler*. Charles Scribner's Sons, 1938.

Melchert, Willi. *My Escape from Germany*. Hutchinson and Company, 1937.

Mosley, Diana Mitford. *A Life of Contrasts*. Time Books, 1977.

Mowrer, Edgar Ansel. *Germany Puts The Clock Back*. Revised ed., William Morrow and Company, 1939.

Mowrer, Edgar Ansel. *Triumph and Turmoil: A Personal History of Our Time*. Weybright & Talley, 1968.

Mowrer, Lilian. *Journalist's Wife*. William Morrow and Company, 1939.

Ossietsky, Carl von. *The Stolen Republic: Selected Writings of Carl von Ossietsky*. Lawrence & Wishant, 1971.

Paassen, Pierre van, (ed.). *Nazism: An Assault on Civilization*. Harrison Smith and Robert Haas, 1934.

Papen, Franz. *Memoirs*. Andre Deutsch, 1952.

Pope, Ernst. *Munich Playground*. Putnam, 1941.

Rauschning, Hermann. *The Voice of Destruction*. G. P. Putnam's Sons, 1940.

Reed, Douglas. *The Burning of the Reichstag*. Victor Gollancz, 1934.

Reed, Douglas. *Insanity Fair: A European Cavalcade*. Covici, 1938.

Regler, Gustav. *The Owl of Miniver*. Farrar, Straus and Cudahy, 1959.

Reynolds, Quentin. *by Quentin Reynolds*. Pyramid, 1963.

Ross, Albion. *Journey of an American*. The Bobbs-Merrill Company, 1957.

Sauerbruch, Ferdinand. *Das war mein Leben*. Kindler und Schiermyer Verlag, 1951.

Schirach, Baldur von. *Ich glaubte an Hitler*. Mosaik Verlag, 1967.

Schmidt-Pauli, Edgar. *Die Maenner um Hitler*. Verlag fuer Kulturpolitik, 1933.

Seldes, George. *Tell the Truth and Run*. Greenburg, 1953.

Shirer, William L. *Berlin Diary: The Journal of a Foreign Correspondent, 1934–1941*. Alfred A. Knopf, 1941.

Shirer, William L. *20th Century Journey: The Nightmare Years 1930–1940*. Little, Brown and Company, 1984.

Sommerfeldt, Martin. *Ich war dabei: Die Verschwoering der Daemonen, 1933–1939*. Drei Quellen Verlag, 1949.

Thompson, Dorothy. *I Saw Hitler*. Farrar and Rinehart, 1932.

Ullstein, Hermann. *The Rise and Fall of the House of Ullstein*. Simon and Schuster, 1943.

Valtin, Jan. *Out of the Night*. Alliance Book Corporation, 1941.

Welles, Bella Fromm. *Die Engel weinen*. Olympia Verlag GmbH, 1961.

The World Committee for the Victims of German Fascism. *The Brown Book*. Knight Publishers, 1936.

SECONDARY SOURCES

Aronson, Shlomo. *Reinhard Heydrich und die Fruehgeschichte von Gestapo und SD*. Deutsche Verlags-Anstalt, 1971.

Bruening, Eberhard. *Mildred Harnack-Fish als Literaturwissenschalftlerin*. Akademie-Verlag, 1983.

Buchheim, Hans et al. *Anatomy of the SS-State*. Collins, 1968.

Bullock, Alan. *Hitler: A Study in Tyranny.* Odhams, 1952.

Calic, Edouard. *Reinhard Heydrich.* Morrow, 1982.

Crepon, Tom. *Leben und Tode des Hans Fallada.* Mitteldeutscher Verlag, 1978.

Dallek, Robert. *Democrat and Diplomat: The Life of William E. Dodd.* Oxford University Press, 1968.

Dallin, David J. *Soviet Espionage.* Yale University Press, 1955.

Delmer, Sefton. *Weimar Democracy.* Mcdonald/American Heritage, 1972.

Desmond, Robert W. *The Press and World Affairs.* Appleton, 1935.

Diamond, Sander A. *The Nazi Movement in the United States, 1924–1941.* Cornell University Press, 1974.

Drage, Charles. *The Amiable Prussian.* Anthony Blond, 1958.

Eckardt, Wolf von. *Berthold Brecht's Berlin.* Doubleday, 1975.

Ekstein, Modris. *The Limits of Reason.* Oxford University Press, 1975.

Eyck, Erich. *A History of the Weimar Republic.* Athenaeum, 1970.

Fass, Paula. *The Damned and the Beautiful: American Youth in the 1920s.* Oxford University Press, 1977.

Fernsworth, Lawrence (ed.). *Dictators and Democrats.* Robert, McBride and Company, 1941.

Fraenkel, Heinrich. *The German People versus Hitler.* George Allen and Unwin, 1940.

Frye, Alton. *Nazi Germany and the American Hemisphere, 1933–41.* Yale University Press, 1967.

Gilbert, Martin. *Sir Horace Rumboldt: Portrait of a Diplomat.* Heinemann, 1973.

Gollo, Max. *Night of the Long Knives.* Warner, 1973.

Graf, Christoph. *Politische Polizei: Zwischen Demokratie und Diktatur.* Colloquium Verlag, 1983.

Granzow, Brigitte. *A Mirror of Nazism.* Victor Gollancz, 1964.

Grunfeld, Fred V. *The Great Cities: Berlin.* Time-Life, 1977.

Hale, Oron J. *The Captive Press.* Princeton University Press, 1964.

Hammer, Walter. *Hohes Haus in Henkers Hand.* Europaeische Verlagsanstalt, 1956.

Hartshorne, Edward. *The German Universities and National Socialism.* Harvard University Press, 1937.

Heinemann, John L. *Hitler's First Foreign Minister: Constantin von Neurath, Diplomat and Statesman.* University of California Press, 1979.

Higham, John et al. *History.* Prentice Hall, 1965.

Hoehne, Heinz. *Codeword: Director.* Coward, McCann & Geoghagen, Inc., 1971.

Hoehne, Heinz. *The Order of the Death's Head.* Ballantine Books, 1971.

Hohenberg, John. *Foreign Correspondence.* Columbia University Press, 1965.

Holborn, Hajo (ed.). *Republic to Reich.* Vintage Books, 1973.

Hull, David Stewart. *Film in the Third Reich.* University of California Press, 1969.

Irving, David. *The Rise and Fall of the Luftwaffe.* Little, Brown and Company, 1973.

Jacobsen, Hans-Adolf. *Nationalsozialistische Aussenpolitik, 1933–1938.* Alfred Metzner Verlag, 1968.

Jordan, Max. *Beyond All Fronts.* Bruce Publishing Company, 1944.

Keegan, John. *The Face of Battle.* Viking, 1976.

Koehl, Robert Lewis. *The Black Corps: The Structure and Power Struggles of the Nazi SS.* University of Wisconsin Press, 1983.

Krausnick, Helmut et al. *Anatomy of the SS State.* Walker and Company, 1965.

Kuckhoff, Armin G., hrsg. *Hans Otto: Gedenkbuch fuer einen Schauspieler und Kaempfer.* Verlag Bruno Henschel und Sohn, 1948.

Lazar, Irma. *Der Fall Horst Wessel.* Belser Verlag, 1980.

Liang, Hsi-Huey. *The Berlin Police Force in the Weimar Republic.* University of California Press, 1970.

Lundberg, Ferdinand. *Imperial Hearst: A Social Biography.* Equinox Cooperative Press, 1936.

Martin, James J. *American Liberalism and World Politics, 1931–1941.* vol. 1. The Devin-Adair Company, 1964.

Maser, Werner. *Hitler: Legend, Myth and Reality.* Harper and Row, 1971.

Nyomarkay, Joseph. *Charisma and Factionalism in the Nazi Party.* University of Minnesota Press, 1967.

Offner, Arnold. *American Appeasement.* Harvard University Press, 1969.

O'Neill, Robert J. *The German Army and the Nazi Party, 1933–39.* Cassel, 1966.

Orb, Heinrich. *Nationalsozialismus: 13 Jahre Machtrausch.* Verlag Otto Walter, 1945.

Orlov, Dietrich. *The History of the Nazi Party, 1933–1945.* David & Charles, 1973.

Pryce-Jones, David. *Unity Mitford.* The Dial Press, 1976.

Riess, Curt. *Total Espionage.* G. P. Putnam's Sons, 1941.

Sanders, Marion. *Dorothy Thompson: A Legend in Her Time.* Houghton Mifflin, 1973.

Schleunes, Karl A. *The Twisted Road to Auschwitz: Nazi Policy Towards the German Jews, 1933–1939.* University of Illinois, 1970.

Schorer, Mark. *Sinclair Lewis: An American Life.* McGraw-Hill, 1961.

Schuman, Frederick L. *The Nazi Dictatorship.* Knopf, 1936.

Schwarz, Dr. Paul. *This Man Ribbentrop.* Julian Messner, 1943.

Sheean, Vincent. *Dorothy and Red.* Houghton Mifflin and Company, 1963.

Swanberg, W. A. *Citizen Hearst.* Scribners, 1961.

Therov, Robert et al. *Pommern 1934/1935 im Spiegel von Gestapo-Lagerberichten und Sachakten.* 2 vols. Grote, 1974.

Tobias, Fritz. *The Reichstag Fire.* G. P. Putnam's Sons, 1964.

Villard, Oswald Garrison. *The German Phoenix.* Harrison Smith and Robert Haas, 1933.

Warburg, Gustav. *Six Years of Hitler: The Jews Under the Nazis.* George Allen & Unwin, Ltd., 1939.

Weil, Martin. *A Pretty Good Club.* W. W. Norton and Company, 1978.

Welch, David. *Propaganda and the German Cinema, 1933–1945.* Clarendon Press, 1983.

Werner, Kurt and Karl Heinz Biernat. *Die Koepenicker Blutwoche 1933.* Dietz Verlag, 1960.

Wheaton, Eliot Barcule. *Prelude to Tragedy: The Nazi Revolution, 1933–35.* Doubleday, 1968.

Wheeler-Bennett, John. *Knaves, Fools and Heroes.* St. Martin's, 1974.

Wheeler-Bennett, John. *The Nemesis of Power.* Macmillan, 1964.

Wulf, Joseph. *Theater und Film im Dritten Reich, Eine Dokumentation*. Siebert Verlag, 1964.

ARTICLES
Abbe, James E. "Men of Cablese." *New Outlook,* December, 1933.

Berliner Illustrirte Zeitung. "Im Konzentrationslager Oranienburg bei Berlin." April 30, 1933.

Bewley, Charles Henry. "Familie Dodd im Ausland." *Deutsche Allgemeine Zeitung,* Beiblatt, August 27, 1941.

Chandler, Douglas. "Changing Berlin." *National Geographic,* February 1937.

Craven, Avery O. "William E. Dodd as Teacher." *University of Chicago Magazine,* May 1940.

Desmond, Robert W. "2000 Dailies Are Suppressed By Hitler." *Editor & Publisher,* April 1, 1933.

Editor & Publisher. "Editors Differ On Censorship." April 1, 1933.

Editor & Publisher. "Reich Gives Warning to Foreign Writers." March 4, 1933.

Eschenburg, Theodor. "The Role of Personality in the Crisis of the Weimar Republic." *Republic to Reich,* Hajo Holborn, (ed.), Vintage Books, 1973.

Ethridge, Mark F. "Reich Press Defeat Held "Degrading." *Editor & Publisher,* April 22, 1933.

Fortune. "Their Excellencies, Our Ambassadors." April 1934.

Fromm, Bella. "Bella Among the Nazis." *True Detective,* February–November 1942.

Gittler, L. F. "Ambassador Extraordinary: A Close-up Portrait of William E. Dodd." *Survey Graphic,* July 1938.

Hanfstaengl, Dr. Ernst F. S. "My Leader." *Collier's,* August 4, 1934.

Holborn, Hajo. "A Wilsonian In Hitler's Realm." *Yale Review,* Spring 1941.

Kammet, Lawrence. "Red-headed Reporter From Texas." *American Press,* May 1934.

Lengyl, Emil. "Blomberg Builds A New German Army." *The New York Times Magazine,* June 2, 1935.

Literary Digest. "Germany's Book Bonfire." May 27, 1933.

Lovett, Robert Morss. "Cassandra: Ambassador to the Third Reich." *New Republic,* March 3, 1941.

Merriam, Charles E. "William E. Dodd as Statesman." *University of Chicago Magazine,* May 1940.

Mommsen, Hans. "The Political Effects of the Reichstag Fire," *Nazism and the Third Reich,* H. A. Turner, (ed.) Quadrangle, 1972.

New Republic. "The Jew In Fascist Germany." April 12, 1933.

Newsweek. "REUNION: Hanfstaengl's Arrival Greeted by 3,000 "Students." June 23, 1934.

Reynolds, Quentin. "Trained to Take It." *Collier's,* October 14, 1933.

Schaleben, Joy. "Getting the Story Out of Germany." *Journalism Monographs,* June 1969.

Thompson, Dorothy. "Good-Bye to Germany." *Harper's,* December 1934.

Thompson, Dorothy. "Putzy-Footing Propaganda." *The Saturday Review of Literature,* July 7, 1934.

Ullstein, Hermann. "We Blundered Hitler Into Power." *Saturday Evening Post,* July 13, 1940.

Wheeler-Bennett, John. "The New Regime in Germany." *International Affairs,* May 1933.

Wilde, Harry. "Rudolf Diels Portraet eines verkannten Mannes," *Politische Studien,* 9:475–81, 1958.

THESES AND DISSERTATIONS

Burke, Bernard. "American Diplomats and Hitler's Rise to Power, 1930–1933: The Mission of Ambassador Sackett." University of Washington, 1966.

Clark, David Gillis. "The Dean of Commentators: A Biography of H. V. Kaltenborn." University of Wisconsin, Ph. D., 1965.

Colwell, James Lee. "The American Experience in Berlin During The Weimar Republic." Yale University, Ph. D., 1961.

Dittmann, Anneliese. "Die deutschfeindliche Meinungsbildung der Vereinigten Staaten von Nordamerika waehrend des Weltkrieges und 1933/34." Heidelberg, 1938.

Patton, Wendy McDonald. "Dorothy Thompson's War With Hitler." University of Illinois, MS, 1965.

Solo, Roselyn. "André François-Poncet: Ambassador of France." Michigan State University, Ph. D., 1978.

Stewart, Barbara McDonald. "U. S. Government Policy on Refugees from Nazism 1933–1940." Columbia University, Ph. D., 1969.

NAME INDEX

Armstrong, Hamilton Fish, 167

Baur, Hans, 59
Bassewitz, Rudolf von, 95, 179–180
Bechstein, Helene, 41, 44
Bérard, Armand, 31, 192–193, 195, 257–258, 277
Bernays, Robert, 172–173
Bertling, Karl-Otto, 101, 159
Blomberg, Werner von, 125, 180, 182
Bose, Hubert von, 275
Bossard, Samuel, 157–158
Bradley, Ralph, 246
Bredow, Ferdinand von, 266–267
Broun, Heywood, 244
Brinkley, Douglas, 159
Bruckmann, Else, 41
Bruening, Heinrich, 74–75, 203
Buelow, Bernhard Wilhelm von, 95

Carnap, Helen "Mammi" von, 108–109, 179
Carter, John Franklin, 166
Cerruti, Elisabeth, 108, 187, 261
Coar, John F., 198–199
Conant, James, 247, 251
Conrady, Otto, 207–208
Cutler, Elliott Carr, 241–241, 250

Dahlberg, Edward, 93
Davies, Marion, 280
Delmer, Denis Sefton "Tom," 31, 59–60, 82–83, 174
Deuss, Edward, 115
Dieckhoff, Hans Heinrich, 158
Diels, Rudolf, 84–91, 97, 100–101, 115, 117, 127, 131–134, 147, 154–155, 157, 175, 199–201, 203–227, 230–232, 234–240, 267–268, 274–275
Dietrich, Otto, 180, 185
Dimitroff, Georgi, 216–218, 232–234
Ditzen, Rudolf "Hans Fallada," 193–195
Dodd, Martha, 9–12, 20–35, 139, 173, 189–196, 198–201, 214–216, 237–239, 257–258, 264, 266–267, 270, 272–274
Dodd, William E., 10, 12–22, 24–25, 129, 139–144, 148, 151, 154–161, 163–166, 189–192, 198–199, 237, 260–264, 266, 269, 272–277
Dodd, William E., Jr., 12, 19, 25–26, 165, 173, 193, 258, 272

Ebert, Friedrich, Jr., 221–222
Eddy, Sherwood, 161–163
Ernst, Karl, 131, 148, 155, 166, 176, 212–213, 232, 269